The Little Book of Hercules

The Physical Aspects of the Spiritual Path

WILLIAM BODRI

Top Shape Publishing, LLC
1135 Terminal Way Suite 209
Reno, Nevada 89502

You can find more books like this at MeditationExpert.com which
offers many free materials for meditation practitioners. You can
signup at the site for a free email newsletter.

ACKNOWLEDGEMENT

Without the teachings of Master Nan Huai-chin, none of this content could have become possible. First, without his guidance I would never have experienced anything along the cultivation trail. Furthermore, without his broad inter-disciplinary teachings, I would not have been able to understand and write about the different cultivation frameworks of multiple schools or the non-sectarian gong-fu experiences of meditation practitioners from various traditions. This is a master whose works you must study, and I hope more translators decide to make his works available in English.

Most people don't realize that the spiritual path is non-denominational; the same spiritual practice techniques are used by the practitioners of widely different religions, their effectiveness depends upon common, non-sectarian, basic principles of spiritual progress, and the gong-fu one achieves or passes through due to spiritual practice includes the same non-denominational phenomena as well. His teachings make this most clear, and I hope this book successfully extends this understanding to encompass the western traditions which are usually ignored along these lines. One might even be agnostic but if they simply learn how to rest their minds according to this non-sectarian framework, they will experience what we normally term "spiritual gong-fu" as well. It is purely a scientific process.

There are many reasons why I tend to repeat topics over and over again in cultivation writings such as this book. When it comes to cultivation and the topic of spirituality or spiritual progress, people tend to know very little and need to hear the same message constantly repeated so that through the repetition they might begin to clearly understand matters. I have encountered numerous individuals who have read dozens of cultivation books and attended my own teacher's lectures on the same subject matters numerous times, and yet they still do not understand the basic principles he keeps stressing.

If practitioners did understand these non-denominational principles, their practice would certainly progress, which is why all cultivation practice should commence with a stage of diligent dharma study. Your practice should always start with a stage of study as well as personal work on policing your mind and behavior. It seems that when it comes to spiritual matters, human beings have a tendency to invent their own habits and dogmas and attach to those mistaken notions they simply like rather than what the ancient sages teach. Hence wrong thoughts and tendencies are very difficult to dislodge. You will therefore encounter much re-emphasis in this book so that you, the reader, might avoid this fate.

Another of my tendencies is due to a background in science, medicine and engineering. That training to be precise pushes me to extreme literary lengths when trying to make things perfectly clear. That's what engineers want – clear explanations that anyone can follow, even if it requires more words. However, when it comes to writing style, this attempt at clarity when dealing with nebulous matters is not likely to win me any awards no matter how valuable or path breaking the information might be. It necessitates expert editors who can turn my lengthy ramblings into shorter explanations of readable English.

My boundless thanks therefore go out to the many volunteer editors who have contributed their time and effort to make this book possible. Without their brilliant rewrites and editing suggestions, you certainly would not have it. Those generous individuals include Marshall Adair, Jeremy Antbacke, Mitchell Houston, John Newtson and Clairemarie Levine, all of whom assiduously went over the work catching errors, providing insightful comments, and causing me to rewrite things as much as possible. It is very difficult to find individuals qualified to edit cultivation texts, and I extend the greatest appreciation to all their contributions because without their involvement this book would not be published at all. They are the ones who have made the *The Little Book of Hercules* possible.

The fascinating thing about *The Little Book of Hercules* is that it has revealed that the ancient Greeks also knew about the gong-fu of the spiritual Hero's Journey. This same story is covered in the Chinese *Journey to the West*, and represented in the emblem plates of the *Atalanta*

Fugiens of European western mysticism, but in the Twelve Labors we find something unique. Many film producers and story writers know about Joseph Campbell's Hero's Journey, but the *The Little Book of Hercules* contains the physical gong-fu phenomenal information they are missing and the common symbols used to represent the most noticeable physical aspects of the spiritual path.

The Esoteric School of Tibetan Buddhism, or Vajrayana, and the tantric yoga and Shaivite yoga schools of India, as well as Shingon, promote all sorts of cultivation practices (pranayama, visualizations, mantra, asanas and exercises, meditation, etc.) to bring practitioners to a kundalini awakening and the opening of their *sushumna* central channel and chakras, on through to dhyana attainments and possibility of spiritual enlightenment. They describe various cultivation technologies clearly, but they only focus on describing a few stages of the process in detail. The Old Testament focuses on describing channels and chi circulations as well, but also leaves out countless details including most of the mental aspects and cultivation methods of the spiritual trail. Christianity and Sufism readily acknowledge various cases of spiritual gong-fu, but fail to link them to a robust framework of spiritual striving that offers any understanding. Chinese Taoism focuses on describing the body's channel openings after the *sushumna* becomes purified, and emphasizes the transformations of chi followed by pristine awareness cultivation and then the emptiness realizations you find in Lao Tzu and Chuang Tzu. Every school, it seems, focuses on something different.

Despite these differences in emphasis, techniques and terminologies used, all these schools (and more) are combined in *The Little Book of Hercules,* which clearly discusses all these gong-fu schemes and more. It strives to transmit a more complete description of the gong-fu details of the spiritual journey along the way to generating the sambhogakaya, or purified Reward Body of spiritual cultivation. It even breaks the silence of many traditions and clearly explains details on the nirmanakaya capability of spiritual masters to help any realm of consciousness via thought projections. It links countless schools, traditions and techniques, and while concentrating on the physical transformations of the spiritual path, still inherently emphasizes the dharmakaya attainment of enlightenment emphasized by Zen, Vedanta, Dzogchen and Mahamudra.

The Little Book of Hercules reveals the universal spiritual path for human beings, and the absence of this knowledge of the true dharma has kept most religious devotees (which means the majority of the world's population) in ignorance for centuries. That is simply a reflection of the bad karma of human beings at this level on the spiritual ladder. In addition to these other schools and traditions, it reveals the understanding of this non-denominational path found in ancient Egyptian, Mesoamerican and European pagan cultures who were not blind to certain spiritual realities. It reveals the non-sectarian road of true cultivation practice and attainments, how it appears in both eastern and western religions, and shows that most spiritual cultures had knowledge of at least the lowest aspects of this process.

Basically our physical body, and its inner subtle chi body, both transform on the road of spiritual practice. Our chi and physical nature both purify, and thus become elevated. You will therefore definitely experience special gong-fu marks and signs as you practice meditation and spiritual cultivation techniques because your body will transform on the road to dhyana attainments. The ultimate achievement, of course, is the final objective of self-realization called "attaining the Tao," which means discovering your true self nature and who, or what, you ultimately are. However, the dharmakaya realization of finding the True Self, while paramount, is only part of the full scheme of complete spiritual attainment. There are also the sambhogakaya and nirmanakaya realizations to be cultivated as well, and the wisdom activity of working for others in whatever realm you find yourself in. Rarely is all this information found together in one text.

In the end, whether one's cultivation is complete or not, whether we are talking about East or West, whether we're speaking of Krishna, Buddha, Confucius, Socrates, Jesus, Mohammed or others, in the end the Path all comes down to behavior. All of consciousness is you, so all of it must become purified; all sentient beings must attain enlightenment in the end and be uplifted in the meanwhile. That compassionate task requires incredible vigor, virtue, patience, discipline and commitment on your part, but especially wisdom and skillful means. Helping other beings is something you often cannot do directly, but must go about indirectly by skillfully working to change conditions and help beings entrapped in their unfortunate situations because of their mental, emotional, spiritual and physical karma.

The spiritual path therefore comes down to the Mahayana path of the Bodhisattva who simultaneously cultivates self-perfection *and* the upliftment of all other sentient beings, which for humans means people, organizations, societies, countries, religions, cultures and conditions formed because of karma. In short, the spiritual path comes down to your behavior and whether it is wise, skillful, virtuous and effective. After enlightenment and prior to enlightenment, it all comes down to your thoughts and behavior and how they are expressed in the realm in which you land.

I have striven to compact as much information as possible in one concise text that discusses all these issues, focusing on the gong-fu phenomena at the lowest end of the spiritual trail, but this required that I leave out many facets I would have liked - even more than I put in! Most religions typically dismiss these discussions as mysticism, but there is nothing mystical about these topics at all as they are all a scientific function of cause and effect pertaining to the realm of spiritual efforts. This statement, because of the information provided and the fact you find the same results in all the genuine spiritual schools, is something I am hoping you will finally be convinced about because that conclusion, in itself, will help revolutionize your own cultivation practice. In any case I hope that this compact synopsis, focusing on the cultivation gong-fu of the spiritual path, can help your own spiritual efforts, or that of your friends should you decide to share it, and that regardless of your background you can greatly benefit from information in *The Little Book of Hercules*.

TABLE OF CONTENTS

PREFACE

There are many books on meditation and spiritual cultivation in the world, but very few deal with the actual physical gong-fu of the spiritual path. *The Little Book of Hercules* afforded me a rare opportunity to explain the trail of spiritual gong-fu that sequentially happens to most spiritual practitioners, in general order and form, as they make progress in their spiritual cultivation.

If you make true progress in spiritual practice then you are bound to experience these phenomena. This is true regardless of your religion or spiritual tradition because these results are non-sectarian and non-denominational. Pagan or agnostic, religious or non-religious, if you practice meditation in the correct way you will definitely experience what is commonly called "spiritual gong-fu" – particular physical and mental signs, markers, special abilities and transformations. If you do not experience these common signposts of the path it is not because they do not exist, but because you have not practiced to their level of achievement. You simply have not practiced far enough yet.

Most spiritual practitioners have heard of the term "kundalini," and the more informed know that kundalini arises within your body as the result of cultivation efforts; it is the deep life force energy from within the body that – when activated or "released" - opens up your chi channels and chakras, and basically kick starts various phases of mental and physical transformation. However, even the most informed practitioners don't usually realize that the Indian term kundalini is the same as the "yang chi" of the Chinese spiritual schools.

As this example illustrates, people are usually unfamiliar with the spiritual information available from different traditions, especially those other than their own. They do not realize that the very same stages of spiritual progress have been described in the ancient Egyptian, Greek, Mesoamerican, Indian, Chinese, Tibetan, Persian, European, Buddhist, Hindu, Jewish and other cultures. At the lowest stages of the path, everyone goes through the same common gong-fu experiences because they happen to everyone. How could it be otherwise? The exclusiveness characteristics people cite about their religion are all the inventions of man.

Ardent practitioners of all religions must eventually progress through these non-denominational stages and phenomena. Unfortunately, they do not know the common methods of spiritual cultivation used across the world's religions that can help their progress. They are also usually unaware of the phenomenological stages of the spiritual path, their expected sequence, the resulting physical transformations of the body, how to cultivate properly to achieve them, how to interpret them correctly and what they basically entail.

This overall ignorance of the non-denominational common results from spiritual practice contributes to the general lack of respect for other religions in the world, and a general lack of spiritual practice by all. And because the worldwide fascination with technology is growing, and the reverence held for spiritual practice simultaneously diminishes as this and other trends grow, it is all the more important to reveal this information now. Too many people and religions are devoid of a clear explanation of the dharma, and it is more imperative than ever to reveal this information.

Through this book I hope you will finally understand the linkage between countless spiritual traditions. In this book I have pointed out the obvious linkages between tantric yoga, Hinduism, Shaivism, Tibetan Vajrayana, Mahamudra, Chinese Taoism, Confucianism, Orthodox Buddhism, Zen, Shingon, Judaism, Christianity, Islam, Sufism, Alchemy, the mystery schools, Paganism and more. Most of these schools do indeed teach some of the transformative physical gong-fu aspects of the spiritual path, and through the Twelve Labors of Hercules you can see where the bits and pieces fit into the overall framework of the pre-samadhi phases of spiritual practice.

Unfortunately, the gong-fu introduced in the Twelve Labors, as high as it may seem, represents just the low level transformations of the path. While fascinating, this level of spiritual achievement did not afford me the chance to talk about true mind cultivation and the teachings of Zen, Vedanta, Dzogchen, Mahamudra, the Great Perfection and Consciousness-Only. Even so, the physical gong-fu descriptions you are about to encounter are revealed in more detail than you are likely to find in any other source.

You literally cannot learn this information unless you experience it yourself. Someone can teach it to you, but to learn it you must experience it, and that means spiritual practice and progress. This book contains very rare descriptions of the completion stages of Vajrayana past the opening of the *sushumna* central channel; you will not find this information printed anywhere else. It links these stages to clear Taoist explanations of how the chi channels sequentially open, and clears up countless misconceptions for those currently trying to practice Taoist cultivation. It explains various stages of spiritual gong-fu revealed within the Old Testament that Jewish Talmudists and Christian scholars have missed because of their own lack of cultivation attainments. It explains the sequences of yoga transformation achieved in the Indian Shaivite schools and tantric traditions of practice, and outlines the purification of the human body's five elements mentioned in Buddhism. It discusses the main cultivation method of watching your mind with mindfulness championed in Confucianism. Nowhere will you find another book that links all these schools, explains their relevant materials in detail, and clears up many of the misconceptions about the path.

The utmost of thanks go to the individuals who gave up their precious time to spend hours and hours going back and forth over drafts to edit this difficult text – Mitchell Houston, Marshall Adair, Jeremy Antbacke, John Newtson, and Clairemarie Levine whose editing skills oversaw the final touches. All credit goes to Mitchell and Claire for their personal devotion to making this the best work possible.

I tend to include as much cross-referential material as possible in my writings in order to give you literally decades of teachings in just one small volume, knowing that seekers are likely to read just one book like this in their lifetime, and this gives editors a difficult job editing my rambling topics. But I see no other way than including as much as possible in as little space as possible. I usually have just one opportunity to help you in this ever busier world, and you need as much information as possible to help you in your spiritual efforts.

It seems that people do not like to read books anymore, and they certainly will not come upon this material anywhere else. Therefore

I realized that I have but one opportunity to educate you as much as possible to help you in your spiritual practice efforts. I have found great value in constant repetition, which is sometimes a subject of complaint by some readers. However, I have seen endless cases where intelligent and ardent practitioners of twenty or thirty or even forty years, who have attended countless lectures and read countless books, still do not correctly understand basic cultivation materials. Repetition is the only solution for accurately transferring as much material as possible in the little time we have together.

In closing, I sincerely hope this book helps not just you, but also the various religious leaders of the world to see the true underlying commonality of the spiritual path. They need to uncover the true dharma and basic cultivation path inherent in each of their traditions and teach their members how to cultivate correctly and successfully. Jews, Christians, Muslims, Buddhists, Hindus, Jains, Confucians, Shintoists, Taoists, … all people must learn how to spiritually practice correctly once again because presently they are not doing so. Nearly everyone has lost the knowledge of how to cultivate spiritual progress, and it seems that the world now prefers sectarian religious ceremonies, disciplinary rules and traditions instead. This is quite useless when it comes to real spiritual attainments. All the dogmas of the world seem to be at war with one another, whereas cultivation methods and the resultant gong-fu are non-denominational.

It is the conclusions that people reach, and the opinions that they hold, that separate us from one another on the road of spiritual practice. Not only should people realize the common end goal of practice and the common features of the spiritual path, but they should come to recognize the wonderful benefits of benchmarking teachings and practices from other traditions. Not everyone has all the answers.

The information within this small book can certainly help to guide and dispel fear as practitioners advance through the various phases of spiritual progress; it is designed with the intent to help everyone reach yet higher stages of attainment on the spiritual journey. Please use it as a guide to become your very best, and as a reference to help you complete your own investigation of the commonality of the spiritual path. I sincerely hope you succeed at spiritual cultivation and become one of the leading lights of your generation, a cultural hero.

Spiritual cultivation is not just a path leading to enlightenment, but a path of noble deeds and dignified behavior. I hope you choose to become a Bodhisattva protector who commits themselves to helping all, benefiting others without attachment to one's own benefit. The Bodhisattvas undertake the responsibility or burden that no one in the world takes, and that is the welfare of all beings. Foremost of their burdens is making sure all people have access to the true teachings that lead to enlightenment.

INTRODUCTION

One of the greatest Greek heroes of all time is Hercules, who was born a mortal but died divine. Known for his great strength and heroic exploits, Hercules was the son of the great god Zeus and the mortal woman Alcmene. Although only half-divine, Hercules eventually attained an immortal body and fully divine status. He was widely honored throughout Greece and Rome because of his many feats, but became especially famous because of his "Twelve Labors."

On the face of it, the various legends of Hercules seem just like good adventure stories. And because of his famous strength, it's easy to mistake him for some ancient version of the modern day Arnold Schwarzenegger-type action hero. However, to do so misses the point of Hercules entirely.

The story of Hercules must be seen in its proper context within ancient Greek culture: it forms part of the framework upon which a vibrant spiritual and religious culture was built. Just like the *Bhagavad Gita* to Hindus, the Bible to Christians and Jews, the Koran to Muslims, the Canon of Sutras to Buddhists or *Tao Te Ching* to Taoists – the stories of Greek mythology were a storehouse of spiritual instruction and moral development for one of the most influential cultures in world history. Hercules' story fits exactly into this mold.

The Twelve Labors of Hercules actually lay out the common human path of spiritual development, but describe it through the images of ancient Greek culture. In other words, it's a "how to" guide for understanding the common stages, results, and methods of spiritual practice regardless of someone's school or tradition. The only difference is that the description of these stages originates in ancient Greece rather than in China, Tibet, or India, which are the typical sources for such information.

Hercules is one of the prototypical heroes of spiritual development for the world, someone we can look to with admiration and emulation just as Tibetans honor Milarepa or Indians honor Rama. The Greek concept of a "Hero" entails the epitome of spiritual development, which is something we find in the stories of Jason and the Argonauts, the Greek hero Perseus, and in the life and teachings of Socrates. Western Civilization has lost sight of the basic spiritual quest, but it is foremost in the story of Hercules and his Twelve Labors.

Each of Hercules' "Twelve Labors" represents a specific stage of spiritual accomplishment on the path of spiritual development. These stages of transformation are non-denominational and are described in many religions. Christians, Jews, Muslims, Hindus, Buddhists, Taoists, Zoroastrians, Confucians ... practitioners of all religions will pass through these same stages if they sincerely cultivate spiritual practice to transform both mind and body. The stages of Hercules' spiritual development are not unique to the ancient Greek tradition, but his Twelve Labors are a unique cultural expression of the universal, non-denominational, non-sectarian common process of spiritual development and transformation for human beings.

Once you investigate the non-denominational stages of the spiritual path and the universality of its methods and principles, your understanding of the storehouse of the world's spiritual literature will start to blossom. Furthermore, you'll begin to realize that the mere intellectual study of this literature will fail to bring you any true understanding unless you personally practice spiritual cultivation. The best place to find your theology is not in arguments but in the results of spiritual practice.

You can only truly understand spiritual literature if you personally practice spiritual cultivation and start to make progress along those lines. If you practice meditation and other spiritual exercises, then you will begin to comprehend the Twelve Labors of Hercules, and after you begin to realize these stages, you will be able see museum statues of religious greats from various traditions – or browse the internet for their pictures - and will immediately understand what the figures truly represent and what you must do to attain those experiences yourself.

Because the physical nature of the human being is a constant for our species and because we all share the same fundamental source nature, we have an equal capacity for the spiritual and physical transformations of the spiritual trail. What is different among us, and what has led to the flowering of so many various spiritual traditions in the world, is the multitude of world cultural traditions that color the human mindset in different ways. Different religions have arisen per the call of the times to address the concerns and mindsets of different peoples and regions. Each tradition talks about the spiritual path with a different emphasis even though all paths are designed to lead to a direct experience of our Source Nature.

Some traditions call this original nature Tao, some call it God, Allah, fundamental source, original nature, Father, True Self, Parabrahman, Buddha-nature, Ein Sof, essence, dharmakaya, and so on. The names are endless. Regardless of whatever we call "It," the one original source nature *is and must be* the same source nature, regardless as to what traditions call it. The ultimate source *is* the ultimate, fundamental, original source by definition. Correct? Various saints and sages may differ as to their ultimate stage of realization of this Source, and thus their teachings may vary,[1] but there is only one fundamental source nature.

One original nature … and countless teachings and religions. How should we view all the differing matters we encounter in this soup?

All the genuine spiritual paths that guide us to an experience of the Source first involve cultivating deep meditation states called "samadhi" or "dhyana." This is a fact often hidden within the stories of various traditions but the practices they employ for spiritual development are aimed at helping you attain samadhi. One of the initial by-products of engaging in spiritual practices is a peaceful, quiet mind empty of distracting thoughts and useless, negative self-chatter. It's a state of open mental freedom largely absent of stress and worry. Since it's a state of internal mental peace and quiet that is absent of rambling thoughts, many schools call it "emptiness" or "empty mind" though of course thoughts or knowing still arise within this attainment.

Correctly following the spiritual path one will encounter various end results, phenomena, or experiences including peaceful mental rest and a healthier constitution. The various phenomena, "marks," "signs" or experiences you will encounter along the way are called the *"gong-fu"* or "kung-fu" of the spiritual path. Gong-fu includes the transformations you feel within your physical body, the opening of energy centers called chakras, feelings of warmth or cold, the softening of the personality, superpowers, visions and the like. Hercules' Twelve Labors are all

---

[1] The details within spiritual teachings will also vary because of the cultural milieu in which they are delivered. They are nearly always adapted to the spiritual maturity of the audience receiving them, and so some teachings are much higher or lower than others depending upon the audience and the skillful expedients used by the teacher.

descriptions of the common gong-fu of the spiritual path shared by the worlds' various religious traditions.

The Twelve Labors of Hercules not only describe various stages of cultivation gong-fu but also instruct spiritual aspirants how to successfully progress through these stages of spiritual development. The descriptions are transmitted in a different way than, say, a Chinese Taoist, Tibetan Buddhist, pious Jew or ardent Sufi would relate them, but they are the same stages and gong-fu phenomena nonetheless. The underlying process is *the same*. Only the language and cultural references differ. Reading the Twelve Labors is therefore essentially the same thing as reading an instruction book for spiritual adherents.

The Twelve Labors of Hercules start out as a tragedy. In a rage of temporary insanity put upon him by the Goddess Hera, Hercules kills his own wife and children. With a heavy heart for his deeds and weary of this world of suffering, Hercules travels to the Oracle of Apollo at Delphi and asks for advice on how to redeem himself.

The Oracle advises Hercules to submit himself to King Eurystheus and complete a set of almost impossible tasks that the King would impose upon him. This was a set of ten tasks given one after the other that eventually became twelve because King Eurystheus did not recognize two of these labors. According to Apollodorus,[2] Hercules was assigned to perform the following Twelve Labors:

> Conquer the Terribly Powerful Nemean Lion
> Slay the Nine-headed Poisonous Lernaean Hydra
> Capture the Golden-Horned Red Deer of Artemis
> Capture the Fierce Erymanthian Boar
> Clean the Dirty Augean Stables in a Single Day
> Slay the Deadly Stymphalian Birds
> Capture the Magnificent Cretan Bull
> Steal the Man Eating Mares of Diomedes
> Obtain the Girdle of Hippolyte the Amazon Queen
> Obtain the Red Cattle of the Monster Geryon
> Steal the Apples of the Hesperides, Daughters of Atlas
> Capture and Bring Back Cerberus, the Hound of Hades

---

[2] The Loeb edition of the *Library* or *Bibliotheca* of Appolodorus, translated by Sir James G. Frazer and published in 1921, is the reference used in this book.

Everyone in the world remembers Hercules for his incredible strength, but it was his completion of these Twelve Labors – which you can also experience yourself on the spiritual trail after you start to meditate - that have made him Greece's greatest hero. Since these Twelve Labors are actually universal stages in the process of spiritual cultivation that everyone must pass through when they start cultivating, Hercules' journey can be taken as a universal model of spiritual development.

You don't have to give up your wife and children to succeed in cultivation as Hercules did. As a woman, you don't have to give up your husband and children either. It's true that the heroic accomplishment of spiritual enlightenment seems to be most often achieved by monks, nuns, hermits and ascetics who leave the family life aside, but success only requires that an individual dare to cultivate meditation despite the responsibilities and dissuasions of the conventional world.

Similar to Hercules' story, Jesus once said, "If anyone comes to me and does not hate his father and mother, wife and children, brothers and sisters, yes, and his life also, he is not worthy of me." This symbolizes once again that the spiritual commitment should take central priority in your life. This is the meaning behind the fact that Hercules loses his wife and child – you must put some of your family life aside and focus some attention on true spiritual cultivation in order to truly succeed in spiritual practice.

Indian culture advises men to put their full energies into cultivation after their children have sufficiently grown up, but the best means of spiritual development is to devote a portion of your life energies to spiritual cultivation in the here and now. This is why Confucianism teaches us to spiritually cultivate, by inspecting the mind, all the time. Spiritual practice is supposed to be the purpose of weekly church, synagogue, temple and mosque attendance, but too often the attendees turn these hours into periods of ceremony, ritual and social time rather than true spiritual practice. It is exceedingly unfortunate that the practice of the majority of religious people has fallen to just ritualism and doctrine. True spiritual practice – which is still available today – will allow you to lastingly get rid of your afflictions such as hate and anger, greed, sorrow and traumas; it will open up and help virtues such as love, compassion, patience and wisdom blossom; it will reward you with peace and stability in the midst of turmoil, and it will remove the barriers between you and the ultimate Source – whatever your tradition calls it.

Like Hercules you must "labor" or work at spiritual practice. You absolutely must engage in meditation as a spiritual exercise in order to succeed in the great feat of spiritual awakening. To engage in spiritual exercises is the process of "cultivation," and this work is necessary on the path of spiritual training, ascension, awakening, divinization, theosis, enlightenment, salvation, liberation, self-realization or deification ... whatever the various religions call it.

The man or woman who accomplishes anything in life is the person who distinguishes themselves by standing apart from conformity, from the ignorant mindset of the crowd. Standing apart is what enables you to become recognized as great, and success in spiritual cultivation is the means for achieving that greatness.

The roster of the greatest heroes of the world, those whose names have lasted countless centuries, is filled with those who have cultivated spiritual attainments and virtuous behavior. The truth is not any simpler than that – that spiritual accomplishments trump the material ones and that the greatest of heroes conquer themselves. Many traditions say that even the great kings and warriors whose names have been placed upon pedestals of glory have received their renown only because in past lives they accumulated sufficient merit from their good deeds and their practice of spiritual cultivation. In short, it is spiritual cultivation which counts in life.

In the field of personal cultivation, every single person can succeed in "becoming a god" as Hercules did. Anyone can follow in his footsteps. You do not need immortal strength or status. You do not need name, wealth, power, or position. You don't even need Jesus' reminder from the Jewish canon that "Ye are gods"[3] because the capability of self-improvement is inherent as your birthright. You just need the willpower to spiritually cultivate in the correct non-contrived, non-artificial way, and then the spiritual stages of gong-fu (states of mental and physical transformation that occur to practitioners on the spiritual path) will transpire just as they did for Hercules. As soon as you awaken to your original nature you will realize you are the Godhead or ground state. You are God or God is you.

If you do the meditation work of developing a free and open mind that does not attach to thoughts or consciousness, then the spiritual gong-fu experienced by Hercules will indeed happen, and you must know that this same gong-fu is also described in countless non-Greek spiritual traditions. If you don't put in the required effort, however, the

---

[3] See *Psalm 82:6* and *John 10:34.*

results won't come no matter how much you beg, complain, plead, or make promises to Heaven asking for assistance. The merit of attaining spiritual progress is solely due to effort, not want.

There are quite a few religions which maintain that self-realization, salvation or spiritual liberation comes from faith alone, or that there is nothing we can do to earn spiritual liberation, or that nothing is required for liberation which is not already within the sect's holy texts. These ideas, usually postulated by individuals without any cultivation attainments themselves, take away the personal responsibility of self-cultivation and are just plain wrong.

In Christianity we say that "grace" comes solely at Heaven's discretion and is a process we cannot fathom. In actual fact "grace" or heavenly help comes as a result of merit, which means you earned it, and merit is earned because of correct effort. If you put in the required practice effort with the correct spiritual exercises, then the help and aid called "grace" will follow just as will spiritual progress.

On the other hand, if a stage of spiritual attainment doesn't manifest to you then it does not mean the stage does not exist, or that you can deny its existence. It simply means you haven't yet reached that level of attainment yourself. It means you have not cultivated far enough.

For a practitioner of spiritual exercises, this might be because you haven't practiced hard enough, long enough, consistently enough, or perhaps practiced the wrong sorts of spiritual exercises or the right techniques incorrectly. Sometimes you do all the right things in terms of practice, but refuse to let go of the wrong views so that you impede your own progress. Sometimes your merit is incomplete, and this holds you back from spiritual progress as well. There are all sorts of reasons why people fail to ascend the ladder of true spiritual ascension. This is why a wise spiritual teacher with attainments is often needed to help guide you on the path.

Cultivation is an effort that sets you apart from the ordinary person. As Confucius said, it is the "great learning" in life. We should also call it the mastering of the science of human beings. Life is all about one thing only – this task of great learning – and so it should remain the single most important occupation of our lives. Unfortunately, many of the orthodox organized religions recite this truth but turn the emphasis into religious practice rather than actual spiritual practice. Thus people often become lost and confused and fail to make the true spiritual progress of the saints and sages we read about from the past.

Because the deeper explanations behind the mental and physical transformations of the spiritual path have been forgotten, even devout religious people feel "lost" today. They are unable to understand how exactly it is that the great saints and heroes within their own traditions were able to accomplish the miraculous feats recorded in spiritual texts. Lacking real cultivation knowledge, people cannot understand their own traditions or those of others and waste their spiritual lives arguing over meaningless details and trivial differences. They never put themselves on the road of genuine spiritual progress themselves.

You will become blind if you let blind authorities lead you in life, and then the blind will truly be following the blind. But if you want to reconnect with the Source original nature of the universe – what we call God or spiritual essence - you must become a cultivation practitioner like Hercules who dared to do what ordinary men would not. His path can be followed. It's been done in countless religions, cultures and traditions by those who dared to separate themselves from the ordinary religious practices. It's just that establishment figures have not told you about these men and women, the path they took, the practices they engaged in, and the gong-fu or labors they suffered. You will discover all this within.

The religious functionaries who are the doorkeepers of religion today are typically men and women of great charm, charisma and intellectual talent who lack any personal cultivation achievements. They typically do not have any extensive knowledge of cultivation dharma (teachings) either. So why then are they your personal guide if they are not even teaching you how the past sages and saints succeeded within your tradition, and what you must actually practice yourself to accomplish what they achieved? These doorkeepers typically ignore the true spiritual path and its objectives, ridicule the path if it gains a foothold, and then attack the dharma and persecute its masters if all those steps fail. It is the "religious" who have most often been the ones to persecute or kill the true saints and realized sages of those very same religions.

Spiritual cultivation is the golden path, the supreme striving hidden openly within the paths of the world's religions. You need but open your eyes to see it and then recognize what all these traditions are trying to teach you. We may not remember Warren Buffet, Oprah, or Michael Jackson in two hundred years time, but we will still remember those who succeeded in spiritual cultivation from hundreds and thousands of years ago, even if they didn't come from our own traditions. No matter how humble their lives, countless spiritual greats from Jesus on through to Socrates, Lao Tzu, Confucius, Mohammed and Buddha are still remembered today without having achieved anything we would normally call "worldly great."

Everyone has the Tao, so everyone can spiritually realize it. The path of Hercules' Twelve Labors simply reveals the spiritual gong-fu – a Chinese term for the phenomena or stages experienced along the path of spiritual practice - he went through in order to tread the path of seeking spiritual enlightenment. Reading the Twelve Labors can help you to understand the spiritual Way, and how to cultivate your mind and body for the highest of spiritual achievements.

THE FIRST LABOR:
CONQUER THE POWERFUL NEMEAN LION

[2.5.1] When Hercules heard that, he went to Tiryns and did as he was bid by King Eurystheus. First, Eurystheus ordered him to bring the skin of the Nemean lion, an invulnerable beast begotten by Typhon. On his way to attack the lion he came to the town of Cleonae and lodged at the house of a day-laborer, Molorchus. When his host Molorchus offered to sacrifice an animal asking the gods for a safe lion hunt, Hercules told him to wait for thirty days. If he returned safely from the hunt by that time, the two would make a sacrifice to Zeus, whereas if Hercules died, Molorchus agreed to sacrifice to him as to a hero. Reaching Nemea, Hercules started tracking the lion and discovered his arrows were useless against the beast. He shot arrows at the lion, but the animal's hide was invulnerable so the arrows simply bounced off. Hercules picked up his club and went after the lion. When the lion took refuge in a cave with two mouths, its den, Hercules closed off one entrance and came in upon the beast through the other, and putting his arm round its neck held it tight till he had choked it to death. Laying it on his shoulders he carried it to Cleonae where he found Molorchus on the last of the thirty days about to make a sacrifice to him as to a dead man. The two sacrificed to Zeus and then Hercules brought the lion to

Mycenae. Amazed at his manhood, Eurystheus forbade Hercules thenceforth to enter the city, but ordered him to exhibit the fruits of his labors before the city gates. They say, too, that in his fear Eurystheus had a bronze jar made for himself to hide in under the earth, and that he sent his commands for the labors through a herald, Copreus.[4]

Hercules' First Labor was to bring back the pelt of the Nemean lion, an invulnerable beast begotten by Typhon. Typhon was known as the deadliest monster in Greek mythology because he had almost defeated the gods of Olympus in battle and was a terrifying composite in form and powers. Since the Nemean lion was Typhon's offspring, this certainly has some special meaning in the legend of Hercules. Once we investigate the details of Typhon's strange body, the significance of this heritage will become clear.

Typhon was the child of Gaia, the Earth, just as we are. We should therefore assume that the legend of Typhon in some way represents our own physical nature since it is also a product of the Earth. This earthly heritage of ours is emphasized in countless cultivation schools which tell us we must transform both our body and our coarse animal nature on the spiritual path. For instance in Chinese philosophy it is said that "man stands between Heaven and the Earth," meaning that he represents a balance between these two forces, possessing the nature of both, but can cultivate to become divine. Thus we can understand why the Greeks said that the upper half of Typhon's body was in the form of a human being that reached upwards as high as the stars.

This half-human form that stretched to the Heavens meant that despite his evil tendencies, Typhon's monstrous nature could eventually become transformed. He had the capability of challenging the gods in the first place because he could himself become divine. Because as humans we possess a dual nature of both heaven and earth,[5] through our actions and behavior we can choose to accentuate our divine nature

---

[4] There are various versions of the Twelve Labors, but the primary descriptions of the Twelve Labors used in this book are based on the Loeb edition of the *Library* of Apollodorus, translated by Sir James G. Frazer in 1921.

[5] You can also think of this duality as yin and yang; earth is yin and heaven is yang. Man, therefore, is a product of yin and yang but he can spiritually cultivate so as to rise to heaven. In other words, he can transform his negative yin energies into positive yang energies, which is what Hercules does throughout his Twelve Labors.

or our animalistic nature. If a person cultivates spirituality then he can reach the divine, but he can also choose to drop into the carnal realm of animal passions and form excessive attachments to sensation. Countless spiritual traditions teach this basic principle, and so it is told and retold in many religions.

Now the bottom half of Typhon's body was composed of a set of gigantic viper coils that could stretch to the top of his head, and each of Typhon's arms had a hundred dragon heads upon it. These features represent the fact that the human body has a set of internal chi channels that run throughout its extent from foot to crown, and the dragon heads symbolize the many major and minor chakras that exist throughout the human body. At the commencement of spiritual practice these channels and chakras are blocked with impure chi, but through the continued practice of meditation and other spiritual exercises they can certainly become purified.

Many of the world's tantric cultivation schools teach that our human body has an invisible etheric component within it composed of chi (qi), prana, or life force. Various chi channels, akin to arteries and veins of the physical body, carry different types of chi energies to all points within this inner esoteric chi body. Along the lines of these channels are chakras, which are nexus points where the channels break off into smaller conduits. Accordingly, these chakras look like little spoke wheeled distribution hubs.

In other words, various chi channels run throughout the human body and at times develop into branching centers called chakras. The way in which they converge into chakras calls to mind the shape of flower petals or spokes on a wheel. Chakras are often symbolized by lotus flowers[6] in many spiritual schools, and the sub-channels breaking away from the main channel are usually represented by petals. If the heart chakra has eight petals, for instance, it means that the main chi channel in that region breaks off into eight minor channels that carry the chi away to other regions of the body.

Most people think there are only seven major chakras in the human body, but there are little chakras everywhere within it. Every so often even the tiniest chi channels have branches coming off them, and those nexus points are chakras. In the schools of Vajrayana and tantric yoga,

---

[6] The lotus flower is most often used to represent chakras not just because of its beauty, but because the beautiful flower always grows in dirty waters, which makes a statement about the cultivation path.

for instance, practitioners are instructed to concentrate on visualizing countless channels and chakras at certain introductory stages of the path. They do this as an aid for developing a stable mind and inner pliancy. Once they stabilize that visualization, they release it to observe the empty nature of the mind and introspect to determine who or what is actually experiencing all this. Hence, knowledge of the chakras can be helpful, but is not necessary.

The tiny chakras along our chi channels serve as distribution centers for the chi flowing through them, and through this network your chi is able to become evenly distributed throughout your body. Because the spiritual path involves cultivating your life force, it involves cultivating your chi along with these channels (called *nadis* in Sanskrit) and chakras, many of which are occluded because of obstructions that have developed over time.

Typhon's body basically represents this uncultivated, unpurified internal chi structure of the human body. It is half human and half divine; it stretches eastward and westward because its true nature is like endless space which also spans the universe. It reaches all the way up to heaven because our human physical nature and our chi can be purified to become divine. If we detach from our lower nature, both our bodies and minds can be purified to become heavenly.

In the Greek myths, Zeus defeated Typhon and trapped him underneath Mount Etna. This symbolizes our human situation of having unpurified chi channels imprisoned within our earthly frame (Mount Etna). This set of internal chi channels becomes the burning bush of Moses after it purifies and blazes with kundalini yang chi, or we can also say it becomes the wish fulfilling tree mentioned in Buddhism. Mount Etna, a volcanic mountain, was said to be one location where the Hephaestus (Vulcan), had a forge, which we will later see has some meaning for our story.

Just as raw gold ore must be melted to become purified and gemstones must be cut and polished in order to sparkle, so can our earthly body become heavenly ... but only if you spiritually cultivate, which starts the process of its purification. Our divine nature is unreachable when our mind clings to thoughts and continues to take our body of five elements (the earth, wind, water, fire and space elements) as our true real self. However, if you begin to cultivate an empty mind of cling-free awareness then the body's five elements – and thus its internal structure of chi channels and chakras – will naturally transform to become like the heavenly bodies of devas or angels.

The imprisonment of Typhon underneath Mount Etna reminds us of the story of Sun Wu Kong in the Chinese epic *Journey to the West*. In that famous story which has greatly shaped Chinese culture, Sun Wu Kong the monkey represents our conscious mind[7] which is always jumping here and there. After causing havoc in heaven, this immortal monkey was punished and imprisoned under a mountain on Earth, called the "Five Element Mountain," to represent the mind's seeming imprisonment within the human body.

Our mind is trapped within a physical body only because we cling to the body, to thoughts, and to the idea that we are the body. Sun Wu Kong was only released from his physical imprisonment when he agreed to help the monk Xuan Zang complete the great task of bringing Buddhist scriptures back to China from India so that everyone could cultivate and reach enlightenment.

In other words, you have to cultivate spiritual exercises such as meditation to become free of attachment to the body and free from identifying the body (or any form) as the self. Meditation is the only way to learn detachment that leads to spiritual progress.

So, to repeat, inside our earthly body of the five elements we have an elaborate structure of chi channels and chakras that spans it and which can be transformed through cultivation to rival the splendorous bodies of the gods in heaven. These are the beings which various cultures call devas, angels, celestial beings, deities, dakinis and dakis, or heavenly spirits. Christianity, Judaism, Islam, Hinduism, Buddhism, Taoism and other religions recognize the existence of these higher heavenly inhabitants who have different ranks and functions.

Perhaps this purification of the human body is possible because, as Shakyamuni Buddha once explained, the template for the human body came from one of the Form Realm heavens, and that body in turn originated in the Formless Realm heavens. Perhaps it still retains the vestiges of these bodies within a shell of coarse physical matter, and they can be reclaimed through the process of cultivation in a reverse form of "ontogeny recapitulates phylogeny." In any case, you just need to know the correct principles of spiritual practice, the right way to cultivate, and

---

[7] In Buddhism he represents what is called the "sixth consciousness" while the monk, Xuan Zang, represents the "alaya consciousness." The various chapters of this famous book also represent stages of cultivation gong-fu, but the public does not know this.

then actually do it to succeed, which brings us back once again to the Nemean lion that Hercules had to conquer in his First Labor.

What does the Nemean lion represent in the first of the Twelve Labors of Hercules?

The Nemean lion in Hercules' First Labor represents your wild, unpurified yang chi at the beginning of the spiritual path. On the first step of the cultivation trail you must awaken your yang chi, which is called kundalini energy in India, but that yang chi kundalini energy is at first impure. You can call this force the "kundalini energy" that sleeps on the *muladhara* root chakra, "yang chi," "vital force," "wind element," "life force," *shakti* or symbolize it as a dragon or snake or lion, etc. Regardless of whatever you call it or however you symbolize it, the first step in cultivation is to awaken that yang chi so that it starts to arise within your body. That's the tale of the Nemean lion.

In many cultivation schools, especially the esoteric schools and Indian tantric traditions that involve concentrating on the body's chi channels and chakras directly, you will often see pictures of masters sitting on the skin of a lion, tiger, stag, or the pelt of a ram. They sit on the skins of animals that represent yang chi to show that they have awakened the yang chi and mastered it, which means they have actually transformed it. If the pelt in cultivation stories is golden or shines with light, such as in the Greek story of Jason and the golden fleece,[8] it means that the entire internal system of channels, chakras and chi has already been purified. This is what was represented by the burning bush of Moses.

Some of the Middle Eastern spiritual schools used the symbolism of Mithras slaying Taurus the Bull to represent the regenerative powers of the yang chi once it's awakened. However, because that symbolism is connected with star constellations and Spring time, people have lost sight of the cultivation connection.

This is what happens to most true cultivation knowledge over time. It eventually becomes lost because so few people really cultivate or succeed on the spiritual path, which is why sages try to incorporate the knowledge in some lasting form for their culture. Despite our modernity, in today's culture spiritual cultivation knowledge is rare indeed, so hardly anyone knows how to cultivate anymore or what the universal spiritual path actually entails. However, with an insider's knowledge of the Twelve

---

[8] The golden fleece was called "a prize of the gods" since it represented the purification of an individual's chi and channels.

Labors you can indeed recover the basic cultivation path and learn how to become a true peer of Hercules.

The point of the ancient Mithras cult was that you *are* in fact Mithras. You *are* in fact repeating the First Labor of Hercules once you awaken your yang chi. You can awaken that yang chi energy (prana or kundalini) through meditation, pranayama or one of a thousand different cultivation methods that all involve cultivating an empty mind as part of the spiritual path. From the peace or stillness of an empty mind, yang chi is activated because yang arises from the extreme of yin and yin from the extreme of yang. Once you are no longer holding on to thoughts which block the free flow of chi throughout your body, the real regenerative forces of nature will start to arise and reassert themselves.

To succeed, it all comes down to persistent personal cultivation of correct meditation practice. You already have everything you absolutely need to succeed in "attaining the Tao," which is the term for becoming spiritually enlightened and discovering your real self-nature or True Self fundamental essence. In order to attain self-realization, you just have to practice letting go of holding on to consciousness, which is often called "false consciousness" since it is not the real you. Letting go of ignorance, ignorance will depart and the Truth will be revealed.

The real you is what is able to witness consciousness, and that real you is what you must find on the road of spiritual practice. You can therefore call spiritual cultivation the path of finding your true self-nature, or True Self, but it is also really the path of "finding God" since God is the underlying nature of all things in western parlance. In the Bible it says "Ye are gods" because everyone is that original self-nature.

Like Hercules you are already half divine, you are already halfway to success in spiritual practice just by virtue of being human, but you will live out an ordinary life and have to reincarnate over and over again, up and down the planes of existence endlessly, if you don't decide to engage in the process of spiritual cultivation and finally succeed at attaining enlightenment and finding your True Self. Success in the Tao is the only thing that brings true liberation. Otherwise, up and down, up and down you'll bob over and over again through countless religions, lives and endless eons until you decide to ultimately succeed on the spiritual path and find your True Self that is experiencing it all.

That discovery will free you from the clutches of karma and reincarnation. It will enable you to control the process of birth and death so that you can decide where you're going to go next and what you are going to do. There's no escaping from the universe, but you can reach a point where you can be in control of the process as to where you'll go and what you'll do, and that's what fully awakened Buddhas do.

If you start down the path of spiritual cultivation, then you can reach what Confucius called the "state of highest excellence" or what Shakyamuni Buddha called "perfect and complete enlightenment." This involves realizing our source nature – the source nature of the entire universe or "Triple Realm" - and becoming free of pain and suffering through that discovery. As a result, you will gain tremendous clarity, purity and bliss. You will be able to control where you are going and what you will do. It all starts with the humble first steps of personal spiritual cultivation, and that involves basic meditation practice.

Both men and women can succeed in spiritual cultivation. Success is not limited to men alone, or races or religions or humans or any other type of classification you might make among sentient beings. For instance, in the Buddhist *Lotus Sutra* there is a famous story about a dragon king's daughter only eight years old who succeeded in attaining enlightenment and who offered Shakyamuni Buddha her precious pearl. The story is there to prove that women – and other types of sentient beings - can just as easily succeed on the path as men, and simply need to try.

Countless women have succeeded in cultivation, such as Yeshe Tsogyal and Jetsun Niguma (Tibetan Buddhists), Mirabai (Hindu), Teresa of Avila (Christian), or Rabia al-Adawiyya (Muslim), all of whom came from different spiritual traditions. It does not matter what gender you are, or what religion or culture or spiritual tradition you come from. If you cultivate correctly and sufficiently, you can succeed just as these women have.

Often you can find pictures of women yogis in Eastern cultures who were sitting on tiger skins or had the heads of boars. These symbols, tigers and boars, also represent the fact that they had overcome the fierce yang chi during their cultivation path. Remember that the wild nature of these sorts of animals not only represents chi, but unpurified passions.

Man or woman, it's not that you engage in some sort of physical yoga or breathing exercises to stimulate your chi in spiritual cultivation. Rather you learn how to empty your mind and let go of passions. As you let go of attaching to consciousness your chi will transform, and at the same time you will be purifying your passions because they will no longer control you. You let go of consciousness by witnessing consciousness and introspecting, or investigating where it comes from, and through wisdom or insight you can arrive at a realization of the source.

Some spiritual schools use a tiger to represent passions and yang chi, although tigers in many schools represent "fierce yin chi" instead. This is the destructive or purifying nature attributed to kundalini energy when it first arises and butts up against obstructions inside the chi channels and produces painful friction as it starts clearing them out. This is the "yin" characteristic of the kundalini energy when it first arises, which is why it is sometimes called the "Fierce Woman" in some cultivation schools.

In other words, kundalini *is* yang chi, but we say it has an unpurified yin nature when it first arises. This is only at the cleansing stage of kundalini arousal, for in the stages of samadhi and dhyana, the circulation of the yang chi within the body feels warm and blissful. In the yin stage of arousal the kundalini feels hot because it is bumping into all sorts of obstructions and encounters friction in trying to remove them. Friction always produces heat and irritation. However, the Chinese Taoists often call chi "no fire" to denote the fact that when your body is truly full of chi your breathing will come to a halt and the feeling will not be of uncomfortable heat anymore.

"Yang chi" is actually synonymous for kundalini, and it always feels blissful and warm when it is purified and circulates freely. However, you only experience this purified stage of kundalini after it goes through an initial process of cleansing the chi channels of embedded or hardened chi obstructions inside. Initially most people only feel the yin effects of its awakening which can take the appearance of itching, heat, perspiration, shaking, and other sorts of sensations. That's the uncomfortable side of a kundalini awakening.

When kundalini first arises in the body it starts pushing through your chi channels, and when the flowing energy encounters obstructions then people typically feel sensations of pain, heat and discomfort. As the *Hatha Yoga Pradipika* mentions, at times there may even be perspiration or shaking of the body as the chi starts to open up the channels. Unfortunately, being just a rudimentary text the *Hatha Yoga Pradipika* does not elucidate upon the very many other types of reactions that happen, but they are catalogued in Buddhism and Taoism.

Everyone will experience different reactions as they start to cultivate, but there will be general types or categories of responses and general patterns to the reactions. For instance, I remember that at one stage in my own cultivation the chi energies were so strong, pulsing throughout my body, that I could not sleep for forty to fifty days in a row during those transformations. You cannot say that everyone will have that same experience or that sleeplessness would last for the same amount of time if you went through that same stage of gong-fu, but the possibility always arises that such things will happen for others on the cultivation trail because it is a common type of gong-fu experience.

In the earliest stages of cultivation almost all your spiritual energy goes into opening and then clearing your body's energy channels from obstructions. As the chi pushes through the channels and expels the dirty, unpurified chi within them, there is friction that produces heat and other uncomfortable reactions. The chi energy has the strength and ferocity of a lion or tiger once it gets started, just like the Nemean lion, and people often feel pain, itching, heat, shaking or other sensations as it clears the channels of obstructions. Buddhism, Taoism and the yoga schools have catalogued countless such sensations.

Of course in some stories that represent the awakening of kundalini and subsequent cleansing of the channels, people don't stress these details. Every story emphasizes different aspects of this stage of the cultivation path, so let me provide an example.

In the Chinese epic *Journey to the West,* for instance, the Monkey King Sun Wu Kong goes down to the bottom of the ocean. This represents the perineum in the body from which the kundalini or yang chi arises. The Chinese call this area the "*hai-di,*" which means ocean-bottom, and we can say it is at the lowest point or bottom of the trunk of our body between the anus and sexual organs.

In the story, which is actually about the stages of cultivation attainment, Sun Wu Kong's trip is just a way of representing the *muladhara* root chakra since it is located above our perineum between the genital organs and anus. This location is why many Hatha yoga books tell practitioners to press upon their anus during special meditation postures, for those instructions actually mean the perineum, which is the lowest point of the trunk of the body. Without instructions from an esoteric master, most people reading these texts never know what the instructions actually refer to.

In the Chinese story, Sun Wu Kong goes down to the bottom of the sea (to the root chakra or perineum or *hai-di*) and there retrieves a weapon called the "will-following golden-banded staff." This unbreakable staff is a magical weapon that he can shrink down to the size of a needle and store behind his ear. To many, who know both spiritual cultivation and

Chinese medical theory, this staff just represents the sexual energies of the penis, which arises due to yang chi, but there is another meaning as well.

Sun Wu Kong's staff weapon is the same as the club of Hercules and the mace of Hanuman (the Hindu monkey deity). It actually represents the strength of your yang chi once it has arisen. As Lao Tzu said, a baby is absent of sexual desire but can have an erection when he fills with chi, and this also represents the same principle. In *Journey to the West*, Sun Wu Kong keeps the staff in his ear to allude to the fact that his yang chi has already traveled up his spine, and thus his *du-mai* back chi channel of the spine is already opened. That's why his staff (chi) can be called upon at will to do his bidding.

Sun Wu Kong could change the size of his staff with just a thought, which is the same as Hercules being able to swing his club whenever he wished; both abilities represent the fact that our chi responds immediately to our thoughts. Our chi transforms as our thoughts transform, and our chi goes wherever our mind wills it. This connection between chi and consciousness is a principle used in many tantric cultivation schools that promote the practice of concentrating on parts of the body.

At the bottom of the sea the Dragon King also gave Sun Wu Kong a headdress with two plumes. You can see videos of this wonderful headdress in the 1986 Chinese movie version of the story which is carried on Youtube. The two plumes indicate that the left and right chi channels of Sun Wu Kong's body, which surround the central or *sushumna* channel[9] within it, also have opened. They open when you practice "prajna wisdom cultivation," which means you realize the empty nature of the mind that is always present with consciousness and continue to let thoughts and understanding arise. For instance, when you drink a sweet drink you never think of the water that's present, and in terms of consciousness we never pay attention to the empty nature of the mind within which thoughts appear.

We can say that thoughts are part of your mind, but they are not the substance of your mind. They are simply things that appear in your mind like the sugar in the water, and you have to discover the essence of your mind to attain the Tao. This is what meditation practice is all about.

In spiritual cultivation it is the true nature of the mind that is the target of realization practice, and Sun Wu Kong succeeded because he cultivated that realization. Statues of Moses also often show him with two horns on

---

[9] Called the *avadhuti nadi* in Tibetan.

his head, and this also symbolizes the same wisdom accomplishment of having opened the left and right channels, too. Projections of some sort on the left and right sides of the head are something you will often see in the pictures of spiritual greats. Alternatively, sometimes you will see a Chinese sage with their beard parted in three sections to symbolize the *sushumna*, left and right channels, though it could also symbolize the *sushumna*, front and back channel, too.

In the story, besides taking the staff from the ocean's bottom, Sun Wu Kong was also given a suit of golden armor by the Dragon King. This is because when you first release your yang chi by unplugging the root chakra, which is what Sun Wu Kong did when he picked up his staff off the bottom of the ocean's floor, it will rise to the top of the head and then start streaming downwards.[10] During the descent, it will coat the outermost skin layers of your body to what feels like an eighth to quarter of an inch thickness. You will actually feel as if your body is being "sealed in" by a layer of chi or liquid that seems to be percolating downwards but whose origins are from below.

When people talk about holy baptism, *this* is actually the first true baptism you must strive to achieve on the spiritual path, and there are many more after this. This chi phenomenon initiates you into the spiritual life and its appearance shows you are cultivating correctly and making progress. You will tend to feel it more as it runs down the front of the body, and to a lesser extent the sides, because it is arising along the *du-mai* chi channel and flowing down the general pathway of the *jen-mai* front channel.

For the first few days this development feels like a protective coating and afterwards you get used to it and then don't notice it anymore. The coating process itself actually feels as if a liquid is flowing down the insides of the body from the top of the head, like water poured from a vase, and somehow sealing the skin whereas it is actually opening up the chi channels in these outermost layers. If you have ever seen a see-through plastic ant farm children's toy, and watched what happens when

---

[10] Unlike what the school of Anthroposophy maintains, cultivation energies always start from below, rise upwards, and then stream downwards. They do not start in the head, but sensations are felt in the head as chi channels open within the skull because of energies streaming upwards. The remedy for such sensations, which sometimes involve slight pressure or discomfort, is simply more meditation until the channels in the head thoroughly open through and through. People who start upon the road of meditation and begin to catch colds easily, because their channels start opening, often find that wearing a hat on the head will help protect them from getting a cold. The aspirin Saridon has been found helpful in cases of headaches caused by what Chinese call "wind invasions."

water is dropped on the sand and percolates down the sides, this is what the process may remind you of.

This "baptismal gong-fu" transforms the outermost skin and connective tissues of your body with a wondrous feeling. Afterwards you feel it for a few days until you get used to the feeling and start ignoring it. In more advanced phases of meditation, you will even reach stages where your bones feel as if they have dissolved and your body feels like an empty sack. That tangible feeling of your body as just an empty sack of skin[11] is a much higher but similar stage of progress from opening the channels. Such sensations never last long.

In Chinese we say that this baptismal stage enables you to feel the "*wei chi*" or protective yang chi that flows through the exterior layers of the body protecting it from outside influences. Just as described in *Journey to the West* and in Chinese martial arts and medicine, this is a chi phenomenon that occurs to all practitioners and so is found in the story of the Nemean lion.

In *Journey to the West*, this inner layer of protective chi is represented by Sun Wu Kong's golden suit of armor bestowed upon him by the Dragon King at the start of the story. Hercules similarly obtains an "invulnerable coat" from the hide of the Nemean lion in his First Labor as well. The lion's pelt is impenetrable and invulnerable to weapons. It serves in the same way that *wei chi* does in protecting your internal organs from the external chi influences that the Chinese call "external wind invasions."

In Tibetan Buddhism it is taught that our mind and our chi go together like a rider and his horse. The rider (our mind) tells the horse (our chi) where to go and the horse obediently runs there. This simple analogy illustrates how the mind and chi are tied together, and why focusing on one part of your body will eventually send the chi there, just as visualization does. Incidentally, horses are used in countless spiritual traditions to represent the chi of the body, or breathing methods that affect the chi of the body, and we'll also find this in the Twelve Labors.

This relationship between our mind and our chi also explains why Sun Wu Kong (the mind) in *Journey to the West* is made manager of the horses (chi) in Heaven, and why in the *Ramayana* of India the "wind god" Vayu angrily started withdrawing all the wind (chi or prana) of the world when the monkey child Hanuman was struck unconscious. "Wind" in all cultivation schools stands for our chi or prana, so in both these stories the relationship between the mind (Hanuman or Sun Wu Kong) and chi

---

[11] This is sometimes called "empty shell meditation."

(horses or wind) was openly recognized. In Hercules' First Labor, it is the Nemean lion which represents the untamed yang chi of the body when it first arises due to spiritual cultivation efforts. At another stage a different type of chi will be represented by a horse, bull, and yet other animals, but for now we start with a lion.

In Greek mythology it is said that Selene, the moon goddess, adored the Nemean lion. This is because the mind is often represented by the moon, and so the mind is connected with the chi of the body as we have already said. Hence, this relationship between consciousness and chi is not only recognized by many Eastern cultivation schools, but was also recognized by the Greeks. This is the mind-body relationship we so often hear about in medicine because chi is what affects our body. Modern science constantly talks about the mind-body phenomena in healing, but scientists never mention the fact that this is basically due to the connection between consciousness and life force (chi) within the human organism.

The mind (the moon) and chi (the lion) always go together just as yin and yang go together, a fact seen in this First Labor and pointed out in countless cultivation traditions. All the aspects of the story show that the Nemean lion represents the chi of the human body, but a special type of chi: the unpurified yang chi, or raw kundalini energy, that first arises from initial steps on the cultivation trail. Many of the Indian spiritual schools refer to the kundalini energy as a serpent, but in this story the yang chi, or kundalini energy, is represented as a lion.

How do you awaken your yang chi on the road of spirituality? Your yang chi arises naturally when you practice meditation. When you practice letting go of your thoughts, which means being naturally aware without clinging to consciousness, your yang chi always arises. The way to make your yang chi arise is to really and truly let go of attaching to the thoughts and sensations (consciousness) that arise in the mind just by witnessing them without getting involved. The moment you truly mentally let go of clinging to consciousness your chi will change instantly - *instantly* - and many people will feel a warmth or vibration in the body at that moment. That sensation should alert you to the fact that you are more correct in your efforts at letting go.

That response shows you are on the road to cultivating emptiness[12] correctly and that your yang chi is immediately starting to open your chi

---

[12] Here we have to add a note about the term "emptiness" and stress that this does not refer to a state of "nothingness." Neither does it imply nihilism, annihilation or non-existence.

channels. This is one of the very first significant bodily transformations which occurs when you start on the correct road of spiritual practice, so you should never try to suppress it.

Other people use more strenuous means such as non-veering (stable) single-minded concentration on special points of the body, or forceful pranayama breath retention techniques, to help stir their kundalini yang chi into awakening. This is typically the emphasis of the Indian yoga schools, Tibetan Buddhism, and many other spiritual schools that approach cultivation through initially cultivating the physical processes of the body and trying to stoke them in various ways. One of the necessities for success on these roads, which many neglect, is that the practitioner must practice the preservation of sexual energies for the best results. There are a lot of preliminary spiritual practices one usually does for the kundalini to awaken, and they are all subsumed under the title of "meditation."

The special emphasis in these schools is on purifying the body and practicing rhythmical breath retention techniques to force a kundalini awakening. In time, this approach can cause people to experience the

---

Sages of different traditions have pointed out that everything in the universe is in a continuous process of change and transformation. Since nothing stays for even an instant, it means that all that you ever experience is just an ephemeral "appearance" that doesn't even have micro-nanosecond existence. All that comes together by causes and conditions (which means all phenomena) is impermanent, and thus there is nothing that can be grabbed or "had" because everything is continually changing even if you can't see the non-fixity. What we have is an endless stream of appearances to the mind that are empty of a non-changing existence. Furthermore, everything is defined by everything else, meaning all of reality participates in the existence of any one thing. Therefore no thing has an independent, self-so real existence. Every thing or phenomenon is "empty" of true reality. Everything is flowing on in continuous transformation, so what you are experiencing in your mind is not the underlying true reality of the universe but a false surface veneer. However, aside from the continuous change there is something always there that is constant, pure and eternal. That backdrop or foundational state is your true Self, or original nature, and it is empty of attributes. Everything arises as a function of that original nature. Sometimes there are sensory experiences, forms, feelings, or thoughts in the mind. Sometimes the mind seems still, calm, peaceful and absent of thoughts, which people usually describe using the term "empty." While these latter states of mental peace are often referred to as "emptiness," the real meaning of the term "emptiness cultivation" refers to finding that always changeless purity called nirvana, or the true Self. The road to nirvana starts out with the meditation practice of letting go of mentally clinging wherein you progressively learn how to let go of all that appears in the mind – even the quiet or "empty" mental states that initially appear due to this letting go. Eventually you can realize with wisdom what is always there behind all the appearances if you continually let them freely arise without clinging. To "cultivate emptiness" means letting go of thoughts, and in turn, thoughts will die down to produce a mental state empty (absent) of thoughts. That state will be an initial image or thought-form of emptiness, and if you do not cling to this or other images, you can eventually arrive at a state absent of all images and experience the true Self of nirvana that we call "emptiness."

fierce type of painful yin kundalini awakening rather than the more blissful sensations that arise from emptiness meditation work which, slowly over time, produces a more peaceful purification of the chi channels. In order to awaken the kundalini you must cultivate meditation for a definite amount of time, and through the Twelve Labors we'll go over the best types of spiritual practice to get you started.

That being said, we have finally thoroughly established what the Nemean lion represents and presented some of the necessary basics you need to know about spiritual cultivation practice. Therefore, with our basics behind us, we can finally start analyzing the First Labor of Hercules in detail.

In setting off on his First Labor to find the Nemean lion, it's said that Hercules journeyed to the town of Cleonae where he stayed at the house of a poor workman, Molorchus. The task of spiritual cultivation is symbolized by Molorchus in the story because his daily duties as a workman symbolize the necessity for consistency in spiritual practice. Spiritual cultivation is like daily labor in that it is something you must humbly work at every day in order for there to be progress.

This is why spiritual masters of all religions have told us to constantly turn our thoughts and hearts over to God or Allah, or however they termed the original nature. They use terms like "constant mindfulness" and "constant remembrance" to indicate we should always be cultivating the path as much as possible. Without regular practice you simply cannot succeed on the spiritual path. Molorchus represents you and me, rather than a king or someone especially gifted in some way, because the lesson applies to everyone. Like him, we all start out at a humble station on the spiritual path, and it is our consistent effort that eventually distinguishes us in the end.

You must work at spiritual cultivation on a regular basis in order to succeed, something seen, for example, in the Islamic requirement to pray five times a day. This gives Muslims five opportunities a day to cultivate, which explains why countless more Sufis seem to have succeeded on the spiritual path than members of other religious groups who "spiritually cultivate" for just an hour or so once per week. You cannot become Superman in one day but must proceed through the stages of spiritual cultivation via step-by-step practice, starting from the most humble beginnings of a day laborer who must work at his tasks on a daily basis.

Whether king or beggar, famous or unknown, all individuals are on equal footing when it comes to the task of spiritual cultivation.

Pedigree, status, power and wealth mean absolutely nothing to realizing enlightenment, whereas putting in the work of cultivating meditation practice means everything. All of us start out on the cultivation trail on equal footing. We start out as poor individuals rather than as the wealthy, so like Molorchus we must conduct ourselves with daily cultivation effort in order to make true spiritual progress. We cannot just spend an hour during the weekend to participate in some religious ceremony, think about "holy" things, see some friends and expect anything to happen.

To make a practice schedule and turn cultivation into a daily habit is the most wonderful asset possible to your practice. Even Hercules had to do this, which is the significance of his visit to the workman Molorchus in this story. If you want to change your behavior or become expert at some skill, everyone knows it takes daily, devoted, continual practice to develop that proficiency. How could spiritual cultivation possibly be any different? The results you seek in any field of endeavor usually don't just happen randomly. You have to cultivate regularly to attain them or to achieve anything in life. How can you learn to perform martial arts, or ice skate, or play golf well, or even cook like a chef if you don't consistently study and practice? Proficiency comes from practice.

The special rule in spiritual cultivation is this:

MEDITATION METHOD + CONSISTENT PRACTICE +
TIME + PATIENCE = RESULT

In this case, all the spiritual cultivation methods in the world involve dropping attachments to thoughts so that you can eventually realize that the real underlying nature of your mind is empty of thoughts. That starting point - of realizing through direct experience that your mind is empty - is called "*seeing the Tao.*" Thoughts simply appear in the mind, but they are not the real you just as the body is not the real you either. They are not actually the mind either, for the mind is the empty medium upon which they are witnessed.

This is a fact that few people realize until they start practicing meditation and eventually experience this realization. The practice of meditation on a regular basis is how you can eventually experience the peaceful, silent, true nature of your mind which is always present but screened by your habit of attaching to consciousness, i.e. mental events that come and go. Mental phenomena ceaselessly come and go until you learn how to stop feeding them energy, after which wandering thoughts settle down and the mind returns to its naturally empty state. To "see" that – and to actually experience that - is a minor spiritual realization that everyone goes through on the road to true awakening.

We usually think our thoughts are the mind whereas the mind is actually the empty screen upon which thoughts are seen or experienced. Yes, thoughts are part of consciousness, or the mind, but it is the emptiness aspect that counts since this is what is always there. It is the underlying empty nature of the mind that we strive to realize in spiritual practice, but the very act of clinging to thoughts and consciousness (which we are invisibly performing all the time) stands in the way of this realization, the first of many obstacles on the road of practice.

In this First Labor, Molorchus tells Hercules that he'll offer a sacrifice to the gods asking them to help Hercules kill the Nemean lion. This is like trying to bribe Heaven to get good fortune, and it just cannot succeed. You cannot buy success in spiritual cultivation from anyone. Hercules therefore wisely asks Molorchus to wait thirty days before making any sacrifice because he has to make the effort to succeed himself. Hercules tells him that if he returns safely from the hunt, Molorchus should make a sacrifice to Zeus, the king of all the Gods, for having made his success possible. On the other hand, if Hercules does not return but dies due to the lion, then Molorchus should sacrifice to him as a hero because he attempted such a great feat.

In other words, all that matters in life is the work of spiritual cultivation. Whether one ultimately succeeds or not, whether one lives or dies, those who devote themselves to the cultivation trail are all the real heroes among men, and like the fallen in battle should be honored. Cultivation is the royal road, so all who tread it are heroes. Forget about whether you will fail or succeed, but just get started and push it for all it is worth. In another life, the opportunity may not exist, and the teachings may be absent as well.

Heroes do not shirk attempting a difficult task because they believe they will not succeed, but take on challenging tasks and work at them without expectations because they are the right things to do and that is the right way to act. Spiritual cultivation is practically the only field of endeavor where you are not just a hero when you succeed but an extraordinary human being just for trying. No other field of human endeavor is like this. In fact, one of the biggest secrets is that many of the greatest men in history rose to heights of prominence precisely because they were self-cultivators.

The story of Hercules' Labors therefore starts off admonishing us never to think that spiritual success can be bought through a sacrifice or ceremony. You cannot obtain it as a favor from heaven. Even fully enlightened beings who incarnate here, called "Buddhas,"[13] must cultivate to attain it themselves. Furthermore, if the enlightened Buddhas of the universe could have liberated anyone they would have done so already, but no one can liberate you except yourself. It is your mind, your consciousness that is stuck in delusion through attachments. You are the only person who can save yourself by purifying your own mind, and so you must do it through your own efforts. You must achieve it by your cultivation efforts.

Heaven can indeed help you in the task of spiritual cultivation; angels, deities, dakinis or devas (they are all synonyms) certainly do help those who tread this path sincerely. However, you must make a personal effort for self-realization because no one can liberate you but yourself, just as no one could kill the lion except for Hercules. People rarely stop to consider that if any Buddha or deity or whatever could liberate you they would have done so already, but the frank truth is that you have to work to attain self-realization yourself. Others can only point out the Truth and the path, and you have to do the cultivation work to arrive at self-realization. It is called "*self*-realization" because you must realize what is your True Self by yourself; you are the one who must awaken because no one can do it for you. Just being the member of a group that considers itself spiritually select, or destined for Heaven after members die, will not spiritually liberate you one bit.

If you do achieve the fruits of cultivation, it is true that you should thank Heaven for its assistance in helping you complete the work. If not, you should still congratulate yourself for the effort and a life lived well achieving merit beyond the ordinary human, for no life is lived well without the personal effort at spiritual cultivation. At the end of your days, you cannot look back and say you have done a good job unless you have during that time engaged in a positive degree of self-cultivation to find your true nature. That effort will carry on to another life where you finally can succeed. Unlike money, power, status, fame or anything else

---

[13] A "Buddha" is a fully enlightened being who has achieved self-realization. The term "Buddha" is taken from Buddhism, but "being a Buddha" does not mean someone who belongs to the Buddhist faith. It simply means an individual who realized their fundamental nature – your fundamental nature, too - and thus became fully enlightened. There are various stages of self-realization, and any sentient being who attains enlightenment is called a Buddha, or alternatively a "sage."

material, the results you achieve in spiritual cultivation can be carried forward to a subsequent life.

People commonly think riches and power and fame matter, but when you die you cannot take them with you and after death you must soon start all over again with an entirely different karma of good and bad circumstances in a new life. Past karma is endless, so you can never count on good fortune occurring in your immediate or far future. Eventually good karma runs out, but the target of cultivation is something permanent and supreme beyond any type of universal good fortune, however great it may seem.

In this world, the only two things that therefore matter are spiritual cultivation to realize the Tao and performing acts of merit and compassion to help other beings, such as teaching them the Tao and helping them in ways that relieve suffering. Acting on behalf of others is what Confucius in *The Great Learning* called "loving the people" and it is actually one of the requirements of cultivation. There is the cause and effect of the ordinary world that rules the realms of chemistry, physics and so forth. There is also cause and effect within the realm of consciousness that produces the happiness or suffering felt by others, and a great being strives to offer kindness, compassion, charity, fearlessness, and of course dharma to help relieve the suffering in this realm and bring about joy. The realm of human behavior is born because of consciousness (our thoughts) and therefore great beings try to teach humans how to watch and manage their behavior to bring about harmony, peace and bliss within human relationships.

In this world, the greatest human beings are not like sheep who mindlessly "follow the crowd." The great heroes of this world are those individuals like Hercules, Krishna, Jesus or Confucius who transcended the world by succeeding at spiritual cultivation. They didn't care what other people thought but set out to succeed on the spiritual path and discover their true ultimate nature, their fundamental source or True Self. That True Self, or fundamental original nature, is beyond both mind and matter because it is what gives birth to both mind and matter. If we try to emulate the cultivation path of such individuals but do not fully succeed, we still merit great respect for treading this road of spiritual advancement, and we do carry our achievements along these lines into the future.

This is what makes a life matter. This is how to find one's true fundamental self-nature in a world of endless falsity or *maya*. Only the greatest people in the world rise above ignorance and the "sheeple" paths of religious dogmas, ceremonies and disciplinary rules of purity in order to really spiritually cultivate and find the True Self of all beings in the universe, and the ultimate source of both matter and consciousness.

Hercules' attitude toward Molorchus' sacrificial offering is therefore the correct attitude to take in regards to spiritual cultivation. You have to set your mind on cultivation and be ready to die to achieve the end. You need the greatest motivation to succeed rather than give up. Like the great spiritual cultivation hero of Tibet, Milarepa, you must be ready to undergo many hardships in order to succeed at cultivation, including even risking death such as fighting the Nemean lion.

How many people are actually willing to do this? Very few have such deep motivation. However, spiritual results will indeed come to you if you take simple first steps in cultivating meditation practice and just keep at it. Progress has to come because it is all a matter of science. Spiritual progress and spiritual states will come if you just learn how to let go, and that is what the Zen masters constantly tell us so that we can achieve the results of the path without effort.

Do you actually think that working five days a week just to make money is worthy of your life? Is that effort worthy of your life essence and if not, how do you make this a life that matters?

One could safely say that the practice of spiritual cultivation for self-realization is the only task genuinely worthy of life, for death is a fate that will eventually claim all of us just as impermanence will claim all our deeds. In the *Diamond Sutra*, Shakyamuni Buddha said that even if you gave away a universe of charity and sacrificed endless lives to help others, the exceedingly great merit you would gain was absolutely nothing, not even a tiny fraction, of that attained by achieving self-realization. Transient, ephemeral things cannot be compared with the eternal.

The most difficult things and the most pleasurable things in life are both soon forgotten. The events of life are like an ephemeral dream you cannot grasp or hold for even an instant. Even the most special of moments are things we cannot make stay, so therefore you have to learn how to mentally let go while still doing everything that has to be done. Events might seem real and intensely alive at the moment, but they are actually occurring as if you are in a passing dream. Feelings, thoughts, sensations, phenomena ... all these things are ungraspable and just endlessly passing through the mind. Pleasure and pain are both there, ceaselessly alternating one after the other until you reach the source nature or True Self and can "abide without abiding" where they no longer exist.

Nevertheless, a human life is extremely valuable for the goal of self-cultivation in attaining the Tao. Shakyamuni Buddha often explained that the gods in heaven don't have it as good as we do here on Earth in terms of conditions perfect for achieving success on the spiritual path. This is because the devas in the various heavens[14] lead lives of extreme pleasure, and when a person enjoys such good fortune they typically choose to play rather than to cultivate. If you look around at many of the rich and powerful in the world today then you will understand this general principle of behavior. Therefore it is actually the great pain and suffering of this world that can help motivate us to succeed at spiritual work.

In this rare time of incredible material prosperity – unmatched by all previous world history – you need only ask yourself one major question: will you remain ignorant and squander the golden opportunity to travel the royal road of cultivation or not? The knowledge of the true cultivation way is quickly declining, so I would personally advise that you grab your chance in this life while the opportunity is still available.

History shows that the knowledge of the true spiritual cultivation path does not last long. Knowledge of cultivation teachings and techniques – as countless masters have warned – is not always humanly available and quickly becomes polluted and altered by false dogmas. The opportunity to cultivate the Tao (enlightenment) because you have knowledge of the spiritual path is exceedingly rare, for when you look around you will also see that few have the correct information. But here, reading this, you have a golden opportunity.

As the world becomes more technological and man becomes even more materialistic, who knows if knowledge of the spiritual path will even exist in future times … or whether you'll still have an opportunity to cultivate? Shakyamuni Buddha predicted that the teachings of spiritual cultivation will definitely die away in time and as we get closer and closer to that prophecy's fulfillment, you will lose even more opportunities to cultivate.

---

[14] Most every religion recognizes the existence of various ranks of heavenly beings, called devas, dakinis, celestial beings, angels, and so on. The fact that there are various ranks of heavenly beings – such as angels, archangels, archai, thrones, cherubim, seraphim, etc. - is connected to the fact that there are different levels of heavens as well, a point also commonly noted in countless spiritual traditions.

It seems that the fate of the ordinary man who does not cultivate is like Sisyphus, who for eternity had to repeatedly push a boulder up a cliff only to watch it roll down again and undo all his efforts. Life after life our efforts at religion devoid of cultivation are wasted. To become able to escape that endless fate is exactly what spiritual cultivation is about.

Spiritual cultivation enables you to break the bonds and barriers of a humble life and turn it into one of universal significance. Those who succeed can choose to do anything, becoming protectors of worlds, religions, races, cultures, countries and cultivation. Just stepping on to the path makes you Hercules yourself and puts you on the road to overcoming the Nemean lion.

Some spiritual schools (such as Taoism and yoga) say it requires not thirty but one hundred days of devoted meditation work for your yang chi to awaken. It's not that hard to stir yang chi into arising with the correct spiritual practices. It just takes the right effort applied over time with patience and consistence. The most important practice is to try to cultivate an "empty mind," which means to let go of thoughts when they arise and cultivate non-clinging since it quiets mentation. You might even try to directly cultivate a state of emptiness by practicing one of the many exercises in the *Vijnanabhairava*, a meditation instruction book from the school of Kashmir Shaivism.

Thoughts always arise and depart within the mind, but if you do not cling to thoughts or mental states and scenarios while remaining open, naturally aware and relaxed, then in time they will die down and you will attain a deep state of silence or peace due to their absence. If you let go of even that empty mental peace that is produced, this is what's called becoming free from the entanglement of mental states. Everything still functions, but the miscellaneous monkey mind and internal dialogue of useless, negative thought chatter drops away so that you can function effortlessly with peace as long as you don't cling. In time your discriminative thoughts will die down completely while your awareness will still remain alive, clear and open without an army of thoughts fighting wars in your mental continuum. If you continue cultivating in this way and shine awareness, observation or witnessing on the mind, you can introspect to ask "who is experiencing all this?," and with insight realize the answer and spiritually awaken.

If you cultivate very hard for even a short period of time, your yang chi *will* start to arise. Pranayama methods can stir the kundalini yang chi into arising, but you must also be celibate for a short while in order to best accomplish the deed in the most efficient fashion. This is hard for young men to do, but youth is a time not to throw away your best chances of making progress because of the inherent strength of your vitality. You must also practice cultivating an empty mind (a mind that does not cling to thoughts but lets them arise and depart freely without interference) for your kundalini to arise and practice patience because meditation results rarely happen instantly.

Just as in the legend of Hercules, you have to stalk the lion for awhile before you can find it. Thus it takes regular daily labor, meaning a practice schedule represented by Molorchus' humble station in life, before you can find the lion. However, you can see results within a short time period if you truly set your mind to it. Everyone can become a spiritual hero regardless of their initial status – men and women both - but you have to work consistently at the task of cultivating meditation.

I highly recommend you create a daily meditation practice schedule, however humble it might be, if you want to succeed along the lines of the Twelve Labors. As you make progress, you can enlarge its scope if you like. This, rather than church, mosque, synagogue or temple services, is what will lead you to genuine spiritual states and the gong-fu you will read about in Hercules' various labors.

This is not to say you should not attend religious ceremonies or services. However, I must reiterate what all the saints and sages from multiple traditions have consistently said: the real spiritual practice is not found in rituals, rules and ceremonies but in personal cultivation practice. Even when you read of a Russian saint like Seraphim of Sarov who somewhat succeeded, you'll find his spiritual progress came from much personal cultivation practice.

How did Hercules cultivate? Setting off from Molorchus' house, the legend says Hercules eventually found the Nemean lion. He started shooting arrows at it, but they simply bounced off the lion's impenetrable hide.

Arrows can represent many different things in cultivation schools. They can mean thoughts, they can mean *kumbhaka* pranayama breathing practices,[15] or they can represent just plain old arrows. In this case the story clues reveal that Hercules probably used emptiness meditation

---

[15] These are yogic breath retention exercises where you practice holding your breath and then expelling it forcefully like an arrow, or slowly according to certain specially timed rhythms. *Kumbhaka* is a term denoting the state where there is neither inhalation nor exhalation, neither in-breathing or out-breathing. Respiration pauses or ceases temporarily. Hence *kumbhaka* practices help you attain states where the breathing stops.

along with anapana[16] or yogic breath retention practices, called *kumbhaka* pranayama, to get started on the path. In those breath retention practices you hold your breath and then finally let it go with tremendous force. The practices are like the pulling back of an arrow on a bow, the holding of the arrow for a measured time, and then its quick release.

Everyone who practices meditation correctly eventually reaches a point where the breath dies down naturally and then seems to pause or stop. You can often reach this stage easily if you if you complement your meditation routine with the practice of holding your breath for a long period of time, as done in the yoga schools of pranayama as well as in Tibetan Buddhism. The state of naturally occurring respiratory cessation is the *real kumbhaka* (breath cessation practice) of the yoga schools despite the fact they practice producing an artificial state of respiratory holding, and it is the time when the real yang chi or kundalini of the body arises.

In Taoism this stage is called "*tai hsi*" or "internal embryo breathing" because the lungs have stopped moving but an internal pulsation originates in the belly and seems as if it is pumping chi. Most everyone eventually experiences the natural *kumbhaka* when they learn how to let go of their thoughts and body during the practice of meditation. If you can maintain that state of respiratory pausation without force, and abide in it without exertion, it will work to greatly transform your body.

After some time doing his stalking, the legend recounts that Hercules discovered that the Nemean lion lived in a cave. The cave had two entrances, so Hercules blocked one entrance and entered the lion's cave through the other.

This refers to the fact that our body has two major chi channels running up its back and down its front, called the *du-mai* and *jen-mai* respectively, which intersect in the lower belly (and top of the head). Meditation practice readily opens the *du-mai* back channel, which runs up our spine, but the *jen-mai* channel running down the front of our body is harder to open until much higher stages of spiritual cultivation.

Entering the cave, Hercules started fighting the lion but simply had no way to subdue it. He finally hit it with his club to knock it unconscious, and lacking any other method he then strangled it to death.

---

[16] A type of breathing practice, followed in Buddhism, where you practice watching, witnessing or observing your breath until it calms down and seemingly disappears. When it disappears, or stops, that's when your real yang chi, or kundalini, starts to awaken. The practice has many nuances whose explanations would require a book in itself. This is one of the two major techniques by which most Buddhist practitioners awakened, including Zen masters, but unfortunately the practice never made its way into Tibet.

This part of the story reminds us that we have to give up thoughts to cultivate an empty mind and then we will reach the state of respiratory cessation, denoted by the strangulation, where we stop breathing. That's how everyone proceeds in spiritual cultivation, and it's impossible to avoid this stage of gong-fu. When thoughts stop your breathing stops, and that's the beginning of true internal chi breathing. That's when your yang chi starts arising.

Hence, when you practice meditation properly and truly let go of your thoughts while still witnessing them like a third person observer, eventually you will reach a state where your breathing stops naturally because your thoughts calm down and seem lacking or absent. That's why we call it cultivating "empty mind" or "emptiness." This state of respiratory cessation is exactly when the internal pulsing of kundalini finally ignites, a process Taoism calls the awakening of the "clumsy fire," and these first stages of kundalini are what is represented by the Nemean lion.

All the details of this First Labor suggest Hercules somehow reached this stage of respiratory cessation that served to awaken his yang chi. He might have used a variety of different *kumbhaka* pranayama techniques in conjunction with emptiness meditation to initially get started – such as the Tibetan practice of Vajravahari's "nine-bottled wind" or some other pranayama method. Given the thirty day time period along with the other story details, this is one possible path he may have followed but we don't know for sure. Everything fits perfectly, but even if he didn't use any of these techniques it still remains true that you will experience this state of respiratory cessation to a greater or lesser extent through the practice of meditation, and when you do, your yang chi will finally start to arise.

This always happens at the very beginning of the cultivation path for those who meditate correctly, and when it happens it kick starts a whole sequence of other spiritual transformations into action. Your only task is to get the process of chi transformation kick started, and then you continue practicing emptiness meditation and let the body transform on its own without any interference on your part. That is the entire cultivation path in general.

Hercules triumphantly returned to Molorchus, who was just about to make a sacrifice to Hercules (whom he presumed dead) because the thirty day period was over. Molorchus then sacrificed to Zeus instead, and Hercules brought the lion skin back with him to Mycenae. Our hero thereafter wore the skin as his cloak, something often seen in his statues, since his yang chi had now opened the outer channels of his skin for the *wei chi* protective coating, and so the first of his Twelve Labors was concluded.

We say the Twelve Labors of our story are difficult Herculean tasks, but you absolutely can achieve them if you practice, especially this first task of kundalini awakening. The story flat out tells us that it only took Hercules about a month to get started once he set his mind on this labor. With thirty days of consistent devoted practice, who knows what you might accomplish? It all comes down to the consistency of the right practice methods in the end.

In summary, the Nemean lion represents the yang chi of the body resting in the root chakra (*hai-di* or perineum). You can awaken this chi by practicing pranayama together with thought free meditation techniques, such as the vipassana practice of watching thoughts so that they quiet down, after which your yang chi will rise up the *du-mai* back channel of your body into your head, and then stream downwards to open the chi channels in the outer layers of the skin. When that happens, it feels like it is coating the outermost layers of your body with a protective coating. That's why the lion had a hide so tough ("impenetrable") that no spear or arrow could penetrate it.

Hercules stunned the beast with his club to knock it unconscious (which tells us to give up our attachments to thoughts on the road of spiritual cultivation) and then strangled it with his bare hands, which shows that he reached a state of breath cessation where the yang chi finally arises.

Pranayama practitioners try to force this into happening through fierce breath retention practices called *kumbhaka* techniques. Emptiness meditation lets you reach this state of respiratory cessation more peacefully and naturally. In my opinion, one should follow both roads of practice. In Buddhism, people commonly follow vipassana or anapana (watching the breath) to reach this state but there are great benefits to pranayama practice, too.

Anyone who practices meditation for a while, and really lets go, will experience an eventual slowing or calming of the breath, and then this stage of cessation quite naturally will occur. Then your yang chi, or kundalini energy, will awaken and start to rise up your *du-mai* back channel. Most spiritual schools will describe the results of this initial accomplishment in terms of experiencing mental peace which they call "emptiness" or the quieting of wandering thoughts in the head. However, here we are mostly describing the physical phenomenon that accompanies the process when the root chakra starts to become unplugged. This degree of achievement is only attained by those who really work hard at spiritual cultivation, and certainly not by lackadaisical meditation practitioners who cultivate randomly without devotion.

The awakening or stirring of the yang chi is the very first step of the cultivation path. Anyone can attain this stage of spiritual practice within a short period of time if they truly set out to be a cultivation hero. You need to practice meditation and breathing exercises to do it. This is what Hercules accomplished in his First Labor. This is what you can do, too.

THE SECOND LABOR:
SLAY THE POISONOUS
NINE-HEADED LERNEAN HYDRA

[2.5.2] As a second labor King Eurystheus ordered Hercules to kill the Lernean hydra. That creature, living in the swamps of Lerna, used to go forth into the plain and ravage both the cattle and the country. The hydra had a huge body with nine heads, eight of them mortal but the middle one immortal. Mounting a chariot driven by Iolaus, his nephew, Hercules came to Lerna, and having halted his horses, he discovered the hydra on a hill beside the springs of the Amymone where its lair was located. By pelting it with fiery arrows he forced it to come out, and in the act of doing so he seized it and held it fast. But the hydra wound itself around one of his feet and clung to him. Hercules could not achieve anything by smashing its heads with his club, for as fast as one head was smashed, two more would return in its place. Furthermore, a giant crab, the friend of the hydra, came to its aid by trying to crush Hercules' trapped foot with its pinchers. Hercules killed it, and in his turn called for help from Iolaus who, by setting fire to a piece of wood to create a torch, would cauterize the roots of the heads each time Hercules smashed one, thus preventing them from sprouting again. Having thus got the better of the sprouting heads, Hercules chopped off the immortal head, buried it, and put a heavy rock on it beside the road that leads through Lerna to Elaeus. He slit open the body of the hydra and dipped his arrows in the gall to make them poisonous. Despite his valor, Eurystheus said that this labor should not be reckoned among the ten Hercules owed because Hercules had not conquered the hydra by himself, but through the help of Iolaus.

The Second Labor of Hercules was to kill the Lernean hydra. The Lernean hydra was a mystical water snake with nine poisonous heads, so right off we know that the snake represents the chi channels of the body and the multiple heads represent its nine major chakras. These chakras are simply major nexus points along the chi channels where they branch into other meridians. In some versions of the story the number of hydra heads varies, but this is not important because many schools emphasize different chakras in the body.

The hydra was the sister of the Nemean lion, so we know that this interpretation of chi channels is right on course since chi and chi channels go together. The Nemean lion stood for yang chi, but the fact that the hydra was female means that this labor will involve the yin energies of the body. Males always represent yang chi, and females always represent yin chi or yin energies or untransformed channels. Sometimes the moon is also used to represent yin energy or the left chi channel of the body (through which yin chi flows) called the *ida* channel in yoga schools, and sometimes it is also used to represent the mind.

It's said that the Lernean hydra was particularly dangerous because if one of its heads were cut off, two would immediately grow in its place. In some versions of the legend it just says that the head would grow back. In one version of the legend, it is also said that the hydra's mouth issued such poisonous fumes that the many fish, which also lived in the river, were all killed due to the contamination. Not only was the hydra's breath lethal, but smelling its footprints could also result in death as well.

Yin chi is like that – it makes you sick just getting near it or passing through a place where it's been. Any areas where there has been much sickness and death, such as battlefields, graveyards and hospitals, are considered areas of heavy yin chi that often make people feel sick or uncomfortable. This is because people can actually feel the yin chi. Ghosts, for instance, are said to be composed of yin chi as well. Yin chi represents death, sickness, poisonous things, criminal activities, nefarious dealings and at times even evil.

It's very simple to identify the stage of spiritual cultivation represented by the Lernean hydra. As the Nemean lion of yang chi arises, your chi channels start to open, thus allowing a stream of dirty yin chi to pour out in log-like sections. The rising yang chi pushes dirty yin chi out of any obstructed chi channels. The impure yin chi that obstructs the channels is exuded from the channels and chakra locations in pieces that look like fat worms, snakes or sausages squeezed out of holes.

The purification process of a channel being emptied reminds me of insects awakening in the Spring time and popping out of a hole one after another. This process of emptying the channels of yin impurities, after the yang chi is awakened, goes on for days until the particular inner chi body (*kosha*) covering that you are cultivating is cleansed of its dirty chi, deflates and is itself exuded from the body.

In Tibetan Buddhism practitioners are even instructed to envision dirty things like snakes, scorpions and poisonous insects exiting through the tips of the toes to help initiate the extrusion of dirty chi from the feet since this region is particularly difficult to cultivate. If the channels don't empty out, they remain filled with dirty yin chi akin to the poisonous fumes emitted by the hydra. Due to the unleashing of the yang chi energies of the root chakra, the polluted chi is pumped forward and starts to empty out of the channels in solidified and semi-solidified segments resembling tubelike sausages being extruded one after another.

This Second Labor of Hercules therefore refers to the "cleaning of the channels" talked about in countless spiritual cultivation schools now that his kundalini energies have awakened, but nobody mentions the particular details like this in order not to frighten people. In Buddhism, for instance, the process is just called the "purification of the body's five elements." Some other cultivation schools correctly identify this as the "awakening of kundalini" but they don't go into the particulars of the process other than mentioning the physical feelings of pain and heat as the channel obstructions are pushed out. Yet other spiritual schools refer to this stage of transformation as the "cleansing," "physical purification" or even the "harmonization" of the five elements of the body without mentioning these details either.

These terms all refer to the same process because it's the exact same event regardless of the cultivation school or spiritual tradition. Everyone who practices meditation, or cultivates other spiritual practices correctly, eventually experiences a gradual purification of their physical body as they pass through this non-denominational stage of cleansing. Yes, EVERYONE goes through this on the cultivation trail after they make progress from a significant effort of meditation.

As one goes past the stage of simply sitting on a mat playing with an array of endless thoughts and finally enters into the realm of profound mental stillness, the physical body will actually begin to undergo a series of life giving transformations. These transformations - especially those due to breathing techniques such as anapana - will not only help to purify the body, but banish illness and extend one's longevity. This is the stage of Hercules' Second Labor.

Most people won't be able to see the dirty chi being expelled from their bodies. Sometimes people are given a vision so they know this is happening. Some who have opened up their third eye (the Ajna chakra between the eyebrows at the root of nose) from various esoteric practices, or from having practiced Taoist inner viewing, can sometimes see something like this, too. It's explained here, in Chinese Taoism, western alchemy, tantric yoga, Tibetan Buddhism and also in other spiritual cultivation schools that describe the physical transformations during the spiritual path and the fact that most of them are basically stages of purification where dirty chi is ejected from your energy channels and your body. Spiritual cultivation schools that place an emphasis on transforming the physical body and its energetic nature are called "form schools" because they concentrate on cultivating the "physical form" of the body in order to speed the road of spiritual progress. You can practice these schools safely, without much risk of going astray, only if you have a good teacher and deeply understand the principles of the path, especially the fact that the "I" that you call yourself is not a physical body.

Whether this route is helpful or not ultimately depends on someone's wisdom. These routes can assist in transforming the physical nature and thus can serve as a pathway to changing your karma, since the physical body is a large karmic burden or inheritance. The state of your physical body tends to influence your mind and behavior due to the link between your chi and consciousness, so transforming your body to a higher stage of purity helps you forget your body and transform your behavior. It enables you to lay a good foundation for better cultivating the spiritual path.

It's interesting that this labor of Hercules is actually analogous to another Greek legend, which is the first adventure of Jason and the Argonauts that occurs when the Argonauts land on the Isle of Lemnos. The story goes that the women on the island of Lemnos had previously killed their husbands. A population of females without men means they were left without yang chi, and having killed them, we can say that the island was populated by impure yin chi.

The story of Lemnos also says that the women were foul smelling as a punishment from Aphrodite, just as the hydra issued poisonous fumes from its mouth. This stench, as in the story of Hercules, represents unpurified yin chi once again. In fact, as your chi channels start to open you might often smell strange odors as poisons are pushed out as a type of detoxification. The odors are different for each individuals based on their genetics and dietary habits.[17]

At the beginning of both these legends we have a representation of the untransformed yin chi of the body, once as the poisonous hydra's breath and once as the women of Lemnos. In terms of the stages of spiritual cultivation, only after your yang chi awakens can it push this dirty yin chi out of the channels. As you continue meditating after your channels have started opening, you start attaining much higher stages of gong-fu as well. But these higher attainments only occur after the dirty chi inside the channels starts being pushed out.

In the case of Jason and the Argonauts, this interaction of the yang chi with the yin chi is symbolized by the fact that the Argonaut men end up sleeping with the women on the island. However, the Argonauts did not stay long at the Island because of Hercules' urging. Hercules wanted to proceed quickly to the next part of their journey because he had already passed this stage by the time of Jason's story.

Of the many chi channels and chakras in the body, it is particularly difficult to open the heart chakra and to purify the throat chakra. It is

---

[17] My Chinese friends used to joke that I smelled like cheese before my cultivation efforts because of my American diet, a claim often made by Americans Indians, too. They would also laughingly tell me that sensitive people say many Chinese smell like soy sauce, but like everyone else, they lose their odor after they start to cultivate meditation and the channels start to clear. Because people are often giving off bad chi like this, we would often have to nonchalantly slide in and sit between our teacher and a guest (without the guest noticing what was going on) to protect him from the bad chi making him uncomfortable. Many people have bodies that are particularly filthy not just because of their diet or environmental exposures (such as working in chemical factories) but because of the lack of cultivation efforts which would drive out the poisons. This is yet another reason why it was a sacrifice to teach publicly, and why it is difficult to find a good partner for certain types of cultivation practice.

also very difficult to open the leg channels that lead to the foot chakras in the soles of the feet. As you start opening all these channels, you'll eventually find that the buttocks and shoulders also represent a particular set of problems, too. When you look at the painted body designs and jewelry hanging on the bodies of Indian avatars, such as earrings and so forth, they often offer clues for cultivation focus to help open these regions. Many things can be used as an object of visualization focus, and this is one of the reasons we are told to visualize the bodies of various Buddhas or specific regions on their body such as a single hair between the eyebrows or point on their chests. These points of focus, incidentally, correspond to traditional chakra locations.

All these different parts of the body contain channels and chakras that open naturally through the practice of emptiness meditation, but sometimes there are little tricks passed down in various cultivation schools to help quicken this process for particularly troublesome areas. Regardless of any visualization you focus on, the key is to develop a stable mind that is focused and non-moving. You are wasting your time trying to open up your chi channels and chakras by imagining that your chi is revolving in orbits within your body. Visualization practice is successful if kept on a single point of focus.

It's true that most spiritual practitioners first open the central *sushumna* channel of the body through emptiness meditation. In the esoteric schools the best practitioners also practice pranayama, mantra and visualization techniques to assist in the process. However, the ability to cultivate an empty mind through a meditation method such as vipassana or "just letting go" is the key to success in this process.

This is why the same non-denominational stages of spiritual development were readily reported by ardent Christian monks who cultivated an empty mind through constant prayer recitation. The correct practice of prayer recitation quiets the mind and, just like reciting mantras, can lead to spiritual awakening. When it is said that a holy man of the past engaged in silent prayer, or searched for God in solitude, you now know that this simply means he used some form of meditation practice to reach a state of cessation, or mental quiet we call emptiness, and then proceeded in his practice from there.

It's important to remember that the *sushumna* central chi channel runs through the center of the heart chakra, which in turn has eight meridians that branch away from it. Some schools call the chi meridians "petals," but they are basically channel branches that separate from the main channel artery, which in this case is the *sushumna*. You can easily open the heart chakra and the *sushumna* central channel by reciting the Zhunti mantra[18] while simultaneously visualizing a bright Buddha or flame on the location of the heart chakra behind the breast bone. This is the mantra I most often recommend because, among other things, it is specialized for this exact purpose.

This method of concentration on the heart chakra is actually the secret method of Shingon mandala practice in Japan, and yet the few who still practice Shingon rarely know this. In the Shingon mandalas, the Great Primordial Sun Buddha Vairocana at the center of the pictures represents the *sushumna* central channel. The eight Buddhas and Bodhisattvas surrounding Vairocana represent the eight meridians branching off from the chakra. People can recite the Zhunti mantra (or an alternative) while visualizing the mandala in the center of the chest behind the breastbone in order to help open this region. For instance, Christian monks would often recite the Jesus prayer at the location of the heart in order to help open up the heart chakra as well.

Once you open the heart chakra you can start to have an experience of the truth of non-ego or no-self which is alternatively called "emptiness" or "seeing the Tao." The mind is quiet or empty of noisy thoughts, and you realize that the mind is empty and that there is no such thing as a self. In truth, the idea of being a self or ego is just a bunch of thoughts we cling to and when those thoughts die down you can realize the true nature of the ego. As the *sushumna* central channel clears, the heart chakra can start to open allowing you to finally have an actual experience of the fact that the true nature of the mind is empty, and that the ego is not something real and permanent.

What you must realize is that only truly healthy individuals have all their chi channels and chakras open. In other words, if they are open it

---

[18] The Zhunti mantra runs: "Namo Saptanam Samyaksambuddha Kotinam Tadyatha Om Cale Cule Cundhi Soha." The last part of the mantra is pronounced "Om Zhurli, Zhuli, Zhunti Soha" in Chinese. In Tibet the cultivation practitioners commonly recite "Ah Om Hung" or "Om Ah Hung" to help open up the chi channels, and there are a number of other popular mantras as well. Hinduism has countless mantras such as the famous Gayatri mantra. Muslims recite "La illaha il allah hu" and Jews often recite "Ani Yod Heh Vav Heh." Some mantras are simply phrases from holy texts, and some are like the connection passwords of various enlightened Buddhas and Bodhisattvas who have offered them as a way for us to connect with their assistance in attaining the Tao.

means you are really healthy (even if you get sick[19]) and if they are not open you are not really healthy no matter how healthy you may consider yourself to be. In cultivating, you become healthy - in fact the healthiest you can become as a human being.

When the chi flow through all your chakras and channels becomes unobstructed, as happens to truly healthy individuals, only then can you begin to experientially realize the teachings of the sages. Meditation is what leads to the opening of the channels and their distribution centers, called chakras. Meditation or spiritual practice, performed correctly and often enough, reduces mental problems and can often eliminate internal illness by opening the channel pathways. The right type of meditation practice eventually leads to health, longevity, and spiritual enlightenment if pursued to the end.

The experience of realizing you are not an ego is not something you think up, but something you finally "see," experience or perceive as the *truth* with enough cultivation progress, just as the spiritual greats in the past have written. After a person purifies both their body and mind, they can achieve a continual state of freedom, liberation, non-ego or selflessness which is the true state of the human being. This realization actually corresponds to the highest state of physical health and excellence you can ever achieve with the human body in that all the chi channels are fully open and your chi and body's five elements have all become purified.

This spiritual accomplishment is called realizing "emptiness" and "breaking through" or "purifying" what Buddhism calls the "conception skandha." The conception skandha is the Buddhist term for the countless fine thoughts that run through the mind, including the exceedingly fine

---

[19] Individuals who have all their channels open will still get the cold or flu, in fact more easily than ordinary people if they do not protect their bodies with the proper clothing, such as wearing a hat outdoors in cold weather, because their channels are all open. At the early stages of the path they often easily get headaches as well due to "wind invasions," and my teacher has found Saridon to be the best aspirin for these cases though the headaches usually indicate that the practitioner caught a cold and didn't know it. Masters who open their channels become very sensitive to matters that ordinary people cannot sense, and throughout history have created principles and warnings from their discoveries that they tried to interject into their cultures. Some masters, in order to help ignorant people adopt these principles, called their findings "the word of God" or something else that would lead to ready adoption. They were actually just discoveries by realized men (or not) who provided their injunctions with fictional heavenly parentage in order to cheat the people to help the people. Many matters of diet, hygiene or discipline fall into this category. As to their own bodies, many masters harmonize it through meditation and also use herbal and other medicines to help balance it. While recognizing it is not the self, it is still the equipment used for manifesting activity and so is protected and taken care of accordingly.

thoughts by which we continually define ourselves as an existing "I." When you reach a state of emptiness in which these thoughts have been abandoned and awareness simply shines, you'll gain a little bit of spiritual insight or awakening. In Christianity we say that you give up the "small ego," or that it dies, but the big ego or True Self (God the Father) remains, and the ultimate goal of cultivation or spiritual striving is to find that True Self which transcends the small false self. Then we can say that ignorance passes away and that you succeed in self-realization, or enlightenment.

When the plug blocking the heart chakra pops open because of your meditation practice—a process described extensively in Tibetan Buddhism[20]—then you will experience a degree of this emptiness realization. The physical result will initially be a continuous streaming of dirty chi logs that start exiting the body through any chakra orifices that are open, and that is what happens in this labor. Eventually you can fully unplug all the chakras and their chi route meridians, but there are a lot of stages to the process which all starts with the kundalini rising, or Nemean lion. These stages all involve transforming the various layers of chi wrapped around the channels and chakras within our bodies. Until they are all transformed you cannot say that you have opened any chakra fully.

In Indian teachings, there are many chi layers of the body which must be purified or transformed, and these layers are called the *koshas*, sheaths or bodies. Hinduism says there are five *koshas* within the human body, identified as follows:

- The *Annamaya kosha*
- The *Pranamaya kosha*
- The *Manamaya kosha*
- The *Vijnanamaya kosha*
- The *Anandamaya kosha*

The *annamaya kosha* refers to our physical body, which is the very densest sort of chi in the universe. We call this chi "matter," but as we know from Einstein's equations, matter is actually condensed energy. The human life is a coming together of energy and on the spiritual path every bit of that energy can become purified. Matter, such as our physical body, is the most solidified form of that energy. It corresponds to the *form skandha* of Buddhism which is the realm of energy, form and appearances.

---

[20] See Glenn Mullin's translation of *Tsong Khapa's Commentary on the Six Yogas of Naropa* for the best explanation to date.

Buddhism states there are five skandhas, heaps or clusters of mental and physical phenomena that serve as objects we cling to in forming the sense of a self, or ego. Just as Hinduism says that the five *koshas* must be purified, Buddhism teaches that the five skandhas must be purified, or broken away from, in order for someone to win enlightenment and gain liberation.

In Taoism and many other spiritual schools, we say that the physical body is composed of the five elements earth, fire, water, wind and space, and these five elements must become purified on the cultivation trail. We also say the physical body is formed from the union of male and female, or egg and sperm, or that it is made out of *jing*. The whole process of spiritual cultivation in Taoist terms is one of transforming this physical *jing* into chi, or life force, and then on to higher stages from there.

If we turn back to Hinduism and Indian yoga, inside this physical body is a more refined layer of prana that composes an inner subtle body of chi called the *pranamaya kosha*. This corresponds to the *sensation skandha* of Buddhism that involves feelings and emotions, and which is often called the affective system of man. The *pranamaya kosha* is the same as the inner chi body of Taoism and countless other spiritual traditions. It basically refers to the chi of the body while the *annamaya kosha* refers to the body itself, made of *jing* or the five elements.

Next on the hierarchy of refinement is the mental body called the *manamaya kosha*. This corresponds to the Buddhist *conception skandha* and a yet more refined layer of chi. This level of chi still involves thoughts and conceptions, but they are much lighter than the coarser thoughts and mental streams involved with the earlier *koshas* and skandhas. So the mental body of Hinduism is equivalent to the conception skandha of Buddhism, which makes sense.

At yet a more purified level of chi is the *vijnanamaya kosha,* which corresponds to the Buddhist *volition skandha*, and then the *anandamaya kosha* corresponding to the Buddhist *consciousness skandha*. In Buddhism the volition skandha deals with karmic forces and all sorts of mental habits, thoughts, ideas, opinions, prejudices, compulsions, and decisions that cause volition. The consciousness skandha refers to consciousness or awareness, the cognizance base that supports all experiences.

You can think of the *koshas* as simply progressively purified layers of chi making up what we conventionally call the individual. The *pranamaya kosha* is just the first one that is less dense than ordinary form and matter, which is the *jing* level of the material physical body - the *annamaya kosha*. It is the one that most people refer to when they talk of spiritual matters because few practitioners are able to progress past the stages of spiritual cultivation dealing with chi in the body.

On the road of spiritual practice you eventually purify all these different layers of chi, and your consciousness purifies in tandem. At the highest stages of the spiritual path, you can even go so far as to transform the dense physical, material body of ours into pure chi so that it can appear and disappear at will. This is the stage of an Arhat in Buddhism, rishi in Hinduism, or Immortal in Taoism.

Many spiritual traditions speak of this attainment. When Arhats are about to pass away from this life, it is common for them to arise in the air and display various superpowers that can even manipulate the physical form of their human body.[21] Typically they rise into the air and then demonstrate their mastery over the fire and water elements of their body, which is something that the Biblical Elijah and Buddhist Ananda did right before they passed away.

Orthodox Buddhism doesn't like to emphasize these aspects of the spiritual path. High stage masters know about these stages and abilities, but any emphasis upon physical transformations or supernatural powers causes ordinary people to start thinking that cultivating the Tao means cultivating the physical form and superpowers rather than looking for the fundamental substrate, original nature or source of the individual. Over-emphasizing physical cultivation and gong-fu abilities constitutes a danger, as our already strong attachments to the physical body are further encouraged, and our incorrect notions of identifying the physical body as ourselves are strengthened. We can also be seduced into the mistake of considering that cultivating the body, or the various amazing functions of the body or mind *is* the path. When you consider that you are not the body, you are left with the essential question: What am I? In spiritual cultivation you strive to find this out by tracing consciousness and then awareness back to their ultimate source or foundation. To do so your mind must be clear, and for that your chi must become purified because the two are linked.

Detachment from the body leads to the purification of your chi and channels, and so letting go of both mind and body is the basic spiritual

---

[21] They can perform what are called the "eighteen transformations" such as being able to emit water from the upper part of their bodies and fire from the lower part, or fire from the upper part and water from the lower part. They can walk about in space, or lay down and go to sleep in space, dive into the earth, or travel at great speeds, and all sorts of other miraculous things. The miracles of Elijah in the Bible are examples of the powers of an Arhat. You must cultivate to a non-denominational stage of spiritual attainment to make them possible.

path. If you let go of your mind then your consciousness will purify, and if your consciousness purifies then your chi will purify. If you let go of your body then your chi will purify, and if your chi purifies then your consciousness will quiet down and empty out, which means it will become purified. Religions simply promote different spiritual practices as ways to do this. One of the big secrets within religions is that most of them are using the very same practices borrowed from one another, and simply change the names and "wrappings" to make them seem "invented here."

The stages of natural purification that result from the process, such as Hercules' gong-fu achievements within the Twelve Labors, build a stable foundation for spiritual investigation, so that you can ultimately trace the mind back to its ultimate foundation, which is the Source or True Self or original nature. A clear mind and body make it easier to "drop everything" and trace the mind back to this ultimate source, or fundamental essence.

The mind is just a bundle of thoughts, and the "I am," "I," ego center, "I"-thought or "I"-consciousness[22] is the root of all of them. When you ultimately see who this "I" is and find out where it comes from, then all thoughts get merged in the original nature, True Self or fundamental essence of beingness. Through self-enquiry, or the application of insight and wisdom to investigating the consciousness of "I am," you can finally arrive at self-realization, or enlightenment.

The process of spiritual cultivation is the journey to discovering the ultimate source of consciousness, awareness and the "I am." The "I am" is like an announcement that comes out of something else, the Absolute, and you must find that something else because the announcement is not real. When you look for the "I" or ego you cannot find it because it does not exist. It is a bit of knowledge that transiently appears, a bunch of temporary thoughts you cling to. It is therefore an illusion rather than something permanent and real or independent that you can take as your solid true self. You can find a body and a bunch of thoughts you cling to and take as the ego, but you cannot ever find a true, unchanging, permanent self anywhere.

The natural underlying state of the mind which experiences all this apparent manipulation, however, is the destination of spiritual

---

[22] This is called the "seventh consciousness" in Buddhism. It is also called the "afflicted mind consciousness," "defiled mind consciousness" or "false ego consciousness" that is the basis of the feeling of "I" or self, which Vedanta calls the "I am." It is a pollution of natural consciousness. It is the wrong identification of the witness with the mind-body.

cultivation - and that natural state, or original essence, is always there. It is what ultimately gives rise to witnessing or the experience of existence. It is our fundamental state that does not come and go but upon which all things come and go as ripples of consciousness. Our True Self is always proclaiming itself as the "I" in the field of manifestation, and you must trace that "I"-consciousness back to its Source to find the Truth of spiritual cultivation. "I" is therefore in a way the ultimate name of God, which is why we have the "I am that I am" of the Israelites.

The Buddhist approach, as well as the approach of many other religions wherein people truly cultivate, is to cut off attachment to the physical body and mind and especially avoid focusing on the physical body from the start – including any of the purified chi phenomena produced along the spiritual path since they, too, are not the real you. One of the four cardinal teachings of Shakyamuni Buddha is that the body is not your real self. Even though the physical nature can be completely transformed on the spiritual road, we must realize that no body that is produced through the process of cultivation, no matter how subtle and refined, is your real and true identity in any sense.

Buddhism takes a different track other than the one of focusing on the physical purification of the *koshas* in cultivation. Rather, it describes the mental scenarios or types of consciousness involved with each of the *koshas*. Instead of saying that the five *koshas* become purified, it describes the equivalent cultivation progress via stages of purifying consciousness, or breaking away from various types of consciousness, to avoid forming attachments to any refined stages of chi. It describes the purification stages of the path as a "breaking through" or "detachment from" or "purification of" a skandha. So, as you purify one of the *koshas,* or inner chi bodies of what seems a physical existence, Buddhism calls it breaking through, escaping from or purification of a particular skandha.

If you break through a skandha you have also purified a layer of chi in order to be able to detach from it. Taoism calls this a transformation of one essence into another. Or you can say you have purified some type of consciousness so that you can detach from it and its workings. Either way you look at it, you must recognize that chi and consciousness are linked to one another. Mental detachment, or "letting go," always leads to the purification of your chi and channels and to the purification of the mind.

In this case we are talking about purifying your chi, channels or a layer/level of chi, but in actuality we are also talking about whether you have learned how to sufficiently let go of the thoughts and impulses that are connected with, or course through that level of chi. If you can break through a skandha and lessen the pull of the consciousness promptings connected with that layer of thought, then it means you have also made progress in purifying your chi and channels yet further. The Indian schools describe the task in terms of chi, whereas Buddhism describes it in terms of consciousness. Taoism describes this in terms of transformations. Other schools don't talk about any of the steps or stages but just tell you to let go.

Remember that chi and consciousness are linked, and this is the mind-body connection we have identified in modern science. Science is still learning about this connection, and has not progressed anywhere compared to traditional cultivation knowledge. The big point is, you can describe the low stages of spiritual process from either of these two aspects of chi or consciousness, and in the Twelve Labors the focus is on chi.

The more materialistically oriented body cultivation schools[23] at times focus on the chi purification aspect of the process, whereas Buddhism, Zen, Vedanta and Mahamudra primarily focus on the purification of the mind. This accomplishes the exact same stages of cleansing or breakthrough as the form schools, and usually entails fewer problems. Nevertheless, in order to make such high stage progress as represented in Zen and these other schools, it is absolutely essential that you first engage in sitting meditation and transform your chi and channels to some extent. No one can experience spiritual enlightenment unless their chi and channels have become transformed.

In the story of Hercules, we are always describing the phenomenological form side, or chi side of the cultivation story, whereas Buddhism, to repeat, focuses on the mental side of the journey and relegates the entire process of purifying the chi, channels and chakras to the "purification of the five elements." The Orthodox Buddhist approach (rather than the Esoteric Buddhist approach) – which is the basis of Zen practice – is a lot higher because it teaches you to cut off all attachments to both the mind and body from the start. Furthermore, it is typically more effective because those people who take the singular approach of cultivating the physical body and its energies to attain the Tao rarely attain the enlightenment

---

[23] These include yoga, tantra, Esoteric Buddhism, western alchemy, Taoism, paganism and more. These are often called body cultivation schools, or (physical) form cultivation schools, because they tend to overly concentrate on transforming the chi, channels and even physical structures of the transient human body, which is destined to pass away, rather than seek the Source.

of self-realization. However, as you learn how to cultivate the mental emptiness of letting go, all these physical changes are bound to happen, so describing them as is done in the Twelve Labors is also perfectly acceptable. If we don't have guides or signposts to the physical gong-fu that can result from our efforts on the spiritual path, many people will become discouraged, or lost, and will cease their cultivation efforts.

If you've previously done lots of full body meditation work that affects the entire network of chi channels in your body – such as practicing the white skeleton visualization, anapana, deity yoga, or tantric visualizations – then with determination, practice, devotion, and patience you might be able to open the heart chakra. The section within the *Six Yogas of Naropa* pertaining to the visualization of little flames or Sanskrit letters on a chakra teaches you how to do this if you've done a lot of the preliminary work. However, without that preliminary work of intensified meditation practices to really learn detachment and cultivate an empty mind, you just cannot accomplish it. It really comes down to mastery of vipassana inner witnessing, or "mindfulness practice," and emptiness meditation in the end.

Once the solidified dirty chi blocking the central channel of the heart chakra pops open, streams of dirty chi logs (that look like feces or tubes of petrified wood) will spill out of the chakras as if they were being pushed from behind by a fire hose. You'll be able to identify the earth, wind, fire, and water chi in the log-like sections as they are being expelled. As each section of chi is ejected, through inner vision you might be able to see different colors or notice different textures. Some of these chi extrusions will even seem as if they are ages older than others.

When the "water element chi" comes out of the channels you will be able to see its watery nature through internal vision, but mostly it comes out as a type of paste or ooze indicating that it is mixed in with the "earth element chi." The impure earth chi seems to have a very hard texture when it is extruded out of the channels. Sometimes it falls off the outside of the channel walls like dried mud cakes, or it seems to drop out of a channel in large clumps or like small grains of sand. At times, what seems like a hardened core of cylindrical rock[24] is exuded out of the channels as they are being emptied and that's the earth element chi, too.

The "fire element chi" is something you usually cannot see directly, but of course you feel it in the heat of cultivation. You may sometimes see a puff of smoke in inner vision to denote when other types of chi

---

[24] They may look like the ice cores you see drilled out of the Arctic or Antarctic.

are being exuded from a channel, but most often the fire element chi is indicated by a reddish or brownish tint in the dirty chi that is being extruded. You might not be able to see the fire element directly, but you can always feel its warmth because all these transformations happen due to a special feeling of heat or warmth you'll perceive in the body.

This is the warmth of the kundalini energy, or yang chi as it arises. Long mantra practice, prolonged pranayama and other cultivation techniques can generate this warmth in the belly, which people can often readily feel. For instance, if you recite mantras out loud for an hour or so, often your belly will start to get warm because the fire element starts to stir as the yang chi tries to work through the channels. Most cultivation schools represent the yang chi with the color red because it is connected with fire and warmth.

Opening the heart chakra and purifying your chi and channels is not really a matter of ability but of persistence and proper practice. The spiritual cultivation methods of the world are readily available and not secret. You just need to choose to practice them and then do so properly and consistently. Furthermore, all human bodies have chakras and chi channels inside them just as they have arteries and veins. We just need to spiritually cultivate to activate our yang chi and that energy will start clearing them out. You just have to choose to cultivate, and you must use the right meditation methods.

Hopefully, you will choose to start cultivating correctly *now* because you can go on for further eons of incarnations without ever coming across clear cultivation teachings again. It takes a lot of merit to come across real dharma teachings so you should not squander your present opportunity. If you cultivate a naturally occurring empty mind by letting go of thoughts, your chi channels will start opening naturally and your body will accordingly reach its highest state of natural perfection. You just need to learn how to be natural, let go, be detached, or empty the mind … however you wish to word it.

The resulting conjunction of mental and physical purification that occurs on the cultivation road is the process of "deification" found in Christianity that will carry you up through genuine spiritual states. Unfortunately, the various Churches have lost knowledge of this simple process. The path and objective is to become as Christ is, as Krishna is, as Buddha is. However, it seems that nearly every religion and spiritual school has somehow covered over the process of true spiritual cultivation with something else entirely different.

If you cultivate not dwelling in mental scenarios and simultaneously practice tantric body transformation techniques, you can quickly purify your mind and body for the spiritual path. However, if you don't master mental detachment then such tantric techniques will be worthless to you because the real transformations won't ever happen at all. If you don't learn how to cultivate an empty mind that lets thoughts be born without clinging to them, you will only achieve a semblance dharma[25] that will seem to resemble the spiritual gong-fu mentioned in classical texts, but which will actually be far off the mark.

Learning how to mentally let go and cultivate an empty mind is the key to all true spiritual cultivation, regardless of the school or tradition. First, you calm your mind by letting go. You continually watch your thoughts and then eventually notice there is a gap between them. That empty space between thoughts is an entryway into realizing the Tao, but is not the Tao.

That empty space between thoughts is still a phenomenon of consciousness, though it is a pause where busy mentation seems to have quieted down. It is not true "no self" or true empty mind but simply an image of an empty state. You have to maintain awareness and witness, observe or watch this silence, and inquire within "who is experiencing this?"

With insight you can realize there is no ego or self doing the viewing, and at that moment of wisdom realization you will immediately detach to achieve a higher stage of spiritual practice. It is hard to let go of consciousness, but by cultivating insight using wisdom analysis, called "prajna wisdom," one can learn detachment and eventually achieve self-realization. As you do this your body will change and your chi will transform, and that story of transformation is embodied in the Twelve Labors.

If you read the biographical or autobiographical accounts of most saints and sages in the various religious traditions, you will find that they commonly talk about internal silence, peace, stillness, empty mind, no self, no-thought and so on. Therefore we must conclude that they

---

[25] The term "dharma" usually means teachings on the spiritual path including deep truths about spiritual training and ultimate reality. However, the term is also used to refer to a factor of mental experience. Thus in this case, a state of gong-fu experience that seems to fit descriptions found within traditional texts, and thus resembles those descriptions, may easily be mistaken for the real thing. Many people think they cultivate high mental states when they find similar descriptions of their experiences in ancient books, but unless they go through many stages of gong-fu and become able to enter and leave such states at will, these are rarely the real thing.

are all experiencing the very same sort of quiet, and that the stages of the spiritual path are non-denominational. To attain these experiences of "empty mind" or "emptiness" they must cultivate detachment from mental thoughts and physical sensations, and so non-clinging is commonly described as a feature of the spiritual path. All these realized ones cultivate detachment, and thereby understand emptiness as the underlying characteristic of the mind.

Even though this is the true basis of religious practice, no one seems to understand the teaching. For instance, in the neglected *Gospel of Thomas* Jesus is said to have described the Kingdom of Heaven as like an old woman who returns home after a long journey. She's carrying all she values on her back, which is a bag full of grain, but a tear in the bag allows all the grain to escape on the way. When she arrives home she discovers that the bag is empty. The parable teaches you to cultivate letting go and teaches you about the end result as well – empty mind – but people don't understand this simple lesson that keeps popping up in religion after religion and from master after master.

When you really understand this from personal experience due to the purification of your chi and consciousness, rather than from just understanding the words, you will have a true spiritual awakening yourself. When that happens we can say you are finally on the Path or "following the True Way" because you have personally experienced or authenticated the path and will know how to practice correctly. Without that personal experience of emptiness or empty mind, your understanding of spirituality can only amount to just intellectual study. Intellectual study is good, but you must always move on to the stage of practice and then realization.

Most saints and sages enter the Tao through the route of mental purification, and they eventually learn that letting go of consciousness is the way. When you let go of consciousness and just let it arise in response to all needs without holding on to it, it's like letting the ripples on the surface of a pond die down until the jiggling water becomes pure and clear, and you can see right through to the pond's bottom.

Consciousness always rises, so you cannot stop it.[26] Therefore, you must learn to detach from it and then ultimately see where it comes

---

[26] Those who seek a cessation of thoughts usually incorrectly practice for attainment, and usually try to suppress consciousness rather than letting it purify or empty out naturally on its own. If you simply let go of consciousness then mind will naturally purify, and when thoughts need to be born they will be born. But if you forcefully practice to produce an empty state, this is incorrect. In searching for the ultimate source of the mind, which Con-

from. After all, you think the mind is "you," so you have to investigate the mind and really see what it is and where it comes from. Meditation, or cultivation practice, is the only thing that will allow you to do this. This is the basic spiritual path.

To find the ultimate Source, which many call "God," is your objective on the road of spirituality. What else would you be looking for other than the source of the small self, the you (or "I"), the ego … and the source of everything else? That one source is also the source of consciousness, so you can trace back consciousness to discover it.

Learning to let go of consciousness is the basic road of spiritual practice, but there are other routes that start off by teaching you to fixate on consciousness or stabilize consciousness as an entryway, such as maintaining stable concentration on an imaginary visualization, until wandering thoughts die down. There are countless techniques available. Nevertheless with all those techniques you still need to know what you are doing and investigate the state of cessation you eventually attain, and from that analysis you will always realize that the spiritual path is about learning to let go and not hold on to the mind because it is naturally empty and gives birth to thoughts as required. It's useless to try to maintain things because they are always changing. The only thing that doesn't change is the real, true nature underlying everything.

You must cultivate letting go, but the fact is that you are always holding on to consciousness without knowing it, so the whole problem is learning what it means "to let go." That's the problem, that's the real issue. People hear the words but don't actually know how to do it. They don't know how to relax, and the habit of mental clinging is so firmly entrenched from countless lives that they don't know how to let go. That's why different schools have developed different techniques to help collapse the clinging. The different schools and methods appeal to different types of karma.

Hence, many cultivation routes have been created to help you get started on the path. In addition to visualization, people often watch their breath to calm their chi. Due to the interlinkage of chi and consciousness, when your breathing calms down your chi will calm down, and when your chi calms down then your mind and wandering thoughts will also

---

fucianism calls investigation, eventually the screens of ignorance will simply drop away by themselves and you will attain the Tao. If you forcefully add another layer of ignorance on top of the layers already there, you will not be able to penetrate through to realize your original nature. In realizing the original nature you can experience the cessation or extinction of thoughts, but it happens naturally as a by-product of perfectly letting go.

calm down. This is another way you can reach a state of peacefulness, silence or emptiness.

On this route, you can learn how to calm your mental states if you learn how to let go of your breathing, and next the energetic sensations of your body which you are always clinging to as your self. Neither your body nor your chi nor your thoughts are the real you, so learn how to let go of them. Thoughts come and go, so there is no need to hold on to them. Chi is energy but energy is like mist or a dream image, so don't try to grasp it because the effort is useless. It is ungraspable. The body is destined to die and is not the real you, so why attach to the body? Though you constantly seem to feel the borders of the body while alive, that's just a set of passing sensations which are not the real you.

Nothing we can know is permanent, so let things that arise within the mental continuum depart since they are not the real foundation to begin with. You keep hearing the term "empty" or "emptiness" over and over again in spiritual cultivation and it simply means that phenomena are ungraspable. What seems like a single thought held for a long time is really a sequence of thoughts occurring so fast that none of them can be said to have a true existence, but just an apparent existence like the ring of light you see when a flame is twirled in your hand. It appears but is said not to be. You therefore cannot say that a thing is existing or non-existing in actuality. You can only say that there is an appearance, and that at the time of the appearance the functioning represents nothing permanent.

Emptiness doesn't mean there are no occurrences in the conventional world but that phenomena – whether they are your five senses, thoughts or realms of seemingly empty stillness – constantly arise and pass ceaselessly. The past, present and future minds are ungraspable, so in life you are always tormenting yourself chasing after some ideal you want to hold. That is why Shakyamuni Buddha said "there is no dharma that can be attained," and why the spiritual path is often summarized with the words "let go, let go." Don't mentally dwell and don't grasp on to forms or appearances on the road of spirituality. If you do, you will divert yourself from the real road of practice because you are clinging to an ignorant state of mind.

Mostly, it's a matter of people not choosing to cultivate in the first place that prevents them from spiritually realizing the Tao. Or, they don't set up a regular meditation schedule of sufficient time commitment and make the right sorts of effort. Most people don't practice to succeed, and so they don't. They don't do the preparatory meditation practices they dislike (that dislike is usually an indication that a meditation method is good for you) or they don't engage in any spiritual practices at all. They don't use wisdom to analyze what they are doing either. They don't look for a teacher who can guide them,[27] or follow the teachings which past adepts have left us, or turn to the spiritual practices that historically have produced the most success stories.

This is one of the strangest behaviors of human beings in that the spiritual techniques in history that have produced the most cultivation successes, such as mantra and vipassana, are the ones people don't want to practice. They always seem to prefer some strange practice that doesn't have a track record of countless success stories behind it, and so they end up wasting their efforts with ineffective practice or techniques. Only a man or woman with the will and desire to succeed and do what must be done, like Hercules, does indeed succeed in spiritual cultivation. If you ultimately succeed in spiritual cultivation, like the Bodhisattvas of Buddhism, you can even become a cultural hero or the protector and savior of a nation. If you succeed, it can have ramifications for millions and millions of people and your influence can last generations.

As mentioned previously, Shakyamuni Buddha wisely just referred to this whole process of Hercules' labors as transforming, purifying or pacifying the five elements of the physical body. In this way, by avoiding an overly strong emphasis on the physical nature, he knew that people would not become attached to the channels and chakras of the body (which are part of its physical nature) and take any body or form as the real "I." The real "I" is the original nature, or Absolute, but you have to cultivate to realize this.

The biggest problems of spiritual practice typically occur in the esoteric schools of yoga, tantra, Esoteric Buddhism, kabbalah, western alchemy, paganism and Taoism, etc. all of which focus on cultivating the energy and form of the body rather than investigating mind, consciousness, and awareness. Any overly materialistic school, or religion, tends to develop a mistaken emphasis in spiritual cultivation and worldly focus. Practitioners in such traditions tend to develop a deep habit of fixating on the physical body and its chi sensations, which is the very problem that must be overcome in the first place. Thus, people develop the errant habit of trying to bring consciousness into the body when the

---

[27] One should always study extensively, work hard at their cultivation, and mantra for a good teacher if they are seeking one.

true mind is everywhere. The body-consciousness is not the real "I" just as the "I"-thought is not the real "I" or true Self. However this sort of practice road ends up strengthening one's belief in the existence of being a false body and ego.

People always get blinded by experiences rather than search for the one witnessing the experiences. Science fails in the same way investigating, investigating, investigating the causes of effects except for the ultimate cause behind all effects, which isn't a Big Bang. Beyond mind and matter is something you can only reach through the path of proper meditation of letting go, since what transcends mind and matter is the Unmanifest, and yet scientists are ignoring this road entirely.

People who excessively focus on cultivating their physical form never achieve the real Tao beyond body and mind, but always end up clinging to their chi or their physical body as their self. This is incorrect, as there is no permanent independent self other than the original nature. That's the underlying True Self of all sentient beings — their real self-nature - and the idea of being an independent entity or ego with independent awareness is just an illusion. Shakyamuni Buddha was extremely wise in not emphasizing all the gong-fu transformations of the body in order not to lead people astray this way or further promote attachments to the body or ego. Zen, Buddhism and Vedanta take the same route of emphasizing pure spiritual cultivation in searching for the source of the false "I" to find the true "I" or true Self.

In the case of Hercules, we are discussing the phenomenological stages of the path in detail as a guide to the whole process, so we absolutely must mention the physical changes of chi and chakras or else we wouldn't have any story. You, too, will experience these things as you pass through the various grades of cultivation attainment. The drama of Hercules' labors tells of a typical cultivation journey through the gong-fu transformations that happen on the spiritual path. That journey is encapsulated in an exciting story that catches the imagination so that it was able to become a surviving part of popular culture. Many cultivation schools encode their teachings this way for posterity, but we are especially lucky to have a tale where the stages of cultivation are revealed in sequence one after the other. Usually things are not this clear.

In early Chinese Taoism the existence of chi channels and chakras was not even mentioned. Later, some Chinese Taoists called the entire set of channels the "three elixir fields" and the whole process of cultivation became the task of transforming *jing* (seminal or generative energy) into chi (prana or life force), chi into *shen* (clear mental awareness) and *shen* into emptiness (no-thought, pure subjectivity because conceptualization has ceased, realization of the Tao). The whole process of gong-fu transformations was represented in an entirely different fashion than portrayed by the Greeks or by Buddhism or Hindu yoga, even though it was meant to capture the exact same story.

This Taoist sequence actually encapsulates the purification of the chi, channels and chakras as well. However, most Taoist practitioners errantly fixate on the physical body to their own detriment and thus never succeed on the path. They think they have some secrets no one else has because of their special Taoist descriptions of internal gong-fu, and special visualization practices from rare books, but they never make it to those stages of attainment because they don't cultivate emptiness, just the body. Let it be said again: It's only through emptiness meditation that you can achieve these transformations at all. You have to reach a state where the mind is unborn – as if void, empty, non-existent, non-produced, without content, not there, free, spontaneous, ready to be born – and you cannot do so by clinging to thoughts and moving them this way and that.

As my own teacher says, who is an enlightened master of Zen, Buddhist Vajrayana, Chinese Taoism and Confucianism, the biggest catastrophes in the form schools of Esoteric Buddhism, Taoism, and yoga come precisely because people concentrate too much on the body and form the habit of clinging to something that isn't the real Self.[28] They practice bringing consciousness into the body and get fixated in that way, tying themselves up into a ball of knots. They form a strong habit of clinging to an identification that impedes their progress for ages, but because they can get superpowers and semblance samadhi from cultivating this internal esoteric structure, and because energies *do* change inside, they think they're correct and won't listen.

In any case, Hercules was able to defeat the hydra in our story, meaning he successfully transformed his dirty yin chi through a process which shows that he used his yang chi, or kundalini, to win the day.

---

[28] The Zen school, on the other hand, rarely ever discusses physical gong-fu. From the very start, Zen students are taught to ignore the body and their physical sensations and concentrate on the ultimate aim, which is why so many ultimately succeed at spiritual cultivation. They are taught not to get distracted by gong-fu. Some scholars have inferred from this lack of emphasis that Zen cultivators do not go through these experiences at all, but this is highly incorrect. One will find many descriptions of gong-fu in the life stories of famous Zen masters, such as in the autobiographies of the Chinese master Han Shan and the Japanese Zen master Hakuin.

When Hercules first arrived at the Lernean swamp, he lured the hydra out of its den by shooting it with flaming arrows. In other words, the hot warmth of his kundalini cultivation, due to some cultivation method, was able to make the hydra stir. Hercules' yang chi, or kundalini, started poking at the yin chi obstructions within his channels, and they started to move.

Of course, Hercules originally initiated the kundalini (yang chi) in his labor with the Nemean lion so now that his yang chi has been initiated, the next sequence of spiritual purification is that it starts cleaning out the chi channels and chakras. It starts pushing the dirty yin chi out of the channels and chakras, which are the multiple heads of the hydra after they are cut off one after the other. This initial purification of the chi channels, now that the kundalini yang chi has arisen, is what's represented by the defeat of the hydra in the Second Labor.

This internal purification of the channels is all accomplished during what is called the stage of "Warmth," "Warming" or "Heat," the first sub-phase of what Buddhism calls the Stage of Intensified Practices within the spiritual path. Buddhism has done a great service for world religions in cataloging the five general stages of the cultivation path. Those five stages of the cultivation path are:

- The Stage of Study and Virtue Accumulation
- The Stage of Intensified Practices, or Preparatory Meditation Practices
- The Stage of Seeing the Tao (Direct Vision)
- The Stage of True Cultivation Practice
- The Stage of Perfect and Complete Enlightenment, or No More Learning

Ordinary people who do no more than try to be good human beings and attend church, synagogue, mosque or temple services, for instance, are only at the Stage of Study and Virtue Accumulation on the spiritual path. For their whole life, if they never engage in meditation, that is where they will always remain - on the first of the five steps necessary for spiritual realization. All their study of dogma and strict attendance to rituals, rules, ceremonies, pilgrimages and worship are profitless unless they start seeking within for the true reality from which all arises.

When people leave behind religious ceremonies, rituals and rules of discipline as the path and really start cultivating meditation, they enter upon the second spiritual stage of Intensified Practices that can gain them some real spiritual progress and spiritual experiences. This stage of practice has four phases to it, and the first phase is the feeling of warmth as the kundalini energies start to cleanse the body and open up chi channels. Unfortunately, most people in the world remain a bit lost at the whole meaning of spiritual endeavors and the fact that there are these stages of necessary spiritual effort. They remain at the beginner's stage of religious study, cultivating virtue and making merit for the path of spirituality, but will never see the Tao in this lifetime if they don't sit down to practice meditation.

If you want to succeed spiritually, you must learn to meditate. You absolutely must engage in spiritual practices other than just participating in ceremonies and book study. You must cultivate the purity of your mind by calming your wandering thoughts, and only then can you experience these things.

When you open up the heart chakra you can attain the stage of seeing the Tao, or spiritual awakening that corresponds to temporarily penetrating through the *conception skandha* and *manamaya kosha*. However, it requires meditation practice to do this, or spiritual practices performed in such a way as to establish the same results as meditation practice.

Usually people think that religious study and religious ceremonies are enough for making spiritual progress. Hence, because they never engage in meditation practice according to the proper principles, they never experience the higher stages of the spiritual road. They simply read about what others accomplished and haven't a clue how to attain those experiences and proficiencies themselves. That's when they try to excuse themselves for their lack of progress by saying it's the result of "grace," meaning it's out of their control, whereas all those "recipients of grace" were cultivating their butts off.

Let's be clear: spiritual progress is something that you can scientifically achieve. It is accomplished through meditation, but there are countless different meditation cultivation practices you can follow. We don't know the exact methods Hercules used in his practice, but we do know that his gong-fu experiences followed the standard course of cultivation progress. His story is a liberation story that traces in mythic and symbolic form the sequential progress stages of the cultivation path.

When the hydra came out of its lair in the Lernean swamps because of Hercules' flaming arrows, Hercules grabbed it and the hydra coiled itself around his feet, making it difficult for him to escape. Due to the poisonous fumes, the legend says that Hercules had to hold his breath while grappling with the animal, an event which stands for the state of respiratory cessation (natural *kumbhaka* or *hsi*) we previously mentioned in order to pass this stage. The hydra even had a friend, a huge crab (crabs represent yin chi) which came out of hiding and kept pinching Hercules in his heel while he was entangled and struggling with the hydra.

This part of the story is telling us two things. First, purifying our chi channels is difficult because the dirty chi surrounding them and inside them is like the hydra being wrapped around Hercules' leg that doesn't want to be pulled off. As we'll find out later, as you purify the chi channels in stages, the best description of the process is that it seems as if you are often untying or pulling an old layer of this impure chi from another layer because they appear to be sticking together. It takes what seems to be some type of pushing of the chi to purify the channels and chakras, but that is not anything you have to force yourself.

Second, this labor correctly points out that it's very difficult to open up the chi channels in the legs, including the energy pathways to the chakras in the bottom of the foot and heel, even for a great hero like Hercules. This is why the hydra wraps itself around his legs and won't let go ... it's difficult to open up the leg channels and so the hydra cannot be peeled away easily. The very first time you make great inroads towards opening the leg channels is when the two channels (think of them as acupuncture meridians) running down the insides of both legs open. When that happens, which is an event that occurs well before this Second Labor, the inner leg channels might feel as if a blast of hot dry air suddenly runs through them. This blast of hot dry chi starts from the big toes and shoots upwards into the head, and the sinus cavities will start draining afterwards so that you develop a runny nose for a short while.[29] That is one of the first major progress signs that the leg channels

---

[29] At much higher stages past the Twelve Labors the nasal cavity channels start clearing at even more profound levels, causing the phlegm to drip into the stomach. What might ordinarily appear to be heartburn, but is the opening of the gastric chi channels proceeding upwards, will also produce a vomiting like sensation for short intense moments of time. Sometimes the whole front of the body will just feel a hotness proceeding upwards, and one will be able to feel the connection to the gastric system at this time. There is nothing one can do at those stages except go through the experiences which only last a few moments. Naturally, one should not mistake ordinary cases of heartburn or nasal discharge with progress on the path, but knowing human behavior I can easily predict that many will think they have reached these stages when they have not yet gone through the Twelve Labors, and thus delude themselves.

are starting to become opened, but as stated, this phenomenon refers to a stage quite prior to the gong-fu referenced in this Second Labor.

Another fact called to our attention in this labor is that it's very difficult to open up the foot chakra and the heel chakra, which the crab was pinching. The labor is calling specific attention to this chakra because after the heel chakra opens, which happens around the time of this labor, you will feel the pulsation of chi in this region.

The heel chakra at the back of the foot has the purpose of pumping your chi upwards to the perineum in a returning circuit after it has descended from above. Part of the chi route within the body entails the descent of chi from your lower trunk region down the inside of your legs to the feet. Then it has to return upwards again, and there is an important pumping station, or chakra, in the heel of the foot.

This is the area the crab was pinching, and its inclusion in the story is a recognition sign for adepts that this pumping you will feel is what is supposed to happen. When first opened you can feel it rhythmically pulsating with the pinching and release mentioned in the story. Later as all the channels open you eventually forget the sensation because the internal obstructions of the channels are removed, and your chi flow becomes smooth all over.

The importance of the heel chakra pumping, where the crab was pinching Hercules, is highlighted in many cultivation schools because it's one of the first really noticeable phenomena of the path where it's impossible to cheat yourself that something unusual isn't happening. For instance, it is also symbolized by Mercury's sandals and found within a famous story from the Egyptian spiritual tradition involving the Goddess Isis.

In the story of the Goddess Isis and the Land of Byblos, there was once a Queen Astarte who had seen an amazing tree (the chi channels and chakras of the body) and asked the king to place it in a garden. Isis eventually comes to tend the tree in the story, and she takes care of the queen's son whom she tries to turn into an immortal.

The Goddess Isis is usually illustrated in paintings and figurines with a sun above her head held by two protrusions, signifying the golden crown chakra (in the head) and the body's left and right chi channels. The reason that Isis is said to "have placed the Sun God Ra in the sky" and is shown with a sun above her head is because she opened up her crown chakra and succeeded in enlightenment. Once again, the sun is just a symbol of the crown chakra, and the two horns that hold it are the left and right channels.

Everyone who achieves enlightenment opens up all the channels and chakras like this, but the wisdom schools of Zen, Vedanta, Buddhism and so forth don't bother to mention it because otherwise people think they have to do something to make this happen. The pictures just catalog this physical accomplishment of the path, but there's nothing you have to do about it because all the chakras and chi channels naturally open when you cultivate the emptiness of letting go. Mention it or not, it's just something that comes along with progress for spiritual practitioners.

It is also said in legends that Isis made "light with her feathers and wind with her wings." This was to indicate that she had achieved success in opening all her other chi channels as well. Isis is sometimes shown in statues with extended wings of many feathers[30] to represent an opened heart chakra together with all the body's other chi channels, the wind element representing chi. Her pictures are similar in symbolization to the pictures of Buddhas with many arms, such as paintings of the Buddha Sitatapatra and "Thousand-Armed Kuan Yin." Kuan Yin's (Avalokitesvara's) many arms represent the fact that all the chi channels in his body, especially those in his crown chakra and around his heart, have opened. The many arms also stand for the multiple cultivation methods he can offer individuals, and his great proficiency in skillful means and nirmanakaya to help all situations.

It's possible, but speculative, that the Egyptian headpiece of the pharaoh with a prolonged upwards extending crown also refers to the crown chakra and the fact that the kundalini has risen to the head. Also, Osiris wore a special hat whose particular tripartite shape might have signified the central, left and right channels of his body being opened, which is why he was known as master of the underworld. His death in Egyptian legends meant the death of the ego and attainment of emptiness, from which all things originate, so naturally he is always born again. This is why he is often called "He who is permanently benign and youthful" as well as the "Lord of silence." In a way he is similar to the ever youthful Buddha Manjushri, who also teaches the essential emptiness of the mind and all appearances.

---

[30] When you examine a feather under magnification you can see countless ribs, veins and shafts. That is why feathers, or wings, are often taken to represent the opened chi channels of the body. When opened they fill with chi, which the ancients compared to air, and thus once again we have a tie-in with feathers and flying.

Continuing with this side lesson, Egypt has many cultivation teachings like this encapsulated into its culture. For instance the god Khepri is often shown with the face of a scarab beetle to denote the initially clumsy nature of kundalini after its awakening and the fact it might feel like a beetle slowly crawling up the spine at the early stages of the spiritual path. The Hindu sage Ramakrishna said its initial movements often felt to him like the wanderings of an ant, fish, monkey, bird or snake, though of course much later a person simply feels blissful all over after all the major and minor chi channels have been opened and the flow of yang chi has become harmonized. Every cultivation school tries to represent kundalini, or yang chi, in culturally appropriate symbols and motifs.

The initial ascension of the kundalini up the spine is the meaning behind the worship of the *shiva lingam* in Hinduism which denotes both the root chakra (represented by the circular base or *peetham*) and the kundalini rising from it. Just the *shiva lingam* stones themselves, however, refer to the yang chi kundalini itself. Hence once again we find the same phenomena represented entirely differently in a foreign cultivation school.

The Egyptian goddess Isis is also sometimes curiously shown with her hawk-headed son Horus on her lap. It is quite possible this means she had also reached the enlightened stage of being able to create transformation bodies, or nirmanakaya, which is the third requirement to becoming a fully enlightened being. It is said that to become a Buddha you must realize the dharmakaya original essence body (the True Self or Source), purify the physical nature and its internal chi structure (which is attaining the sambhogakaya reward body as Hercules is doing here) and then become able to emanate countless projection bodies (known as nirmanakaya emanation bodies) for other sentient beings. These projections of consciousness can perform tasks in the world such as helping to teach, protect and foster sentient beings in various ways. That is why Horus, likely an emanation body, becomes the protector of Egypt.

The various representations of Isis show that she accomplished all three Buddha bodies of enlightenment, and so she was called the "great mother" because she succeeded on the spiritual path and became a fully enlightened being. Just as Typhon was born of heaven and earth, Isis was said to be the daughter of the earth (Geb) and sky (Nut) to show once again that as human beings we stand between earth and heaven and can cultivate from these beginnings to realize our true nature.

While Isis has two protrusions from her head, in Tibet we have a bull faced Buddha called Yamantaka who has two large horns representing his opened left and right channels. The pictures of Yamantaka are often elaborate illustrations whose complexity indicates that he has opened up many other chi channels in his body as well. Basically he has opened up all the channels and chakras in his body due to his great efforts at spiritual cultivation. Yang chi is often represented by a bull, so his fearsome bull face simply symbolizes the highest achievement of yang chi purification.

Typically the termination points of the left and right channels we see over the head of Isis become extra faces in various Buddha illustrations, and it's a pity that scholars don't know this. The three-faced goddess Hecate (a "Triple Goddess") in Greek mythology, for instance, shows the same stage of accomplishment in opening up the body's central, left and right channels. Hecate is also often shown holding two torches representing the left and right channels of the body, and naturally the extra two faces are their termination point on each side of the head.

When you look at ancient statues of Anahita (the Persian Lady of the Beasts) or ancient Sumerian and Celtic goddesses as well as various Hindu deities, you often find special headdresses denoting an opened crown chakra. Any animals on their clothing are usually symbols which represent the flow of yang chi, and feathered wings and other symbols are often used to denote an opened heart chakra along with all the other chi channels in the body. These are all stages of cultivation you pass through which we'll see shortly as we unfold the story of Hercules and his Twelve Labors.

In the meantime, one need only go to the internet to look up pictures of these various Buddhas and deities to see how various ancient cultures represented the same fruits of cultivation achievement for their people. When you're there, take a peek at the "Canticle of Brother Sun and Sister Moon," written by the Christian cultivator St. Francis of Assisi. We know St. Francis attained some degree of cultivation success in purifying his body and transforming his chi channels from his spiritual practice because his body did not decompose after his death. That is a common result, found for many saints, of truly purifying your chi channels from spiritual cultivation. His "Canticle of Brother Sun and Sister Moon" is a testament to the transformation of the body's five elements that are purified on the cultivation road, as well as the opening of the left (moon) and right (sun) chi channels of his body. In his own spiritual cultivation he discovered the same non-denominational stages of purification that everyone else experiences, and the existence of the major chi channels as well.

Everyone who cultivates sufficiently eventually discovers these phenomena. This is why multiple cultures represent them in statues, stories, poems, pictures and myths. It's always the same thing, always the same thing.

When you cultivate far enough to open up your *sushumna* central channel along with the left and right *ida* and *pingala* channels, then you will immediately recognize their representation within the pictures of those who have spiritually succeeded in the past. You can and should look up pictures of various gods and goddesses on the internet to see how different cultures represented the same non-denominational, non-sectarian, non-religious stages of spiritual achievement, emphasizing this or that phenomenon that is part of the normal set of spiritual gong-fu achievements. It's always the same story because spiritual gong-fu is non-denominational and the purification of the inner chi body happens to everyone according to a certain sequence, just like the stages of going through puberty.

The elaborate pictures of many hands, heads, hats, headdresses, parasols over the head, or headrests you see behind Isis (Egyptian), Sitatrapatra (Buddhist), Durga (Hindu), Vasudhara (Tibetan) and many other female deities are simply illustrations denoting a stage of purified chi channels for women who succeeded in their cultivation. In many statues and illustrations of the Hindu goddess Durga, for instance, you can readily see from these images that she opened her crown chakra. Wings with many feathers, such as seen with Isis or in western Madonnas, and illustrations using countless arms or breasts represent the petals of opened chakras and opened chi channels as well.

In any case, in this interesting story about Isis and the tree, Isis disguises herself and goes to Byblos where (in a reference to chi channels) she teaches the palace maidens how to braid hair. Isis also gets a job as gardener for the wonderful tree which Queen Astarte had planted in her garden (a reference to the network of chi channels in the body, often called a tree), and eventually becomes caretaker of the Queen's children because of her elegant grace and learning. One night Queen Astarte walks into Isis' bedchamber and finds her holding the queen's only son, Dictys, by his heel over the fireplace. His body seemed to be all afire, which is our stage of Warmth from the kundalini cleansing process.

This heel location where she held him is the exact same spot where the crab pinches Hercules because it refers to the heel chakra. When the boy Dictys is on fire, Isis said she was trying to make the child Dictys immortal by burning away his mortal parts, which is what kundalini does in its task of purification. Yang chi, or kundalini, pushes out the dirty chi from the body, as is happening in this Second Labor, so this fire symbolism was quite apt.

It is through the warmth of kundalini cultivation - symbolized by torches, fire, forges, boiling kettles, cooking and so on in the world's cultivation schools - that the body becomes purified. In Hercules' battle with the hydra, he had to use a torch to defeat the monster. There are multiple ways to indicate the warmth of kundalini as it pushes through chi channel obstructions and transforms the body. They are all fine as long as they refer to blazing heat.

Once discovered holding the baby over the flames, the Goddess Isis reveals herself to the queen and says that had she not been interrupted, in a few minutes more Dictys would have become immortal. This, too, is eventually what happens to Hercules at the end of his life after all these labors and more. By the end of this book, you'll be able to figure out the "how" and "why" of this yourself and why some individuals, like Enoch or Melchizedek of the Bible and various sages, really can cultivate an immortal-like body that "ascends to heaven." This is just one small facet of what is called "cultivating the sambhogakaya" in Buddhism, but no body is immortal because all things end in impermanence.

In Buddhism, the purification of the physical body that naturally produces the sambhogakaya becomes an extreme focus in the Vajrayana tradition, and this is due to the fact that tantric yoga influences from India entered and entwined with the original Buddhist tradition that had passed to Tibet. Attaining the sambhogakaya involves changing every cell of your body, even your bones and marrow, and the process starts from the raising of the yang chi kundalini and then the subsequent purification of all your chi channels and chakras. Hercules has started on this path in his First Labor, and we will see the subsequent phenomenological stages of physical transformation in the other labors to come.

Only if you attain enlightenment can you achieve the full set of physical transformations necessary to achieve the perfect reward body, or sambhogakaya. The process entails purifying the impure karma of the human body, beset with pain and suffering, so you can simply think of it as transforming the body to become healthy. In Taoism they describe this process as getting rid of illness, lengthening one's lifespan and eventually achieving immortality or ascension. If you awaken your kundalini yang chi and succeed in opening your channels and purifying your chi, which is the meaning of the Greek hero Jason finally gaining the Golden Fleece, you are on this very same road to spiritual accomplishment.

All these stories bear witness to the importance of opening up the channels to the feet after the initial yang chi arising at the stage of the Nemean lion. This task of opening the chi channels in the feet is emphasized again and again in countless cultivation schools because it is both extremely hard to accomplish and a highly recognizable signpost for the path. Most people entirely neglect cultivating their feet so many schools call attention to this fact to help remind students to concentrate on the matter.

In Chinese Taoism it is stated right out in the open that you can only become an "Immortal" if you clean your intestines and open up the channels to the bottom of the feet, just as we have seen represented in the Egyptian story. Taoism also says that the "true man," the healthiest man, breathes with his heels while ordinary men breathe with their mouths, once again referencing this very same accomplishment of opening the heel channels. For instance, Chuang Tzu said, "The men of old breathed clear down into their heels," but ordinary people don't understand the meaning of this because they never achieve the cultivation stage of opening the channels into the feet.

Part of this opening of the foot channels involves the initial pumping sensation felt in the heel chakra where the crab pinches Hercules, though of course you will actually feel the chakras in the bottom of the feet as well. Later as you make more progress you can initiate the same type of heel pumping in the wrist chakras and sometimes near the tailbone as well, but this only lasts for a very brief period of time. At even higher stages of cultivation you will eventually feel an oscillation back and forth between the left and right channels of the body after they open, and later even more profound sensations as the body slowly becomes able to experience the bliss of the first dhyana. At the stages of the dhyana, your channels are all opened so these previous coarse sensations disappear and you only feel sensations of bliss.

These explanations suggest why the "invincible Achilles" was finally killed during the Trojan war by an arrow that hit him in the heel. In the story of Jason and the Argonauts, the importance of the heel chakra was also highlighted in the battle against the bronze man Talos whose ankle plug was opened so that his life force could drain out. The Greek hero Perseus wears flying sandals whose flapping denotes the opened heel chakras as well. All these stories, including the pinching crab that attacks Hercules as he is battling with the hydra, refer to opening the chi channels in the body at the heel after the kundalini first arises, yet they represent the achievement in entirely different fashions.

The importance of the feet channels in meditation is so important to cultivation gong-fu that Shakyamuni Buddha makes a special point of telling people to start the white skeleton visualization by focusing on the left big toe in order to make sure they don't neglect the feet. Many schools of Indian yoga pranayama[31] also tell you specifically that when holding the breath in *kumbhaka* exercises you should visualize your feet, toes, heels and ankles as shining brightly in order to send the chi there and help open those channels ... especially the big toes.

If you are doing Indian pranayama practices, you should visualize the big toes as shining with a bright silver light. You should also sit cross-legged in meditation whenever possible because this knotting of the legs forces the chi to try to open up the channels to the feet. Although uncomfortable, sitting in a lotus posture is the easiest and most efficient way to help open the chi channels in your legs. People like to joke that the initial pain in mastering the lotus posture for sitting meditation helps burn off your hell karma, and there is some truth to this as well.

Now in our story of the Second Labor, it's said that every time Hercules smashed one of the hydra's heads that two more heads would grow in its place. Some say that a head would simply grow back. As we have seen, this signifies that once your root chakra is unplugged and the dirty chi gets a chance to escape, streams of impure chi are pushed out of the channels one after another by the kundalini energy (yang chi arising) until they are all emptied. After certain sections of the body are emptied of dirty chi, they seem to deflate and must be discarded. It seems as soon as one layer of dirty chi is discarded, there's another layer beneath it, which is why another hydra head always grew after the previous one was chopped off.

Hercules finally gets over the dilemma of new hydra heads constantly arriving every time he smashes one or chops it off. He came up with the tactic of cutting off a head with his ax, having Iolus cauterize the wound with a burning torch to seal it, and then proceeding on to the next one. In other words, it was because of the kundalini experience that he could get through this purification process. The idea of the torch was just a way

---

[31] Such as in the *Hathatatvakaumudi*.

of indicating that at this stage you'll feel a lot of heat as the kundalini starts pushing the impure chi out of the channels.

Using this technique Hercules was finally able to destroy the hydra heads one by one, signifying that the chakras would empty themselves of their dirty chi one after the other. Hercules eventually killed the ninth immortal head of the hydra, meaning he was able to unwrap the chi from all of the major chakras, and finally triumph in this Second Labor.

In some schools this process is called the initial "unfolding of the chakras" (Indian) or "untying of channel knots" (Vajrayana) rather than the "purification of the channels" or "harmonization of the five elements" (Buddhism) even though it's all the same thing. This reference to untying, which is represented by the hydra curling itself around Hercules' foot, is due to the fact that only after the channels empty of their impure contents can a larger covering of dirty chi unwrap itself from being bound around the chakras-channel system. It seems like you are experiencing an emptying of the channels of dirty chi and then an unwrapping of several layers of chi for each of the *koshas*. It's like disrobing a layer of clothes and then throwing them away piece by piece.

You must undergo this purification and unwinding process many times when cultivating the initial stages of the path. The exact number of purification sequences is difficult to pin down because the process for going through all these chi layers is so tiresome that you lose count. Taoism uses the number nine, the largest single digit, to indicate that you must go through many repetitions of this process. In any case, this chi that comes out of the channels is – like the hydra's breath or the foul stench of the women on the Island of Lemnos – dirty, polluted, or impure. Basically it's old yin chi that causes sickness and disease and which encases and blocks your channels and chakras. This expelling of the yin chi is the "poisonous" part of the story and as my teacher once told me, if you don't transform it then it easily causes cancer.

In summary, the snakelike hydra with nine heads symbolized all the impure (as yet unpurified) chakras and energy channels of our physical body and the way they are filled with dirty, impure, untransformed yin chi and wrapped with similar gunk. If you open one of the chakras, the chi inside its channel will spill out of it in tube-like squeezes one after another, a seemingly endless process that lasts for days. Thus, if the hydra's head was cut off, two would grow in its place.

Dirty, poisonous chi just keeps coming out of the chakra orifices if you initiate your kundalini yang chi and don't lose it through sexual activities at this stage. That's the process of the cleaning or purification of the channels. Once initiated, the yang chi can open up the chi channels and push clear their internal obstructions. Dirty chi will pour out of all the orifices possible, and you cannot achieve real physical health and longevity if you do not accomplish this feat, which is why some people practice pranayama in the first place. Scientists think they can invent some magic pill to extend the lifespan of individuals but if they don't solve this problem of expelling the life force (chi) poisons from the body, healthy, quality life extension is just impossible.

Hercules was eventually able to defeat the hydra's heads by slicing them off and sealing the wounds with a torch, which just means that he experienced the hot kundalini energy and continued cultivating while the dirty chi was expelled from the channels and chakras one by one. The Stage of Warming, the phrase used by Buddhism to denote this stage of spiritual practice, is simply an early stage of emptying the channels to a preliminary degree. It involves discarding the dirty chi everywhere in the body that's possible. All the world's cultivation schools, including western alchemy, remind you that the earliest stages of the physical purification process involve warmth like that from a fire, a furnace, cooking and so on. They are just referring to the initial arousal of the kundalini yang chi in the body that will push away channel obstructions while causing friction, heat and irritation in the process.

Once the channels are preliminarily emptied, then you can continue your spiritual progress to transform your yin chi into yang chi. As you chi continually transforms, you can start opening and purifying your channels and chakras at higher levels of attainment. Back and forth you go in sequence, first activating a degree of yang chi, next letting it clear your channels, and then letting it transform to a new degree of purity where it starts working on your channels again. In the earliest stages of cultivation, this type of physical purification sequence happens over and over again, and at times you will feel both the yin chi and yang chi in turn.

Everyone thinks they can just open their channels and chakras by concentrating on them and there are countless misleading books and courses on this process. The actual truth is that they unravel or unfold through many repetitions of this cleansing process. What purifies them is yang chi poking through them and pushing out obstructions, and that kundalini arises because you cultivated the emptiness of letting go. There are many layers of dirty chi that must be purified in the body, and every time Hercules wrestles with someone in his journeys it usually refers to the unwrapping or untangling of one of the layers or refers to his purification of some particular set of chi channels.

In short, unlike what most people believe, you cannot see the true shape of the chakras until a very high stage of cultivation because they are impacted with many layers of impure chi that must be stripped away. The whole process of physical purification at the earliest stages of the path involves the purifying of these channels. When yang chi (kundalini) arises it pushes out the obstructions, and we can call this the "transformation of yin to yang" or simply the cleansing of the channels.

Ultimately, you are not a body – neither the physical body nor purified chi body (like an astral body) that you might think you carry with you to another life. Ultimately there are no forms or attributes in your Real Self, so there is no body at all. The awareness that you functionally are has no body or center or form, but is empty of essence – or we say its essence is empty. That empty essence, which has awareness as its function, manifests a world of transient relativities that lack any true substance, and thus the realm of changing interdependent origination (the dependent arising realm of manifestation we call the universe) is one with its true emptiness nature. Unfortunately, only those people who reach enlightenment ever realize this in the experiential sense.

Those who start down the road of concentrating on the channels and chakras end up believing they are ultimately real, and become trapped in new realms of form rather than letting go of everything altogether. This is something that my teacher often warned against and being an *enlightened* Esoteric master himself, he refused to teach much about the yoga, Taoist and Vajrayana practices that focused on chakras and the like. Like Shakyamuni Buddha, how wise was his decision. Nevertheless I am revealing all this information not just because it is useful but because in the West, in order for the cultivation path to take hold and flourish, revealing such esoteric information will help establish a foundation for spiritual cultivators. That's what people tend to believe in, and this is also the type of information most often preferred by busy minds.

To realize the Tao is to realize that the ultimate substance or essence of all matter and mind is empty. As the *Heart Sutra* says, in reality there is no form, no matter, no chi, no consciousness, no five skandhas, no sensation, no anything. All these things are an illusion from the standpoint of the Absolute nature. Only a true cultivator who detaches from physical form and the energy we call "chi" can ever attain the stage of spiritual enlightenment where they realize this, so don't become attached to any phenomena along the way.

Who therefore succeeds on the spiritual ladder? It is rarely anyone who wrongly practices the esoteric traditions or clings to phenomena. It is those who turn within and search for the ultimate basis of the mind, which is the common basis of both mind and matter in the universe.

THE THIRD LABOR:
CAPTURE THE GOLDEN-HORNED HIND OF ARTEMIS

[2.5.3] As a third labor Eurystheus ordered Hercules to bring the hind of Ceryneia back alive to Mycenae. Now the hind was at Oenoe; it was a special deer that had golden horns and bronze hoofs, and was sacred to the Goddess Artemis. Wishing neither to kill nor wound it, Hercules hunted it a whole year trying to capture it. Eventually the deer became weary from the chase, and took refuge on the mountain called Artemisius. She then made her way to the river Ladon and was about to leave the region. Hercules shot her just as the deer was about to cross the stream and get away, and catching it he put it on his shoulders and hastened through Arcadia. Along the way he was met by Artemis and Apollo who would have wrested the hind from him. Artemis rebuked Hercules for attempting to kill her sacred animal. Howbeit, by pleading necessity because of the command of the oracle and laying the blame on Eurystheus, Hercules appeased the anger of the goddess and carried the beast alive to Mycenae and the king.

The Third Labor of Hercules was to capture the golden-horned Cerynian hind, sacred to the Greek goddess Artemis, and bring it back to King Eurystheus alive. Not wishing to hurt it, Hercules pursued the deer for one full year before he was finally able to capture it and bring it back to the palace.

What was the Hind of Artemis? A hind is a female deer, so right away we know that Hercules was cultivating the yin chi of his body (yin is always represented by the feminine) now that his chi channels were opened to some degree. Deer usually represent yang chi in spiritual traditions, but in this case the deer was female. Because the hind was also red, which is the traditional color of yang chi, we have several indications that his yang chi was starting to transform his channels during this labor, and many of the story elements support this interpretation.

In his First Labor Hercules stimulated the root chakra and got his yang chi to arise. Next that yang chi started running through his chi channels, and so the chi channels started emptying out their impurities. Various blockages and obstructions were pierced and removed because of that energy. Now that his channels are opened to some degree, he must once again experience the opening of more chi channels, the arising of more chi, and the purification of that chi and those channels within his body once again. That is what this labor entails.

Back and forth we'll see in the labors that no sooner than Hercules achieves a certain degree of channel opening, along with a higher stage of purification, than another set of channels opens up and the process begins all over again.

This transformation of yin obstructions within the body is a task that doesn't take brute strength, but patience and humility. It requires that you cultivate an empty mind and let go of the sensations that occur as your chi starts to move, refusing to block them or attach to them. Then the transformations that are meant to occur will happen naturally without interruption. The more you can let go of the body, the faster this can all occur.

If you read Lao Tzu's *Tao Te Ching (Daodejing)*, the spiritual path is all about how to cultivate your chi by being natural and "not acting," and this is just another way of describing the cultivation of letting go, detachment or emptiness. Traditional Taoism teaches it takes about one year to transform the chi of your body, and that's how long it took Hercules to accomplish this labor.

Shakyamuni Buddha often compared spiritual cultivation to the work of a potter who must carefully toil at creating his pots without destroying them. Similarly, in this labor Hercules must work at capturing the deer without hurting it. He has to be very careful in his cultivation for a long period of time so that he doesn't lose the past results of his practice. The process of spiritual cultivation is like cooking rice over a fire; you always have to adjust the cooking temperature according to the circumstances, and this requires some wisdom and skillfulness.

In the *Atalanta Fugiens* (a western alchemy book by Michael Maier that also uses many Greek myths to explain the process of cultivation), there is also a picture of a potter in one of the emblems to emphasize this aspect of the path.[32] This analogy simply indicates that it takes steady work, time and patience to normalize, balance and purify all the elements of the body, in particular the water and wind elements involved with the chi and channels. You cannot cook a meal all at once, and so it takes time for you to undergo all these various sequences of purification.

The entire school of Chinese *feng shui* reminds us that the wind (chi) and water elements in nature do not always harmonize, and the same principle extends to within the human body. Not just the wind and water elements, but all five elements of the body are initially impure and unbalanced at the very start of spiritual practice, but eventually they will become normalized and purified as you start cultivating to the higher stages of the path. That eventual purification and harmonization is part of the reason why people usually get healthier when they start meditating.

Your *jing*, or seminal essence within your sexual organs and the cells of your body (represented by the water element), and your chi or life force (represented by the wind element), must become transformed on the spiritual road. This is a process Taoism refers to as *jing* transforming into chi whereas other schools simply call this the purification of the body, opening of the channels, opening of the chakras or purification of the body's five elements. As previously stated, different schools identify the same process and stages using different descriptions and symbols. Each body will react to this purification in a different way, but also according to a common general pattern.

In the New Testament, for instance, Jesus tells Nicodemus that a person must be born of water and spirit - referring to the transformations of *jing* and chi once again - in order to "enter the kingdom of God." People normally stay away from this passage because they don't know the meaning, which is obviously esoteric, but it simply refers to this very same fact that you have to cultivate spiritually so that the *jing* and chi of your body starts transforming, which are your water and spirit (wind) elements accordingly. Only if your *jing* transforms into chi can you attain

---

[32] See Emblem 15 of the *Atalanta Fugiens*.

samadhi, which Jesus often spoke of using "the kingdom of God" or "Heaven." If your *jing* and chi do not transform, it is because your mind is not pure[33] and you therefore cannot attain samadhi or even be reborn in the highest heavenly realms.

Putting it another way using a different angle that represents the same thing, you have to reach a stage in your spiritual practice where your chakras and chi channels become purified, or the wind (chi) and water elements of the body start to transform and become purified, or *jing* transform into chi, in order to succeed on the spiritual road. This is Jesus' meaning of "water and spirit." It's unfortunate that the Bible has many spiritual teachings like this and yet people don't know these are lessons on cultivation.

Now the outward appearance of the Cerynian hind of Artemis is also of special significance to our story because it indicates that Hercules was cultivating his channels and chakras to a yet higher level of attainment than in the first two labors. First, the deer had golden horns, which represent the golden crown chakra of the body at the top of the head. Many schools represent this with an especially large hat or parasol, and almost always associate it with the colors gold, yellow or silver.

The deer also had hooves of bronze, which was a way of pointing out again that it is particularly difficult to transform the chi and channels at the bottom of the feet. It's as hard to open up the feet as it is to deal with dense metal. It's almost as if they are dead until you open them with spiritual cultivation. That feeling of wanting to get your chi to pass through that region is one of the reasons that some cultivation practitioners feel a strong urge to curl their toes during sex. Their sensation is as if some energy is stuck in the foot, because the chi has run down to the foot channels, and they unconsciously wiggle their toes and try to move their foot bones in order to help open up the area.

---

[33] Consciousness (meaning thoughts or the mind) does not become pure unless you practice the meditation practice of inner watching and other cultivation exercises. If consciousness does not purify from calming down, your chi also cannot purify to the necessary level of accomplishment indicated by Jesus. Chi purifies when *jing* transforms into chi via the process of meditation and spiritual exercises. As you cultivate, *jing* transforms into chi, chi opens up your channels, and thus the water and wind (air) elements of your body purify. Chi is often called "spirit" and consciousness is also often called "spirit" in some traditions. However which way you look at it, the dialogue refers to the processes of cultivation that an ordinary person must achieve to be truly treading the spiritual path. When Jesus said "Blessed are the poor in spirit, theirs is the Kingdom of Heaven," this poorness also refers to the loss of egoity (the "I-notion") and the purification of consciousness necessary on the road of spiritual practice. This refers to emptiness practice, of course. From all angles the same lessons continually come out, and from different traditions as well.

Even pictures of ghosts, whose bodies are composed of yin chi, attest to the difficulty of opening the foot channels. You rarely see the feet of ghosts in pictures (they fade out) for the simple fact that even these yin chi beings cannot open their leg channels without engaging in cultivation. This is also why the Christian images of the "devil" are traditionally represented with hooves as well, for the "dead" nature of hooves signifies untransformed yin chi.

In Hinduism and the yoga schools, we are often specifically shown pictures of sages whose foot chakras have been opened. These pictures teach us once again that we shouldn't neglect this part of the body in cultivation. For instance, pictures of Shakyamuni Buddha often show his opened foot chakras as well. In his instructions to practitioners, Shakyamuni Buddha often told students to practice the white skeleton visualization technique to help open up all the chi channels of their body and enter samadhi. What's important to note about this is that he specifically instructed them to start their visualization practice at their left big toe, *so as not to neglect the feet,* and then to work upwards. Only when you open the channels in the feet can you initiate the full microcosmic and macrocosmic chi circulations[34] within the human body.

It took Hercules one year to capture the deer, which is about the amount of time it takes to slowly transform the chi of the physical body. Hercules then brought it to King Eurystheus but released it at the request of Artemis and Apollo, divine twins that stand for the left and right (or yin and yang) chi channels of the body, respectively. Whenever you see a pair of male and female gods in a spiritual tradition, it usually stands for the yin and yang chi of the body, or left and right yin and yang chi channels.

This is why in the *Atalanta Fugiens,* a genuine western alchemical book, you often see male and female gods paired together, such as Mercury or the sun (Sol) appearing with Venus. All these representations reveal the physical aspects of cultivation, but rarely the mental aspect which is paramount for success. For this you need to turn to Zen, Mahayana Buddhism, Vedanta, early Taoism, Mahamudra or Confucian introspection-witnessing practice.

Yes, all these physical transformations described in the labors of Hercules can occur to you on the spiritual path, and they are important

---

[34] The microcosmic orbit is a circulation that runs upwards starting from the perineum, up the spine to the top of the head, and down through a middle line on the front body, back to the perineum again. When the legs and arms and other orbits join the circulation, you have the complete macrocosmic circulation.

benchmarks for successful cultivators who need some confirmation that everything is okay when they occur. But these are just the signposts of physical transformation that naturally occur on the path rather than markers of real progress in spirituality. The objective of all religions and roads of spirituality is to search for the fundamental essence of the universe from which all matter and consciousness originates. Another way of saying this is that you cultivate or search for the true nature of the mind, or the "true mind" that births all appearances.

As you start to achieve success along this route, which involves learning how to detach from thoughts so as to realize an empty mind where clear awareness still functions without attachments, your body will naturally start to transform as you mentally align yourself with this perfection.

As a summary, in this Third Labor of Hercules we find that the goddess Artemis (Diana in the Roman Pantheon) owned a little female deer which had golden horns and brass hooves. The deer and its special features clearly represented the chi and channels of the body. Hercules found it a challenge to capture the hind without hurting it but eventually caught it after a year of effort and then safely carried it back to King Eurystheus.

This labor represents the stage of cultivating *jing* (seminal energy) to chi (life force energy) in the body, a process also known as transforming yin chi to yang chi in the Taoist tradition, and produces a further opening of the chi channels. It represents a further step forward in the physical transformations that occur due to spiritual cultivation. Hercules just cleared the channels a bit in the Second Labor, and in this labor his chi can start to traverse the channels and become purified a bit. Success for this stage takes just about one year of effort, so this purification of chi and a subsequently higher stage of cultivation is the essential meaning of this labor.

THE FOURTH LABOR: CAPTURE THE FIERCE ERYMANTHIAN BOAR

[2.5.4] As a fourth labor Eurystheus ordered Hercules to capture and bring back the Erymanthian Boar alive. This was a fierce wild boar that lived on a mountain called Erymanthus, but which would come down to terrorize the people and the land. Passing through Pholoe on the way to the mountain, Hercules was entertained by the centaur Pholus, a son of Silenus by a Melian nymph. Pholus set roast meat before Hercules, while he himself ate his meat raw. When Hercules called for wine, the centaur said he feared to open the jar because it belonged to the centaurs in common. But Hercules, bidding him be of good courage, opened it, and not long afterwards, scenting the smell, the other centaurs arrived at the cave of Pholus, armed with rocks and firs angry that someone was drinking their wine. The first who dared to enter, Anchius and Agrius, were repelled by Hercules who threw a shower of burning sticks from the fireplace at them, and the rest of them he shot and pursued as far as Malea. Thence they took refuge with Chiron, who, driven by the Lapiths from Mount Pelion, took up his abode at Malea. As the centaurs cowered about Chiron, Hercules shot an arrow at them, which passing through the arm of Elatus, stuck in the knee of Chiron. Distressed at this, Hercules ran up to him, drew out the shaft, and applied a medicine which Chiron gave him. But the hurt proved incurable because the arrows had been dipped in the hydra's poison. Chiron retired to the cave and there he wished to die, but he could not, for he was immortal. However, Prometheus offered himself to Zeus to be immortal in his place, and so Chiron died. The rest of the centaurs fled in different directions, and some came to Mount Malea, and Eurytion to Pholoe, and Nessus to the river Evenus. The rest of them Poseidon received at Eleusis and hid them in a mountain. Pholus, drawing the arrow from a corpse, wondered that so little a thing could kill such big fellows; howbeit, it slipped from his hand and fell on his foot, killing him on the spot. When Hercules returned to Pholus, he therefore found Pholus dead. He buried his centaur friend and proceeded to the boar-hunt. After he had chased the boar with shouts from a certain thicket, he drove the exhausted animal into deep snow, trapped it, and then brought it back to Mycenae.

For the Fourth Labor, King Eurystheus ordered Hercules to capture and bring back alive the huge Erymanthian boar that had killed many men with its fierce tusks. The Erymanthian boar was a ferocious giant wild boar that lived on Mount Erymanthos, a mountain sacred to the goddess Artemis located on the borders of Arcadia and Helias. Periodically, the Erymanthian boar would come down from the mountain to attack men and animals and dig up farmland, wreaking havoc and destruction wherever he went.

Boars in general have a particularly aggressive nature. They are known to be remorseless when they attack, not hesitating to take on animals much larger than themselves. If one attacks you it can cause dismemberment or even death. The fact that they will attack larger animals who might threaten them gives them a reputation for a fearless, ferocious temper.

Boars also have a brutish ugly appearance, and are known as "razorbacks" because their back is covered with bristles. Their snout has small tusks normally used in foraging for food but they can also be used as weapons. While poking at the ground you can hear them snorting as they dig up the earth looking for their next meal, but they are always ready to chase other animals that come near. If you surprise one it may rush at you and try to slash you with its tusks.

The large boar in this story therefore stands as a symbol of man's wild, brutish, aggressive, and unrefined lower nature. Hercules previously opened his root chakra and ignited his kundalini yang chi, partially cleaned out some of the chi obstructions in his chi channels, and just started to transform his yin chi into yang chi. Now he stands poised for the arrival of more yang chi coming up, and the arising of so much unrefined chi will irritate him and cause his aggressive tendencies to arise.

In the task of conquering the Erymanthian boar, Hercules must now deal with the raw, unrefined yang chi that is now arising due to his cultivation. Now that he has opened his chi channels, the process of chi circulation escalates and lots of yang chi starts coursing through the channels. This is not a smooth process but sometimes quite irritating at the earliest stages. The yang chi that arises is not refined but raw and impure. This stage is almost too much for most people to handle without succumbing to angry outbursts, unless they cultivate emptiness to let go.

You've opened your chi channels, initially transformed some small degree of yin chi to yang chi, and now more and more unrefined yang chi starts coming up. As a result, due to the increasing volume of unrefined chi all sorts of angry, aggressive, irritating qualities start to emerge, so how do you deal with this?

The task of spiritual cultivation is a process of mental, as well as physical refinement that reoccurs at progressively higher and higher degrees of purification. You are certainly not done with purifying your body, mind or behavior just because you were previously able to stimulate a little yang chi into rising and were starting to open your channels and their chakras. You have to undergo many stages of purification countless times over many years, a process Taoism has referred to as the "multiple refinings." The rule or principle is as follows:

DIFFERENT TIME, DIFFERENT SECTION, DIFFERENT DETAILS, DEFINITE SEQUENCE.

In other words, there is a definite sequence of gong-fu transformations that occurs on the spiritual path. Different channels or sections of the body open up in a specific sequence, according to a specific timing and lasting for a specific length of time, and when a particular section options there are different phenomena, details or responses that occur than for other sections or pathways.

When it starts arising so profusely at this stage of the path, an individual is likely to get carried away by this excess energy until the channels open a bit further and the yang chi finally becomes more purified. Often they will engage in angry outbursts or just get easily irritated for what seems no reason at all. When a cultivator has reached this stage, anger, irritation, impatience and so on are all symptoms of unrefined yang chi rising rather than due to personality flaws. All sorts of things can provoke you at this stage of cultivation, but of course this does not mean that bad behavior is to be permitted.

My teacher once told me of a head monk who had reached this stage of cultivation, and all day long he cursed and cussed at his disciples because the slightest thing they did wrong irritated him. Perhaps he also had what is diagnosed as a liver energy imbalance in traditional Chinese medicine because when people have liver problems there is an emotional tendency to get angry easily. Regardless, until you can refine your yang chi at this stage by letting go and letting it purify, it's easy to lose your temper and engage in all sorts of aggressive tendencies.

Many people at this stage of cultivation ingest herbal liver medicines, liver drainage herbs, or dredging herbs to help clean their gall bladder, liver and blood since imbalances and toxicity in these organ systems can contribute to the problem. A popular Chinese formula for mental irritation due to liver stagnation is "Lung Tan Xie Gan" pills. You can also take certain herbal formulations for the gall bladder such as the Chinese medicine "Li dan" or "Break Stone" (*Chanca piedra*) and other herbal combinations.[35] When the chi reaches the back of the head and cannot pass through, so that your dreams start to bother you, there is Chinese medicine for that as well.

---

[35] People often take the health supplement nattokinase for one or two months to clear their arteries of blood clots. Nature's Pure Body can be taken to clean the skin and connective tissues of accumulated poisons, and enzyme products such as Vitalzym do the same. Twenty years from now, even better products will be created to help with physical detoxification, and hopefully detoxification will become a yearly routine in most human cultures. Right now, Candisol and Oregacillin are available to help kill off yeast infections that can cloud a clear mind. L-Glutamine can be taken for detoxification purposes and to help heal the stomach and intestinal linings. The Pekana homeopathic remedies of apo-Hepat, Renelix and Itires are also a great way to start the process of organ detoxification and drainage for those with cleaner, more refined chi. As to cleaning the colon and intestines, there are many herbal formulas and techniques available such as colonics and herbal remedies, but none of these are taken at later stages of the path because they cause you to lose too much energy. As time goes on, far better products and approaches will be created by various companies to help detoxify our bodies. In today's world loaded with chemicals, detoxification should become an annual process but remember that no drug, herbal formula or combination product – no modality of any type other than meditation - can help you attain samadhi.

Anything you do for physical detoxification will definitely help your progress at these early stages of the path because nearly all your chi energies initially go towards dredging your chi channels and clearing them of poisonous filthy chi. You must remember that just because the ancients lived on natural organic vegetarian food doesn't mean they didn't have to go through this process of channel cleansing and detoxification. It is a necessity for everyone because the human body is filthy. The ancients often referred to our body as a big dirty tube that we keep filling with food.

Additionally, in ancient times the various medicines, massage, acupuncture and other healing modalities we have commonly available today were not readily available to the sages who cultivated, and so they went through tremendous suffering as the poisons were expelled from their bodies.[36] Skin problems were quite common because it was often used by the body as a channel of elimination, a fact that the records of many schools commonly verify, and my own teacher told me it took him nearly twenty years for such difficulties to die down. I, too, suffered such problems for years.

On the other hand, lives were simpler in ancient times, so the mental barriers to spiritual cultivation were far fewer than those we experience today. Today the mental barriers are the biggest obstacles to cultivation – the modern day pace of life with stress overload, anxieties, multiple responsibilities, etc. – whereas the medical modalities available to help transition the body are abundant. This is the way it will always be – there will always be barriers to cultivation, either of the body or the mind.

One other thing we should mention at this point is that while you can use substances to help clean and detoxify the body, no chemicals, herbs, drugs, hormones, vitamins, minerals, or physical modalities of any type

---

[36] My teacher often told me of Taoists who would slice a cut across their fingertips right beneath the nail line when heart poisons finally were being pushed out of the heart channels. You could see the poisons collect under the nails at a certain stage, and the blood letting afforded them a ready avenue of exit from the body. All sorts of methods of detoxification were developed. Chinese medicine also has the method of blood letting from the top of the ear lobes to help eliminate poisons that accumulate due to stagnation. It is not that such methods are found due to clairvoyance, psychic abilities or anything like that. Cultivators simply invent or accidentally discover remedies for all sorts of situations that arise, and these become part of overall body of cultivation knowledge, namely human being science. If they find that a certain posture reduces back pain, it becomes part of the cultural body of knowledge. If they find that castor oil packs eliminate cysts, it is added to the body of knowledge. The western scientific method of studying every possible thing to understand interrelationships will in time produce its own body of such wisdom knowledge that, when mixed with knowledge from the East, will hopefully in time produce yet another renaissance in human culture.

can help you achieve the spiritual states of samadhi. No electrical means, magnetic means, vibrational means, gemstones, orgone, whatever - no type of energies can help you attain samadhi states of mental peace and quiet. The most any physical substance can do is help cleanse your body tissues of wastes and poisons so that your kundalini energies have less work to do when they start working through physical tissues, but the real work of attaining samadhi is only achieved by thought-free meditation.

Personally, I have collected and researched many dozens of rare books on special Indian, Tibetan, and Nepalese siddha medicines and tested many such preparations from various countries. I have tried hundreds of western herbs and special concoctions as well, and my teacher has tried hundreds more special Chinese formulas (including many rare, secret formulas that would be practically impossible for others to hear about or obtain) for all sorts of things. His conclusion, as well as my own, is that nothing can help you enter into samadhi or transform the body other than chi, as past sages also state, and after you go through all this gong-fu you will also understand why. It must be this way. If someone says otherwise, they are just cheating you. Among other things, people will make all sorts of outrageous claims to sell jewelries, herbal formulas, "psychic interventions," and expensive equipment.

As an aside, many Medicine Buddhas and Bodhisattvas of the past have often tested medicines on their own bodies to see the actual first-hand effect of those substances, and this is proper when care is taken. They could not rely on reading research studies and reporting on their results. You must be careful doing this yourself, however, as many individuals have died as a result of ingesting the wrong types of substances, especially if they mix this with excessive alcohol consumption or sexual dissipation.

In any case, based on first principles, absolutely no substances or modalities should be able to help you attain samadhi other than meditation itself. I must bring up this point again because someone in the future will no doubt use various false marketing claims to try to cheat you into buying their expensive product or concoction saying it will in some way help you attain the Tao. It is a waste of your time and money to travel this mistaken road – which also includes the road of psychedelic drugs and alcohol.

I also frequently have people who excitedly show me some new martial arts exercise, stretching position or yoga asana that helps unwind restrictions in the body, and they tell me it's helped their practice. I always laugh because while making the body more comfortable and healthy is one of the keys to being able to meditate longer, this type of effort can never open the central channel or ignite the River Chariot rotation. After the chi starts rotating, then all the channels will unwind and open, but this type of physical emphasis will never take you there. Nevertheless, people are always excited when they find some new physical secret for this physical body of ours that is doomed to decay and pass away.

Once you attain the rotation of the macrocosmic and microcosmic chi circulations within your body, you will quickly find that any supplements or medicines you take might actually *interfere* with the cultivation progress you've already made, including stimulants like ginseng, mushrooms, various adaptogens and mineral formulations. Some of the nutritional supplements seem to clog up the chi channels rather than lighten the body, and some over-stimulate sexual desire so that you end up "losing your elixir" and subsequent cultivation progress. At the higher stages of cultivation, losing one's *jing*, or semen, can result in damage to the kidneys, eyes, waist channel and knees. In advanced cases of dissipation, it can even lead to death. This is not theory but actual fact, for advanced cultivators will actually feel the harm of loss and then personally prove to themselves the warnings of sages that men need to preserve their *jing* as a treasure. With women the injunction is less severe because their bodies are different and designed to absorb sexual essences.

Despite what people may advertise to help sell their products, no physical substance or energetic modality of any type can help you attain samadhi. Emptiness cultivation is the only thing that can help you attain samadhi. Furthermore, no such substance or modality will be invented in the future either, despite claims that "science has progressed," and when you pass through these stages yourself you'll understand why. The dharma teachings already tell you this as well.

On the other hand, the physical detoxification of the human body is another issue entirely. In our modern times with the fact that we are bombarded with an overload of synthetic chemicals, pesticides and pollutants that our livers simply cannot handle anymore, it is a crime not to detox the body once or twice a year for health reasons. Aside from its value in cultivation practice (because most of your energies at the initial stages of the path become devoted to cleaning out the body), annual detoxification regimes are something that would go a long way toward cutting down on illness, disease, and debilitation in modern society. Whether one uses supplements, kidney and liver flushes, or other modalities (such as fasting or far infrared saunas) to help pull accumulated poisons out of the body, this should become an important habit for the public, helping people to reduce or even eliminate their chronic illnesses and improve their quality of life.

As an incidental note, pranayama practice helps push poisons out of the body as well, so it has this extra benefit for cultivation practice.

The only true way to create and extend a quality illness-free life is to combine an annual detoxification routine with pranayama breathing practices and emptiness meditation. In ancient legends, most of those who were said to have attained longevity (some examples being Methuselah of the Bible or Peng Zu of China) *were connected with spiritual traditions,* which is a lesson telling us that the longevity was the result of cultivating spiritual practice such as meditation. Those of whom it is said they attained the same stage as a Taoist Immortal who could continue living for thousands of years – such as Ancestor Lu in Taoism, Pindola of Buddhism and several of Tsong Khapa's students - all practiced anapana and pranayama breathing exercises to make this possible. They cleansed their intestines, opened their network of chi channels including the chi channels running to the feet, and practiced emptiness meditation so that their chi could run smoothly without obstructions in the body.

Another area of the body that must be transformed in cultivation is the region of the throat, which is often symbolized in Chinese culture by stupas of multiple stories. Though not explicitly mentioned in this labor of Hercules, the throat chakra is particularly difficult to open when the yang chi starts arising because of all the glands in the region. Only someone who opens the throat chakra can ultimately succeed in some stage of enlightenment. Jesus showed that he had opened his throat chakra when on the cross he offered forgiveness to those who had crucified him. As people get older the chi channels in the region of the throat tighten and close, and only an enlightened master can open them fully to be able to do this.

An Indian story that illustrates the difficulty involved in opening the throat chakra involves the god Shiva who swallowed a poison created by chi. This poison came about when the Indian gods started churning the Ocean of Milk to obtain amrita, the nectar of immortality. In the churning of that chi, a poisonous substance arose called *Kalakuta.* Shiva swallowed the poison to get rid of its poisonous influence, and it left a blue mark on his throat where the throat chakra was located.

There are many meanings to this story and quite a few deal with the difficulty of opening this particular chakra. In many cultivation schools you will also encounter this symbol of stirring. You will often see the symbol of two fish swimming in water, arrayed like a yin yang symbol, to denote the stirring of the life force, transformation of *jing* to chi in the body, and circulation of the chi through a circular orbital pattern up the *du-mai* and down the *jen-mai*.

To recap, at the earliest stages of cultivation nearly all one's energies go into transforming the chi of your body and its chi channels, collectively known as the "five elements" of your physical nature. It is all a process of purification which leads to the balancing or harmonization of the body and its energies. Internal poisons are expelled through the process and natural chi flows are also re-established that had become warped because of clinging and the wrong use of your mind over time.

Thus, any supplementary detoxification efforts at the earliest stages of the path – including eating less meat and substituting cleaner and more natural, wholesome foods in the diet - will help deal with the problems that arise from unpurified yang chi coming up and causing uncontrolled outbursts of behavior. Sometimes a vegetarian diet helps at this stage, and sometimes it doesn't. Overall, it is better to eat less meat than more in the diet, but whether or not someone can become a vegetarian has a lot to do with energy needs, the cultural environment and personal circumstances. Many people simply cannot follow a vegetarian diet correctly to maintain their health as required for cultivation attainments. As the cases of Milarepa and Shakayamuni both show, extreme diets and ascetic deprivation will not win you the Tao because it is only after the body becomes healthy that you can achieve enlightenment.

The only real remedy to dealing with the arousal of raw yang chi is patience and the meditation practice of letting go of any urges or predispositions that arise to push or impel you. These impulses are not you so you do not have to follow their provocation, which is something you soon realize if you practice any sort of mental witnessing mindfulness. They are due to body currents of raw, unpurified yang chi that provoke emotional responses and impel you toward behaviors, but only if you follow them.

This is why meditation stresses detachment. You are not these energies or forces or even your thoughts but stand apart from them. The real you is behind even the awareness that sees or knows them. They are just passing by so you do not have to react to them. You just have to know them which is called being mindful of the mind. If you know them, you can certainly leave them alone (that's "detachment") and they will naturally depart. When you detach from them, you actually change your karma or life fortune and in addition, by letting go of those energies (especially sexual urges) they will be freed to work toward opening up chi channels.

As Jesus said in the neglected *Gospel of Thomas*, one must "be a passerby" and not attach to the transient thoughts or impulses. You should let them go by learning non-attachment since they are already fated to leave. Vipassana meditation encapsulates this lesson, for by practicing internal witnessing you learn to be like a hotel manager who stands there in the lobby watching all the guests come and go, but who doesn't move at all. He doesn't get involved with the stream of visitors but just maintains a motionless stance watching the scenery pass by. Pure witnessing means you watch the events within the mind without taking part in them.

For instance, have you ever heard a musical song play in your head and you could not let it go? That is an example of attachment or clinging – you find that you just have to follow the music, rather than let it play, and you find you are anticipating every part of the melody. That's what it means to not be detached from mental arisings. If you could just let the music arise and simply experience it while it plays, but without trying to hold it or reject it, that's the meaning of non-clinging. If you anticipate with intense expectation the next few bars of a melody that plays in the head, that's attachment.

This explanation should help you understand the meaning of being a passerby who doesn't get involved. It does not mean not to help people or to forgo compassion, but simply means to let go of thoughts while still acting as you should and must to institute what is good and right. You must respond appropriately to all situations, and you respond because of thoughts, so thoughts must not be suppressed.

The world is one of impermanence, so thoughts cannot stay. They will arise naturally and depart naturally, so you don't need to blot them out, or try to restrain them because any thoughts necessary for a situation will arise as required. You just need to know your mind and act on the thoughts that are appropriate. Hence, you can relax and simply do what you need to do without much fear or anxiety or stress.

It's impossible for thoughts to stay, so the correct spiritual road is to cultivate the empty awareness that knows thoughts, and not act on thoughts if it's unwise to do so. Sometimes stupid thoughts, errant thoughts, incorrect thoughts or even harmful thoughts arise … and "wisdom" or "insight" means acting on the correct ones. No one said that the right thoughts always arise, just that thoughts always arise and that you need to practice discrimination by acting on the right ones. Usually that's your first thoughts, but then again, not always. To practice discrimination in determining what to do is spiritual practice, too, because it is the exercise of your wisdom. What Jesus meant is to just let thoughts pass without feeding them any extra energy or clinging to them. Act as necessary but do not cultivate a mind that clings.

If you set out to cultivate a mind that does not cling to all the scenarios of consciousness that pass by, your chi will change and spiritual gong-fu will happen just as is documented in the Twelve Labors of Hercules. It isn't necessary to try to force the gong-fu into happening, and you shouldn't waste your time trying to experience this or that. You do not need to try to bring the results of the path into the causative process of the path as is practiced in Taoism and Tibetan Buddhism. Various gong-fu experiences will occur naturally as you practice detachment with observation, which this story has amply documented, such as the manifestation of great irritation or violent outbursts at the raw yang chi stage represented by the Erymanthian boar.

You just need to know about these things if you are truly an ardent spiritual practitioner so that you are not confused and think you are retrogressing when such things occur. These are all temporary stages you pass through and sometimes just the knowing helps you get through the difficulties because you understand the problems are temporary. Spiritual gong-fu like this is entirely non-denominational, so you should seek knowledge about it and how to deal with it from whatever source is available. Benchmarking is the name of the game for true spiritual practitioners.

Chi and consciousness are linked at the lower stages of the cultivation path, so it's understandable that when this wild yang chi arises it will be reflected in outbursts and aggressive urges. However, these will die down as the yang chi begins to circulate more and more without obstruction, a process which by its very nature will tend to open the channels, eliminate the irritations, and purify the chi. Through such peaceful circulation, your yang chi will clear your chi channels of further obstructions and in turn it will purify and refine itself.

Hence, the wild boar in this story represents raw, unrefined yang chi that has been released after you start opening up the network of chi channels within the body and start transforming your yin chi and channels, as represented by the Hind of Artemis. It's the very next stage of cultivation. First, you start cultivating your chi and channels, and next your yang chi can start arising more voluminously, which of course will produce a new set of consequences. The true source of yang chi, or kundalini, is that it arises from the perineum, and you already opened that in the First Labor of Hercules.

In real life you can practice mantra recitation plus the skeleton meditation, pranayama *kumbhaka* breathing practices and vipassana meditation (along with sexual discipline, or non-leakage) to get to the first of the Herculean labors. If you know how to engage in spiritual prayer according to the right cultivation principles and thus develop an empty mind, while also practicing celibacy or conservation of sexual energies, that could also accomplish the feat as well. There are countless spiritual avenues that will work, but they all depend upon the same basic cultivation principles.

What people usually follow as spiritual cultivation is what is usually available in their religion, however, these may or may not be the most efficient practices available that you might use. Once again, benchmarking is in order – take the best practices from somewhere else if your tradition is barren. To get the quickest results you must use science and logic combined with a consistent practice schedule of effective meditation techniques practiced according to standard cultivation principles. What's most effective? It varies on a case-by-case basis, but it's best to start our cultivation with those practices that have produced the most success stories in the past rather than exotic, rarely known and rarely used methods. The search for novelty and wish to claim uniqueness is a big reason why many people fail in cultivation as well.

Once your yang chi starts rising remember that it is at first just raw, unpurified chi that is now starting to circulate. As it arises and circulates in the body, pushing here and there, all the human traits associated with raw yang chi will tend to arise with it. These pulls might include anger, aggression, brutality, irritation, sexual desire, strong appetites, and violent tendencies in general. Don't let this mystify you. It takes a long time to purify your body's yang chi just as it takes time to refine your yin chi. When your yang chi is active at this stage it's easy to strike out at others because people have a hard time controlling these urges due to the chi provocation. It's just like a wild boar running rampant. That's the meaning of this particular labor.

In this labor, Hercules' encounter with the centaurs is also significant. Centaurs are half human and half horse, the horses representing both strong yang chi (that can run wild) and also our lower untamed animal nature. Centaurs also hate men. Therefore they are once again a perfect description of unpurified yang chi at this stage of the story. This story is all about purifying unrefined yang chi, a task which is highlighted time and again.

Horses represent yang chi or breathing methods in most cultivation schools, so a half-man half-animal type of chi – unpurified human chi - is indeed indicated here. The reference to centaurs in this labor means your lower nature must be transformed, and that is what happens because the centaurs get killed. This is a side story in this labor that has puzzled most scholars, but now you will understand the meaning of these deaths.

To capture and subdue the wild Erymanthian boar, Hercules visits his centaur friend Pholus ("caveman") who was eating raw meat (a reference to unpurified yang chi once again) and starts a fire to cook it for Hercules, which of course represents the warm kundalini energies. In the story the caveman Pholus also opens a jar of wine, which belonged to all the centaurs, in order to share it with Hercules.

This wine is also a symbol, for once the yang chi is released and starts ascending the spine it sometimes activates the pituitary gland in the head which produces a sweet tasting hormone in your saliva. Taoism calls this saliva "sweet dew" whereas other schools, such as the Greeks, called this the "ambrosia" of the gods. This is also the sweet "Grail wine" of medieval European legends, but the yoga schools in India simply call it sweet saliva. It is said to banish sickness and extend your longevity, and all the cultivation schools tell you to swallow it. Since it first originates from the pituitary gland in the head, Pholus is said to live in a cave to represent the skull as its origins. The Labors of Hercules do not mention the fact, but feelings of physical coolness within and along the surface of the body usually intermittently appear along around the time of the sweet saliva due the transformations of *jing* to chi. The Confucians call this Springtime feeling *ching an* (lightness and peace) while Tibetans relate it to pliancy.

The other centaurs smell the wine after the jar is opened and come running to attack because they think someone is stealing it. This symbolizes the fact that the secretion of the pituitary hormone is accompanied by yet more yang chi arising within the body, so all the centaurs come running to the cave. The chi runs into the head, which contains the pituitary, to cause this secretion.

Hercules attacks the centaurs with burning sticks from the cooking fire, which of course refers to kundalini energies once again. After a long battle the attacking centaurs are defeated, which means the channels open and the aggressive tendencies die down. Pholus also gets killed in an accidental way because, friend or not, the chi and channels involved with aggressive tendencies and our lower nature must be transformed in this labor.

Hercules is still in the Warming phase of the Stage of Intensified Practices during this labor, which is the second stage of the overall cultivation path. This second stage of the cultivation path is what the Tibetans call the preliminary practices, which simply means you are an ardent cultivator working on a schedule of meditation practices. In the stage of Intensified Practices there are four sub-phases of cultivation progress: Warmth or Heat, Peak or Summit, Patience or Forbearance and then Highest Worldly Dharma. The first phase, which Hercules is going through, is the stage of Warming.

Hercules at this stage still feels the hot kundalini yang chi energies opening his channels and transforming his body, readily swallows the sweet saliva, and lets go of his lower urges by cultivating emptiness or detachment until the channels open and the chi purifies. This is how he passes this stage.

Most people do not notice the mental component of this stage, which is represented by the fact that he catches the wild boar in a snowdrift. Snow, because it is white and pure, is used extensively in many cultivation schools to denote emptiness or mental purity. In the western cultivation schools it is also used as a symbol to represent mental purity. While there are many cultivation stages where the chi feels like a cool vapor, which can arise from the feet or the head, this is not what is being referenced here.

Snow is white, which in turn represents emptiness or purity of mind, and this is why Hercules was finally able to get the boar under control. By continuing to cultivate mental emptiness at each and every stage of the spiritual path, which means letting go of the habit of clinging to thoughts, you can finally attain each stage of spiritual gong-fu and reach the highest spiritual attainments including complete and perfect enlightenment. As I was many times told by my teacher – who is recognized as an enlightened master of many schools - the cardinal rule in spiritual practice is emptiness cultivation from start to finish, emptiness cultivation each and every step of the way, letting go all the time. Detachment, letting go, not clinging but keeping awareness live and bright and doing everything you have to normally do. One need not go into seclusion or become a monk or nun to cultivate, but shutting yourself off from the world simply makes some of these aspects easier to master. The Tao is the only thing worthwhile to attain in life, and a monk's or nun's life is simply easiest for the activity of cultivation.

The use of wine is excellent in this story because not only does it represent this sweet dew of Taoism that we're talking about – a special sweet tasting hormone secreted because of a chi awakened, rejuvenated pituitary gland - but the fact that men who become drunk tend to lose their heads and let their lower natures come out. The presence of centaurs in this part of the story is also really quite good because it allows the same lesson to be repeated over and over again in different fashions. That lesson is that your lower animal nature must be transformed. Your unpurified yang chi must be refined at this stage of practice and certain channel obstructions, which cause irritation, must be purified away.

Thus, in this Fourth Labor of Hercules, we see that when the unrefined yang chi is first unleashed that it can be too raw like the meat that Pholus ate, or untamed like the wild centaurs and fierce Eurymanthian boar, and can provoke emotional outbursts just as rising liver chi often does. It sometimes leads to strong, wild, and aggressive urges that are difficult to control.

Quarrelsome and violent qualities will surface as yang chi pushes and prompts us into behaviors that reflect our lower selves. Happily, this stage is quite temporary and passes quickly if you cultivate an empty mind. In time, the unruly traits will disappear and balance will be restored.

The yang chi which arises at this stage will also cause the body to secrete a sweet tasting hormone in the saliva after the chi enters the brain to stimulate secretion, and it is impossible not to notice this. Our lower nature is transformed as the raw yang chi gets purified at this stage and chi channels open, and this is represented by *all* the centaurs dying from the poison arrows, including Hercules' friend Pholus.

In short, at this stage and life in general urges will sometimes arise in the mind but if they are errant, just pay them no heed by ignoring them, by not following them. Don't hold on to them, just let them go and don't act on them. Despite their promptings, you must come to recognize that they are just thoughts rather than the real you, and you don't need to follow your thoughts or impulses when they are incorrect. They are just phenomena that pass through the mind like the countless other thoughts in the course of a life time. Is this not a skill one should learn for life in general?

You must learn to choose which thoughts to follow through your own wisdom, and this too is part of the path of true spiritual cultivation. This is the meaning of Confucian introspection and Buddhist mindfulness practice, and even the Greek injunction to "know thyself" though in the truest sense it means to find your original nature. It takes time for your chi to become purified on the path of spiritual practice so that these impulses stop arising and pushing you into irritation. The Chinese call this process of purification the chi "returning to its true nature," but during the meantime you have to suffer the chance that rising yang chi will provoke angry outbursts, antagonism, sexual desires, and other lower urges.

As an ordinary human being, society tells you that your duty is to check these tendencies through the discipline of proper conduct. As a cultivation practitioner, you must match the societal rules of good behavior with cultivating an empty mind of detachment that does not cling to thought impulses that arise. You need to learn how to let go of the entire visage of your mental scenario and only act on what is right and proper. That's what "emptiness cultivation" means. It does not mean escaping from the world but acting in it with both wisdom and compassion. As you detach from clinging to your mental continuum – because your own consciousness is all you ever experience in life – you will in time develop peace in the midst of activity.

Just know your thoughts and feelings as they arise, but do not give in to them when they are improper. You should always witness (observe or know) them but don't let errant thoughts provoke you to action. Don't follow their lead by dropping into anger, lust and the other tendencies of our lower animal nature. Spiritual cultivation helps you rise above all this. If you do not drop into these tendencies then the relevant thoughts will pass, your chi channels will open, and your lower nature will become transformed into something more spiritual. Raw yang chi can and will become transformed for those who cultivate. It is a hero's destiny if you simply let go, which means in whatever you do, do not dwell. You must learn to act without attachment on the spiritual trail.

How do we know Hercules used this method of letting go and cultivating empty mind to capture the boar? As mentioned earlier, the legend tells us that Hercules finally caught the boar by chasing it into white snow, which represents a clean, pure mind. The *Atalanta Fugiens* uses this very same symbol of white snow to also represent mental purity, and it's used in other spiritual schools as well (except those originating from, of course, desert or arid countries). A mind of purity is a mind empty of thought. It's a mind Confucius called "absent of desires." When Hercules finally cultivated a clear mind – a mind pure like snow known as the empty mind of meditation - he was finally able to capture the wild boar and complete the Fourth Labor.

To others who suffer your uncontrolled outbursts and attacks at this stage, they will certainly seem a vexation. To yourself, they will seem like a terrible affliction you cannot shake off that will cause tremendous personal pain and suffering. The only way to get rid of them is to cultivate a clean, pure, empty mind whereupon the yang chi will naturally refine itself because you don't cling. Then you can proceed to the next higher stage of spiritual attainment. Everything proceeds step by step in spiritual cultivation, and you simply have to pass through these stages of progress by cultivating emptiness at each phase along the way.

In summary, for this labor Hercules had to capture a wild boar, which represents the need to transform his wild unrefined yang chi that is now voluminously arising. He killed several centaurs during the course of his task, which represents conquering his animal nature or lower urges. He eventually chased the wild boar up a mountain (the chi ascended the channels of his body) into a snowdrift (an empty clean mind born of meditation), whereupon he captured it with a net and brought it back to King Eurystheus.

The moral or lesson of this labor is to cultivate an empty mind, and do not give in to the impulses of your lower nature when your yang chi arises. As the raw yang chi ascends it might provoke, prompt or impel you to follow unusual urges but keep an empty mind and your body will transform from the ascending energies, and your mind will purify as well. This is how a true cultivator treads the hero's journey.

THE FIFTH LABOR:
EMPTY THE IMPACTED AUGEAN STABLES IN A SINGLE DAY

[2.5.5] The fifth labor Eurystheus laid on him was to clean the dung out of the cattle stables of King Augeas in a single day. Augeas was king of Elis. Some say that he was a son of the Sun, others that he was a son of Poseidon, and others that he was a son of Phorbas. He possessed many herds of cattle, more than anyone in Greece, and over the years their dung had collected in a stable that had never been cleaned. Hercules went to Augeas and without revealing the command of Eurystheus, said that he would clean out the dung in a single day if Augeas would give him a tenth of the cattle. Augeas was incredulous, but promised to do so. Having taken Augeas's son Phyleus as a witness to the deal, Hercules made a breach in the foundations of the cattle-yard, and then, diverting the courses of the rivers Alpheus and Peneus, which flowed near each other, he turned them into the yard, having first made an outlet for the water through another opening. The waters entering the stables thus rushed through and cleansed them of their impacted filth. When Augeas learned that this labor had been accomplished at the command of Eurystheus, however, he reneged and would not pay the reward. In fact, he denied that he had promised to pay it at all, and on that point he professed himself ready to submit to arbitration. The arbitrators having taken their seats, Hercules called Phyleus to testify and he bore witness against his father, affirming that he had agreed to give Hercules a reward. In a rage Augeas, before the voting took place, ordered both Phyleus and Hercules to leave the kingdom. Returning to Eurystheus, the king would not admit this labor either among the ten Hercules had to do, alleging that because Hercules had asked for a reward it had been performed for hire even though no reward was received.

For his Fifth Labor, Hercules was ordered to clean the stables of King Augeas in a single day. King Augeas, whose name means "bright," was the son of the Sun (Helios) or Poseidon (God of the oceans). This solar heritage might refer to a chakra blazing with chi, such as the heart or crown chakra, and the Poseidon heritage to the *jing*-chi of the body.

King Augeas had a vast herd of cattle - more than anyone in all of Greece – and an enormous amount of cattle dung had built up in the stables over the years because it had never been cleared away. Yet Hercules was given the task by Eurytheus to clean the stables of King Augeas in a single day! How would this be possible?

What this labor symbolizes is very clear. Inside our bodies is a central channel, called the "*sushumna*," that runs from the perineum (*hai-di*) to the crown of the head. It runs directly up the center of the body through the belly, heart, throat and crown chakras. Because they are on the *sushumna*, these chakra regions are often points of visualization focus in many spiritual schools and religions. We also have the back and front chi channels in the body called the *du-mai* and *jen-mai*.

Flanking the *sushumna* closely on its left and right sides are another two channels called the *ida* and *pingala* respectively, or the "left" and "right" channels.[37] The left channel is also known as the moon channel, white channel or yin channel and is usually symbolized by a female god. The right channel is often known as the sun channel, red channel or yang channel and is usually symbolized by a male god.

Whether it be Persian cultivation, Indian cultivation, Chinese cultivation, Tibetan cultivation, or the western cultivation schools, the images of the sun and moon, or male and female, are repeatedly used to represent these two channels or alternatively, the concepts of the mind

---

[37] These are also known as the *lalana* and *rasana* channels in Tibetan Buddhism.

and chi (also called "vital breath"). In other words, if you see a depiction on relevant spiritual pictures of the sun and moon, or male and female, these are usually referring to the *ida* and *pingala* left and right channels.

Naturally there are many more channels than this in the human body – the science of acupuncture doesn't even catalog all of them - but for the preliminary stages of cultivation these are the only major channels you need to know. In fact, to succeed in cultivation you don't need to know about chi channels at all, but this information serves as guideposts for when you start experiencing spiritual gong-fu because of your efforts. Many people who experience these things wonder what they are all about and seek explanations to allay their fears, or they misinterpret things because they didn't have the teachings and then start cultivating wrongly because of attachments to their body.

The importance of the *sushumna* central channel is that after it opens, samadhi attainments are finally possible. The problem is that the central channel is impacted with impure or dirty chi just as the Augean stables were clogged with dung and feces.

That is exactly the meaning of the Augean stables in this labor – they represent your unopened central channel. In order to attain samadhi and high spiritual states from your chi running freely through this channel, you absolutely must clean the *sushumna* of all the impacted, solidified *jing*-chi obstructions that have built up within it over time.

The compacted cow dung that had built up in the Augean stables basically represents the dense unpurified chi that fills and solidifies within the central channel over time, making it difficult to remove. It has to first be made pliable through warmth in order for its discharge to become possible. That's why the heat of kundalini is a necessary accompaniment of the cultivation path, and why pranayama and mantra practice are popular ways to prepare for its opening.

In the yoga and tantric schools, practitioners use all sorts of forced pranayama breathing techniques, mantras on chakra spots that line the *sushumna*, and visualizations to try to finally clear the channel. All this activity warms the channels and helps soften this solidified chi, a process Tibetans call "melting the bodhicitta," so that at the appropriate time it can be pushed out due to the force of the rising yang chi from below.

Now you know the secret as to why most esoteric cultivation schools will teach you to focus on visualizing the *sushumna* central channel, perform pranayama breath retention exercises, or recite mantras. They all help soften the garbage chi that has become densely impacted inside this and other chi channels. Prolonged mantra practice will do this and so will *kumbhaka* pranayama practice or the peaceful anapana practice of following the breath. Once opened the *sushumna* can be compared to an uncapped fire hydrant that releases a torrent of water due to all of the pressure inside. All sorts of dirty chi will spill out of it and pour forth for days, just as in the case of the Lernean Hydra. However, opening up the *sushumna* central channel is very difficult.

Hercules set about this daunting task by tearing big holes at opposite ends of the cattle yard. Next he dug wide trenches to two rivers nearby which flanked the stables on both sides. He diverted the course of the two rivers so that when the flow of the river waters reached the yard, the water rushed in, picked up the wastes and flushed out the stables in a short while. All the impacted cow dung was carried away by the current, pushed out through the other end of the yard, and Hercules performed this task in less than a day!

So why does this represent the cleaning out of the *sushumna* central channel?

The natural chi flow of the left and right side channels of the body is downwards whereas the natural flow of the chi within the central channel is upwards. The two side channels are easier to open than the *sushumna*, so several spiritual cultivation schools instruct students to specifically concentrate on this task through *kumbhaka* pranayama combined with visualization. If you open up these side channels, their energies will flow through the *sushumna* and open it in turn.

Here's how it works. When as a result of spiritual practice you open the left and right channels, which connect with the *sushumna* channel at its base, the subsequent pressurized flow of chi downwards from these side channels into the central channel at its base will cause the dirty chi within the *sushumna* to be expelled upwards and out. It is finally ejected from this channel. That's why it clears out, and it is not that hard to reach this stage if you cultivate sufficiently. All the preparatory cultivation work you normally see done in spiritual schools is to help prepare students to reach this stage. Students usually don't notice the previous progress they make, recounted in the first four labors, because the experiences are more subtle and there's no one to tell you that such and such is a symptom of a certain stage of progress.

You usually don't start feeling specific chi channels in the body until during and after this Fifth Labor. Therefore it's hard for cultivators to connect any earlier experiences they might have due to cultivation with the spiritual path itself or any definite stage of gong-fu progress, even though it is occurring. They tend to dismiss the earlier signs of progress as nothing special because they just don't know they are making progress at all or that those experiences are definite stages to be expected. Most people cannot feel their body's internal energies at all unless they start cultivating meditation and their chi channels start to open. But even for meditation practitioners, it is easy to dismiss the signs of the earlier Herculean labors as anything significant since they are not overtly striking and can stretch out over a long period of time. That's not the case with this labor, however, for the signs are impossible to miss, occur over a very short period of time, and the subsequent stages of gong-fu are unmistakable as well. Thus the Esoteric school signifies that the opening of the *sushumna* is the start of something different from all previous stages of practice work, and calls it the commencement of the completion stage of the path. But is it really that the completion stage can be passed through in a short period of time? We should just consider this stage a signpost or marker because there are many more stages and years of cultivation experiences to go through before one can attain the Tao. To say that one will definitely attain the Tao after this stage or that completion is assured is actually an announcement of hope rather than a reality one can count on. One needs to continue devoted cultivation work, with the right view, to the very end which may take years more of meditation practice.

After opening the *sushumna* there is still a long cultivation process ahead of you. Just because you opened up the central channel it does not mean self-realization is assured. You can become a great man or woman if you continue to cultivate, but how far you go is all up to your efforts. One should never be self-satisfied with their current stage of cultivation attainment. No Buddha or Bodhisattva considers their cultivation complete because all of consciousness is not yet transformed, and it is all you. For one to assume they'll get samadhi or attain enlightenment just because they opened up their *sushumna*, as yoga and Tibetan Buddhism sometimes insinuate, is a foolish assumption. And yet definitely you must open it. However, do not afterwards assume that success is assured. As Shakyamuni explained in his many years of teaching, especially in the *Surangama Sutra*, there are countless ways one can still go astray.

When someone does succeed in opening the central channel it is just as in the Bible where Jacob describes his vision of angels climbing up and down a ladder stretching to Heaven[38]— you can see the chi ascending the central channel to the crown chakra in the head, but at the same time you can also see a substance descending down the left and right channels to its sides. You can initially see (what appears to be) unpurified *jing*-chi dribbling down through two side channels upon this event, and that's what is represented by the angels descending in this story whereas the rising chi represents the angels ascending.

In Tibetan Buddhism there are descriptions of various signs you can sometimes see as the central channel begins to open, such as the inner vision of the channel becoming as black as charcoal when it is just about ready to open, but in the legends of Hercules these signs are omitted and just the opening is described instead. The big secret is that the visions and voices one experiences during these transformations, including Jacob's, are all fictitious. They are visions provided as nirmanakaya projections by other cultivation beings. They are often just imaginations which often make use of one's subconscious memories or knowledge of cultural symbolism in such a way as to get you through this stage and keep motivating you to cultivate and progress forward.[39] Because they are illusory and denote just temporary phases of purification, this is why most masters rarely describe them except those in the tantric paths that concentrate on purifying the body, for these appearances are illusory bodies or nirmanakaya projections.

In spiritual matters the central channel, where it connects with the left and right channels below, is often represented by the trident spear of Shiva or Poseidon[40] while the straight *sushumna* itself is often represented by Krishna's flute or the string on Rama's bow. All these channels are represented in different ways by different cultures. Symbologists have

---

[38] Genesis 28:11-19.

[39] Despite books delineating certain signs or marks, there is no standard for what you will see at certain stages of the cultivation path although you will pass through the same stages of purification. However, in some traditions you are trained to have the expectation of certain visions. Because those expectations will be in your subconscious memories they can easily be accessed and projected into your consciousness as enticements, confirmations or motivations. A lot of the experiences one reads about in religious texts are really just such projections. This secret should help clear up much confusion that has for centuries plagued the various traditions.

[40] Poseidon is god of the sea, or ocean depths. The Monkey Sun Wu Kong retrieved his magic staff from the ocean's bottom, or *hai-di*, which Chinese also says represents the perineum, a general area where *jing* transforms into chi. Poseidon's fish tail might even be construed as representing the sacral chakra right above the tail bone. The pumping of this chakra reminds me of cartoons showing a beaver's tail hitting the water, though of course the pumping is actually felt vertical-horizontally rather than horizontally. The wriggling of a fish tail's would be another excellent symbol to represent this chakra's pumping sensations.

missed the commonalities because they are not cultivators themselves and are not familiar with the results of cultivation practice either.

You should think of the body's channel system as a set of closed hydraulic loops with the chi circulating to a tiny chakra bulb intersection point at the top of the head. The *du-mai* back channel and *sushumna* send chi heading upwards to this point while the front *jen-mai* channel and the *ida* and *pingala* left and right channels take the overflow and send it downwards. That is why energy becomes available to open the central channel after the *ida* and *pingala* left and right channels open. But those channels, in return, cannot open unless the front and back have also been somewhat opened, too.

There are other main branches to this circulatory system as well, such as the two leg systems which proceed downwards into each foot. However, most schools stress opening the *du-mai*, *jen-mai*, left and right and *sushumna* central channels, and then simply say that the peripheral systems will open afterwards.

Some schools describe our chi channel circulations by referring to the orbits of planets, and some just refer to the whole system as a tree or bush with many branches, which is the method used in the Jewish tradition. There are lots of ways to represent our internal system of chi channels, or *nadis*, and the symbolism employed by a teacher or school depends upon which features of the system are being emphasized and the culture fostering the tradition.

In the Chinese cultivation schools practitioners usually concentrate on opening the front and back chi channels of the body, called the *jen-mai* and *du-mai* respectively. The *du-mai* corresponds to the spinal cord of the central nervous system while the *jen-mai* corresponds to the autonomic nervous system and the visceral organs. The traditional Chinese herbal medical system, or TCM, has developed elaborate correspondences between these channels, health conditions and herbal remedies one should use when sick.

In the Indian and Tibetan cultivation schools, however, practitioners usually concentrate on the left and right channels in their cultivation. It is not surprising that these schools share a similar emphasis since most Tibetan tantric yoga practices originally came from India. The difference in emphasis is due in part to differing medical systems and cultural concepts. When the front and back channels open, however, be assured that the left and right channels will open as well and vice versa. In truth, you almost always feel the back *du-mai* channel opening before anything else.

In the yoga schools and Tibetan Buddhism, practitioners are explicitly taught how to do pranayama breathing exercises, combined with focused visualization on chakras and bright points, to force the chi within the left and right channels into the central channel through an opening at their base. After this happens, the chi rises in the central channel and the dirty chi obstructions that have been inside it are pushed upwards and out.

What is particularly important to success, and stressed in other cultivation schools as well, is that practitioners first spend some time concentrating on the region of the heart chakra just behind the breastbone. You can recite mantras on this location. You can visualize a Buddha (such as Zhunti Buddha) or spiritual other Avatar, or a moon or diamond point of light on the spot. You can create a stable visualization of a Sanskrit, Hebrew or Persian letter at that location while reciting mantras concentrated on that spot (and several other mantra locations as well to help open all of them simultaneously, which is a basic principle in many tantra practices). In all cases you must concentrate on that region to bring chi to the area, which will help open up the tiny channels in the vicinity, while developing and holding on to a stable visualization.

The practice of reciting the Jesus Prayer on this spot, as documented in many Eastern Orthodox Christian accounts, definitely helps loosen up the *sushumna* and heart chakra channels in this region. If one succeeds in the practice, one can sometimes see a little (chi) flame arise in the area, which happened to me from reciting the Zhunti mantra along with visualization. When that happened my teacher, whom I never informed of the progress, immediately called me up to his apartment and gave me a special set of clothes to commemorate the progress.

In India the tantric yogis are taught various pranayama breathing techniques to help prepare for the opening of the *sushumna* channel. They learn alternate nostril breathing and train specifically to hold the breath for long periods of time. This forceful breath retention is a pranayama practice called "*kumbhaka*" that helps open up the chi channels. However, most yogis who succeed emphatically tell you that the real *kumbhaka* is when your breathing stops naturally and you stay in a state of breath cessation without effort, just like in Hercules' First Labor. That's when the real kundalini arises, a state called "*hsi*" or embryo breathing in the Chinese cultivation schools.

In fact, if you simply watch your breath (a meditation practice called anapana) while letting go of your thoughts and your body, in time your coarse respiratory breathing will slow to a halt, the internal embryo breathing called *"hsi"* will commence to start pumping (later with progress that sensation dies down) and your central channel will start to open. Simply cultivating awareness will do this. However, no one believes that it's this simple to accomplish, yet all you have to do is relax your body and know the breath is going in and out your nostrils while letting go of clinging and interpretation.

First you relax the body and let it fill with chi. After you are relaxed and your chi becomes full because you let go, you will eventually experience a slowing of your respiration. Eventually you will experience a pausation or cessation of your breathing for short moments of time. You are not doing anything but resting and your breathing will seem to stop, so since this is natural don't worry about it and clench up when it happens but just let it occur. The body knows what it wants to do, so don't "freak out" when it happens.

As your breath fills your body, those periods of cessation will become longer and deeper. All the while you simply watch the breath without attachment, which means without clinging to the feelings of the body, or body-consciousness, or sensations within the body.

This non-forceful method of simply "watching your breath," by simply "knowing" that it is moving through the nostrils without any attachment or analysis (you just know it's there),[41] should be practiced while the body is totally relaxed. It's as if you are almost half asleep, and this practice of observing the breath will in time also open up the *sushumna* central channel and take you into dhyana. It's so simple, however, that few believe in it and therefore few people practice it as everyone wants more complicated cultivation techniques. But this is how to cultivate all the chi of your body and open up all the channels and chakras at the same time. That is, *if* you learn how to let go of the body while practicing the technique.

This is one of the fastest ways to open up the central channel. The Zen school simply says that if you unite your breath with your mind, and the two become one, you'll open up your *sushumna* central channel

[41] At higher stages you practice noticing the breath when it's in the mid-nose, and then later with much progress you can observe it at the region of the third eye. The important point is to start from the aspect that you are bodyless awareness, and to observe the body from this vantage. You observe the breathing from the aspect of being a dimensionless center of observation that has no body. So you must dis-identify from the body without trying to blot anything out. By dis-identifying from the body your chi and channels can transform quickly, and at the same time you practice remaining aware of the energies moving but detached from the sensations. As you succeed in the practice you do become detached from the energies and the breathing often slows to a halt.

naturally. To effortlessly just know that your breath is in your nostrils is the meaning of "uniting breath with your mind" – you don't have to forcefully unite anything by pushing anything together because when you know the breath is there then breath and the mind are united. You *witness* that your breath is in your nostrils, so you *know* they are connected.

The instructions are not anything esoteric but as simple and plain as that. You just know, and keep your awareness on the knowing while detaching from the sensations and everything else that flits through the mind. Stay centered on the knowing, but without clinging or pressure. It's effortless, but people don't understand this instruction of practice and think it involves some type of forcing rather than just clearly knowing something, which is awareness. You are basically practicing awareness or witnessing and when breathing eventually slows or stops due to this practice, you will reach a state of cessation or halting of mental busyness. When that happens you simply continue to shine witnessing on the emptiness, looking for the perceiver or ultimate source of the perception. The witness simply registers the presence of experience and remains ever unstained because it is not an experience it. It underlies consciousness and becomes "I am" when thought arises.

This method of anapana is extremely effective, the teaching is true and clean, but it's so simple that hardly anyone believes in it. Hence people without much wisdom, despite the fact that many in Shakyamuni Buddha's day achieved samadhi with this technique, typically turn to more artificial and forceful techniques when they don't need to.

In any case, the opening of the *sushumna* central channel and the side channels is symbolized by the angels ascending and descending Jacob's ladder in the Old Testament story of his awakening, for of course angels don't need a ladder to get in and out of heaven. When was the last time you saw an angel climbing a ladder? This was just a symbol for this phenomenon of cultivation. There are many stories in the Bible representing particular stages of cultivation achievement, but the majority of Christian and Jewish adherents have lost the direct knowledge of cultivation teachings, thus blinding them to the *modus operandi* behind genuine spiritual attainments. Unfortunately, this leaves them incapable of correctly interpreting the depth of their scriptures and leaves them blind to the highest spiritual teachings.

In Tibet the spiritual practitioners are taught vase breathing exercises and the nine-bottled *kumbhaka* wind practice of Vajravarahi to help open their left and right chi channels. They are also taught to visualize their energies entering the *sushumna* channel while dark, dirty poison chi is expelled from the channel. Once the *sushumna* channel opens, then one can start to open up the other extra energy meridians in the body and attain the River Chariot rotation, which is the microcosmic circulation spoken of in Taoism and chi-gong, though given a different name in yet other schools. In many schools this rotation is symbolized by the flow of a river.

This opening of the channels and circulation of the chi is also described in the Old Testament *Song of Solomon*. The key point is that it is the same story, same journey, same events, same chi phenomena, same spiritual gong-fu, same set of labors over and over again regardless of the spiritual school, sect, or religion. The results of spiritual cultivation are non-denominational so the gong-fu is common, non-sectarian, or non-denominational as well. You can experience the same thing and prove this to yourself, but only *if you bother to cultivate*!

It is a well known fact, represented in different ways in various spiritual traditions, that the left, right and central channels are at first somewhat obstructed when you start on the path of spiritual cultivation. With time and effort at proper meditation practice these three channels eventually open, including the front and back channels, too. The school of Chinese Taoism, in correspondence with Chinese cultural concepts, once represented the obstructions in the three channels by saying they were inhabited by "worms" or ugly spirits that thwarted people's cultivation efforts, and who left the channels after sufficient meditation practice.

In Greece this idea of the three worms (obstructions) within the channels became the three ugly old blind witches, or Graeae, who shared one eye (the Ajna chakra) in the story of Perseus. Perseus met these three witches when seeking out some way to kill the monster Cetus, which like Typhon possessed a monstrous body. The fact that Perseus succeeded in outsmarting the Graeae and then killing the snake-headed Medusa was an artistic way of saying that he had cleared his three channels and then the many other chi channels in the head. His story also contained symbols of what happens as you transform the physical body on the cultivation path. Of course, Perseus also eventually killed the monster Cetus, which meant that he triumphed in transforming his physical body like Hercules.

Now in the story of Jason and the Golden Fleece,[42] his opening of the central channel was represented by his famous journey with the

[42] The golden fleece, or prize of the gods, represented the purified chi and chakra-channel system of the human body, as did the "burning bush" in the story of Moses.

Argo (his ship) through the Clashing Rocks (the "Symplegades") at the Bosphorus. These two rocky islands, known as the Clashing Rocks (a clear reference to breathing process of in-breaths and out-breaths), were set close to one another and would often clash together to crush any ships that got between them. This represents the difficulty for chi to pass through the central channel. However, the hero Jason released a white dove when he approached the cliff faces and as the dove made it through the narrow passage without being killed, Jason knew he could get through the passageway safely if he rowed fast enough. Rowing with all their might, his crew of Argonauts was able to speed through the tight passage and forever after, because of their success, there was open and free passage for all others to pass through.

The Symplegades were opened permanently because of his feat, which represented the opening of the central channel. Once it finally opens, your chi can finally traverse through all sorts of other circulations within the body's complicated structure of channels, and you are in reach of samadhi attainments if you cultivate further.

The idea in Jason's story was that there was a small crack between the two rocks and you had to squeeze through it by rowing with tremendous force to attain speed.[43] The Argonauts had to row furiously, while Hercules had to use the force of two rivers to clean the cattle yard in one day. With pranayama practice you have to use force to hold your breath

---

[43] In China there is the legend of a famous enlightened monk, Ji Gong, who lived in Hangzhou near Linyin temple. Ji Gong was an Arhat who had succeeded in his cultivation, but who spurned the purely academic and ceremonial methods of Buddhist practice that had enveloped the times. Like a mahasiddha or tantric master of India, he wore tattered robes, drank wine, ate meat and displayed countless superpowers, all of which went against the normal rules of religious discipline for monks. In a famous story, when the main hall of the Linyin temple was destroyed by a fire (kundalini), the abbot asked Ji Gong for help. Through his supernatural powers, Ji Gong enabled the timbers (representing the wood element, or chi) from far away to be hauled up through a tiny well (*sushumna*) in the middle of the temple grounds, a story that reminds us of the necessity for *yang* chi to squeeze through the central channel and the heart chakra. If you go to Hangzhou you can still visit the temple well and will marvel at its small diameter. Whether the story is true or simply another fanciful legend, one can say it hints of the importance behind opening the central channel in cultivation. Some people take the famous Ramayana story of Hanuman's tail, that burned the palaces of the evil Ravana after it was set on fire, as a similar lesson on how the rising kundalini fire and heat will destroy the yin chi of the body and burn it away. The dangerous cobra around Shiva's neck represents the ascension of kundalini up the body's chi channels, too. The Biblical story of the building of Solomon's Temple that housed the Ark of the Covenant, with the two left and right pillars named Boaz and Jachin, also refers to similar lessons on the esoteric anatomy of the human body. You don't have to be Jewish to understand the meaning of these two pillars, or to be able to establish them within your own body (temple). All these schools speak of the same lesson, which is that you simply must cultivate and then you will attain the relevant gong-fu whereas if you don't cultivate you won't attain any gong-fu.

until the *sushumna* shakes, rumbles and then finally opens with a sudden flash.

Incidentally, when you concentrate on chakras at this stage your chi is sometimes seen at those locations, through inner vision, as having a bright silvery color. This is what's represented by the white dove in Jason's story. When a little bit of chi can finally squeak through the central channel to open the heart chakra, that's when it can finally open and a person can gain an experience of emptiness or "no self."

Tibetan Buddhism catalogs many of the stages of this process of opening the central channel and the heart chakra. The crucial moment to the process of opening the heart chakra where it intersects the *sushumna* is that there comes a time, provided to you through inner vision, when a blackness as dark as charcoal comes flooding down and starts to cover the center of the *sushumna* central channel at the center of the heart chakra.

Once again, the big secret is that the visions are given to practitioners by spiritual beings who wish to help them through the process of cultivation, and while they may not necessarily accurately represent what is happening, they can help lead practitioners through the process at critical moments. This is something you finally learn only after completing (going through) the Twelve Labors and cultivating further, but in the meantime there are lots of ways in which you will be deceived to lead you onwards and it will seem so real during the process.

True or false, visions in an appropriate cultural motif are often given to practitioners at many stages of the process, including during *abhisheka*, but most people don't realize this and think the inner vision they see is the actual event rather than a representation. It's just a nirmanakaya projection. Even in dreams and near death experiences, the same usually holds; if you think angels have wings you'll see angles with wings, if you believe in Mesoamerican deities you'll be shown Mesoamerican deities; if you believe a deity has the head of a bull you might be shown a deity with the head of a bull, lion or whatever is appropriate for your cultural training and background. Sometimes the experience is real or the representation accurate, but in most cases it is not. Only a master will know for sure, but regular human beings will not be able to differentiate between a projection in consciousness and genuine sensory input from the five senses.

As explained in the Buddhist sutras, this is how an enlightened individual intervenes to help ordinary people, projecting millions and billions of nirmanakaya, including helpful thought solutions in emergencies or strength at crisis moments, and acting in other helpful fashions as well. Such interventions all depend upon your merits and openness to receiving assistance. The famous Taoist cases of future adepts falling asleep and dreaming their entire life stories that end in tragedy, or dreaming they entered the world of a painting, are similar examples as well.

Sometimes an individual might see spiritual beings in the sky or in the room and think they are interacting with them. They might see their master talking to past spiritual greats in a transfigured spiritual light, and might somehow recognize them without having ever met them. While the interaction with other spiritual beings is possible for those with samadhi attainments, for ordinary people these are usually just nirmanakaya projections that only they can see. The projections are to your individual consciousness, and so true or false, they can be anything the other wants. A master might even cause you to see something in order to frighten you from doing something wrong.

Many, many things in the Bible (all the way to *Revelations*) are examples of the nirmanakaya projection process; they do not exist in truth but only were only appearances produced to impress the recipient (for an immediate effect) and not meant to be taken as literal standards for centuries. The Zen school calls most of these things illusions, or *mara*, and tells practitioners to ignore them. Unfortunately, people without great wisdom and lacking deep cultivation knowledge and attainments don't realize this. Other easily understood examples include the multi-armed or multi-headed deities of India often seen in visions. Such fanciful images are further examples of skillful means produced for a specific situation in order to impress the individual and bring about a special intended effect. They are examples of expedient methods employed by Bodhisattvas and deities to help a certain individual, based on what is already in their mind, and only relevant to the individual's personal psychology and situation. This is another reason why the descriptions of spiritual things vary across cultures, and why similar stages of gong-fu are described differently.

You can find the instructions for how to open the central channel in all sorts of tantric texts, such as *Tsongkhapa's Six Yogas of Naropa*, which requires plenty of previous cultivation work as the Hercules tale readily indicates. Basically you are instructed that you must concentrate on a single diamond point, visualized within the central channel, and go through many stages until you reach the stage of "proximate attainment." This is a stage where blackness fills the vision and one must keep concentrating without losing consciousness. This is a detail stressed over and over again within the tantric Vajrayana instructions on how to open the *sushumna* channel at the critical moment.[44] You fix your mind on a single point of concentration and ignore everything else as it finally opens.

To get to this point of opening the channel, practitioners engage in countless preliminary practices beforehand - such as meditation, breathing exercises and reciting the Zhunti mantra or other mantras while visualizing images at the heart chakra - in order to soften the occluded obstructions within the central channel and prepare for that moment when the yang chi can burst through them. Those who succeed

---

[44] You can read the descriptions of the stages of "appearance," "very empty" or "proximity," "great emptiness" or "proximate attainment" and so forth in various Vajrayana Esoteric Buddhist texts such as the *Six Yogas of Naropa*. I had written down the details of many of these stages in a diary every few minutes as I was passing through them, and the following are diary excerpts concerning just the stage of proximate attainment: "Slowly, slowly darkness arises in my internal field of vision. It just slowly slides everywhere, sort of like the darkness is filling everywhere but coming from the sides and from top down, covering the visual field of what I see in my mind internally when my eyes are closed. The darkness just sort of arises everywhere and appears to obscure everything. At first it seemed a bit shiny and grainy like coal, but then it just became like a dark cloud or smog. It's not really a cloud or smog but it covers everything like that - it's covering things like a curtain. The blackness covers everything. ... Now blackness is descending. Wow, it's like dumping a bucket of coal dust into a chimney and having that dust come down on you, only this is dark vapor - it's streaming down the central channel over the heart chakra. STREAMING DOWN - like a blanket of coal dust - that's the only way I can describe it. It's like there's a tube and this thick black smoke comes falling down the tube, like a cloud of black thickness, to cover the bright point at the heart chakra in the channel that I'm concentrating on. It's descending into the whole channel over my concentration spot. ... My gosh is it black. Before it was dark, but this is black BLACK. Pitch black. Vairocana presses the palm anxiously with force showing me to "Focus, Focus, put all your effort now into focusing." The blackness tries to blot out the flame at the heart chakra, my point of focus, but I succeed in generating it and holding to it within the blackness. I'm straining my concentration like you wouldn't believe. I'm focusing so hard because I can tell Vairocana is worried for some reason, so I just throw all my efforts into it because of his worry. I tell you it's difficult - the concentration required is difficult ... the blackness makes you want to give up, you want to give up - it's covering consciousness. But I persevere because I can sense Vairocana is nervous so I know that whatever this is about, it's critically important. He's pushing his index finger against the fingers of the other palm held straight up, as on a single spot, and somehow I know this means I should be focusing intense concentration on a point, so I struggle and struggle to maintain that single point of focus, that single point of diamond light, that single silvery chi flame in a tiny, tiny flame point. The black pouring over it cannot extinguish it. I succeed; I did not lose consciousness. The blackness quickly lifts this time, it clears. It just sort of lifts across the vision, as if evaporating. The sky or vision gets bigger again, the sky returns and it seems wider open - it reminds me of an empty morning day where the sky is totally clear and the air is clean. While it seems as if it's a bright morning the air also seems to have some lingering humidity or thickness in it which you can't see but only slightly feel, as if it had rained. Somehow it seems a little heavy. It's got a sheen to it, this view. ... Happiness arises in my mind. During this process, only for a few short seconds I could tell that a pristine wisdom had sort of half arisen - something similar to when I saw that earlier stage of emptiness. It was very similar, but not clear and seemed only half there in the field of the mind, the other half seemed covered over somehow."

in this can eventually attain samadhi and are truly the great heroes of the human world.

The fact that Hercules was able to clean the Augean stables has given rise to the common phrase "Herculean task," which is equivalent to saying that a task is almost humanly impossible to accomplish. Opening up the central channel fits this description, for few individuals cultivate hard enough with spiritual practice to accomplish this. Individuals that open up the central channel, called the *sushumna* in India or *"zhong mai"* in Chinese, perform a heroic feat that few ever work at achieving. Once they open up the central channel they are in reach of being able to see the Tao and complete the rest of the cultivation journey.

In summary, countless cows lived in the stables of King Augeas, and the stables were compacted with filth because they had never been cleaned. This refers to the *sushumna* central channel of our bodies which is initially closed off because it is impacted with dirty yin chi. Hercules was assigned the task of cleaning the stables, or opening the *sushumna*, in a single day. He accomplished the feat by bending the flow of two flanking rivers so that their dual waters flowed into the stables and swept out the filth.

The story simply means that the left and right chi channels of his body, which were blocked, finally opened at their bottom into the *sushumna* central channel. That opening finally allowed a flow of chi energies through the *sushumna* to clear it of obstructions so that yang chi would eventually, in time, be able to reach to the crown chakra in the brain. Hercules did this in a day but you can only experience this if you work at lots of prior preparatory cultivation practices whose accomplishments are symbolized by the completion of Hercules' previous labors.

THE SIXTH LABOR:
SILENCE THE TROUBLESOME STYMPHALIAN BIRDS

[2.5.6] The sixth labor Eurystheus enjoined on Hercules was to chase away the Stymphalian birds. At the city of Stymphalus in Arcadia was a lake located in the deep woods. To it countless birds had flocked for refuge, fearing to be preyed upon by wolves. Hercules was at a loss as to how to drive the birds from the woods, so Athena gave him brazen castanets [krotala or noisemaking clappers], which she had received from Hephaestus, the god of the forge. By clashing these on a certain mountain that overhung the lake, he scared the birds who took to flight. The birds could not stand the sound, but fluttered up in a fright, and in that way Hercules shot them with bow and arrow.

After cultivation practitioners open their *sushumna* central channel, they can often bump into experiencing a minor taste of samadhi, which is a state of profound mental peace, quiet and calm. Once the central channel opens some of your chi energies can now ascend directly into the brain, your thoughts will start quieting down even further, and you start always experiencing a more profound type of mental peace than previously attained. This state of cessation, emptiness or mental quiet is more profound than when just the chi from the *du-mai* channel of the spine reaches the brain. It is a more permanent reduction in mental chatter, a sort of "turning down of the volume," that is all due to your prior meditation work.

In samadhi the mind seems quiet because it is emptied of most gross discriminative thoughts. In initial stages of transformation from meditation practice, sometimes there is even a physical coolness you feel in the head[45] that accompanies the quiet, and that coolness is due to the opening of chi channels and the transformations of *jing* to chi. Wandering thoughts die down so the monkey mind comes to a rest and seems internally more peaceful and quiet. This quieting is what most cultivation schools mean when they mention "emptiness" or "empty mind" although this is just a preliminary form of emptiness. It means a quiet mind, but in samadhi the best term that describes the state is "void" or "empty" rather than just still, peaceful or silent.

All that internal dialogue that you have running around in your head quiets down when in samadhi, so we say that the mind becomes empty and you are cultivating emptiness. The miscellaneous thoughts of the wandering monkey mind, the internal blaring orchestra of self-talk, all this internal dialogue quiets down and eventually disappears. Your mind becomes empty of discriminative thought chatter, hence the term "emptiness." While the mind becomes quiet, it is not like sleep because there is still awareness or attention. It is quiet, and because that quiet is an experience (you know there is quiet), it is still a mental phenomenon.

When you finally open up the *sushumna* you can reach truly profound states of mental stillness or "emptiness" where thoughts seem totally absent. The most profound states of empty mind or "no thought" are traditionally called the four dhyana and have various specific characteristics. Taoism talks about them, hatha yoga discusses them, Hinduism mentions them, and so does the school of Buddhism. The Jewish prophets cultivated them, Sufi saints cultivated them, Confucians cultivated them, and they appear in the writings of many Christian saints and so on it goes. If you do not know about these states you are missing something major in your religious instruction. Through every genuine religion with realized adepts you can find the same descriptions

---

[45] This coolness, which feels like the vapor from dry ice, can originate from the bottom of the feet. It can proceed upwards starting from below, or descend starting at the head. The stage of emptiness reached when it ascends from below is usually more long lasting and more profound than stages of cessation experienced after one feels the chi in the head. In ancient times natural air conditioning was generated by letting running streams of water evaporate within a building, and that analogy of transformation may serve to explain some of this feeling of coolness.

of samadhi and dhyana attainments. If a religion or path you subscribe to does not have these things, you better rethink your practice.

In the first dhyana, your coarse thoughts start to drop away, and you feel immense mental joy and physical body bliss because of all your opened chi channels and the fullness of refined chi circulating everywhere. In the second dhyana, your chi stops but the state of mental peace you experience is yet deeper and your states of joy and bliss even more refined. In the third dhyana, your mind is even more quiet because the state of mental joy has dropped away, whereas the physical bliss experienced by your body becomes even more refined due to the chi and channels having become further sublimated. In the third dhyana the pulse stops. In the fourth dhyana, it seems as if there is no longer any self because both body and mind no longer seem to exist. They seem to have passed away. These are advanced stages of cultivation,[46] and Hercules only gets a small inkling of what samadhi is like in this labor. The stage of quiet he reaches is no doubt a mundane stage of quiet rather than a stage of spiritual samadhi attainment. In Buddhism it is called a minor calming of the sixth consciousness, or discriminative mind of conscious thought. Nevertheless he is sure to bump into those stages now and then as he proceeds through the Twelve Labors.

In fact, after someone opens the central channel they may be able to gain an experience of the "clear light" mentioned in Tibetan Buddhism, which is indicated here. This state of selflessness, non-ego or emptiness is called "clear light" because the mind remains aware, or illuminated,

---

[46] Because chi and consciousness are linked, and because the five *koshas* refer to more refined states of chi, I have often wondered whether there is a tie-in between being able to attain the four dhyana and the purification of the upper four *koshas*. A correspondence with the five skandhas also seems plausible, but since this is not confirmed in any scriptures or sutras the idea should be deemed questionable. Nevertheless, one should recognize the difficulty of cultivating the four dhyana; those who attain the dhyana have spiritual attainments past ordinary men but they still may not have attained enlightenment. I once asked my teacher about the number of individuals in the world with dhyana attainments and he closed his eyes and counted up just over thirty samadhi masters at present whereas it used to hundreds in the far past. About sixteen to eighteen had been able to finally cultivate the first dhyana attainment, seven or eight had reached the second dhyana attainment, about three or four had been able to cultivate the third dhyana, and two or three the fourth dhyana attainment. People always think enlightenment is easy, but it is indeed difficult to cultivate the Tao and such self-less individuals and the dharma should be protected and supported regardless of their tradition. Unfortunately, people tend to persecute them because their truths usually worry vested interests and rub against the orthodoxy. As to perfect and complete enlightenment, only five or six individuals have achieved complete realization of all three Buddha bodies since Shakyamuni's day. It is often said that to become fully enlightened all future Buddhas must eventually come to this world of coarse matter, which is a perfect training practice ground for the goal, so do not waste your chance to cultivate while you have it.

while experiencing a state of profound emptiness, quiet or no-thought. The mind seems broad and expansive as an empty sky, thoughts seem absent, and yet there is awareness present so everything can still be known. This is equivalent to the Christian Eastern Orthodox or Hesychast idea of experiencing the Unborn Light, which is the empty awareness nature of the mind. We call it "light" not because there is any physical lights or colors you might see, but because awareness still shines even though thoughts seem absent. The mind is quiet, empty, open, free, expansive and aware, and so people usually refer to this as emptiness, awareness or light.

Because of physical light you can see things even though you do not see the light, and because of awareness you can know and experience but never recognize the underlying clear base nature of awareness. Awareness is still present and perfectly active rather than suppressed during a state of no-thought. That is why you can know that the mind seems empty.

In Buddhism this is also called a state of non-production, and is like a tiny peek of what it is like when you truly free yourself from the conception skandha, but the actual freeing oneself from the conception and all other skandhas takes many years to accomplish. This is not yet the Tao or enlightenment, but just a minor glimpse or peek into the true empty nature of the mind.[47] That's why it's called "seeing the Tao." At this stage you are only getting a small peek of what "emptiness" means, and there are many more years of cultivation to go to actually break free of, purify or transcend all the five skandhas that shield you from a direct experience of true reality. The reason you cannot experience your true nature is because you are always holding on to something in consciousness and that holding obscures a never moving awareness.

When you know what is going on in your mind, we call that consciousness or conscious experience (as opposed to unconsciousness).

---

[47] Practitioners train to gain a glimpse of this experience by various "bardo" practices, which concentrate on the transition between two mental states wherein there is a gap or momentary stilling of consciousness. Most people think that bardo practice only means cultivation during the time between dying and a new rebirth, but any intercessionary period is a "bardo period" that can be used as a point of focus in some form of cultivation. The practice of witnessing thoughts and noticing the quiet gap between them, which is basic vipassana or Buddhist mindfulness practice, is a bardo practice. To focus on the transition state in consciousness between the sleeping and waking states is the basis of the bardo dream yoga practices. When you concentrate on the pause between respirations, this is the basis of bardo pranayama breathing practices (see the *Anapanasati Sutra* for instructions), and the mental experience during the dying process as the personality consciousness is disintegrating is the basis of bardo death practices wherein one can also experience the clear light, or underlying empty but aware nature of the mind. The school of Kashmir Shaivism suggests many bardo practices for spiritual practitioners, as does Tibetan Buddhism.

Beyond the mind there is no such thing as experience; without consciousness there is no such thing as experience. Perceiving is consciousness, but you are not consciousness or its content. They are just its functions. You have to find the source of consciousness to fathom what you truly are, and to fathom what is the true essence or true body of all existence. In other words, that which makes perception possible is the only thing that is real and you must find that *Real One* through the vehicle of spiritual cultivation. You do this by watching mind so that it eventually quiets, and by observing the silence, which is an image of emptiness, one can eventually find an underlying awareness that starts the spiritual journey. As you make progress in this effort, of course your chi and channels will change because chi and consciousness are linked.

Now in the Sixth Labor of Hercules, our hero was given the task of driving away a flock of troublesome and dangerous birds which had gathered near a lake near the town of Stymphalus. Because of their noisy nature and flapping wings, birds usually represent thoughts or mental chatter in spiritual schools because they are always flying about or making a ruckus. So in this Sixth Labor, Hercules is finally silencing these thoughts to reach some state of emptiness experience. The symbols of dogs scratching themselves or chickens running on the ground are also used in various spiritual schools to indicate the wandering thoughts of a busy mind.

In this case, the Stymphalian birds had metal beaks and feathers they used as arrows to kill men. Their dung was also toxic, which is not surprising since they were pets of Ares (the God of War). They could scratch you with their long nails, and harm you in many ways.

All this means, of course, is that the thoughts running around in our heads vex us, bother us and cause trouble to no end, otherwise Ares would not be involved. If we could silence our incessant internal dialogue, then we would experience peace because it would be a great blessing. These noisy toxic birds had arrived on Lake Stymphalia in Arcadia to escape a pack of wolves, indicating in no uncertain terms that they are a yin condition that must be transformed away.

Everyone knows you can have no peace of mind with wild thoughts running around in your head, and every spiritual school attempts to lead you to a state of internal peace where wandering thoughts disappear but your awareness remains wide awake rather than silenced in stupor. Your mind is awake and aware, so thoughts still arise when necessary, but when not necessary all the useless chatter is absent. You are always resting in emptiness, but are clear about everything because thoughts arise when they should. In not attaching but just letting the mind function this way, you transcend the contents of the mind and are always at peace even during the most vexing of situations. You still give rise to thoughts, deeds follow the thought, but you do not mentally perpetuate the mental response. Action becomes effortless. Spontaneity becomes natural as the mind quiets and becomes open and free of clinging.

In spiritual training you are not supposed to cultivate trances, dullness, stupor or any state where the mind is suppressed, blocked, inhibited or not fully awake and aware. Most people don't know this basic principle and try to cultivate a lazy mind or hazy mind to suppress thoughts. They turn to drugs, shamanistic trances or all sorts of incorrect avenues they think are spiritual cultivation, but which actually produce lethargic mental states of ignorance and stupor. This is the wrong way to cultivate what's called emptiness, quiet or "cessation."

In proper spiritual cultivation, there is always natural awareness or attention but this witnessing or observation does not engage in clinging. Thus we say "the mind is bright" (connotations to light once again) because we are clear about whatever arises.

To denote this, some schools say the mind "abides in emptiness" which means that your mind is naturally empty but alive, awake, aware and ready to give birth to whatever thoughts come up, and thoughts will always come up because that is the nature of the world of manifestation. You witness thoughts without clinging. "No thought" does not mean to suppress thoughts but to reach a state where the mind is naturally quiet or empty, gives birth to thoughts when necessary, but you simply don't cling to them. If you thought that "no thought" meant suppressing thoughts then you might as well try to imitate being a rock. This is not what spiritual cultivation is all about for if it were, you would never realize the true source of mind and matter that way. Holding on to a blankness you create, you would just become a simpleton. While detachment, which means no effort, is a natural spiritual path, holding or attachment is not. True emptiness is a state uncluttered like the joy of open spaces and is like something ever new and fresh that has infinite potential for manifestation.

As the great master Tsong Khapa of Tibet therefore also warned, cultivating a mind of drowsy stupor and ignorance is incorrect, and cultivating dullness can easily lead to rebirth as an animal. It sounds incredible but some people don't know enough about cultivation theory and actually try to cultivate a state of mental dullness. They do this, trying to suppress thoughts or block thoughts or cling to a hazy state of mind, because they think this is the meaning of emptiness and the absence of thoughts.

Some spiritual practitioners can cultivate a somewhat empty mind but then they try to cling to it as a spiritual triumph. This false path has been criticized in Zen and many other schools as a wrong spiritual way as well. You must cultivate an empty mind, but must always let consciousness be born. Therefore you do not cling to the emptiness. Consciousness is there with life, it's there for a reason. Do not cling to consciousness, but do not suppress it and cultivate a stale emptiness or silence like a hollow cavern.

To attain the real emptiness spoken of in spiritual schools, you do not cling to images of emptiness either. You just stop feeding energy to attachment by learning how to witness without clinging, and then in time as your expertise grows the excessive thought disturbances of the mind will drop away. You just have to try it to prove it as this is the basis of meditation practice.

Consciousness should just flow through the mind like the images that pass across a mirror without sticking. Even if the images linger for a bit, the mirror does not cling to them. Even if the images linger for a long while, still the mirror does not cling to the images but is always free and open to reflect whatever new thing arises. It is fresh every moment even if the images do not move. It just reflects things as they are and when the images are gone they are gone; there is no trace of what went before, there is no clinging to the prior images, and no clinging to the present state either.

Our mind has no dwelling place because it is actually non-local, everywhere, so "not dwelling" or "non-abiding" is the actual meaning of emptiness and spiritual cultivation. You cannot just believe the sages about this fact, but must cultivate to a high stage to discover this for yourself. Otherwise it sounds unbelievable.

"Not dwelling" is the way to arrive at an experience of emptiness, and not dwelling is the natural outcome of having regained the right use of your mind. If we realize we are experiencing some form of emptiness, this is okay at low stages but not correct at the highest stages of cultivation either because it means we are attaching to an image, which is dwelling. The mind should be like a bright mirror in that whatever arises through perception or conception is reflected in it, seen in it, but whatever appears in the mirror mind should not become an object of attachment.

Of course it is hard to get to this stage, so the initial stages of spiritual attainment have you cultivating and experiencing empty mental states until you finally get there and reach the ultimate substrate of the mind. As your chi purifies your mind purifies, and as your mind purifies your chi and channels will purify. Back and forth will the progress be, and you will reach higher and higher (or more "purified") mental levels or realms until you finally realize the Tao, which transcends all realms of consciousness.

In cultivation your mind should be clear and aware and always able to give rise to an understanding of what's going on, something we call insight, prajna wisdom, knowing or understanding. You know, you understand, you comprehend, you can analyze and make decisions. Take juggling, for instance. A juggler must watch his balls in the air and make constant tiny adjustments, but a good juggler doesn't need to see the entire path of the balls at all times. He can see just the apex of a ball's trajectory and then estimate the adjustments he must make because of his experience and understanding. As another example, would you ask your boss for a raise when he's angry? Probably not, and that understanding of what to do or not do, or when to do it or how to approach it, is wisdom. Wisdom doesn't mean you are psychic or are omniscient. Possessing wisdom means you have a good understanding of the principles of a situation and how you should conduct yourself to achieve what you want to achieve. Because of wisdom you can understand situations and anticipate things better than chance, and therefore can judge how to act.

If you know you are confused, this is a type of prajna to know that you are confused. No one ever said a Buddha always had to know an answer, or even the right answer. A Buddha is simply clear about his mind. He knows all the thoughts in his mind stream. It does not make any difference to awareness that you know something or are temporarily confused and ignorant, for awareness is there whether you are clear or confused or inattentive. In spiritual cultivation, it is that ever present, ever functioning pristine awareness you must find because that's the first step to discovering what you are. That awareness is beyond thoughts and consciousness. It is therefore beyond the concepts of being and non-being.

Thoughts always arise; you should never block thoughts. Furthermore, on the road of cultivation you ultimately find that you have no body; there is no body that is you. You are bodyless; you are the pristine awareness of all that happens to the body and mind. However, thoughts always continually arise, which we call consciousness, and those thoughts produce understanding, or insight. That consciousness is just an automatic functioning that arises due to the situation, and consciousness is known because of an underlying foundation of universal awareness that is filtered through the deceptive filter of the I-notion. Cultivation brings you to a direct experiential realization of that underlying universal, pristine empty awareness that is the common ground of knowing for all beings and a function, or characteristic, of their singular absolute nature. It's always there, permanent and eternal. It can never be destroyed. The nature of the True Self is self-illuminated.

This empty essence is what you truly are, for there is no individual, self, or individual being in existence. There is just this one functioning that works, runs or shines through the apparent forms of all sentient beings. From the highest realms down to the lowest, the thoughts of being an individual have become a dense habit over countless incarnations (bodily transformations) that now screen the true self of the Source. It is because you have not penetrated through to once again recognize the Source, and thus cling in a binding way to this ignorance and self-deception, that a realization of the non-moving underlying universal body of awareness goes unnoticed. There is one underlying real nature or True Self for all (apparent) sentient beings that has the function of awareness, and that's what you are – call it God, dharmakaya, Parabrahman, Ein Sof, Buddha nature or whatever you wish. Mind arises because of It, the original nature. Thoughts, though unreal, will always arise in the mind because that's the function of consciousness, which should not be blocked but purified, and because thoughts arise you will always have understanding of a situation. That understanding, that ability to know is called insight or prajna wisdom. The more you study and train the more appropriate the thoughts that will arise for your situations and circumstances, and hence the greater your prajna wisdom. The more you learn the greater your natural prajna.

People always get confused about this. Prajna wisdom does not necessarily mean you know the answer to a question or situation, but just that you are clear about your knowing and know what you know or don't know. The size of your wisdom has to do with your life experience, your study, and also how far you have escaped being tied to consciousness because of spiritual cultivation. Prajna wisdom also has connotations that you know, or understand, the best answer or the best response of what to do in any situation. But the big meaning is that you are clear about the contents of your mind. From that clarity and your own wisdom, you often will know what to do, and if you attain enlightenment then your prajna wisdom will explode and you will know better what to do than anyone else because you will be outside the realm of consciousness and yet can access whatever thoughts are necessary, from which your actions will naturally follow.

Buddhism is the foremost of the various spiritual schools in terms of prajna wisdom (the one way in which it is far different than other spiritual traditions) because it teaches how to directly cultivate the mind and offers explanations of almost every phenomenon you encounter in cultivation – all the states of consciousness, gong-fu, superpowers, heavenly beings, and pitfalls on the path. Many people turn to it simply because they can find answers and explanations to most of their cultivation dilemmas whereas complete answers may be difficult to find in many other paths. Buddhism can offer all these answers because Buddha had very high stage students, and so he could teach much, whereas most religious founders have uneducated audiences and therefore could teach very little of the highest spiritual matters. This is a point people often don't recognize.

The application of prajna wisdom to investigating the states of emptiness that appear to the mind means that when you realize a state of quiet that you analyze it with insight to see where it comes from. Through introspection you can look for the foundation of the self and progressively become more empty and clear, via awareness with detachment, to ultimately arrive at a realization of the True Self or self-nature. That's enlightenment when you discard everything else to discover the ultimate root, essence, foundation, nature or host from which all comes, both matter and mind. Some religions call this God, but Buddhism calls this the "original nature" because it is beyond the notions of a personal being with a body, voice and intelligence. That is an image usually presented to ignorant people to lead them.

You *are* that original nature. You are the undifferentiated consciousness, called pristine awareness, of pure being which is of itself completely pure in character, uncontaminated by thoughts, emotions, sensations, names, labels, memories, objects, appearances, marks, stains or anything at all. It transcends them; it is beyond them. In realizing your fundamental face there is not even a witness left anymore because mind and intellect have left you, so you cannot even call it an experience. It's just an awareness wherein the dualistic knowledge of subject (the "I-am") and objects has been destroyed.

In terms of the dhyana and samadhi states, which are the quiet states of the mind, they are the common or shared stages of the spiritual path equally available to all beings, all spiritual schools and all religious practitioners, so nearly every genuine spiritual school and religion has them to some degree. There is nothing denominational about them, and they are not the province of any set of practitioners or religion. The big problem is how to achieve them, and that is what the spiritual path with thousands of practices is all about.

When you see colorful pictures of Buddhas like the thousand armed Kuan Yin, the countless arms and hands not only represent the opened chi channels of the body but uncountable meditation techniques which the Buddha can offer to practitioners. Buddhas, which means enlightened beings who have completely succeeded, often offer mantras to practitioners who can recite them as a method to quiet the mind. As all consciousness is one, those specific mantras cut through the infinite clutter of consciousness to connect with the power of that enlightened being for cultivation assistance. This is why I always recommend mantra recitation, and countless masters who have succeeded in the world's different spiritual traditions did so in part by using them as one of the bedrocks of their practice. Reciting mantras is always a wonderful spiritual practice for quieting the mind, and through mantra practice alone it is possible to arrive at a very high stage of mental calming.

Now most of the wandering thoughts in our mind are actually negative self-talk, and to become rid of this wandering internal dialogue is a blessing as well as a necessity for reaching the higher stages of spiritual attainment. Christian monks and nuns often talk of spiritual states where their ego seems to disappear. They are usually talking about samadhi when they mention mental states of great internal peace, quiet, silence and bliss that they attain after prolonged spiritual practice, such as prayer.[48] Clinging to thoughts and consciousness, rather than letting go, is the main barrier to progress in spiritual cultivation but you cannot rid yourself of thoughts by suppressing them or trying to push them away.

---

[48] Prayer recitation is actually a form of mantra practice. Done correctly it can produce profound spiritual progress. Done incorrectly it is just repeating thoughts in the mind, and only wins you a little merit from not having done or thought evil things during the time of practice. If one engages in prayer, they should understand how to do so correctly in order to gain the most benefit and spiritual progress from such practice. Otherwise it is just repeating thoughts in the head whose content is largely irrelevant. Thus prayer, performed in the right way, can be a type of meditation and powerful spiritual practice. Performed the wrong way, it is just another time when you stir up internal "talk in your head" for no advantage.

You can try to force your chi up the *du-mai* or central channel to silence thoughts, as many yogis try to do, but this is a coarse, crude way to cultivate and involves artificial methods rather than the natural true way of spiritual cultivation which produces results that last. Forceful techniques that involve pushing your chi energies in any way cannot help you reach the highest state that is non-artificial or Real.

The real path is one of letting go along with introspection to search for the ultimate source of consciousness and the "I"-thought. What you really should do in spiritual practice is just watch thoughts without becoming involved[49] and they will simply disappear by themselves. That will naturally open up the central channel, and that's how you attain samadhi.

How does Hercules get rid of his thoughts?

Hercules has previously opened his *sushumna* central chi channel from the labor of cleaning the Aegean stables of impacted cows' dung, but his body's yang chi must now rise within the *sushumna* and proceed upwards to reach his brain. The kundalini energies from his *dan-tian* ("*hara*" in Japanese) – which contains the *muladhara* root chakra - must ascend now that the channel is opened. They already ascend the back a little, and now a little amount of chi can flow up the *sushumna*, too.

This is what is represented in the Sixth Labor of silencing the Stymphalian birds by a gift of divine clackers or castanets given to him by the goddess Athena. In the story the castanets were made by the "God of the Forge," so originating from a god they definitely refer to some type of cultivation phenomenon. Since a hot forge is a common symbol used in many traditions to signify the pumping of chi energies from the *dan-tian* – and you'll see this symbol in various schools over and over again - this identifies the origin of the chi used to silence the birds. Many of the cultivation schools dealing with the physical body[50] identify the *dan-tian* as a type of forge, furnace or cooking pot within the body that has a set of bellows attached to the side.

These bellows represent the pumping of a chakra to push the chi upwards, which in other schools is represent by (sitting or standing) sexual congress or the wiggling of a fish's tail, and this pumping is the same as the clicking of the castanets. The bellows, which open and close just like Hercules' clackers, denote both the in and out phases of our

---

[49] You just witness or observe them without clinging to them, attaching to them, or dropping into their flow.
[50] Taoism, yoga and western alchemy to name a few.

breathing and the pumping of the chi up the central channel due to this chakra.

Once the chi starts ascending upwards, it also passes through various areas in the body which sometimes produce various clicking sounds, such as in the back of the head, although I don't think this coincidence is what is signified by the clackers. It is just something you need to know sometimes happens. When the chi passes through the occipital region of the brain people tend to see visions, and when it passes through the chi channels in the ear you tend to hear sounds including voices. You should always ignore such phenomena because they are illusions. The book *Tao and Longevity*, by Nan Huai-Chin, explains this quite clearly including the fact that they arise from deep psychological tendencies.

In any case, Hercules in this Labor used the gift of castanets (*krotala*) from the God of the Forge to scare away the birds, meaning he started experiencing the independent pumping of his chi upwards (what's often called internal embryo breathing) so that it entered his head channels to help calm wandering thoughts and silence his mind. He was successfully able to attain a degree of mental quiet which is the next stage in the hero's cultivation journey after opening up the central channel.

Hercules attains some degree of mental quiet in this Sixth Labor, just as you can also achieve yourself, by following the simple path of meditation. This accomplishment, rather than his feats of strength, is what makes Hercules a hero worthy of our admiration. You need only to put time into the meditation practice of just watching thoughts go by and then in time, like Hercules, you will experience the silencing of the birds as well.

THE SEVENTH LABOR: CAPTURE THE MAGNIFICENT CRETAN BULL

[2.5.7] The seventh labor Eurystheus enjoined on Hercules was to capture and bring back the Cretan bull. Acusilaus says that this was the bull that ferried Europa across for Zeus, but some say this was the bull that Poseidon sent up from the sea when Minos promised to sacrifice to Poseidon what should appear out of it. They say that when Minos saw the majesty of the bull he decided to keep it in his herds and sacrifice another to Poseidon instead. Poseidon got extremely angry at this and made the bull savage and run wild. To attack this bull Hercules came to Crete, and when he requested aid from Minos in capturing it, Minos told him to capture and conquer the bull by himself. Hercules caught it and brought it back to Eurystheus, and having shown it to the king he let it afterwards go free. But the bull roamed to Sparta and all Arcadia, and traversing the Isthmus arrived at Marathon in Attica and harried the inhabitants.

After getting rid of the Stymphalian birds, Hercules next challenge for his Seventh Labor was the task of capturing the Cretan bull. To this point Hercules has opened up his *sushumna* channel, the chi has risen to his brain and his thoughts have subsequently calmed down, so that he is now experiencing some mental stages of quiet or emptiness.

In this labor we can surmise that he is going to reach a more advanced stage of chi cultivation for as we know, bulls stand for yang chi and Hercules is dealing with a beautified bull in this labor. Back and forth we go in these stories between the purification and arising of yang chi to a new level, a resultant further advancement in chakra and channel openings and purification, and then the repetition of the opening and purification process all over again. We just had a stage of mental silence, and now we have another stage of chi purification due to that new stage of emptiness.

The story behind the Cretan bull is essentially the following. At one time a bull rose up out of the sea in front of King Minos. At the moment the bull arose out of the ocean waters, King Minos was vowing that he would sacrifice anything that came out of the sea to the god Poseidon. However, once he saw the magnificent bull Minos wanted to keep it for himself, and he decided not to offer it. He went directly against the practice of "letting it go" or giving away, one of the cardinal principles of spiritual cultivation.

Naturally, the bull in the story refers to the cultivation or arising of yang chi since the bull belonged to a god, namely Poseidon. The fact that it was the ocean god's bull may also be referring to the well known fact that *jing* (a water element) transforms into chi (a wind element) during the process of spiritual cultivation. Your generative force is transformed into life force, and this is what opens your energy channels.

Throughout Hercules' Twelve Labors we find a recognition of the transformation of the water and wind elements of the body, or *jing* and chi elements, by a reference to Poseidon. Some schools, such as Chinese Taoism, represent this by the transformation of "*jing* to chi"[51] while other schools, such as Hinduism and Buddhism, represent this as the purification of the wind and water elements of the body.

Poseidon got mad at King Minos for breaking his vow of sacrifice, and caused the bull to run away into the forest, from which it would at times come forth to terrorize people. This is a lesson showing that you cannot hold on to your yang chi even if you want to; you should simply let it circulate in the body wherever it pleases. The whole problem of the Cretan bull in this story arose because Minos got too attached to his chi circulation and didn't want to let it go. He clung to his beautiful chi, or channels, or stage of attainment.

---

[51] This type of descriptive scheme is fully explained within *Tao and Longevity, Working Toward Enlightenment* and *To Realize Enlightenment* by Nan Huai-chin.

Basically, the Cretan bull in this Seventh Labor represents a yet further transformative stage of *jing* (your seminal essence or generative force within your body cells) to chi after the opening of the *sushumna* channel, and then the circulation of this new stage of purified yang chi through the channels system.

You've opened up your central channel and cultivated a bit of mental quiet, so your level of chi purification has progressed. If you cultivate enough, the water and wind elements of your body will also transform to a higher degree of purity, and eventually your chi will become resplendent. However, you must not cling to any of these stages of chi transformation or the resulting chi circulations within the body, even when your chi becomes more refined. You must let it transmutate and circulate freely. Unfortunately, many people (like Minos) try to hold on to their chi during spiritual practice, which Tsong Khapa was getting at through his warnings against suppression, and thereby inhibit their cultivation progress.

In particular, this is a typical mistake most Taoists, athletes, yoga practitioners and martial artists tend to make. They tend to cling to their chi circulations rather than letting them flow freely within the body to transform it, opening the channels at deeper and more subtle levels. Your chi is not you and the body is not you, so let them do as they please as they naturally unfold the process of physical purification during spiritual cultivation. To realize emptiness, use whatever tricks help you to let go. But of course don't use any methods that hurt yourself or another.

In Christian monasteries, monks would practice "giving everything over to God" to help them let go. They would ignore bodily sensations while practicing humility until that letting go of the body and ego transformed into selflessness, and thus emptiness. They would recite prayers until their minds calmed down and they reached an internal mental degree of quiescence. Combined with chastity, such methods could, would and did indeed lead to spiritual attainments. Did that progress have to do with Christianity itself, or with the methods employed? By now you should have a firm educated opinion. Such it is with all traditions.

Some modern day people tell me they would imagine themselves jumping out of a plane and experiencing free fall to shake up their mental holdings so they might learn to let go. Some traditions teach you to imagine that you are dead so you can learn to let go of consciousness, or teach you to directly practice extreme relaxation (but without falling asleep). Others tell you to investigate the source of the ego or self so that you eventually abandon the holding on to all phenomena which are not the self. The practice of "neti, neti" (it's not this, not this) from India is another similar technique. Countless methods can be used to get you started on the path. You never know which particular method will work for you, and so countless methods, which work according to different principles, are available that can help you cultivate and make progress from different angles.

One of the major reasons people make any cultivation progress is because they simultaneously cultivated many different meditation methods and spiritual practices,[52] and refused to fall into a rut clinging to some concept of what "empty mind" might be. This is a mistake most practitioners do not avoid, for they usually start mentally abiding in some mental state they eventually cultivate, and they fall into a holding pattern by repeating the same clinging over and over again *for years*. This is why their chi and channels take so long to transform, and why they never seem to achieve anything.

If you are always holding on to consciousness then you are always holding on to your chi, and if you are always holding on to your chi, your channels will never transform and you will never experience any significant stages of gong-fu. Most unsuccessful cultivators do not study the principles of the path, don't apply them to practice, and they don't keep their practice fresh. They always continue clinging to the contents of the mind without realizing it. They never work to break free of that rut, by mixing things up and always investigating their mind freshly, because they always think they're practicing correctly when they are not. Think for a moment: if they truly knew the true meaning of "let go," "no effort," relax, be empty, do nothing at all, and stop clinging, would they not already have some significant measure of attainment?

Unfortunately we're always clinging to consciousness and our mental scenarios, so we need some skillful ways to slowly learn how to let go. When we truly stop clinging to mentation, we will no longer interrupt

---

[52] The major practices people should try to master include the basic "Meditation 101" practice of watching the mind (mindfulness, vipassana, recollection, contemplation, etc.), the white skeleton visualization, pranayama, mantra and anapana practice. Once you are through the Herculean labors, for samadhi attainments people typically drop all tantric techniques and switch their focus to emptiness meditation, anapana practice and Kuan Yin's method of listening to sound to awaken. To make basic progress, however, as long as you keep from falling into a rut by practicing meditation techniques that work on different principles, and by trying different methods of cultivating emptiness from time to time, this constant newness will usually help you open your channels and make progress more quickly than sticking to one method alone. I always advise individuals to create a meditation practice schedule that employs several different techniques, and which always includes mantra and offering.

our internal chi flows and they can start to open our channels. Our yang chi will awaken when it is no longer suppressed because of a busy mind. The best way to stop internal clinging – with countless conventional benefits as well - is to learn how to observe or witness thoughts, and so I always recommend the Confucian practice of watching your mind which Buddhism calls "mindfulness" (vipassana) and Christianity calls "contemplation" or "recollection."[53]

For the quickest results in spiritual cultivation you should approach the path by simultaneously practicing different techniques because you never know which will work best for you. By cultivating different methods that work through different principles or angles, you give yourself the best possible chance of realizing what emptiness means. Visualization practice, for instance, works by tying up your wandering thoughts until you reach a state of quiet, calm concentration which you then let go of. In regular meditation practice where you introspect by watching the thoughts of your mind (mindfulness witnessing practice), thoughts die down via dissolution since you stop continuing them with energy but just watch their comings and goings like a third person observer. This method works on the principle of subtraction, for your thoughts naturally subside when they lack any new energy input of continuation. Mantra practices focus the mind on one thought, the mantra, and in this way other thoughts tend to go away. Additionally, reciting mantras from enlightened beings taps into their promised assistance for your efforts to become spiritually enlightened. As to pranayama practice, countless cultivation schools say it helps the physical body and your cultivation efforts, so you can help yourself from this angle as well. You never know which of these angles will be most effective for your progress, so by creating a practice schedule of several such methods, you are always looking for emptiness in different ways, "shaking the glass so it cannot settle," and cultivating a freedom that will allow your chi and channels to more easily transform so that you eventually realize a genuine state of

---

[53] This practice is so common that every religion or spiritual school gives it a unique name so that the school can "claim" it. Benjamin Franklin's method of watching his thoughts so as to be able to change his behavior, and the famous Chinese ledger of merits and demerits for introspection introduced by Liao Fan, are other examples of the basic technique which should be taught to everyone, young and old. You must learn how to know your own mind, and how to watch your thoughts as a basic life skill, so this should be taught everywhere as it is non-denominational and non-religious. The benefits of such practice can virtually ripple thorough and rejuvenate whole societies because people will naturally cut down on their errant thoughts and evil deeds once they learn to know their own thoughts through mental watching, and can then detach from those thoughts and intentions that are bad or evil.

emptiness. That's when we say you "see the Path" and can understand what it's about, and how to correctly practice.

Basically, you need some way to help you let go of holding on to your thoughts and consciousness so that your chi can finally start to circulate freely, while you don't impose any mental restrictions on its movements, and if you feel any sensations due to the resultant transformations that occur during this process, once again you should also just let them proceed without attachment or interference. Everything in spiritual cultivation should proceed naturally and without force or mental clinging, especially when it comes to the subject of the body.

In the Seventh Labor, Hercules was ordered to go to Crete to capture Minos' bull and bring it back to Eurystheus. However, rather than receiving any aid from King Minos in this difficult task, Minos told Hercules he had to catch the bull by himself. This symbolizes the fact that you *must* cultivate your chi yourself – no one can help you do this, just as no one can save you or enlighten you. An enlightened being cannot save you but can only point out your true nature. You have to spiritually cultivate to realize it and thus liberate yourself.

As a result, in this labor Hercules sets out and successfully captures the bull without any external aid, and then he does indeed take it back to King Eurystheus. After presenting the bull to Minos, Hercules let it go free and it was said that the bull roamed throughout all sorts of other regions.

Neither Hercules nor Eurystheus hold on to the bull because you must always refrain from holding your chi during the process of spiritual cultivation. As all these channels start to open, just let it roam where it wants and don't try to hold on to it or guide it, which is the mistake modern Taoists make. You simply put all your efforts into having it arise, some schools stirring it into awakening through force and others encouraging it to arise through the mental non-abiding we call emptiness cultivation. To not attach or not abide is one of the main lessons of this labor. When your yang chi arises, just let it course through your channels and open up what it wants without trying to guide it.

To fully analyze this story and extract some more cultivation lessons, let us start off with what we know with some certainty. This entails a bit of repetition, but bear with me until the new material. Since Hercules was dealing with a bull in this story, we know he was dealing with yang chi because bulls are a strong representation of masculine yang energies. That's pretty much a given. Some details within other Greek stories suggest that the bull might have been white in color, which is a sign of purity in most traditions as well. The white bull does not mean that chi is white but is only a symbol of purity.

We also know that Hercules had previously reached a stage of mental quiet when he opened up his *sushumna* central channel (the cleaning of the Aegean stables) and was able to quiet down his thoughts (he chased away the Stymphalian birds), so now he definitely is in a position to reach a more advanced stage of spiritual progress. That progress in turn means a further transformation of his chi and channels, and more transformation of *jing* to chi, which is why this bull can arise out of the waters.

Taken together, the facts unequivocally suggest that this story has something to do with a more purified state of yang chi, namely the beautiful bull, that arises in full force. The fact that the bull rose from out of the sea represents the transformation of *jing* to chi within the body to produce more chi, or purification of the water and wind elements of the body. Because of his previous opening of his central channel an even better (or "higher") stage of yang chi transformation has been reached in the Seventh Labor than anything previously attained. This is the beautified bull that arises out of the ocean waters, and this full measure of powerful chi traverses everywhere opening up all the chi channel circulations within the body. That is why, when the bull is eventually set free, it then travels all over Asia.

This is as simple an explanation as it gets. However there is another related but rarely discussed cultivation phenomenon we should introduce here because it also transpires around this stage of cultivation and has many similarities to the main features of this story. In fact, this phenomenon is even mentioned in the Old Testament, but few westerners have ever recognized this stage of kundalini purification. It is a stage of chi transformation or purification seen in visions that occurs exactly around this stage of attainment.

During the stage of spiritual cultivation that follows the opening of the central channel, a cultivator will start to generate or eject what are called the "impure illusory bodies" mentioned in Tibetan Buddhism. What most people do not realize is that the phenomenon of the illusory body is not particular to Tibetan Buddhism or the eastern spiritual schools in general because it is a non-denominational phenomenon inherent to the purification of the human body. If you cultivate to this level of spiritual attainment, you will start to discard the dirty chi coatings of your inner channels, which are part of what's called the impure illusory body. This happens regardless of your religious tradition, gender, and regardless of your race or any other category.

This is a non-denominational purification process for all spiritual cultivators to go through who cultivate far enough, which is why you'll even find this stage of purification mentioned in the Bible. Yes, the Vajrayana generation stage of the impure chi body is in the Old Testament. This is because regardless of gender, race or religion, the necessity for the cleansing of the chi channels does not differ since the results of spiritual cultivation are totally non-sectarian and non-denominational. The spiritual gong-fu transformations we have discussed are simply *part of the science of human beings*. It is just unfortunate that most of the western religions do not recognize this fact and that so few people cultivate to experience these stages so they cannot identify them.

Shakyamuni Buddha was quite magnanimous in declaring that the paths leading to the ultimate achievement of self-realization can be very different from one another; therefore, he said, there was no definitive dharma that he could teach. He never declared that only his set of teachings, which he compared to a raft, was the only one that could ferry you across the river to the other side (take you to enlightenment). This was quite unlike the organized religions today, each fanatically maintaining that they are the best of the world and that all other spiritual traditions and their practitioners are wrong or inferior. Wars have been fought because of these differences, yet practitioners of all these paths always go through the same stages of achievement. The question is, with the religious path you are following, are you on the road to these achievements? Worship, ceremonies and disciplinary rules will not get you here.

The major purpose of religion should be about leading you to enlightenment, which means helping you realize your true fundamental face, and there are many ways to do this. As explained with the example of Kuan Yin, there are countless practices that you can follow. The ultimate target should be to help you realize the foundational state of everything, which the western religions call "God," because there is no higher goal or objective. You don't worship God because you are, in essence, God, and God needs no worship. Worship is just a method used within religions to train people. What you must do is strive to realize the foundation of being, which westerners call God, and then you'll know what you must do to help others. That is the process of striving for self-realization, for the essence of God (or the "original nature") is your True

Self. That fundamental essence is non-fabricated, pure, blissful, eternal and possesses the ability for consciousness or awareness.

If your religion does not aim to help you attain self-realization, however, then to put it directly, you are wasting yet another life and who knows whether the next incarnation will be as good as this one in terms of both access to cultivation teachings and having the opportunity for practice. Enlightened beings who teach constantly say that a human life is rare, dharma teachings are even rarer, and having the opportunity to practice the teachings is rarer still. You might consider whether you are squandering your blessings and whether a personal meditation schedule is in order.

Since there is no one absolute model of spiritual teaching or spiritual training that is best for helping us to realize our True Self, there is ample room for many religions, spiritual traditions and practices that can lead you to the Tao. However, you can also correctly say that some traditions have been, or are, far more effective than others for leading practitioners to achieve self-realization. This is simply a fact. It is just plain true. If your religion is deficient in this respect, one should have concern that another life is not being wasted. It is wholly proper to employ cultivation practices from other traditions because this common sense borrowing, which I call benchmarking, is logical and has always been done in the past.

The eastern religious traditions have definitely led more people to enlightenment than the organized religions of the West, partially due to the presence of accomplished masters and the absence of an overarching religious authority that could censor information and persecute "religious heresy" or unorthodoxy. If we were to rank the world's religions on a scale of openness and completeness of spiritual teachings for attaining enlightenment, then because of the lack of interference and corruption by a power structure, on this scale the eastern paths would definitely win. To learn about the Tao, one must always turn to the East.

Many individuals within the western organized religions often trumpet the fact that there is a common goal to all spiritual paths. However, when the view starts gaining ground that there are non-denominational ways to achieve spiritual liberation, various functionaries within the organized religions immediately pull their support from this magnanimous view. They suddenly draw back and shirk away out of fear they are going to lose something. Western religious functionaries instinctively know that there is much that is false (and even harmful) in the world's religions, and if some of these key dogmas were to be found false in the light of day then many western roads would simply collapse along with their proclamations. They cannot let that happen because part of their message is how lucky you are to be in their group.

If they hear that you will definitely experience non-denominational spiritual gong-fu after you start to cultivate, oh boy are they in trouble … especially if they have not experienced anything themselves. That would mean the blind are leading the blind. And if other paths offer these routes, one might expect to lose adherents and financial contributions in the long run as patronage is made elsewhere. Better it would definitely then be to suppress or ridicule that type of message!

If the logic of this message is followed to its conclusion, cherished dogmatic claims that separate one religion from another will have to go down the tube. People say they want this, but they don't in actuality because what they really want is for what they personally follow to remain standing at the top. Hence many religious people fear to hear that there is a common, non-sectarian, scientific way to cultivate the spiritual life because it might mean that their present way is "wrong" or deficient. Many of the false notions people believe in might just have to be discarded, and few want to admit they have previously been wrong or misled, and that their prior investment in beliefs must go up in smoke. For most this is much too painful.

What we usually hear from the pulpit is typically only lip service to the idea of ultimate spiritual unity. When it comes down to the actual knowledge and application of the universal principles of spiritual practice, the organized religions still each cling to their own dogmas and beliefs with adherents secretly thinking, "We are superior and the others inferior. We are right and they are wrong." Jobs, opinions, positions of status, money flows … all sorts of things like this are at stake. Ridicule, persecution, threats and worse therefore follow people who teach the true dharma. Often they have been killed. To tread the cultivation path, you must increase your own level of prajna wisdom and come to openly recognize this. The true path always requires your support, but hardly anyone ever lends a hand which is why so few people inherit the dharma.

The stranglehold of orthodoxy is also one of the reasons why the true spiritual path is hardly ever made available to the masses and accordingly, hardly anyone in the West ever reaches self-realization. Despite the overwhelming numbers of people in the western religions, the track record within these groups is that fewer numbers have reached high spiritual attainments within these avenues as compared to practitioners in eastern paths who simply learn how to let go of their minds. Consciousness is ultimately one, but all these groups are trying to segment it out into bunches of believers.

Most of the organized religious activity we see on the weekends is basically the busyness of individuals involved in the Stage of Study and Virtue Accumulation where people study holy books, attend ceremonies of religious worship, and try to live life in more virtuous and compassionate ways. This is commendable and has all sorts of societal benefits. The East has this as well, for this is the ordinary man's stage of religion that can indeed help one to be reborn in a heaven or attain a better life now and in subsequent incarnations. But after that merit is used up, what then?

The actual attainment of spiritual progress, such as a more purified stage of consciousness and the spiritual gong-fu mentioned so far, is only possible when religious adherents move on to the Stage of Intensified Preparatory Practices. This is when they start to intensively cultivate spiritual exercises rather than depend on ceremonies, rituals and religious rules of purity[54] and discipline as the main road of spiritual practice.

---

[54] To strictly follow or enforce religious purity rules and disciplinary codes in a fervent, unbending, ultra-orthodox fashion, and to take this as the spiritual path, is considered a lack of spiritual wisdom and the lowest level of practice on the spiritual ladder, sometimes even a negative level. Such rules are always invented by men – sometime men of Tao or just intelligent ordinary men - for immature minds lacking discernment. Religious followers who concretely hold to these rules or ceremonies as the spiritual path continue exhibiting that initial deficiency of wisdom. Not understanding the Tao, such people are usually quite extremist, prejudiced, and tend to persecution. They bind themselves in all sort of artificial injunctions that don't exist in reality. Adhering to these guidelines because of attribution to higher authorities, they sin against Reality and the necessity of wisdom and compassion as required in all situations to fulfill the needs of the moment. They build a mythology as to how the world is supposed to work, but of course it doesn't work that way. Due to their rigidity, if people with such notions assume the leadership helm of societies they typically bring violence, misery, repression and persecution rather than harmony, prosperity, peace and social order. When such religious notions usurp the leadership helm of nations, those countries quickly weaken. The universe is endless, as are incarnations, and there are five errant perspectives which must be eliminated on the road to enlightenment, and such adherents violate three in particular. These include eliminating the view that you are the body, eliminating one-sided or extreme views, and to stop taking religious rules, ceremonies and disciplinary codes as the spiritual path. On the road of spirituality one must cultivate an open mind that can function freely anywhere, matching all situations perfectly and adapting to situations and circumstances. On the Mahayana path you must learn to be flexible and hear things you don't want to hear, say things you don't want to say, do things you don't want to do, and suffer things you don't want to suffer to help liberate all sentient beings. Individuals living based on a strict radical orthodoxy are not yet qualified to take such a great road, show they don't understand the ultimate target, and in subsequent lives what they denied themselves due to forcibly binding restrictions often manifests in extreme desires and mad personality disorders to fulfill those repressed tendencies (since they did not cultivate them away naturally through emptiness and wisdom). "In one life good, in the next life bad." The tantric path actually forces you

Spiritual practice is personal, so one should always be watching their mind because that IS true spiritual practice.

To be pious in itself will not win you the Tao of enlightenment but only worldly and heavenly merit that has a constricted limit. In other words, true spirituality requires genuine meditation practice and other spiritual work to cultivate and then experience the genuine spiritual states and attainments. Just the study of religious texts or the attendance of religious worshipping ceremonies won't bring you to this end. *Real spiritual cultivation practice* is what is missing in the organized religions today even though it is the underlying crux and essence of the road of religion.

It is extremely easy to find countless quotes from the realized saints of various spiritual traditions, including the western streams, stressing the need for more actual spiritual practice instead of worship and ceremony. Only spiritual practice can lead to self-realization and this is the important thing that matters for enlightenment. The sad truth is that most ordinary religious functionaries lack any significant inner experiences. Therefore they can only offer ceremonial methods of worship and ritualistic or disciplinary modes of living to help guide people because they lack true knowledge of the real spiritual path. When this is stressed over any path of cultivation, that sect or tradition has lost its spiritual wisdom and cannot help you for the Great Learning.

---

to break any clinging to artificial rules so that your channels can all open, and so that both consciousness and behavior can purify to a degree people cannot comprehend. Once you attain samadhi, to maintain it you are always following a stricter path of discipline than any set of rules or regulations stipulated by religious authorities, yet people don't understand this because they don't understand the purity of mind one attains, often called "the mind of Heaven." It is amazing that in the records of history it is the ultra-orthodox, who think they are championing true religion, who are usually the ones who kill the only people who succeed on the road of spirituality – the men of Tao. Sages of the past simply invented rules and guidelines to help guide simple people, and attributed them to higher sources only to help them become accepted and take hold. It is like governments today deceiving people in order to guide and govern them. To inflexibly take such recommendations past their original intent, or to carry them forward when they are no longer needed, has created more suffering in the world than can possibly be described. Part of spiritual wisdom is relying on virtuous life principles for guidance – common sense rules that are beneficial, make us happy, and do not hurt others regardless of societal conventions. One should strive to make others happy and try to avoid hurting feelings or making things worse for others because that consciousness is also you. And if science can provide better guidance rules for living than established religious rules of conduct or discipline you should defer to science. If justice conflicts with religion or cultural tradition one should also defer to justice, and so on. This is the correct way to live according to wisdom. It is sometimes said that "the law is an ass" and when circumstances are such that the law is truly an ass, one should certainly not enforce it.

That is our pitiful world today, and hence one of the many reasons for writing this book. You need to see the universal nature of the spiritual gong-fu that awaits all those who truly cultivate, regardless of their particular religious school or denomination. As the world becomes increasingly fascinated by the capabilities of science and the modern inventions of technology it subsequently spawns, such as genetic manipulation and bioengineering, if this information does not now become available then the cultivation trail may disappear entirely. No one will be motivated to cultivate anymore when technology offers up all sorts of competing mental fascinations.

In any case, the appearance of impure illusory bodies is one of the many types of non-denominational spiritual gong-fu that can happen to everyone during the natural process of spiritual cultivation. It is simply because they have not cultivated far enough that even religious functionaries don't understand the phenomenon, which simply represents a further stage of the cleansing or purification of the chi, chakras and channels.

There are many phases to the process of purifying your body during spiritual practice, and many phenomena occur within this long process. The generation of the illusory body is that you will often see what appears to be an inner chi body break away from the inside of your physical body as it passes these stages of purification, and then rise up out of it and then disappear. You might also see smaller images of your body that appear and then drop their chi skin coating to reveal a core of transparent gel-like *jing*-chi inside that looks like a crude, unformed stalagmite. It just vibrates there a bit and then also seems to rise and disappear into the air.

These experiences are actually teaching visions to help lead you forward at this stage of the path, and these events that you see are all called "illusory bodies" because they are illusions peculiar to body chi purification. What you see and hear is your imagination, which is why Vajrayana directly tells you they are "illusory" bodies. Whether or not you can see these things depends upon the extent of your prior cultivation efforts, your wisdom, your teacher and your merit.

What you see is also dependent upon the tradition you were training in, because the cultural expectations of what you should see are what can be readily used from your subconscious to denote this stage of purification. Hence Taoists will sometimes be shown an immortal fetus rising into the heavens, Tibetan Buddhists will often see deity images rising, western practitioners without a tradition will often just see their own body and channel systems drop away, and so on it goes. The Bible also has records of prophets seeing particular things during their cultivation, and modern interpreters in both Jewish and Christian traditions cannot figure out the meanings not just because they never went through the process themselves, but because the events (seeing thrones, wheels, divinities with animal heads, etc.) were only appropriately invented for those individuals.

Such recountings get passed along and cause a heap of trouble for later generations who aren't privy to these explanations of the purification stages of the path, and don't cultivate far enough to go through them and get first hand experience of such phenomena. Such visions are only a type of skillful cultivation assistance that is appropriate for the individual in question, and thus are different for each individual according to their background. They are an illusion that has nothing to do with a prophecy of future events. In Christian theology there is even an entire branch of study, called pneumatology, to help individuals interpret human encounters with spiritual beings, visions, prophecies and so forth, and the common theme once again is that most should be ignored. It doesn't say particular phenomenon didn't arise - it just says to ignore them. Most all schools, especially the Zen school, rightfully tell people to ignore such things as illusions, but at least you now have some minor explanations behind the process.

In Tibet it is explained that a wisdom dakini (deva, or heavenly being) might create such a vision in order to help some adept with their concentration exercises, and the method used, invented on the moment, might be so successful that this skillful expedient means was carried forward in the lineage to help other practitioners. This is how "Heaven helps" individuals who cultivate, giving them visions as appropriate. The history of Christian medieval monks and their visions illustrate this type of phenomenon as well. This explains why other traditions might be lacking the same visionary symbols, which is usually unlikely unless the information was communicated as a shared technique. This tradition has this, that tradition has that, and so the expected marks or signs and visions differ. All these visions are just a focus of attention to keep the mind occupied in one-pointedness for awhile, to acknowledge the cultivation progress, and to entice practitioners forward. After you've been through this many times and seen all the types of forms and experiences that can be invented, you'll know it's true.

Sometimes visionary experiences represent the present cultivation stage of the practitioner to inspire him or her onwards, and sometimes they are projected for other reasons. In some cases what is projected at the moment is meant to simply keep you mentally busy and detached from being fixated on certain processes which are occurring. Thus visions tend to cheat you in order to distract you. Whatever can grab your attention, because of your memories and cultural expectations, is often used at these stages of chi channel purification. The deception is done in a helpful way and in fact eventually helps you learn to rely on your own wisdom. Since only cultivation practitioners who reach relatively high stages can encounter this sort of help, there is not much we can say about it.

Although these visions serve to validate that your chi channels are opening and that your subtle body is being purified, what you see is often just a symbolic representation of the process rather than a documentary of the way it is really occurring. The images shift the focus of attention. In any case, these internal visions of chi bodies being ejected out of the physical are the generation of the "impure" or "unpurified" illusory bodies talked about in Tibetan Buddhism, and the immortal fetus talked about in Taoism which represents a new life because the old physical body is being purified and rejuvenated from all the chi. They are not an astral body one inhabits at all.

It takes many years to completely transform your chi, channels and chakras on the spiritual road, and your physical and subtle body will go through many different sequences of purification during this process. This phenomenon only lasts a few days as your chi is being purified after the central channel opens. At higher stages of cultivation you will experience yet different phenomena, such as a rush of memories and emotions as the chi and channels open up in particular areas of the brain and vital organs. As you go through the opening of new channel conduit systems, the chi, and therefore consciousness, bound up with those sections must transform.

There are all sorts of steps and stages to the entire purification of your inner subtle body but in this labor we are only at the initial foundation of the transformations. Even though the initial steps during the Herculean labors are just the beginning, these steps are still very critical and include some of the most unexpected manifestations; thus, many religious traditions have written about this subject so that practitioners might be forewarned and encouraged to keep going forward.

As you cultivate your body's chi and channels to increasingly higher stages of purification, it is like pushing out obstructions from inside the channels and purifying successive layers of impure chi from around the channels. This is usually represented as an unwinding, unbinding or untying in internal visions. Each time you complete an unwrapping or unbinding, the skin or covering of this discarded structure, which is now considered "impure," seems to fall off from inside like the dropping of a robe from around the physical body. Next, a body of impure chi seems to rise in the air and disappear. Don't ask where it goes, whether it disintegrates or whether it is reabsorbed inside the body because what you see is actually an illusory vision that appears during the process of purification. This is one of the attached meanings of the term "illusory" in "illusory body." What you see is just an illusion. As to where it is coming from, you'll find out quite soon.

Only Esoteric Buddhism[55] has extremely explicit teachings on the impure illusory body although it is a phenomenon sometimes described in various schools as a meeting with deities or "rising into heaven." The dirty chi from around the channels and chakras seems to be ejected from the body, and fictional visionary experiences often accompany the process that may or may not include heavenly beings. You might see angels, Buddhas, dharma protectors, deities, Biblical cherubim with heads having the faces of animals, all sorts of things like that. There are indeed sentient beings behind the projections, but what you see are usually illusions.

You don't need any instructions to pass through the process, although you need lots of cultivation work at intensified preliminary practices to get this far. You don't actually need the visions either (which is why some cultivators do not experience them) but only need to keep cultivating meditation, maintaining an open mind, and letting go while remaining celibate. You might sometimes have visionary experiences of the process during this stage, depending upon your tradition, training, merit, wisdom and teacher, but the *sila* or discipline of the path does not allow for an entire explanation behind the phenomena.

In any case, this all happens right around this stage of Hercules' Seventh Labor. As his chi became more purified, there were transformations to his body's water-wind element or *jing*-chi essences. After the *sushumna* has been somewhat opened, the yang chi became able to pass through entire sets of other interlinked chi channel circulatory routes that were previously inaccessible. This is definitely one of the meanings of the bull being set free to roam all over Asia, for in the final analysis it means

---

[55] Most of the teachings of Tibetan Esoteric Buddhism detailing this originated from various schools of Indian tantric yoga.

that Hercules' yang chi ran everywhere throughout his body to open up various new sets of channels.

The other phenomenon that might be seen by those who open up the *sushumna* channel is the vision of illusory bodies being ejected out of the body after each cycle of channel purification is completed. Whether the ejection of a full human body, the birth of a baby at a chakra location (as related by Taoism), or the arising of a deity, it is all illusion. This is often one of the special natural phenomena that occurs, but it is not necessary that you see this illusion. It simply represents the purification of the inner subtle chi body for practitioners who reach this stage of spiritual cultivation, and it happens simply because you cultivate an empty mind of letting go from which your yang chi can arise and open your subtle channels.

In the Biblical *Song of Solomon* 5, the writer of the *Song* describes many of the same details related in Esoteric Buddhism that are involved in opening up the *sushumna* channel and heart chakra, after which he experienced this very same generation and ejection of the illusory bodies. Imagine that! The author experienced the same thing as described in Esoteric Buddhism, but Biblical scholars don't know this because they have never gone through these stages to be able to make the identification.

The author of the *Song of Solomon 5* described this same gong-fu phenomenon when he wrote that he took off his robe (the impure chi coverings drop away), and then asked, "why should I put it on again?" Next he lamented that his lover leaves him and disappears, which is the rising and then disappearance of the impure illusory body as described. The watchmen of the town next beat and bruise him as he wanders around because this stage of transformation is accompanied by painful body transformations that make you sore all over.[56] The watchmen were said to take away his cloak, indicating yet another round of the impure chi falling off (like the disrobing), and the process was repeated. In actuality, you will go through around a dozen or more generations of the illusory body during this stage of experience.

This section of the Bible is absolutely, one hundred percent for certain talking about a particular stage of spiritual cultivation gong-fu, which is why it is included within the Old Testament. The details within the *Song of Solomon* unequivocally describe the process of opening the *sushumna* and heart chakra, the subsequent subtle body purification and the gong-fu that happens to one's chakras and channels and physical

---

[56] Specifically, the "Big Knife Wind" which we'll discuss in the next labor.

body as they are purified during this stage of attainment. Once you go through this process you will be able to identify the relevant Biblical passages immediately without any possibility of error.

Although there are many details within the *Song of Solomon* that identify this stage of cultivation, we don't have space to recount all the details and correspondences here.[57] Suffice it to say, that to an initiate the text unmistakably reveals in symbolic form the initial opening of the heart chakra and the coursing of the yang chi through the *sushumna* and other tiny chi channels in the body. This is why the story is included within the Bible in the first place. It even describes the ejection sequence of the illusory body as the inner chi body starts going through these requisite steps of purification.

The Tibetan school of Esoteric Buddhism calls these events the "generation" of the illusory body, but basically the impure chi of the subtle body is pushed off or out of the chi channel system and then is discarded. In internal vision you seem to see it rise up and float away due to the pumping of the root chakra energies from below. At least that is what you see in interior vision, which the school of Vajrayana calls the arising in/of an illusory body. It is actually just a standard pattern you are shown to keep you practicing at these crucial stages of cultivation so you do not slack and lose momentum. The pumping of those energies at this time are so strong that you cannot sleep for days, and additionally, for a short while everything you say will sometimes come out in rhyming pattern or rhythmical verse. Some schools therefore call this a stage of inspiration, and others call this an opening of consciousness.

Commentators who read *Song of Solomon 5* cannot fathom its true meaning because they have never reached these stages of spiritual practice themselves, and don't know anything about cultivation gong-fu either. The teachings of these stages are not even within the Jewish, Christian and Moslem traditions for practically no stages of spiritual gong-fu are recognized in the orthodox side of the western religions. The people who actually succeed in the western paths are shunted aside and derogatively called "mystics" or some other belittling term in favor of the orthodox worship vehicle. Thus "religious authorities" take the *Song of Solomon* as entailing other meanings they can understand. They resort to all sorts of interpretations about love, Israel or Jesus that have absolutely nothing to

---

[57] I hope to be able to put these details, and explanations for many other Old Testament gong-fu stages of spiritual cultivation that have escaped scholars, in another "Little Book" title.

do with the stage of cultivation being described even though the invented meanings are quite clever.

To add some more details to this process, every time you eject the impure chi, it seems to mark the closure of another completed cycle of chi and channel purification. The process afterwards seems to rest for a bit, usually a half day or so. During these resting periods prior to recommencement, the dirty chi on the insides of your physical body will continue to fall away in interior vision. The pumping power of your root chakra, which you will strongly feel at this time, is what essentially does this by pushing your impure chi through the channels.

Orthodox Buddhism doesn't bother to talk about the specifics of this process other than to once again say that the five elements of your body undergo a process of purification during the path of spiritual cultivation. Other than that it, too, remains silent. That's the most it ever says about any particular processes within the whole sequence of body transformations. Whether you are Buddhist, Hindu, Sikh, Jain, Taoist, Muslim, Jew, Christian, Confucian, Zoroastrian or from any other tradition, however, everyone will go through each and every one of these stages without having to specifically follow Tibetan Vajrayana (Esoteric School) instructions. The five elements will express themselves in different fashions through the body as they undergo these purification transformations, but the general pattern of purification responses can be described.

Taoism simply describes the whole purification process by saying there is a transformation of the essences from *jing* (generative or seminal energy) to chi (life force energy) and chi to *shen* (spirit). Taoism also says there are many repetitions of the refining process and during this process you can often feel the body's chi circulating within its channels, but it does not say that you can imagine this into happening.

The yoga schools also summarize the purification process by talking about external physical symptoms such as heat, itching, and perspiration as the energy channels clear and eventually, of course, you attain samadhi. Samadhi is the end result of all these processes if you keep cultivating. The tantric schools, which concentrate on the details of physical purification step-by-step, are of course the ones who explain all these tiny phenomena one after the other.

As to all the cases of spiritual gong-fu we read about in the labors of Hercules, you must always remember that these are just the normal transformations that occur to your inner body of subtle energy, with corresponding physical effects, when you put yourself in tune with the Tao. What happened to Hercules happens to everyone else, only the Greeks described it through their own cultural analogies, namely a beautified bull that rises out of the water and eventually roams free. As we've seen many times, every school takes the same phenomena and processes but describes them differently according to their own cultural milieu.

Thus in this Seventh Labor, a beautiful bull that once rose out of the sea, representing purified yang chi, was captured by Hercules and then taken to King Eurystheus who set it free. Afterwards, it roamed wherever it wanted because it was coursing through all sorts of different chi channels. The bull represented a new stage of yang chi development within Hercules's body after the critical *sushumna* channel had been opened, so in our next labor we should expect to see the results of this improved circulation.

At the same time that this happens, an individual going through this stage of attainment might also experience the generation of illusory chi bodies, born from the wind-water *jing*-chi elements of the inner subtle body being purified, that also rise and disappear.[58] This phenomenon simply indicates that your physical body is being transformed and reminds you not to cling to any type of chi on the road of spiritual cultivation.

In our next labor we will be able to see the result of non-clinging now that the yang chi has access to a more complete set of channel circulations and can start coursing to a fuller extent within the body.

---

[58] As to the importance of these *jing* to chi transformations, which represent the purification of the water and wind elements of the body, Jesus also told Nicodemus that unless a man is born again of water and spirit he cannot enter the Kingdom of Heaven. Individuals without any knowledge of cultivation or personal gong-fu accomplishments don't understand that he's talking about specific spiritual stages of cultivation transformation in this dialogue. It is impossible to attain the Tao without going through these transformations because no one attains the Tao without first cultivating mental purity, which would naturally bring about physical transformations on the path.

THE EIGHTH LABOR:
STEAL THE MAN EATING MARES OF DIOMEDES

[2.5.8] The eighth labor Eurystheus enjoined on Hercules was to bring back the mares of Diomedes the Thracian to Mycenae. Diomedes was a son of Ares and Cyrene, and he was king of the Bistones, a very war-like Thracian people. The strange thing about his mares was that they were man-eating horses. To capture them, Hercules sailed with a band of volunteers, and having overpowered the grooms who were in charge of the horses, he drove the mares to the sea. When the Bistones in arms came to the rescue, Hercules committed the mares to the guardianship of a youth named Abderus, who was a son of Hermes and a minion of Hercules. Unfortunately the mares killed him by dragging him around until he was killed. Hercules fought against the Bistones, slew Diomedes and compelled the rest of the men to flee. He founded the city Abdera besides the grave of Abderus who had died, and bringing back the mares he gave them to Eurystheus. But Eurystheus let them go, and they came to Mount Olympus, as it is called, and there they were destroyed by wild beasts.

In his Eighth Labor, Hercules is sent to obtain the man-eating horses of Diomedes, and this represents yet another stage of spiritual gong-fu that is particularly easy to identify. Once you go through this uncomfortable stage, which lasts a few days, there is no way of mistaking the description for anything else.

Before we start discussing this stage of cultivation gong-fu, however, first a reminder. While many of the gong-fu experiences we have already discussed sound like excerpts from a science fiction movie, they will indeed happen to you if you cultivate far enough. They are described again and again throughout countless spiritual traditions *including* the orthodox religions for those who bother to look, because they do occur.

The stage of gong-fu introduced in this labor does indeed happen as well, and the reason why becomes apparent after one understands it. Always we are going back and forth between opening up a set of chi channel circulations and then having the chi run through them, which produces reactions you can feel. After awhile, as the circulations normalize, the reactions die down and cannot be felt any longer. When another set of chi circulations opens then another set of symptoms arises based upon the chi that arises and the areas of the body (channels) which are affected.

Special techniques are not really needed to initiate any of these gong-fu reactions. They naturally occur as a consequence of the natural purification of the human body during spiritual practice. Call it body purification, call it the opening of the chi channels, call it the removal of obstructions in the body, call it the transformation of *bindus*, chi, and chakras and channels, call it the purification of the subtle body, call it the harmonization of the body's five elements, call it the body becoming healthy and the reaching the best of its physical perfection or however you wish to word it - it's all the same thing. It happens to everyone if you cultivate sufficiently in the right way. This is why common descriptions are found across traditions, and all these things happen because you just learn how to let go and rest the mind.

The only people who ever reach these stages of spiritual transformation are the ones who learn how to deeply rest their minds and detach from desires. They let thoughts and desires arise without suppression, but that does not mean they act on them. For instance, if you let sexual desires arise without acting on them, those energies will help open up the chi channels in the body and the desires will eventually dissipate. This is not wasting energies, but making use of the body's natural energies to become healthier. One should not blame themselves that sexual thoughts or desires arise because this is natural. All sorts of good thoughts and bad thoughts arise in the mind without your doing, and certainly natural urges as well.[59] What is incorrect is to perpetuate the bad ones or act on errant thoughts when it is not appropriate.

All the gong-fu stages we have discussed so far are totally natural phenomena. They are the process of physical purification that accompanies the resultant purification of the mind when it stops clinging to realms of consciousness. We can also say that these processes are the only thing that will produce truly healthy bodies because through these processes your chi channels will all open. That is the measure of a truly healthy constitution.

In any case, all these physical and spiritual results are non-denominational. Thus, many of these same stages have been reported even by various Christian monks and nuns, who in lengthy prayer sessions practiced letting go of their thoughts and "giving all their concerns over to God." Many Christian saints cultivated an empty mind free of grasping at thought from these practices, which is why they were able to succeed in spiritual cultivation and describe various phenomena such as kundalini or samadhi.

In spiritual practice you must learn how to continue being aware of all things without being tainted by or attached to them. This is called "letting the mind give birth" since you don't suppress thoughts to achieve an empty state, and you continue to let understanding arise. You let your mind function freely and actively but never become stuck in anything. That's what realized Christians accomplished through methods not unlike those found in dozens of other spiritual traditions.

The repetition of prayers, for instance, is a cultivation means like mantra practice that silences the usual mental chatter inside us so that we can experience silence. From abiding in silence we can next realize that awareness is still present and "knows" the silence, and that we should be cultivating this natural *awareness that lets us know* without clinging to whatever is recognized as consciousness. Many other meditation techniques will take us to similar states of silence, known as "cessation," which is the basic state of beginner's spiritual practice.

---

[59] The higher you cultivate the less that bad, evil or errant thoughts will arise, to be sure. However, one must not blame, criticize or punish themself when bad thoughts arise at the beginning of the path. All sorts of garbage will arise, and you will simply start to notice it for the first time because of cultivating awareness. Just do not cling to errant thoughts to perpetuate them, and do not act on them. This is why mantra practice is important, for it can help you learn how to cut off errant thoughts, symbolized by the sword of Manjushri. Your actions in the world are important and should not follow your errant thoughts when they arise, which is why all religions stress the importance of cultivating harmonious human relationships. It comes down to knowing your mind, and then choosing the correct course of action for all circumstances rather than just blindly acting on passions.

Since you now know the basic principles of practice, the next thing to realize is that it is the continual working at an effective, virtuous spiritual practice like this that is important rather than the tradition or religion to which you belong. Your religion actually means nothing because it gives you absolutely no "leg up" over anyone else in any type of spiritual progress despite what most of what the western religions like to claim.

The process of spiritual cultivation is *always* accompanied by transformations in the chi (life force energies) of your physical body, as well as by a purification of consciousness we refer to as an "emptying out" or "cessation" of excessive wandering thoughts. This is what produces deep states of peace, silence, stillness or emptiness that the eastern cultivation schools call empty mind, cessation, stopping, halting, quieting, abiding, purity, disappearance of thoughts, or no-thought. The terms vary across traditions, but they all refer to the same state of mental calming, or quiet.

Once excessive thoughts die down, a spiritual practitioner should always practice witnessing or observing the quiet mental state that's reached. Witnessing or observing it means you also examine it, or scrutinize it, and that is why the practice is often called insight meditation. You have to come to realize, verify or authenticate the observations that sages in the past have made about the nature of the mind, so here is your chance to match your own direct observations and experience with their teachings.

All spiritual practices involve these two principles of cessation and witnessing, and as one travels the path they unify these principles at higher and higher levels of purity. Then they become the principles of samadhi and prajna wisdom which must become unified to an equal degree.

Witnessing is so important to this process because the witnessing or observation of consciousness is not in the realm of consciousness. Rather it is out of consciousness in order for there to be witnessing. When you are in a position to witness consciousness you are out of consciousness. Consciousness is being watched from the standpoint of the absolute, which is why you never try to deaden your mind and destroy witnessing awareness in cultivation. The True Self is actually the illuminant of everything and its awareness must always be allowed to shine. This witnessing awareness ability is a function of the absolute nature that actually does not require the creation of a false observer, (in which case the original nature simply witnesses itself), but the world of dualities arises in manifestation when there is one. This is what we call the realm of sentient beings.

When your mind becomes naturally calm, tranquil and at rest because of spiritual practices such as meditation, you are bound to eventually experience your chi. Because of quiet, which is a state of yin, your kundalini will arise, which is a stirring state of yang chi. When that happens, you can start proving the truthfulness of all these experiences yourself and will be able to identify them when you read of them in other traditions. It all starts with cultivating mental quiet; quiet gives rise to yang chi; yang chi opens the channels; impurities leave and the chi, chakras and channels purify, physical sensations arise as this happens, and then the process of purification repeats itself all over again at higher and higher levels of refinement.

This process is known in Taoism as the "multiple refinings." Of course this doesn't mean that "multiple refinings" or "purification cycles" only happen to Chinese Taoists; the phrase was coined to denote this exact same non-denominational process that occurs to practitioners in all traditions.

People tend to make the mistake of thinking that spiritual gong-fu only happens to individuals within the tradition that describes that particular gong-fu, but the *same* gong-fu happens to everyone - whether it is described or not is all part of a school's emphasis. Some spiritual schools, such as Zen, don't even bother to record the low level physical gong-fu stages of the path we are discussing; some schools only focus on the changes in the mental realm; and some schools only call attention to certain parts of the purification process, but practitioners go through it all nonetheless.

The mares of Diomedes in Hercules' Eighth Labor refer to one of these common, non-denominational stages of purification. These mares had a reputation as wild and uncontrollable horses. Usually horses stand for yang chi, but these are female (mares) which indicates that there is some connection between both yin and yang chi here. We're talking about some yin aspect of a yang chi phenomenon, and it is pretty strong because the horses are described as wild.

The strangest thing about these horses was that they were said to feed on human flesh, which is the big key to understanding the story. Another clue to their identification is that these wild, fierce horses were owned by King Diomedes, who was a son of Ares the god of war. Diomedes was also ruler of a very warlike people, the Bistones in Thrace. These clues together suggest a form of wild, fierce yang chi since Diomedes is a warlike ruler related to Ares, and when yang chi is fierce in a painful way we call that fierceness its yin aspect.[60] For instance in Chinese fortune telling each of the five elements earth, wind (wood), fire, water and metal (space) have a yin and yang aspect, as does electricity or any other form of energy. Chi can therefore have a yin or yang nature, and its fierce side that cuts away at obstructions is usually called its yin aspect.

We know from this labor that we are now dealing with a special form of chi that "eats men's flesh" or somehow tears it open, and it is described as "wild" because it does not run in a regular predictable fashion. It does not feel smooth and tranquil. "Wild" means the chi flow is strong, unpredictable and runs everywhere. Some versions of the Eighth Labor say that the horses even expelled fire when they breathed, as is also sometimes said of the Cretan bull, and these are obvious references to the warmth of the kundalini purification which is felt at this stage.

You need warmth to cultivate all the various stages of spiritual attainment within the Twelve Labors, and in all these transformations Hercules has never left the phase of Warmth within the stage of Intensified Practices. The hot chi felt at this stage of the hero's journey that cuts through men's flesh is called "Maitreya's Big Knife Wind" in Buddhism. That is what this Eighth Labor represents: the phenomenon of Maitreya's Big Knife Wind cutting open all the tiny chi channels in your flesh and organs and producing terrible sensations during the process. It only lasts a few days but you have to pull yourself back to your meditation cushion each morning to finish the process and go through it quickly, sacrificing any hold you have on your body so that the chi can open up the channels and finally pass through.

Michael Maier in his western alchemy book, *Atalanta Fugiens*,[61] represented this stage of cultivation by the picture of a man who was being eaten alive by a wolf. That is because in this stage of kundalini purification you feel like your flesh is being cut into tiny pieces. You are sore all over, you are hot everywhere, and your body feels beaten and broken. It feels as if you are actually being cut into small pieces because all the tiny chi channels that cross your body like a net become filled with

---

[60] The real nature of kundalini, or yang chi, is warm and blissful. This real nature of purified yang chi is experienced after the chi channels open. However, a yin kundalini awakening refers to the pain that occurs when the energies push through partially blocked chi channels, encountering obstructions and producing hot friction. Tibetans therefore call kundalini the "Fierce Woman" to recognize the yin, cutting through aspect of the transformation process rather than the blissful, warm, true peaceful nature of kundalini experienced during samadhi and dhyana. Various religions show deities with knives, choppers, tridents and so forth to represent this cutting through, poking type of action.
[61] See Emblem XXIV of the *Atalanta Fugiens*.

chi and pry open. It just feels like you are being sliced by a network of channels all at once.

This filling of the obstructed channels with chi pushes aside their internal obstructions, so you experience pain and heat from the simultaneous frictional cleansing of countless channels at this time. The process, which is uncomfortable but in no sense life threatening, only lasts a few days. In fact, it leaves you much healthier, younger and more flexible than ever before. Scientists always dream they can create a pill that will let you banish sickness lurking inside your body or help you to extend your lifespan, but unless you go through this type of cleansing process you will never achieve that objective. Large chi channels have to open in the body, small channels have to open, and they must open in a definite sequence. If they don't open and clear out you will never be able to extend your lifespan to the mega-ages that scientists talk about because the body is just so dirty and collects impurities over time. This is a process that cleans the body and helps purify its life force, but unfortunately scientists know nothing about it.

Practicing the white skeleton visualization method taught by Shakyamuni Buddha (who developed it from cultivation methods pre-existent in India) is a very good preparation for the Big Knife Wind[62] because it helps you prepare your body for opening up countless chi channels on the road of cultivation. Esoteric Buddhism is filled with pictures of various Buddhas, Bodhisattvas and protector deities standing on white skeletons to emphasize the importance of this preparatory practice for achieving the higher physical stages of spiritual attainment. If you want to cultivate to success, I always recommend the white skeleton visualization practice for about fifteen to twenty minutes a day, if not more. The benefit of this technique is not limited to just developing the habit of one-pointed concentration. Because you are actually engaged in visualizing your internal skeleton, you end up cultivating the full extent of your chi channels as well.

The white skeleton visualization technique actually ties in quite nicely with the Christian practice of Ash Wednesday where your forehead is anointed with ashes and you are reminded that your body will one day become ashes and dust. This is also the final visualization phase of the white skeleton practice where you imagine that the dust of your disintegrating skeleton is blown away and only empty space remains. Visualizing that your skeleton is burning brightly or shining

---

[62] "Wind" or the "wind element" is the Buddhist term for chi or prana.

with bright white light, and then becomes dust, and then emptiness, is a great practice for people who are terminally ill because it helps raise their yang chi and clear away channel obstructions. This is one of the few meditation practices, other than just empty mind meditation, that can help cure sickness and produce "spontaneous remissions."

The Christian *Book of Common Prayer* (1662) actually contains funeral rites that tie in quite nicely with the white skeleton visualization method and the cultivation target of transforming our body to the sambhogakaya: "Forasmuch as it hath pleased Almighty God of his great mercy to take unto himself the soul of our dear brother here departed, we therefore commit his body to the ground; earth to earth, ashes to ashes, dust to dust; in sure and certain hope of the Resurrection to eternal life, through our Lord Jesus Christ; who shall change our vile body, that it may be like unto his glorious body, according to the mighty working, whereby he is able to subdue all things to himself."

It was not necessary to add this part to our story, but I'm always scratching my head as to how one might make basic cultivation practices more acceptable to people within different religions. I always encounter people who won't engage in the best spiritual practices available because they believe they are illegitimate if they don't already exist within their own tradition, despite the fact that most of the spiritual techniques within their own religion have already been borrowed from elsewhere. In any case, this example just goes to show that the white skeleton visualization technique can easily be practiced by Christians, or any other groups, if they really want to succeed in spiritual practice. It is a practice based on science, so once again it is a non-denominational affair.

In the Greek story of Jason and the Argonauts, there is a part of the journey where Jason must yoke a pair of fire breathing oxen and then plough a field with these beasts. This plowing of the field and cutting up of the soil using fire breathing oxen is yet another representation of the non-denominational Maitreya's Big Knife Wind. I don't think I've ever come across a finer symbol than this. This stage of purification rips open your body's chi channels within the flesh, just as a plough rips open the soil, rather than the larger channels that act like large veins and arteries.

After passing this test of yoking the bulls, Jason next has to throw dragon teeth into the field which sprout as skeleton men, and he must defeat them, too.[63] Those skeletons might refer to the aforementioned

[63] In the 1963 film version of the story directed by Don Chaffey, it is King Aeetes of Colchus (owner of the Golden Fleece) who throws the dragon's teeth into the ground to produce

148

skeleton meditation, but they most probably represent another phenomenon that Hercules doesn't mention. Following the Big Knife Wind you seem to start ejecting the hardened bone chi out of the body, and sometimes you will see visions of living skeletons during this stage to indicate what is going on, which is that your earth element chi is being transformed. These skeleton images indicate that the difficult to alter earth chi within and around the bones is being purified and transformed.

This ejection of the skeleton chi (and there are many stages of this process, for different levels of bone chi or "earth chi" seem to be ejected at higher and higher cleansing cycles) is one of the reasons you see living skeletons in esoteric pictures from Tibetan Buddhism, for they point to this very phenomena. In the Chinese cultivation schools this stage is not represented by skeletons but by fish, scorpions, lobsters and other pertinent symbols that carry the overall shape of the bone chi skeleton as it is ejected out of the body.

There are many stages of transformation where the impure bone chi of the body seems to be ejected, and this is where that set of sequences start to happen. Sometimes it seems as if you just eject the bone chi of the skeleton to discard it, and that's the end of the story. Sometimes after it's seemingly ejected a practitioner might be given a vision as if the bones are independently alive for a short while, and the purpose is to teach the practitioner that this is a stage of earth chi purification, or the chi (life force) that flows through the bones. The earth element of the body, like the space element, is extremely difficult to purify. These are the two most difficult elements to transform.

There is a stage where the skeletal bone chi of your spine is seen in vision to rise out the top of your head; due to the resemblance of our sacral bones to the tail of a fish, and since the skeleton chi struggling to rise upwards and out the top of the head is akin to a fish that is swimming against the stream, we can now understand an otherwise inexplicable Chinese legend of a fish swimming against the stream to become a

---

the skeleton warriors. Although the movie poetically changes a number of key events from the legend, this is still a great movie. A famous video interview between mythologist Joseph Campbell and Bill Moyers once dissected the film *Star Wars* in terms of mythic themes, and within it George Lucas acknowledged a great debt to Campbell's *The Hero With a Thousand Faces*. The basic structural plot of *Star Wars* contains the path now known as the "hero's journey" which has since been used in countless other movie scripts and stories, especially Disney animations. If a true understanding of the nature of Hercules' gong-fu attainments were made known to movie writers and producers, this would revolutionize movies by providing new symbols of the hero's spiritual journey that audiences could resonate with.

dragon. When you reach this stage, sometimes a little effort, force or push is required to help the process keep going.

At a later stage the spinal system bone chi that is ejected resembles a lobster in shape because the finger bone chi seems enlarged and undifferentiated. The chi of an enlarged hand, like a boxer's glove, sort of resembles a lobster's claw when it is ejected with the rest of the skeleton, and hence the analogy. A yet higher stage in another cycle of ejection resembles a scorpion with a red tipped stinging tail because a discarded covering of the *du-mai* chi channel accompanies the ejected bone chi, and its red tail end previously terminated at the *hai-di's muladhara* root chakra. None of these more advanced stages are mentioned by Hercules or Jason. The idea of a skeleton is good enough and does not complicate the story too much. When going through this stage it will seem as if some parts of the skeleton chi will be pushed out the head, and other parts out the feet, and you will find out which is which after you reach this stage of earth chi purification.

Hercules's attainment of the Big Knife Wind requires us to speak a little more about this phenomenon for there is even a third indication of this phenomenon in the story. This is the fact that his companion Abderus is dragged to death by the wild horses, which is yet another way to describe what you feel like during the experience. At this stage of chi cultivation I must emphasize again that you will feel heat, pain, soreness and friction in every part of your body. Your head will feel heavy but you will be clear enough to function and know everything that is going on. You will feel the hot yang chi coursing everywhere in your body, and at times it will feel as if you are being cut up in pieces everywhere, and you will feel absolutely sore everywhere. Sometimes it feels like sections in the shape of a net are opening, but it all seems more peripheral than deep inside the body although that is happening as well. You can often feel the chi moving from region to region opening all the tiny channels everywhere as it goes. As I previously said, to drag yourself to the meditation cushion requires a heroic effort.

When you get up in the morning, because this lasts for several days, as soon as you start meditating again the volume of hot yang chi starts increasing again and floods your system to complete its work until after a few days the stage is completely over. Even though it is hot and painful, and all body parts feel sore, you should ignore your parched lips and not drink cold liquids at this stage or you'll impede the process.

This cultivation stage of the Big Knife Wind is the meaning of Diomedes' wild horses that eat men's flesh, for the horses (chi) are gnawing open all the chi channels in the body (the flesh). This is a stage of chi that involves opening all the *tiny* channels throughout your flesh and organs to start purifying that aspect of the physical body. The equivalent structures in the blood circulatory system would be the tiny capillaries and micro-capillaries that crisscross everywhere rather than the big veins and arteries.

There are similar stages of chi channel cleansings later on the path, but none seem quite as uncomfortable as this one.[64] Every cell feels like it is being worked on at this stage of full body cultivation that seems to "cut open men's flesh." That's Maitreya Bodhisattva's stage of the Big Knife Wind in a nutshell, and of course only your chi channels are being opened; no flesh is being cut, no blood is being spilled and no harm or damage is being done. You are simply feeling tremendous heat and soreness as a frictional response to the yang chi encountering obstructions in this set of channels, and pushing through them.

In the Bible's *Song of Solomon* this same stage is described in conjunction with the opening of the heart chakra, as previously mentioned. It mentions a man wandering everywhere about town, getting beaten up by the watchmen and having his cloak taken away. His wandering signifies the chi coursing through all his channels without any discernable pattern. Feeling sore all over from being beaten up is exactly how you feel at this stage, so the Biblical description got that exactly right, too. As to the other match-ups with this account, we can discuss them later.

The process of feeling cut up is due to a slow flow of chi that spreads throughout the body, inflating and pushing through chi channels that were previously obstructed, and the force is unstoppable, like a fire hydrant that has been opened where the pressure keeps pushing out the water. The only thing you can do at this stage is submit yourself to the process and surrender to the transformation. Just relax and let go, or give yourself over as if you are dead, and the process will proceed more quickly

---

[64] Opening up the head bones and ear channels is also quite painful, but in a different sort of way. In the Big Knife Wind you suffer heat, thirst, soreness and discomfort whereas in opening up parts of the cranial region you tend to feel a burst of sharp pain for just a few minutes. This more advanced stage of opening the cranial bones usually lasts for a few minutes intermittently whereas the Big Knife wind lasts a couple of days, fluctuating with intensity during that time. You are extremely sore, but it is not as if you are uncomfortable with a high fever. Some people mistakenly call this stage the actual kundalini awakening because they simply were not aware of all the other stages of chi transformation prior to the Big Knife Wind.

the more you let go. Also, one must be celibate and not lose any semen during this stage as well, a common rule for all these transformations despite the rise in sexual desires due to the voluminous yang chi. The yang chi (kundalini) will then be able to proceed everywhere cutting open all the tiny channels in the flesh. Having gone through the process, the best analogy I can think of is that at times it seems to proceed to various body regions like a sheet of rain that starts wandering down the street and heads to one region or another.

Don't try to stop or impede Maitreya's Big Knife Wind when it happens. Just surrender and offer everything away. In that way you will pass through it more quickly and attain a more complete stage of chi channel opening. The physical body is not you and your body will never do anything to harm you in the process of cultivation, so just let it go because it's an entirely natural process. Emptiness cultivation, which means letting go, is the basic principle of spiritual practice from the very start and all the way to complete and perfect enlightenment.

The white skeleton (body impurity) visualization practice of Buddhism, or the Christian practice of imagining that your skeleton turns into dust and then you are left with empty space, is one of the easiest ways to prepare for this stage of cultivation because it affects all the chi channels of your body running throughout its entire dimensions. The other good preparation to reach these stages is pranayama practice, anapana meditation practice (watching/observing the flow of breath/chi everywhere in the body, especially through the nostrils and chakras), as well as certain types of other stable visualizations.

Once you accomplish Hercules' very First Labor, which means you initially arouse the yang chi of the body, you've stepped on the spiritual trail with firm steps. If you keep cultivating an empty mind that knows thoughts but lets go of them, you are bound to reach this stage and start opening up all the tiny channels of the body. Of course this opening of the Big Knife Wind is still at a superficial level of chi cleansing because there are far more advanced stages than this which take many years to complete. This is still just a coarse dredging when the tiny chi channels are first cut open. This phenomena is what people usually think of when they hear the term "kundalini awakening."

Higher stages, such as the Arhat's ability to disperse his body into space and then instantly reappear elsewhere at will, involve more advanced degrees of chi and channel purification. At those stages absolutely all the channels are open and the body's chi flows are so pure and even that thought seems non-existent. Everything proceeds step-by-step in the process of physical purification that accompanies spiritual cultivation, so to get to the highest stages you must really cultivate well. You cannot attain the higher stages of body purification, such as the attainment of the sambhogakaya, diamond body, immortal body or rainbow body mentioned in Buddhism or other cultivation traditions unless you go through these preliminary stages first. It is very hard to cultivate all three Buddha bodies, but in the endless universe this is the only thing worthwhile. As my teacher often told me, over the last two and a half thousand years since Shakyamuni there have been only five or six individuals who have attained perfect and complete enlightenment, or Buddhahood.

The meaning of this Eighth Labor is unmistakable with the description of wild horses that eat men's flesh, but we get yet further confirmation of this stage through other details of the story. Hercules' companion Abderos, who was the son of Hermes,[65] gets killed by the horses. Some versions of the story say he gets eaten, others say he loses control of the horses and gets dragged behind them to his death, his body becoming broken and torn to pieces in the process. This is again the same stage of the Big Knife Wind. It is a process necessary before all your chi channels can open and your physical organs and even cells of your body can become transformed.

In the story, we also have the fact that the warlike Bistones come to fight Hercules to prevent him from stealing the horses, and our hero has to fight off all these men while simultaneously battling Diomedes. Doubtless, this is a task where he is being attacked and pummeled on all sides, just as happens to your body from the ascending chi at this stage of gong-fu. So we have countless indications, including the references to Ares, pointing to this same stage of physical purification. This is the stage of kundalini that most people refer to when they say it is cutting open the body, but many schools skip descriptions of the earlier stages of transformation because practitioners were not clear enough to know what was going on.

After a long time Hercules eventually defeats the warlike King Diomedes in battle and then what does he do? The legend says Diomedes is thrown to the horses, who eat him, and then they eventually calm

---

[65] Hermes is a clear allusion to chi once again because Hermes is often paired with wind, meaning chi. He is commonly used in the western schools to not only represent the mind, or thinking, but the flip side of consciousness which is chi, prana or the "wind element" of the body.

down. In real time the intensity of the whole process usually lasts for at most three or four days if you don't resist and keep letting go as it happens, continuing to meditate. It lasts for a short while and finally ends after the preliminary opening of the channels at this superficial level is done. We call this a superficial level because this is the first time the tiny, tiny *nadis* in the flesh become free of obstructions. Usually you're working on the *du-mai, jen-mai,* and other larger chi channels at the earlier stages of cultivation, but now the energies can be diverted to cleaning out the really hard to reach places because the branch circuits leading to these circulatory orbits have been cleared.

Of course, there are many stages of physical transformation after this, but this one is probably the most uncomfortable except for the opening of the cranial bones and head. When the chi passes through the bones of the head, some masters feel like they want to die because it's so painful. When this happened to the Second Patriarch of Zen, a voice from the sky told him to bear it a little while longer, and explained that the chi was passing through and transforming his skull bones. It's a very painful stage compared to this full body heat and soreness, but it does not last long at all. For me it was just intense pain in regions of the head, for an intermittent few minutes of time, that often had me doubled over holding onto my knees or lying on the floor to bear it. That particular opening didn't last hours but only a few seconds or minutes at most each time it happened. Afterwards the head felt refreshed and opened.

At another stage I felt like I might lose my eyesight when the chi was going through the visual nerves and eyes, but I never experienced anything like my teacher. When the chi reached his eyes, he told me that he actually started seeing things upside down and also went blind for a few days, but knowing it was all natural he just relaxed and it went away. When the chi went through his heart chakra there was an explosion that was heard in the room, and that's the type of thing that happens for very high stage cultivators with lots of vitality.

These are all natural changes, like the transformations that happen as you pass through puberty, so while they may sound extreme they are natural purification processes that are supposed to happen, always go away, never hurt you in the least and definitely leave you healthier in the process because your channels have been cleared. Being younger, or a better cultivator, you may tend to have stronger reactions than older cultivators who have lost a lot of vitality because this is all due to the rising of yang chi in the body. Nevertheless, even older practitioners will experience a greater or lesser degree of these purifying transformations.

The pain that arises from yin kundalini openings is simply due to the friction of the yang chi encountering obstructions in the body and trying to push through them. As blocked channels are pushed open by this yang chi, pain results from the friction of chi impurities inside the channels being forced outwards. That's why many schools make a point of saying that the obstructions must be melted, for heat always accompanies the process and helps soften and quicken the process. As an example, if you simply chant a mantra out loud for one or two or three hours, you'll often feel that your belly gets warm, which is due to a minor opening of the channels. That's a good way to get a taste for various chi transformations.

At the *real* stage of yang chi kundalini which is past these yin stage kundalini openings, the body feels warm and blissful rather than painful. That is why one can finally experience various stages of physical bliss that characterize the four dhyana, and these are the states one wants to cultivate. All in all, you are simply going through what Shakyamuni Buddha called a process of purification, the balancing of the five elements of the body. None of this is anything to ever worry about or fear because it is a natural body process.

As explained in *How to Measure and Deepen Your Spiritual Realization,*[66] most people don't know that there is a "yin" type of kundalini awakening and "yang" type of kundalini phenomenon. The reason most spiritual autobiographies contain stories of the painful yin stage awakenings is because these are some of the most colorful or memorable events during the early stages of cultivation. Cultivation autobiographies and biographies are just like the daily news on TV which emphasizes painful stories and problems because they attract more attention and interest than happy events. This focus doesn't mean that good stuff is not happening, but just that the unusual or painful stories are much more memorable.

Yang chi in these early stages is spreading everywhere opening up all sorts of channels to produce all sorts of physical reactions. While the painful yin aspect of kundalini at this stage is why Tibetans call it the "Fierce Woman," in China they call kundalini the "clumsy fire" to denote its tendency at this stage to stumble around everywhere. Even if you are just a lacksadaisical beginning meditator, in time you are sure to feel various sensations in the body (perhaps in the belly, back or head)

---

[66] Available at www.MeditationExpert.com.

indicating that your yang chi is stirring and starting to open up chi channels at some superficial degree.

Those who are young, virile and chaste and who engage in the pranayama *kumbhaka* breathing exercises of Hatha Yoga tend to experience extremely pronounced yin type kundalini reactions due to the friction of channels being forcefully pried open, a sensation that feels like your flesh is being ripped apart. Once they ignite the "kundalini fire" in this way, the process usually continues for years. If those individuals first practiced emptiness meditation for some time, which is the meditation practice of letting go of thoughts and trying to realize the empty nature of the mind without clinging, they would have fewer difficulties on the path. Everything would proceed faster because emptiness meditation opens many channels in a peaceful way ahead of time so that you don't even know it is happening. You still have to go through these phenomena after you finally open the *sushumna*, but if you practice emptiness meditation the progression is a lot easier. With emptiness meditation you have less need of a spiritual master, too, but that's not the case with forceful tantric techniques.

Those who do a lot of preliminary meditation work to realize the meaning of "empty mind" have fewer problems because they tend to open up many chi channels before this stage commences. Full body tantric concentrations (Heruka, Guhyasamaja, Chakrasamvara, Vajrayogini, etc.) that cultivate all your chi, channels and chakras simultaneously, and meditation methods such as anapana practices where you witness your breath going in and out your nostrils, deity visualizations, and the white skeleton meditation technique that also involves a full body visualization, prepare you for an easier time during this stage because they accomplish a lot of work in preliminary openings. But if you don't practice emptiness meditation, no matter how many of these other practices you do and no matter for how long, the reactions will not occur. It all comes down to whether you can cultivate an empty mind of giving up everything in the end.

All of these stages arise because you continually cultivate mentally letting go of thoughts and sensations, letting things arise in the mind without attaching to them, throughout all the meditation techniques you use. You must let go of thoughts and cultivate an empty mind, with perhaps the best way to practice this being vipassana mindfulness (watching thoughts and sensations like a third person observer who does not cling to them) or one of the many meditation methods found in the *Vijnanabhairava* of Kashmir Shaivism. This is an excellent Indian text that lists a variety of meditations to help you learn how to let go, and the meditation topics can be adapted to most any religion.

People usually practice a different "emptiness meditation" from the *Vijnanabhairava* each week so that the practice of letting go stays as fresh as possible all the time. By revolving through a variety of practices that require a fresh wisdom approach each time for figuring out "how to let go" or "what it means to let go," they quickly break out of any fixed habit patterns that may have developed from prior efforts to cultivate emptiness. That is why I often recommend this text.

In Buddhism practitioners often analyze their mind (mental phenomena) during a state of witnessing or watching using the categories of the five skandhas so that they can learn how to let go of everything that mentally arises,[67] but sometimes it's smart to switch practice techniques for awhile to break up the routine. The target is for your mind to become free of all clinging. To be detached, or free of clinging to thoughts as they arise and depart, actually makes you super capable because you will be detached from all phenomena in the midst of phenomena. If you actually are perfectly detached from all mental phenomena as they arise in consciousness, you can reach a stage of attainment called "direct cognition" where there does not even seem to be an "I" anymore involved in the process of perception.

The Zen, Mahayana Buddhist and Vedanta method of spiritual cultivation is just to let go directly and see what everything turns out to be. You just give everything up[68] so that there are no attachments anymore but let the mind stream continue and react as it must. Thoughts will always come up, but you just reach a stage where you have dropped any attachments to their appearance or disappearance.

Constantly dropping attachments to your mental continuum will eventually result in realizing the Tao, or recognizing the fundamental substrate that underlies consciousness. Consciousness is everything you

---

[67] This is called wisdom or insight analysis. Your mind quiets but your awareness remains because you still witness your mental states. You reflect to yourself, "Hey, I am still experiencing such and such" in order to help let go. Or, you try to look for the ego/self, or try to realize the nature of the mind directly, or try to determine who is actually experiencing consciousness. The Buddhist sutras or lessons from Vedanta masters tell you the answers, but you have to do the exercises yourself to discover that the ego cannot be found and the natural mind of awareness is actually empty. Because of such cultivation discoveries you can eventually let go of mental quiet realms so that you find their fundamental substrate via awakening.

[68] This is the real meaning of the Christian practice of poverty or renunciation as spiritual practice, but most Christian practitioners do not understand this and take the materialistic aspect of poverty as the meaning. It is also the meaning of "Blessed are they who are poor in spirit."

are seeing, hearing, feeling, thinking, etc. this moment. Dreams are also consciousness. Dreams are no different than the ordinary waking state we call reality because both dreams and what you are experiencing right now are both visages within consciousness. Both dreams and wakefulness are states of consciousness, so in that way they are equivalent. We know not to get attached to dreams because they are not real, so why should we get attached to the wakeful state since it is fundamentally equivalent to dreams and just as changeable and ungraspable? Just function freely as you are supposed to do without getting attached, whether in dreams or during ordinary wakefulness, and you can attain a state of fundamental peace while so living.

Are there any other spiritual methods you should practice, other than letting go and vipassana, if you really want to succeed in cultivation? I always tell people that to succeed in spiritual cultivation they should recite a mantra on a daily basis, such as the Zhunti mantra or Gayatri mantra.[69] Even the Jesus Prayer, or Prayer of the Heart, is fine to recite continuously when you know what you are doing. You can continually recite a mantra in your mind anytime and anywhere without other people knowing, so you are never losing a moment's time if you use mantra recitation in your cultivation.

This is something I highly recommend, especially the practice of the Zhunti mantra for changing your fortune or opening up your heart chakra. Many people owe their success in spiritual cultivation to the fact that they mantra-ed a lot, which is one of the easiest ways to enter the stream of the path and lay a good foundation for success. The fact that you constantly mantra shows you are committed to cultivation and really want to succeed at enlightenment, and when you show consistent diligent effort all the enlightened beings will work to help you succeed.

Second, I almost always recommend that people do some form of full body cultivation, preferably twice a day if they have the time, if they want to succeed at attaining a high stage in this lifetime. Perhaps the skeleton visualization and pranayama and anapana practiced together since these are methods that cultivate the chi of the body and require you to develop a stable mind. Many of Buddha's highest students succeeded because of anapana practice, but this technique never made its way into Tibet and few practice it today.

---

[69] The Zhunti mantra runs as follows: "Namo Saptanam, Samyaksambuddha, Kotinam Tadyatha, Om Cale Cule Cundi Svaha." The standard Gayatri mantra runs: "Aum Bhur Bhuva Svah, Tat Savitur Varenyam, Bhargo Devasya Dhimahi, Dhiyo Yo Nah Prachodayat." The pronunciation of each mantra is easily found on the internet.

You can take the road of cultivating your chi energies to help transform your body for spiritual practice, but only if you have the right view of emptiness, non-ego, impermanence, and ceaseless transformation in the first place – the realization that the world is like mist or a dream you cannot hold on to and that there is nothing material to gain. If you don't attain the right view, however, then like the Fifth Zen Patriarch said to the Sixth Patriarch of Zen, all your cultivation work will be in vain. The famous Tibetan Milarepa warned his student Gampopa that if he didn't realize the true nature of his mind in the deepest sense, then even if he attained samadhi, superpowers and wonderful experiences, he was wasting his time. Shakyamuni Buddha once told his cousin Ananda, "Right at this moment, even if you attain all the possible samadhi you still will not end all mental defilements or achieve enlightenment." Unfortunately, true to Shakyamuni's warnings many religious greats of the past only attained samadhi rather than enlightenment.

In addition to mantra/prayer practice and stable forms of full body visualization (the white skeleton method, deity yoga, tantric visualizations), people who really want to succeed in spiritual cultivation should be spending 80% of their practice time cultivating an empty mind by trying to learn how to let go of our "invisible" habit of clinging to mental states, i.e. the mental continuum. What arises in the mind as mental phenomena are the five skandhas – appearances, sensations, thoughts, impulses and consciousness itself. They are all empty, destined to depart, so let them come and let them go freely without clinging to them. Let them arise and let them depart with out trying to hold them since you can't actually grasp them anyway even though you think you can. As long as you need a certain type of thoughts they will be there because they always arise in response to need, so it is not necessary to use energy to hold on to them to make them stay.

Vipassana, watching your thoughts, letting go, searching for the source of your mind, Buddhist mindfulness, remembrance, giving everything over to God, practicing the many emptiness meditation methods of the *Vijnanabhairava* to experience a mind of bright awareness but empty of wandering thoughts - all these are possibilities for learning how to cultivate an open mind of naturally letting go. The natural mind is never holding on but always in a state of non-abiding.

As to this stage of Maitreya's Big Knife Wind in Hercules' labor, it only lasts a few days at most so as the labor indicates, when the mares were fed Diomedes they eventually calmed down. This teaches you to just let go and submit yourself to the process without trying to fight it, and be as if dead so you don't cling to the body at all as it is being purified. In the story it also says the mares wandered around after being released until they eventually came to Mount Olympus, the home of the gods, where they were eaten by wild beasts or became tame on their own. This part of the story was meant to show that this stage of transformation just fades away after a short while and disappears, just as happened to the horses. That's the meaning behind this fate after their release.

The opening of the tiny chi channels in the body's flesh and organs at this level, while still superficial, actually drives out illnesses and chi winds that would later cause disease or impairment if left in the body. You will never find a better mechanism at banishing latent illness in the body, and thus transforming bad karma, than spiritual cultivation. The process of opening the chi channels at this stage, while uncomfortable, is not damaging at all and actually leaves you with a much healthier body since the five elements of the body (the earth, wind, water, fire and space elements) are being purified. It's a painful stage of cultivation that involves being hot and sore for a few days, which is why some schools represent it with the image of a man cooked over a fire, but it's a wondrous stage of cultivation after which the body can really become transformed.[70] So it's nothing to dread or fear.

In fact, this stage connects us to a very important topic. What do you do when you encounter pain and uncomfortable feelings in cultivation, or in life in general? Spiritual advancement always entails cultivating in line with the correct view and at each and every step you have to step back and evaluate if this is what you are doing. So what do you do when painful sensations arise on the path because of chi channels opening, or because of some unfortunate event in life?

When pain crops up in the body - whether through chi opening up channels like the Big Knife wind or from simple things such as sitting cross-legged – most people are typically swayed by these sensations. They get dragged by their aversion and clinging - in this case to tactile sensations (what we call the body consciousness) - and become further enmeshed in the view of being a body instead of freeing themselves of it. You are not the pain because the recognition of pain is a thought. Because the real you is separate from the pain, you can realize that pain

---

[70] Many masters who cultivate only attain the dharmakaya through wisdom cultivation. Many don't want to cultivate the physical body to attain the rupakaya (the transformed physical body and sambhogakaya or purified beautified body of purified chi) and nirmanakaya, a task which is necessary for attaining perfect and complete total enlightenment.

is only happening to the body and that you are not the body nor your thoughts.

In cultivation, you have to watch painful and blissful sensations alike with equanimity, a process which we also call detachment (to represent non-clinging to whatever arises) or awareness (since awareness has no characteristics other than empty stationary clarity). This principle extends to form, your body, emotions, sensations, consciousness and all phenomena that arise in consciousness, namely the five skandhas. You must watch them without adding craving and aversion, without forming further concepts or grasping for permanence.

If like or dislike arises, you let these emotions arise but you simply don't cling to them but just know them and react naturally. If you don't like oranges, for instance, then you don't like oranges; you don't try to block or suppress that thought or emotion to be empty or pure or "better" but simply act according to it when the thoughts and emotions are not errant. In this way, by using the wisdom of observation and understanding, and the principle of letting go, you will free your mind from all kinds of mental fetters and gradually approach enlightenment if you are diligent … and you'll be spontaneous and natural in every worldly reaction just as you should be. This is how to approach the Big Knife Wind as well. It's there, you accept it, let go and pass through it quickly using your wisdom.

Hence in summary, during this Eighth Labor King Diomedes, leader of the warlike Bistones, had a team of horses who fed on human flesh. These horses represent the cultivation stage of Maitreya's Big Knife Wind, which is what people typically identify as the kundalini awakening of painful sensations. In this stage the kundalini, or rising yang chi, is now cutting open so many tiny chi channels in the body's flesh and internal organs that you feel like you are being cut to pieces, beaten by clubs or trampled by wild animals, dragged behind a chariot or eaten by a wild animal as this network opens. The fact that Hercules engaged the warlike Bistones in battle, and that his friend Abderos was killed by the horses, all speak to this same unmistakable stage of transformation.

Hercules passed this stage by killing King Diomedes and feeding him to the horses because the only thing you can do at this stage, once it's started, is submit to the process and let it complete the transformation. This made the horses tame, and Hercules lead them back to King Eurystheus to complete his labor.

THE NINTH LABOR:
OBTAIN THE GIRDLE OF THE AMAZON QUEEN

[2.5.9] The ninth labor King Eurystheus enjoined on Hercules was to bring back the belt of Hippolyte, who was queen of the Amazons. The Amazons were a tribe of women warriors who dwelt about the river Thermodon. If ever they gave birth to children through intercourse with the other sex, they reared the females. The Amazons pinched off their right breasts that they might not get in their way when throwing the javelin, but they kept the left breasts that they might suckle. Now Hippolyte had a leather belt from Ares in token of her superiority in skill to the rest of all the Amazons. Hercules was sent to fetch this belt because Admete, daughter of Eurystheus, desired to get it. Knowing he could not get it by himself, he took with him a band of volunteer comrades in a single ship.

Having put in at the harbor at the land of the Amazons, Hercules received a visit from Hippolyte, who inquired why he had come, and hearing his story she promised to give him the belt. But Hera in the likeness of an Amazon went up and down the multitude saying that the strangers who had arrived were carrying off the queen. So the Amazons in arms charged on horseback down to the ship. When Hercules saw them in arms, he suspected treachery, and killing Hippolyte stripped her of the belt. After fighting the rest he sailed away and touched at Troy.

It chanced that the city was then in distress consequently due to the wrath of Apollo and Poseidon. For desiring to put the wantonness of Laomedon to the proof, Apollo and Poseidon assumed the likeness of men and undertook to help fortify Pergamum for wages. But when they had helped strengthen it, Laomedon would not pay them their wages. Therefore Apollo sent a pestilence, and Poseidon a sea monster, which, carried up by a flood, snatched away the people of the plain. But as oracles foretold the deliverance from these calamities if Laomedon would sacrifice his daughter Hesione to be devoured by the sea monster, he exposed her by fastening her to the rocks near the sea. Seeing her exposed, Hercules promised to save her on condition of receiving from Laomedon the mares which Zeus had given him in compensation for the rape of Ganymede. On Laomedon's saying that he would give them, Hercules killed the monster and saved Hesione. But when Laomedon would not give the stipulated reward again, Hercules put to sea after threatening to make war on Troy. After several other travels, Hercules brought the belt back to Mycenae where he gave it to Eurystheus.

After all the tiny channels in the body have had a preliminary round of being opened up by the Big Knife Wind, your body can start working on clearing the really large chi channels of the body such as the "eight auxiliary channels" of Taoism. Most cultivation schools mention the chi channels of the body in some form or another, and it's not that there are just about a dozen chi channel meridians. In fact, the number of chi energy channels within the body is often said to be 72,000, a symbolic figure used to denote a large number.

Don't get caught up on the exact number of chi channels in the body. The important point is that now you can start opening up some of the other major channels, and you can feel much of this activity in the trunk of the body from the waist upwards.

The world's cultivation schools and medical traditions emphasize different chi channels because of their practice techniques. Chinese medicine, for instance, recognizes twelve large meridians, or chi channels, that nourish the internal organs (such as the liver, stomach, lung, large intestine, heart, etc.) in addition to the eight auxiliary channels, also known as the eight extraordinary flows. The schools of acupuncture and acupressure are based upon stimulating critical points along these channels to enhance chi flow.

In India, yoga instruction manuals usually focus on describing the left and right channels instead of the front and back channels emphasized in China. However, the Indian practice of stimulating *marma* points" (called *bindus* or secret dots in ancient texts) is akin to stimulating Chinese acupuncture points, and visualization exercises on these points were incorporated into esoteric yogic manuals, many of which made their way into Tibet to help form its tantric literature.

Sometimes the same points and channels are emphasized within certain traditions and sometimes not. Since each channel serves a different function and carries a specific type of chi energy, just as veins and arteries in our body perform certain flow functions, cultivation schools have developed various techniques that place emphasis on certain chi channels and chakras. Those teachings vary according to the findings of each school and the purpose intended by those practices.

In any case, the number of meridians or chi channels in the body is extremely large. By the time you reach the level of this Ninth Labor, you can start opening up the major channels in the waist, chest and elsewhere. This is an entire army of channels ... channels that cannot fully open until after the front, back and *sushumna* channels are opened and the tiny supporting channel structures are somewhat cleared with the Big Knife chi.

Even though you feel as though you are being ripped apart by the yang chi of Maitreya's Big Knife Wind, you must remember that the uncomfortable signs of heat, thirst, soreness and pain are still within the preliminary stages of physical body transformations and only constitute a "superficial" cleansing of the chi meridians. There are as yet many higher stages of physical body purification to go through – where even the physical body seems to drop away - because there are many channels and levels of chi to transform.

In his Eighth Labor Hercules accomplished the coarse dredging of his tiny chi channels which allowed him to proceed to the Ninth Labor of opening the major secondary channels. The attainment of spiritual gong-fu always proceeds in a step-by-step fashion. You open channels, chi goes through them, there are transformations, you reach a higher stage of transformation or purity, and then the process repeats itself.

As with passing through puberty, the body accomplishes all the necessary transformations in stages that might seem uncomfortable, but which are temporary and never endanger the human being. They even make the individual healthier, younger and more capable in the end. You might not personally be able to predict what will happen next as you go through the stages of spiritual transformation, as happens when you go through puberty, but the stages of physical purifcation always happen according to a general, highly recognizable pattern. We are revealing the general pattern to the physical transformations of the spiritual path using Hercules' labors and showing the various descriptions of these general stages from countless different cultivation traditions. Religions may differ, but if you spiritually cultivate correctly within any religion, you will definitely pass through these stages. They are just another of the many non-denominational aspects of the spiritual path. Of course there are common mental stages of purification, shared by all religions as well, that equate to higher and lower achievements of the spiritual path as well.

This stage of opening the other major chi channels besides the front, back and left and right channels is the meaning of obtaining the girdle of the Amazon Queen, a female warrior, and conquering the other Amazon women. That's the Ninth Labor of Hercules – to obtain the golden girdle of Hippolyte, the Queen of the Amazons, who wore it across her chest.

Since we are talking about a queen in this Ninth Labor, this clearly refers to another stage of yin chi transformation, but it is higher than the previous stage as indicated by the involvement of a queen. The Amazon Queen Hippolyte is leader of a tribe of women warriors who represent many of the other unopened energy channels in the body along with their untransformed yin chi. Since they are warriors they represent the fact that yin chi can be transformed into yang chi. It was said that the Amazon women were not only beautiful but skilled in archery and fighting on horseback, and these qualities have connotations to yang chi and the practice of cultivation as well.[71]

In his Ninth Labor, our hero Hercules was ordered to bring back the golden belt of the Amazon Queen Hippolyte, which was a gift from Ares signifying her authority as the queen of the Amazons. Hippolyte used to

---

[71] Archery often represents breathing practices, and riding on horses often represents cultivating the breath, or chi. The archer's bow is sometimes used to represent the spine and the bow string the thin *sushumna* central channel in front of it.

wear this golden belt across her chest signifying the subsidiary channels of the body that normally don't open until after the prior major meridians are cleared. And because the girdle was a gift from Ares (the male God of War), we know there is a transformation of yang chi involved somewhere in this story.

When Hercules' ship arrives at the land of the Amazons, Queen Hippolyte came down to greet him and asked him why he had come. Hercules explained his story including the fact he needed the belt and that he had come to ask for it. Without any lengthy deliberation, Hippolyte immediately agreed on the spot to give him the golden girdle.

This symbolized the fact that many of the auxiliary channels in the body readily open at this stage without any difficulties because all the necessary preliminaries have already been accomplished. It just happens naturally without any special effort due to the prior cleansing action completed by Maitreya's Big Knife Wind. Just as the body's purified chi and chi channels in the story of Jason and the Argonauts are represented by the Golden Fleece (the pelt of a ram, which is a yang chi animal), the transformed chi channels here are represented by a golden belt.

All did not go well during Hercules' visit, for it's said that the queen of the gods, Hera, went amongst the Amazon women and spread the rumor that Hercules was planning to capture their queen and take her away. Hera always poses as an obstacle for Hercules since she represents the most powerful yin obstructions, matching the yang forces of Zeus. Listening to this fabrication, the Amazon women got on horseback and then charged at Hercules and his men.

Fearing he was betrayed, Hercules kills the Amazon queen and takes away the golden belt. The fighting signifies that there is still some effort required to open up these auxiliary channels and Queen Hippolyte dies because the yin chi, however willing or amenable to change, must be transformed just as earlier the centaur friends of Hercules died, too. In the end, Hercules succeeds in his quest by obtaining the golden belt.

In short, the meaning of this Ninth Labor is that after the primary major meridians of the body open, the secondary or auxiliary meridians start to open and your body's yin chi is further transformed. Thus you can finally start to transform all the yin chi of the body as well as the other chi channels, which are aptly represented by the Amazon women. Yin chi will be transformed into yang chi, and so the queen was killed so as to proceed to the next higher stage of cultivation. Hercules cannot carry off the Amazon queen and keep her, nor can the yin chi represented by the queen remain untransformed.

As to the other parts of the story concerning Apollo and Poseidon (yang chi) who become workmen to help build the city of Troy, these refer to various subsequent transformations of the yang chi and water element of the body along with chi circulations that can now go through these channels. After these channels open there is a further flood of chi throughout the body as it adjusts itself with its new structure, and, of course, the dirty yin chi has to be driven out again. There is really no discernable pattern to this flooding other than to say that the body always has to adjust itself once again after a new set of channels open, so this part of the story does not offer a lot of useful information.

In summary, for the Ninth Labor Hercules traveled to the land of the Amazons where the Amazon Queen Hippolyte readily agreed to give him her golden belt peacefully. This represented the fact that many of the great subsidiary chi channels will present no major difficulties opening after the major channel circulations have already opened. However, because of the influence of Hera, Hercules still ended up having to fight the Amazons and even had to kill the queen before leaving with her golden belt. The new channels open easily, but they must still be cleansed of impure chi obstructions.

Afterwards, there was some discomfort as the body's energies adjusted to these newly opened structures and impurities were driven out. In time, homeostasis was achieved, and Hercules proceeded on to a new adventure. The main point to remember is that all these stages of chi purification and channel opening occur only after a spiritual cultivator opens the *sushumna* central channel and experiences the Big Knife Wind.

THE TENTH LABOR:
OBTAIN THE CATTLE OF THE MONSTER GERYON

[2.5.10] As a tenth labor Hercules was ordered to fetch the kine of Geryon from Erythia. Now Erythia was an island near the ocean inhabited by Geryon, son of Chrysaor by Callirhoe, who was daughter of Oceanus. He had the body of three men grown together and joined in one at the waist, but parted in three from the flanks and thighs. He owned red kine, of which Eurytion was the herdsman. Orthus, the two-headed hound begotten by Typhon on Echidna, was the watch-dog. So journeying through Europe to fetch the kine of Geryon Hercules destroyed many wild beasts and set foot in Libya, and proceeding to Tartessus he erected as tokens of his journey two pillars over against each other at the boundaries of Europe and Libya. But being heated by the Sun [Helios] on his journey, he bent his bow to shoot at the god, who in admiration of his hardihood gave him a golden goblet in which he crossed the ocean. And having reached Erythia Hercules lodged on Mount Abas. However the dog Orthus, perceiving him, rushed at him. Hercules bashed it with his club, and when the herdsman Eurytion came to the help of the dog, Hercules killed him also. But Menoetes, who was there pasturing the kine of Hades, reported to Geryon what had occurred, and he, coming up with Hercules beside the river Anthemus, as he was driving away the kine, joined battle with Hercules and was shot dead. Hercules, embarking with the kine in the goblet and sailing across to Tartessus, gave back the goblet to the Sun.

Passing through Abderia he came to Liguria, where Albion and Dercynus, sons of Poseidon, attempted to rob him of the kine, but he killed them and went on his way through Tyrrhenia. But at Rhegium a bull broke away and hastily plunging into the sea swam across to Sicily, and having passed through the neighboring country since called Italy after the bull (for the Tyrrhenians called the bull *italus*) came to the plain of Eryx, who reigned over the Elymi. Now Eryx was a son of Poseidon, and he mingled the bull with his own herds. Seeing the bull gone, Hercules entrusted the kine to Hephaestus and hurried away in search of the bull. He found it in the herds of Eryx, and when the king refused to surrender it unless Hercules should beat him in a wrestling bout, Hercules beat him thrice, killed him in the wrestling, and then taking the bull drove it with the rest of the herd to the Ionian Sea. When he came to the creeks of the sea, Hera afflicted the cows with a gadfly, and they dispersed among the skirts of the mountains of Thrace. Hercules went in pursuit, and having caught some, drove them to the Hellespont; but the remainder were thenceforth wild. Having with difficulty collected the cows, Hercules blamed the river Strymon, and whereas it had been navigable before, he made it unnavigable by filling it with rocks. He herded the kine back to Eurystheus, who sacrificed them to Hera.

For the Tenth Labor, King Eurystheus ordered Hercules to bring back the herd of red cattle belonging to the monster Geryon, who was a strange being indeed. The cattle lived at Erytheia, the "red island" of the sunset, which is the furthest westward part of Hercules' travels.

Red is always used to denote yang chi in cultivation schools[72] so we know right away from the color of both the cattle and the island

---

[72] See Michael Maier's *Atalanta Fugiens* emblems, Taoist texts and hatha yoga manuals for obvious examples. Yang chi is active and usually warm, as is fire, so the color selection is usually the same in most cultures.

that Hercules must be dealing with some type of yang chi. The task set before him in this labor is that he must reach the stage where his yang chi circulates through all his body channels fully and peacefully now that they have been cleared of the larger obstructions.

If you are very natural in your cultivation then a full circulation of chi throughout all your channels will eventually happen naturally. It will not happen immediately, however, because it takes quite some time to progressively open up all your channels. This happens in a sequential step-by-step process, as do most bodily functions. People often think they can cause the channels to open by visualizing the circulation of chi within their bodies, but they delude themselves and never reach any of these stages that way.

This is a misconception that has particularly taken hold of Taoism because practitioners have read the descriptions of the channel circulations left by previous masters, and subsequently felt they must imagine those results occurring in order to make them commence. They forget that the highest masters in most every school, including the Taoism which they are taking as their guide, never describe specific chakras or channel circulations at all. If you search the writings of Lao Tzu, for instance, you will find nothing about this sort of visualization or chi channel practice. Rather, he talks about being empty with natural mind. With Chuang Tzu we can find descriptions of the stages of attainment, but as to the channels he is quiet as well.

The natural empty mind is hard to arrive at, however, especially if you've cultivated a busy mind all your life. Therefore in all the full body visualization methods such as deity yoga, the white skeleton meditation, Vajrayana Buddhist tantras and the like, people practice to first develop a steady mind by trying to form stable visualizations. Then they try to let go of that provisional construction to experience their natural mind of empty awareness. They first try to switch attention from the sensations of the body to absorption in an imaginary cognition, whereby they can ignore the sensations of the body and other wandering thoughts, and then they release that stabilized cognition to experience an empty mind. Initially that emptiness is akin to an image of space, but with progressive efforts with other practices as well they might be able to achieve true emptiness without any attributes. Since space is known by the fact that it has borders, and by the fact that you have an image in your mind that is identified as space, it still has attributes or characteristics.

This practice method for forming stable visualizations is yet another cultivation technique for learning detachment that starts from a provisional imaginary focus. The methodology is to develop a stable mind (which means it is relatively absent of wandering thoughts), and then release that state of concentration to experience some degree of emptiness. For some people visualization practice is excellent and for others it is a nuisance, so in cultivation you try a method one to three months, see if it helps, and if does not, move on to one that does.

The attainment of spiritual gong-fu on the path of cultivation proceeds in stages, step-by-step, and cannot be forced or hastened. Yang chi, or kundalini energy, is awakened according to first principles – the prolonged emptiness meditation of "letting go" that results in a relatively "empty" or quiet mind. From that stillness of yin, yang is born. From emptiness practice, which is attaining stillness or peace through the mental witnessing of non-attachment and non-clinging or non-involvement, your chi will arise. So just by cultivating a quiet mind, through detachment, your yang chi or kundalini will arise. Of course to help this happen quickly you typically also practice pranayama, mantra and other techniques to help transform the body and clear away preliminary obstructions, but empty mind is the path in basis.

The most pertinent question on the spiritual road is therefore how to properly and quickly cultivate that necessary emptiness, quiet, silence, peacefulness, calming or cessation of thought, however you wish to word it. Visualizations are one such way, but other methods exist, too. For instance, one might even use sexual intercourse to further open up the *du-mai* and other chi channels of the body quickly, and attain a higher stage of emptiness if one knows how to do so properly. Several mahasiddhas had consorts to help them transform their bodies in this way, and of course they were helping their consorts as well. Some people can use sex in the path and others cannot. It depends on the individual. Most people cannot.[73]

---

[73] My teacher told me that in the Esoteric school, after a master reached enlightenment and wanted to transform his body quickly, then a real dakini might arrive to help him. He would go into some remote area with his most trusted students, set up a tent with all manner of niceties for her stay, and for several days and nights the students would stay outside and continually mantra for protection and success while the two practiced. Inside, he and she would work together using sexual practice to help further transform his chi, chakras and channels by cultivating a full infusion bliss and deeper, fuller rotation of the chi through all the meridians. One does not only feel the strong River Chariot rotation but full, deep, overflowing rotations through all the channel orbits simultaneously, and even the body cells feel full of chi and bliss. The rotation of the chi, opening up of the tiniest channels, and transformations of the most refined subtle chi levels are the quickest way to transform the five elements of

Mantra and prayer recitation are common methods for reaching a state of mental silence, too. All religions call the objective of emptiness (non-attachment) something different, but they all require you to cultivate "empty mind" since it means you are letting go of consciousness and not imposing your will on your chi. Hence they all describe the same thing.

Whenever you reach a stage where the mind is relatively quiet and you are not clinging to thought, your chi will then become free to circulate. Your chi and your thoughts are linked because chi and consciousness are linked, so give up the tightness of thought and your chi will start to flow. It will become free to circulate as it should without any bias or interferences caused by mental clinging. Thus, it will start to open up your blocked chi channels since it is no longer strongly connected to consciousness and bound up with wandering thoughts. When this labor therefore talks about the capture of the red cattle of Geryon, representing the flow of yang chi, we know that it really has nothing to do with clinging or actually leading chi in a particular direction.

So much for the underlying meaning of the Tenth Labor, but why is the monster Geryon in the story? Usually we are dealing with some monster that is the offspring of Typhon, and who thus represents something within the human body. In this case, we have Geryon who was the son of Chrysaor and Callirrhoe. Who were his parents, and what does this tell us?

Chrysaor had sprung from the body of the Gorgon Medusa after Perseus beheaded her, and Callirrhoe was the daughter of the two Titans, Oceanus and Tethys. From this description we might think that Geryon represents the throat chakra because a head is chopped off at the throat. Furthermore, the throat chakra is traditionally said to deal with the water

---

the physical body. People might often see rainbows surrounding the tent when the practice succeeded. An example of an enlightened female who used such techniques, and many more tantric transformational methods, can be found in the example of Yeshe Tsogyel, whose story can be found in the book *Sky Dancer*. She not only used sexual cultivation but herbs, minerals, mantra, formal meditation, tantric visualizations, yoga, pranayama, fasting and severe asceticism to help transform her chi, chakras and channels. A woman's body experiences some different types of gong-fu than men on the cultivation trail. As explained elsewhere, while young they must practice to a point where their menstruation stops (indicating a particular stage of transformation of their chi and hormones), and then continue cultivating past that point until it appears again. They should never try to halt menses through artificial means such as herbs, acupuncture, low cholesterol diets and so forth. As the examples of Milarepa and Shakyamuni show, you need to be healthy to succeed on the cultivation path. If you go to ascetic extremes in your cultivation, it is only after you once again return to a normal life of balance that progress can be achieved.

element, which might be represented by Oceanus. However, the meaning of Geryon is not that simple.

Geryon was a strange looking monster, and is basically described as a creature with a human body that has extra limbs. In some accounts Geryon is said to possess three upper torsos and three sets of legs all joined at the waist. In other versions of the story Geryon has one set of legs and three upper bodies all joined together at the waist. There are other alternative descriptions as well, but they all suggest three unique bodies somehow joined together.

The colorful descriptions remind you somewhat of the pictures of heavenly beings found in Hinduism. Tantric yoga texts from India, for instance, have pictures of various deities with multiple limbs who are said to reside in our chakras. However, none of these pictures show beings with extra body trunks.

Geryon's body also calls to mind the various transformation bodies of Buddhas and Bodhisattvas you see with multiple heads and arms, but once again there is always only one body in all these pictures. For instance, the wrathful bull-faced Yamantaka is a nirmanakaya emanation body of the Buddha Manjushri used for one-pointed visualization practice, and like Geryon has multiple arms and legs together with the head of an ox. But Yamantaka only has one body trunk. Therefore what does this strange creature Geryon represent?

The meaning becomes clear when in the story Geryon grabs three shields and three spears to fight Hercules. The three round shields clearly represent three chakras, and the spears represent the chi passing through them.[74] The fact that Geryon has three bodies joined together represents three chakras along the same line of chi circulation each with their own set of complicated circulatory systems, and so the mystery is finally solved with this explanation. The big question then is: which three chakras are represented here?

The answer is probably the throat, heart and solar plexus (belly) chakras – the three main chakras on the *sushumna* channel between the root and crown chakras. We are not including the root and crown chakras because they are dealt with elsewhere with their own stories of unfolding. These three chakras, out of a traditional set of four, are subjects

---

[74] When you see pictures of Buddhas or other enlightened beings with spears in their hands, this most often represents the chi poking through a chi channel or chakra. For instance, Shiva's trident not only represents the bottom of the *sushumna* channel where it connects with the *ida* and *pingala*, but the chi actually poking through the channel and ascending upwards.

of visualization focus in the "Six Yogas of Naropa"[75] and countless other spiritual schools and traditions. Many schools and traditions – including tantric yoga, Vajrayana Buddhism, Sufism, Judaism, western alchemy, and even the Hopi Indians – use four chakras along the *sushumna* in visualization practices. The common adoption of this technique across traditions speaks to its power and effectiveness in spiritual transformation.

This is what you find represented at the center of the ten sephirot in the Jewish kabbalah tree of life, and you can also see this type of visualization focus in Emblem 17 of the *Atalanta Fugiens*, too. Hercules previously opened his *sushumna* central channel, and because of that he was able to open all sorts of auxiliary circulations. Therefore in this labor, there is now the possibility for the three major chakras along the *sushumna* to start functioning in fuller measure because a full chi flow can finally reach them. That chi flow goes up the *sushumna* and clears or "unfolds" their circulatory paths, and hence the monster Geryon will be conquered.

Congratulations to our hero! Hercules has now reached the stage where, after all the subsidiary channels have opened, these major chakras can reach a higher stage of unfolding. Chakras are a critical component of the chi circulatory system within our bodies. No matter where it is located, each chakra in our body is like a multi-spoke distribution station surrounding the channel that runs through it. Each chakra basically has a different number of channels (called petals) extending away from its center. You can count the major petals, but if you also consider the number of subsidiary branches coming off those major petals then various cultivation schools will disagree as to the number of total petals.

In this story, Geryon's body with many arms and legs is just a single figure used to represent three major chakras, above the root chakra, along the ascending line of the *sushumna* channel. If you said he represented a single particular chakra, the difficulty is that the number of his limbs, or limbs and heads, doesn't match any of the chakras we know about. But with three chakras along the same *sushumna* trunk line, the story makes perfect sense as it fits the known details of our esoteric structure exactly.

The heart chakra in the chest (behind the breastbone) is commonly recognized to have eight petals, whereas the throat chakra of our body has twelve petals and the root chakra has four petals. This is why you often see pictures of eight or twelve Buddhas in circular mandalas, or why you often see square shaped mandalas from India and Tibet with four doors on

---

[75] See Glenn Mullin's *Tsongkhapa's Six Yogas of Naropa*.

the sides. They are representations of specific chakras and given as objects of visualization focus to practitioners in tantric cultivation traditions. Sometimes a single mandala represents several chakras all stacked on top of one another. As to the sex chakra floating above the sacrum whose pumping is like the wiggling of a fish's tail as if it was swimming upwards, this powerful chakra is said to have six petals like the six trunks on the white purified elephant of Samantabhadra. One might therefore think the sex chakra was represented in this story, but the multiple shields and other parts of the story don't quite fit in with this identification.

Geryon is in charge of herding red cattle – red being the standard representation of yang chi arising from the perineum – and because he is carrying multiple shields they represent a set of chakras along the *sushumna* channel which Hercules previously opened. This interpretation fits all the evidence and one in particular which is the most important – it represents what *actually happens* at this stage of cultivation. Now that most of the body's chi channels have been opened, these chakras can really start to pulse with life until their chi flows smoothen.

Various cultivation schools use a variety of methods that in some way involve focusing on or visualizing chakras. These methods include visualizing letters on the chakras (Sanskrit, Hebrew, etc.), reciting mantras on the chakras, imagining rhythmical movements or lights on the chakras, visualizing lights of different colors one after the other, and other techniques superimposed on what is assumed to be the location of a chakra. Most of these methods originated in the Indian tantric yoga schools and slowly made their way into Tibet to mix with Esoteric Buddhism. Taoism developed its own concentration methods on "elixir fields" rather than chakras, though in time it developed techniques related to the Indian influences, too.

When you go into other spiritual schools and traditions – say the Taoist, Shaivite, or even Jewish mystery schools – you will often find that there are specific exercises for working on chakras if previous masters have passed down useful practices along these lines. Quite often these were considered "secret" teachings although this should not be the case anymore. They were usually called "secret" to prevent people from hurting themselves on the spiritual path because most people would not understand them enough to use the information wisely. Quite often people can ignite (or clear) the chi circulation in a specific region of the body from concentrating on a chakra, and then feeling the newly arising chi energies bouncing against obstructions (since they never bothered to cultivate the full body) they will start to worry and wonder what they did wrong. In most cases these concentration exercises on chakras are therefore misleading practices since they result in worries about the path, and can produce chi imbalances rather than physical and emotional harmony. Most people cannot use them to succeed without a lot of merit, study, the use of other cultivation techniques and the presence of a wise master to oversee their practice.

In actual fact, information on chakras is neither secret nor a "high" teaching although most people assume so since the information is rarely seen. The information on this topic is so scarce because it is unnecessary, because so few people truly cultivate to experience these things, and because, as stated, it is misleading for most practitioners. You can iopen dozens and dozens of books on chakras today and quite frankly, you will find almost all the information useless. What it comes down to is that most people simply cannot succeed using visualizations focused on chakras unless they first do a lot of preparatory cultivation work and learn how to let go rather than force energy here or there within the body. The necessary preparatory work of intensified spiritual practices usually includes mantra or prayer recitation, pranayama *kumbhaka* practice, the vipassana meditation practice of inner silent watching we call "mindfulness," the white skeleton or some other full body visualization-calming technique, and merit-making. You cannot succeed along a tantric cultivation path unless you are also trying to perfect your errant habits and bad behaviors. Virtue and merit accumulation are always necessary requirements for success at spiritual cultivation.

As an example of my own initial ignorance about these techniques, in my early years I would cart up dozens of Tibetan cultivation books and argue with my teacher – who is an enlightened master of the Vajrayana school - that the special chakra instruction materials provided in Tibetan tantric texts were high stage materials because there was nothing like this elsewhere, and the information contained all sorts of secrets about the esoteric structure of the body.

He would patiently laugh and tell me I'm mistaken, and that all those teachings were just the extremely low level stuff. In response I would think he just didn't know what I was talking about because this material was only available in Tibetan and English, so he might not have read the materials to see the contents. My teacher did know the truth. His great knowledge is why he has been recognized as an enlightened master by multiple cultivation schools, in this case Vajrayana, Zen, Buddhism,

Taoism and Confucianism. Most people convince themselves that the pageantry or uniqueness of Vajrayana techniques somehow makes these methods more powerful than other cultivation techniques in the world but this is just not true. Even so, these rare teachings, which saved some of the best materials from now extinct Indian cultivation traditions, should be treasured, preserved, and respected … but also understood and practiced in the right way.

After years of effort, after studying countless cultivation schools and having many experiences myself, I can confirm his comments were one hundred percent on the mark. The esoteric yoga techniques, as in most of preliminary practices of the Vajrayana school, are just used at the beginning stages of cultivation. Their usage is equivalent to trying to strike a match to light a fire, and after it's lit you don't need the match anymore. A match doesn't immediately light when you touch a striking surface, so you at first slowly drag it along a surface with some pressure as you increase the speed and it finally lights, at which time you lift it off at the end. Thus there are many materials within this school that must be cleaned up with this proper understanding. Many tantric teachings primarily deal with the body rather than with the real attainment of penetrating through consciousness to realize the Tao, or the use of your awareness and energy to conduct wise compassionate activity in the world to help others. Those are the most important things on the path of spiritual realization.

Unfortunately, too many people in the world mistakenly assume that the color and uniqueness of the Tibetan Buddhist, Vajrayana, and many Taoist and tantric yoga methods, makes them the high stage materials. They are simply attracted to the multi-dimensional pageantry of these schools, and not having found such tantric materials elsewhere, think they must be supreme because of their rare contents. People also too easily become misled by the experiences that arise from pursuing these paths, which are not the marks of self-realization. If one pauses to really think deeply, they will realize that many other schools don't use these materials because they are simply not needed, or simply contain the very same teachings in a different format, or because they can too easily lead people astray. These materials are extremely beneficial and helpful, but it takes a lot of study, merit and wisdom to tread these paths correctly. As the Fifth Zen Patriarch said to the Sixth, if you don't first see the Tao then all your work along these lines is in vain.

In terms of Vajrayana itself, the great Vajrayana masters will always say that the real esoteric part within the Vajrayana (Esoteric) school is

Zen rather than any focus on chi, channels or the body. Zen focuses on enlightenment to the exclusion of all else, and for enlightenment you must jump out of all teachings including the scriptures (after you have laid your foundation, of course). After you attain self-realization you can concentrate fully on transforming the body but in pursuit of Zen enlightenment, you typically ignore the body and all its transformations other than what you would normally do to adjust yourself.

Zen recognizes that the physical body is not you and the transformations of the spiritual path which happen to the physical body occur naturally without any efforts required on your part other than meditation. Those transformations happen on their own when you just do the right thing. You don't have to force anything into occurring; you should put all your effort into searching for the ultimate source of your mind.

The highest Vajrayana stages are openly found within the Buddhist Mahayana sutras, and a Zen adept who studies the sutras will be well informed about the highest accomplishments of the Buddhas and Bodhisattvas, many of which I have already cited. Ordinary people usually don't believe in the Buddhist sutras, always thinking their own religion is the truthful one, but these encapsulate the highest genuine stages on the spiritual trail. Furthermore, the miraculous abilities recounted within the Buddhist sutras are factually possible, which is why they are commonly found in other schools as well. However, the beauty of Buddhism is that it offers explanations and the ability to understand such phenomena in depth. Buddhism differs from most other schools by offering countless explanations of the phenomena and processes connected with spiritual cultivation. Most other schools just offer some injunctions to believe or have faith with the fictitious reassurance you are chosen and that worship is the path of spiritual practice, and that's about all.

In any case you don't necessarily need these tantric teachings because as Buddhism, Taoism, Vedanta and many other spiritual schools point out, emptiness cultivation (just letting go of thoughts rather than clinging to them) is enough to eventually open all your chi channels and chakras without error. If you just become mindful of your breathing, you can also go a long way to attaining samadhi and the Tao. The opening of the channels just happens naturally when you let go as you are searching for your True Self, the original nature, the true source of *both* mind and matter. However, some people with complicated minds need a school with all this extra material because that is the only thing that can attract them to the spiritual path of cultivation, or give them a focus for their attention, and hence the Esoteric school founded by Nagarjuna and Padmasambhava proceeds along these lines. It's like a sausage which is stuffed full of all sorts of tasty meats and spices ground up together. However, not everyone likes to eat sausage. After all, some people are devoted vegetarians and would get indigestion eating meat. Therefore the world is full of very different cultivation paths you might follow to attain enlightenment, as well as different religions to match your merits and wisdom levels for getting you started. Whatever your karma, that's where you start. Depending on your wisdom and merit, that's where you turn. The path you originally get is due to your good or bad karma, and if you look outside of it for something better that wisdom is due to your intelligence and merit.

The Confucian practice of introspection (similar to vipassana meditation or Buddhist mindfulness), which is to constantly watch your thoughts and behavior and cut them off or correct them when errant, will result in the same set of openings and chi purifications when practiced long enough and in the correct fashion of employing the detachment of letting go. Mencius followed this path, and then subsequently ended up cultivating his chi, just as he described.

Like Confucius, Mencius described the natural process of cultivation in a humanistic way that is a different form of presentation than what religions usually use. He said that you must first start with the desire to cultivate. Spiritual cultivation, he said, is about only desiring what you should desire, and we should call this kindness. For example, desiring to save the whole world versus just desiring a lot of money, food, sex, and so on is kindness. The compassionate Bodhisattva vows that you make when you get started on the road of cultivation are also examples of kindness, which Confucius called "loving the people."

From that type of motivation, which is the correct type of motivation because it is acting for the people, you start always watching yourself and the desires of your mind. You watch your mind for what's right or wrong rather than what's legal or profitable. You watch your thoughts, which is the practice of meditation, and then act from that basis of awareness. In time you get better at this practice and you become able to gradually establish trust, confidence, faith and belief in your cultivation and in yourself as your skill builds. Acting correctly proceeds from cultivating awareness.

In time, from introspection or mindfulness practice done in the right way, Mencius said that your body will begin to transform. The body will begin to feel full or rich - a stage he called "beauty" — because the chi channels all start to open and your chi becomes full. Your yang chi will then be eventually felt all over your body just as we have been describing. You will have ignited the River Chariot rotation and opened the eight extra meridians to achieve this, so the warm chi will be slowly pulsing everywhere but not completely through the central channel. True dhyana is still a bit out of reach.

Your body will not only feel full and rich and glorious at this stage but your mind will feel open and expansive as well, which he called "grandness." It becomes so grand or large or big or empty that there's no boundary, which Mencius called the stage of a saint. When the saint's cultivation level is so high that nobody knows how high it is, that's the stage of a "shen," which is like the tenth level Bodhisattva bhumi in Buddhism.

This represents a stage far beyond an ordinary person because no one can speculate on what you are at this level of cultivation. Because no one can put you in a box that way, or put a name or label on you, no one can know who or what you are or what you'll do next. In olden times, that was the accepted description of a "god" though today we call that the stage of an enlightened sage because those are the ones who really get that stage, and gods don't. The gods or celestial beings are just heavenly denizens with higher samadhi attainments than ordinary beings, and most aren't enlightened at all.

So even in Confucianism it is recognized that any type of "letting go" in conjunction with maintaining a stance of open witnessing, instead of mental suppression, will allow the natural resumption of chi flows in the body, and thus lead to the cultivation of your chi. Your chi will indeed purify, and your channels will open, if you learn how to relax your mind. Along this route there are no special dangers, and you will not miss a thing either. At the very least the practice of vipassana or mindfulness – watching your mind as a type of silent witness - will help you to avoid mistakes in business and life and will even help you transform your personality in the way you most desire. It really should be taught in schools as a basic skill for human beings and not taken as a religious practice at all.

Whether or not there are specific yogic teachings on chakras in a spiritual school is a matter of whether it had adepts who recognized their existence and thought it important enough to leave some instructions for posterity. You actually do not need to know anything about these things at all but simply cultivate correctly and let whatever happens occur without interference. As I always mention, it is just like going through puberty; you don't know what is going on and cannot control or hasten the process, but the change is proceeding naturally according to a definite type of general time frame and pattern.

Along these lines, it is proper to record these transformations for posterity. The information can be quite helpful in diminishing the fears that arise in people when they make spiritual progress and their gong-fu starts to occur. For some people, knowledge of their esoteric anatomy will indeed encourage them in their cultivation efforts, and that is to be applauded. However, one must never confuse cultivation reading, study or memorization with practice effort. The spiritual path all comes down to personal practice in the end, and that means ample sitting meditation where you simply watch your mind. For the kundalini yoga visualizations on chakras and the like, *brahmacharya* or celibacy is necessary for the best results, too.

This topic of chakra cultivation highlights a particular historical problem in the field of spiritual cultivation. Many people in the past who attained some stage of the Tao did not teach what they had learned and thus did not pass on the tradition. Some practitioners became arrogant about their attainments and even locked up teachings. In those cases they surely retained selfish egotistical thoughts, thus indicating a far from complete stage of accomplishment on the path. In the *Lotus Sutra*, it is even recorded that five hundred enlightened Arhats once walked out of Shakyamuni Buddha's lesson because he announced that there was a higher stage of accomplishment than the emptiness realization they had reached. That higher stage meant devotion to the Mahayana path of compassionate service and teaching to the unenlightened, which is something they did not want to follow.

The highest result of spiritual practice is the road of compassionate service for others that is most clearly elucidated in Mahayana Buddhism, and to a lesser extent in Christianity. Christianity rightfully teaches us to sacrifice ourselves for others. The nirmanakaya attainment provides the ability to help millions or billions of beings along these lines. Mahayana Buddhism stresses that purifying your behavior and acting selflessly on behalf of all sentient beings, which it calls "compassion," is the heart of the spiritual path. You are encouraged to read the Mahayana sutras to gain a deep understanding of what the spiritual trail really entails and the sacrifices that the great enlightened ones continually make for us.

In the end, the spiritual path is all about benevolent behavior and righteous, compassionate activity in the world because everything is you, and so it behooves you to improve things. This includes teaching others the path to enlightenment, improving their lives, and helping them counteract their bad karma. This is what Mahayana Buddhism is all about with the foremost objective of helping others attain the Tao. The Bodhisattva path also involves endless acts of merit as well as improving your own knowledge, wisdom, skillfulness, and behavior since they are essential to accomplishing these ends. Hence the true spiritual path also calls for a commitment to self-improvement and personal excellence. This is the Mahayana path of sacrifice, service and offering taught in Buddhism, and also emphasized in Confucianism and Christianity. Spiritual cultivation is not done for a tribe, or even the world, but for the universe at large because it is all you and will also go on forever.

The methods one can use in spiritual cultivation definitely differ in terms of their efficiency or effectiveness for each individual. Whether or not you have access to correct spiritual teachings and efficient methods in the first place is all due to your karma or merit. If you have not accumulated sufficient merit from prior compassionate actions, vowing to help all beings, and actually performing the three different types of charity,[76] it is hard to come into contact with correct spiritual teachings, high spiritual teachings, and efficient cultivation teachings that will help you to realize enlightenment. You might have to search for them rather than have them come to you easily, and this should remind you to always be supporting true self-realization paths with your own charitable efforts.

There are many worthwhile causes in the world, but only cultivation frees people from helplessly suffering in the endless rounds of cyclic existence. When people learn how to act better, in terms of their relationships with each other and the world, this, too, helps reduce the level of suffering in the world so that more joy, peace and bliss can be born and experienced. To find more joy in life, you must change your own behavior. But just doing good deeds for others, and just perfecting one's own behavior or helping society adjust and perfect its own behavior by codes and rules of conduct is not enough. Spiritual cultivation is necessary to produce true peace in society, and necessary for you to be able to find true peace in the realm of endless existence.

If you have not made any efforts to support such teachings, it will certainly become difficult to come into contact with them in the future.

---

[76] Giving fearlessness, material help and especially spiritual teachings to others.

Most people in the world are therefore deprived of the truest and most helpful spiritual teachings, and it is usually of their own doing for failing to make the effort. They have been following fruitless paths for a long time, and steeped in the habits of ignorance, it is hard to break out of the rut. It is an effort even to get the right information to such individuals whose minds are so closed. Even if they were following a true road of self-cultivation towards spiritual realization, you should also know that without practicing virtuous ways and accumulating merit through good deeds, it's almost impossible to succeed in the Tao or even be reborn in a heaven either.

You must cultivate a clean mind of purity and become generous in offering[77] if you want to succeed on the spiritual path. If you say "I will when I become a Buddha" but you are not doing anything along these lines right now, you are just kidding yourself and making a mockery of cultivation and what it entails. You have to act appropriately in whatever circumstances arise in life. You must help others wherever you might help. Sorry, but you cannot succeed at any spiritual techniques if you lack determined cultivation efforts along with activities of virtue and merit.

You must think about this if you believe that an individual can simply go isolate themselves in the mountains, meditate and succeed. Perhaps a sage can do so because of countless past lives of merit, which even afford him or her the opportunity to do so with support and without worries, but do you already have the merit of a sage? The first stage of the spiritual path is one of Study and Virtue Accumulation because if you don't know the way you will certainly not achieve self-realization and if you are not a good person who practices kind deeds and wants to improve himself then it is nearly impossible to succeed.

After this foundation of recognizing that you truly want to purify yourself and achieve spiritual enlightenment, next comes the second stage of intensified spiritual practices, or intensified cultivation yoga. Only if you engage in this second step of practicing meditation can you reach the third phase of spiritual awakening, or seeing the Tao. This book is all about the gong-fu results achieved during this second stage of practice and effort.

Hercules is definitely at the stage of intensified practices, experiencing the gong-fu of the path, and in this Tenth Labor he sails westward to Erythia, where Spain is today located, in order to obtain Geryon's cattle.

---

[77] Practicing charity, giving, good works, service, kind words, compassionate action, dharma teaching and so forth.

Naturally this represents a stage of cultivation achievement as we'll soon see. Many months go by and he has many adventures along the way, eventually coming to the place where North Africa and Europe meet. This is where the smaller Mediterranean ocean becomes connected to the vast Atlantic.

In some stories it is said that Hercules smashed through the Atlas mountains at this location to create two sides, thus forming the Strait of Gibraltar. Other stories say he simply set up two pillars at this location. In any case, this far westward journey, after his previous labors, suggests that his chi is now traversing as far as possible within his body. This is because Hercules' extra meridians have all opened and his chi can start coursing everywhere. Therefore it can even run more freely through the *sushumna*.

When this starts to happen, the existence of a far left and right chi channel within the body becomes clearly distinguished because yin and yang chi finally become clearly differentiated from one another. Before this stage it's hard to separate out the function of the left and right channels from the rest of the chi channel circulations, but now the location and functioning of these two channels can be clearly felt, and the sensation is surprising at first. This is the meaning of the part of his journey where he erects two pillars, or splits a mountain in two, at the boundaries of Europe and North Africa.

We say in cultivation that the two types of chi (yin and yang) or the two left and right channels, become "discriminated" or "differentiated" because their existence is now felt on opposite sides of the body. At this stage, you can now feel the length of the two channels far apart from one another without any chance of delusional mistake. Thus, you can start to experientially verify teachings on the existence of yin and yang. On the road of spiritual cultivation you must read about the theory and study it, but then you must cultivate to attain the stages and prove everything you read about. It's never a matter of belief but of proving, verifying and authenticating the path through personal attainments. At this stage you prove the teachings on yin and yang because you will feel the different nature of these two types of chi.

Chinese Taoism typically represents this stage of "yin and yang becoming discriminated" with the image of an egg because the egg white and yellow yolk represent two complementary pieces of one whole. The two parts match each other perfectly just like a Chinese yin and yang symbol, which also shows a whole divided into two pieces. The image of an egg is also used in western alchemy[78] to represent this stage of yin and yang chi differentiation in the body. Differentiating yin and yang means opening the bottom interface point between the left and right channels and allowing the chi to flow in the left and right sides of the body fully. Also, during this process, one will sometimes have full body sensations of either yin chi or yang chi, which some cultivation schools represent by the image of young boys or girls.

Ever since the legend of Hercules, the two land masses forming the Strait of Gibraltar have become known as the "Pillars of Hercules" to commemorate this Tenth Labor. It is really something remarkable to reach this stage of attainment where the yin and yang chi become clearly differentiated from one another and the existence of the left and right chi channels becomes apparent on opposite sides of the body. Your chi will often oscillate alternately on the far left and right sides of your upper body trunk when this happens. You will feel the chi switch back and forth in these two channels, which feel rather wide in diameter, and then the phenomenon will die down, or appear again, based entirely on your practice efforts. This is the stage when you can verify for yourself why pictures of Isis are shown with left and right horns and why many other deity figures have similar representations on their head.

Most cultivators eventually feel the existence of their chi channels, and this can become a problem when they start to cling to the experience. If you let go of the tendency to cling, and allow the chi to simply course through the channels, you will eventually forget the sensations of pulsation entirely; the smoothness, or evening out, is due to further opening and constitutes real cultivation progress. However, people who keep clinging to the channels, chakras and chi flows always get lost. My master says that they represent the great catastrophes of the cultivation path that are frequently seen in Tibetan Buddhism and other esoteric schools that concentrate on the body's energies and abilities of the mind while bypassing the search for the ultimate Source. He has seen so many catastrophes among practitioners along these lines that he does not teach this material, even though he is recognized as an enlightened Vajrayana master. The following stories may help explain this and the errors to be avoided when it comes to cultivating the body.

My own teacher had achieved enlightenment at the incredible age of twenty four. This amazing accomplishment at such a young age is a testament to his many positive qualities and cultivation efforts. It is also

---

[78] See Emblem VIII in the *Atalanta Fugiens* of Michael Maier.

testament to his exceedingly high wisdom along with the proficiency of Zen school training. The Zen school instructs practitioners to ignore the body and everything else during meditation and to instead search for the ultimate source of the mind. It directly targets the main objective and doesn't get distracted by gong-fu along the way. Because of his great talent my teacher was able to quickly detach from all five skandhas, including consciousness itself, and penetrate through to discover the original nature.

At one time when I was very sad at my own lack of progress, he told me that he also cried after his enlightenment because he felt he had been cheated; he couldn't fly or do anything like you read in scriptures and ancient stories. This was because the physical transformations of chi, chakras and channels had not yet caught up to his enlightenment. As the Bodhisattva Samantabhadra once explained, the transformation of the body proceeds step-by-step according to the timeframes of the karmic realm of cause and effect, and so the physical body requires time to transform. It is absolutely true that your chi, channels and chakras must transform to a certain extent for you to be able to realize the Tao, but after their enlightenment most masters go into retreat so that they can complete the transformative process undisturbed. After his Zen enlightenment my teacher went to Tibet to learn the Vajrayana school and became an Esoteric master while offering Tibetans the Chinese dharma equivalents that had not yet made it there.

Most people who focus on cultivating their chi and channels, even if they achieve these Herculean stages and beyond, never achieve enlightenment unless they meet an already enlightened master who points out their mind. You would think that all who attain samadhi thereby achieve enlightenment but this is not true, and Shakyamuni mentioned this several times during his teaching years. Samadhi attainments are not the Tao but just a helpful preparation for enlightenment. Countless cases have come down to us from history illustrating Shakyamuni's warning - individuals with samadhi attainments and superpowers galore who did not attain the Tao but needed help to attain awakening, or who never awakened at all.

The Hindu sage Papaji told of an Indian yogi he met who could levitate, understand the language of plants and animals, produce a body double (*yang shen*), travel to other worlds, produce any food he liked at will and all sorts of other samadhi yogic feats called *siddhis*, which are mentioned in ancient texts. The young adept said his teacher had warned him these abilities came from the mind only and were not the ultimate achievement. His teacher said that the highest accomplishment was true knowledge of the self-nature but admitted he did not have this attainment himself even though he also possessed these samadhi abilities. His teacher said that an enlightened sage was exceedingly rare and that if he ever found a man of Tao who could help him attain this awakening, then even a lifetime of service to him could not repay the debt of liberation. This is correct.

Papaji helped this samadhi yogi realize his true mind right there on the spot and then left, just as in the story of the Zen Boat Monk who enlightened the gifted Chia-shan and then immediately departed as well. When the Sixth Zen Patriarch was awakened through the words of the Fifth Patriarch reciting the *Diamond Sutra*, he, too, immediately departed as did the Fourth Patriarch after bringing the mountain monk Niu-tou to his awakening. The important thing in life is to finally achieve liberation, or enlightenment, which is not a samadhi itself yet is often attained by cultivating the path of samadhi. Some students who awaken stay with their teacher and some depart. Sometimes the teacher leaves as soon as the transmission of the mind dharma is accomplished. The important thing to recognize is that the enlightened don't want anything from you, but are simply there to help you, and that often means correcting you.

In China there once was a Taoist adept like Papaji's "student" who could also fly in the air and had all sorts of supernormal yogic powers. He, too, had countless superpowers from cultivating his chi, chakras and channels and thought he had achieved the ultimate attainments. This Taoist immortal, Lu Chunyang, had cultivated his vitality and chi to such a high level that his physical life could last for hundreds or thousands of years, which is a common attainment of those who particularly cultivate their chi once the channels are opened.

One day Lu Chunyang was flying around in the sky with his famous sword and noticed a strange aura on a mountain, so he descended to find a simple Buddhist monk giving a lecture. He got into a challenging discussion with enlightened Zen master Huang-lung Nan, who laughed at and mocked Lu Chunyang's attainments but appeared as nothing other than an ordinary monk.

In their verbal battle which ensued, Lu Chunyang remarked, "A single millet grain contains the world," announcing that he reached the point in his spiritual cultivation where he had realized the witness and recognized that it was like a tiny point of pure awareness which creates the universe for the individual.[79] He realized the one underlying pristine awareness as a droplet of knowingness, a small speck of consciousness that has all the universe within it. Creation, manifestation, or "the universe," is nothing but a vibration in pure consciousness, and pure consciousness is what we call empty, pristine awareness. The "I am" is a tiny defiled aspect of pure awareness or pure consciousness that lets one experience a world, or we can say creates a world, and this is what Lu Chunyang had realized. Through a conversation that bandied about, Huang-lung Nan

---

[79] All you are ever conscious of is your own mind. You only experience your own mind. Everyone therefore lives in their own little world of subjective consciousness. When you penetrate to the root source of consciousness, which is a single body of awareness, you find that one pristine awareness is the cognizer of all consciousness. The filter is the consciousness "I am" that arises between base awareness and the body. "Individual minds" are just waves on the ocean of one body of consciousness, and so as separate entities or existences in themselves they don't actually exist. Through the road of spiritual cultivation you can find that underlying, always present, empty, pristine awareness that can know all consciousness. That awareness is pure being, and as an individual, which is just a false assumption, you must try to untangle pure being from the tangle of experiences by abandoning false thoughts and attachments within your consciousness. By doing so, first you find yourself as bodyless, dimensionless witness only, and then realize that ocean body of pure awareness that is both mind and consciousness and beyond them. Then you become pure beingness wherein there is no difference between *samsara* and *nirvana*, between interdependent origination and emptiness. You don't become that – it is what you have always been, "hidden from view" because of mistaken clinging. The functions of the Source are no different than the Source but effervescent, impermanent, not lasting, and so individual consciousness and aggregate consciousness are unreal. In the *Real One* is peace, purity, permanence, beingness-existence, awareness and bliss (no suffering). This is the Self, your True Self or true identity. Its awareness functioning is always changeless, always in the now, always presence. Upon enlightenment you shed the mistaken identification with the false self and realize your true pure being which needs nothing to rest on. That's what you are. An identity still remains upon shedding the identification with the false self, so the functioning personality can still say "I am," but the identity is inherent in the underlying reality itself – the "I am" is the announcement of the Self. That identity is not a person, and yet when spiritual greats say they are "one with God" we think they are talking about their person. This is an incorrect assumption since a person does not exist. You are not a person. You are It. You are God, Allah, Ein Sof, dharmakaya, Parabrahman, the Matrix Womb, Buddhahood itself. You are the Reality of All and are experiencing a world through the small filter of an individual self because of the incorrect habit of wrong clinging developed through countless lives. That is the habit of ignorance caused by attachment. The higher spiritual realms have less and less of this clinging and therefore higher spiritual attainments where inhabitants experience greater degrees of bliss. Everything still operates upon awakening. Nothing changes except you no longer hold on to delusions that have been binding you. So what you think is a person – yourself – is actually different than what you believe the self to be. You cannot say what you ultimately are because it is beyond consciousness (and thus experience), and because you would need consciousness to know attributes. It is formless and free of attributes, *and yet you are* so you can announce "I am." All consciousness, all thoughts, memories, forms, bodies, all existence is your own. You are separate from nothing, hence you are All. There is no "my self" or "their self" but the one Self of all, the only Self, the One Without A Second. The Self is just experiencing Itself. The words "I am" address the conventional world, but emanate out of this True Self, which is what you, who are reading this, are. You certainly aren't the body, but just don't know what you truly are because of delusion which one lets go of, and which thus dissolves away, on the road of spiritual practice.

parlayed and thrust and enabled Lu Chunyang to finally realize the Tao. Lu Chunyang afterwards said,

> I throw away the gourd and drop the shattered zither (symbols of his efforts at physical cultivation)
> Right now I don't long for the gold in the mercury (other symbols of the physical body's essences that transform on the spiritual path).
> After I once saw Huang-lung (after the Zen master helped me awaken to enlightenment)
> I finally realized that I had always been using mind wrongly.

There are so many cases of people who attain samadhi and superpowers from cultivating the body, but who miss the Tao completely and cling to their attainments, becoming catastrophes of the path. This is actually the general pattern rather than the exception for it is very hard to achieve the enlightenment of self-realization, especially when people mistakenly concentrate on cultivating the body too much. Once again, as these stories amply illustrate, it is very easy to miss the true cultivation path. The orthodox religions, in terms of their offerings of teachings, are even worse. They might tell you that you are God, but do they tell you what that ultimately means and how to reach or realize your true nature?

You really need to have lots of knowledge, wisdom and merit in order to successfully utilize esoteric practices, but this doesn't mean that you have lots of wisdom or qualifications just because esoteric practices come your way, so tread with caution! It's not that people don't have the capacity for it, but that they usually don't have sufficient wisdom because they have not studied dharma teachings deep enough and lack sufficient devotion to the Mahayana path. You really need to master cultivation teachings to a deep level before you throw yourself into specialized Vajrayana practices, otherwise you will go astray like these practitioners and there may be no enlightened sage there to save you.

Naturally this does not mean you should not practice the white skeleton visualization, vipassana witnessing practice, anapana, pranayama and so forth but that one should not take the fruits of physical cultivation as the path or prime objective. There have always been individuals who have become enlightened without resorting to contrived methods, such as Hui-neng the Sixth Patriarch of Zen or the more recent Indian sage Sri Ramana Maharshi, so the physical cultivation path is neither the ultimate path nor absolutely essential. Nevertheless, a helpful path is a path and poison can serve as medicine if you take it correctly. To cultivate the Vajrayana path, Taoism or tantric yoga and so forth all comes down to your wisdom, or your master's wisdom and instructions. If you have great wisdom you can use all sorts of tantric techniques to help transform your body, as did the female Tibetan master Yeshe Tsogyel, but even then they do not guarantee the highest Tao, for Yeshe herself only reached the second Bodhisattva *bhumi*. The real practice, as Buddha and the Zen school point out, is Mind-Only to discover the original nature, and only after success on this path can you concentrate as Yeshe did on transforming her chakras and channels.

Now, whether we say that Hercules created two mountains or erected two pillars to commemorate his having reached the Strait of Gibraltar, both representations serve the same meaning. This is no different from the two pillars, Boaz and Joachim, mentioned in the story of the building of the Temple of Solomon. In many religions, people commemorate the spots where their spiritual leaders attained some cultivation breakthrough by erecting a temple or some other memorial, and thus we have the Pillars of Hercules. In the earlier mentioned story of Jacob in the book of *Genesis*, subsequent to the dream about of angels climbing the ladder, he mentioned that "God told him" that all these lands to the north, south, east and west were his and his descendants forever. However, just as the splitting of the Atlas mountains in the story of the Pillars of Hercules does not refer to worldly land or pillars, Jacob's story does not refer to worldly lands either.

Buddhas, Bodhisattvas and heavenly beings will help you in your cultivation attainments when you work hard enough, providing visions and other types of assistance wherever they can to help you to change your behavior, open your chi channels and purify your consciousness. They will provide all sorts of visionary motivations to keep your cultivation strong at certain critical stages and to distract you from clinging to the body's chi sensations at that moment of time. However, as to specific interpretations about land ownership, military movements, societal rules, political decisions, and so forth, this universally comes from the human realm of aspirations rather than edicts that are heaven sent. The human mind creates all sorts of justifications for acts it wants to accomplish, and smart people often try to lead the ignorant by blessing their goals or actions with a fictitious heavenly mandate. This is something that has been seen in history time and time again. Similarly, religious rules and societal rules are often created to help the affairs of the world go on smoothly, which is sometimes so that powers above can still control the populace, and hence those rules do not necessarily mean the true benefit of the people.

The big secret is that many of the visions one experiences when going through these various stages of purification – including the visions described by Tibetan Buddhism as the central channel is being opened - are provided by Buddhas, Bodhisattvas, and devas who are trying to help affirm practitioners' efforts and help motivate them to continue with their progress. All sorts of masquerade illusions are thereby projected. If you are a Christian practitioner and see visions of angels, the Madonna or Jesus, it is normally the very same deceptive process going on rather than the actual visitation of angels, Jesus or Mary. If you are a Hindu and see visions of Krishna or Lord Rama, the same holds again. If you are a Taoist and see the Three Pure Ones, or a Buddhist and see the Buddhas, or a Confucian and see ancient sages, once again what you are most often encountering are nirmanakaya projections by a dharma protector to help you.

The image of all sorts of past saints and sages might be hijacked for this process, though of course sometimes what you experience is the real thing. The images of deceased dear ones might also be used as well and because your consciousness and memories are like an open book to those with higher attainments, whatever they say to you will be correct in representing recognized mannerisms and events of the past. This sort of masquerade is always done out of compassion to help lead practitioners forward in their spiritual cultivation. It is an acknowledgement of your practice and progress, and used as an enticement, but as masters from all the traditions commonly warn, don't be cheated by these things. Now you know why as the veil has been lifted to help cultivation no longer remain in the realm of the mystical.

The images or visions provided to practitioners will always correspond to their cultural, religious and educational backgrounds and beliefs. If you think angels have wings you'll be shown angels with wings, but don't ever for a moment believe that's how they really appear. Whatever you can understand is what can be cobbled together from whatever is already in your memories, so the masquerade almost always employs traditional images from your own cultural teachings or religion. Nevertheless, one should ignore such visions because what you see is not necessarily as things really are. This is why Vajrayana calls these phenomena the generation of the illusory bodies.[80]

---

[80] Are there other ways to cultivate without this happening? Yes, but we are revealing the most typical teaching patterns and images shown to individuals cultivating the lower stages of body

All these body visions are illusions. You do not actually arise in an illusory body, like an astral body, but just see all sorts of things like this because the images are given to you by those undertaking the *abhisheka* empowerment. One must not attach to these things as your self or take these visions as absolute teachings or accurate representations in themselves. In actual fact, the majority of visions given are fictitious representations simply provided to lead a practitioner forward. Whatever is in your memories can be used to fabricate a vision to help you continue practicing.

Therefore, while the cultivation path is the same and the gong-fu milestones are the same, Greeks, Indians, Chinese, Persians, Hindus, Jews, Muslims, Buddhists and Christians – however you wish to partition cultivation adherents - will all experience culturally pertinent visions on the path. They will see visions that dharma protectors make up to help lead them a bit forward because Heaven does indeed want to help those who cultivate, but the surprising secret is that most of these visions are not trustworthy at all. All sorts of visions will be projected just to help explain the process which you yourself cannot see, in a way you might be able to understand, and to motivate you to continue cultivating forward. There are many other reasons as well, such as interrupting your focus of attention at times so that you do not cling to the body. In any case, visions are just expedient inventions that do not necessarily represent things the way they really are, nor do they represent accurate predictions or prophecies of the future.[81] They are expedients designed to keep you on the road of concentration and moving forward while the kundalini is still at peak activity, because its fullness will indeed rise and fall based

purification. The key importance is to keep the practitioner going because once the momentum of transformations has begun, any interruptions in practice can severely delay the entire sequence of transformations. This is why one should go into retreat at this time. Because the visions given are particular to the individual, a Chinese Taoist would therefore be shown different signs than those practicing tantric yoga in India, and a Christian, Muslim or Jewish spiritual practitioner would experience different visions as well. They'll be shown whatever explains the process in a way they might culturally understand, and which keeps them going. Practitioners following the Vajrayana school of Esoteric Buddhism in Tibet, Persian cultivation, Muslim cultivation, Christian cultivation and Jewish cultivation, etc. would also therefore be shown (see) entirely different cultural images. It's all a matter of showing a practitioner something they can understand, which somewhat explains the process or stage of gong-fu, and which works because of their background, training and culture. These projections are why nirmanakaya emanations are called compassionate activities, and why thoughts are called nirmanakaya. Just as the same human symbols are often commonly employed across different religions, races and cultures, many of the signs of cultivation progress people see are common patterns used by the enlightened or dharma protectors because of their effectiveness.
[81] The future can always be changed because karma can always change and is being changed all the time.

on your activities and efforts. It is crucial to keep a practitioner going at some critical stages of the path.

These are really big secrets I am revealing so that the era of superstition and mystery in cultivation matters should end. You need not believe me, but I've done my best revealing what will help those few who get this far. Naturally all cultivation stories and results, and even my explanations, will seem to fall into the science fiction fluff-fluff realm until they occur to you personally (but of course those from *your* own spiritual tradition are true from the start). Then you will be searching for answers and will remain clueless without this vital information that explains what the representations in Taoism, Hinduism, Esoteric Buddhism, and so forth are all about.

While this information may itself sound like unproven superstitious hogwash, since it is actually what happens when you progress far enough, you will call the explanations "scientific" when you realize those stages yourself. The world is extremely lucky to have *Tao and Longevity*, by Nan Huai-chin, that explains many of the stages of the path using Buddhist, Confucian and Taoist terminology, and I hope this further information on the Vajrayana or tantric yoga stages of generation and completion – which involve the stages prior to and far after the opening of the *sushumna* – can also help you in your cultivation regardless of your religion or spiritual tradition. You don't have to experience all of these phenomena yourself, but when some of these signs occur you will now have some guidance to help you with interpretations. As in *Tao and Longevity*, the information is actually quite non-denominational which is why we can explain it from so many angles and find it in countless traditions.

Hence once again the reference to "all the lands" in Jacob's vision represents all the chakras and chi channels inside Jacob's body, which Taoism declares is like an entire world system unto itself. Various Indian cultivation schools also declare that the body is an image of the macrocosm like a populated world with the organs and chakras as lands or residences. Therefore, people always misinterpret this Biblical story because they lack the requisite cultivation attainments themselves and can only interpret spiritual things in a material way. Far too many spiritual teachings have been destroyed because of this materialistic emphasis stressed by individuals without any knowledge or attainments.

You must remember that Jacob awoke from this dream and said "surely this is the gate of heaven" not because the physical land was special as some gate, but because the central channel *is* the spiritual gate to heavenly attainments, namely samadhi and the Tao. The yoga schools of India explicitly state that you cannot attain samadhi or enlightenment unless you open up the *sushumna* central channel. Pick up a copy of the *Hatha Yoga Pradipika* and you will find, "only when the *prana* (chi) flows through the *sushumna* will there be samadhi." Other spiritual schools similarly assert the importance of the opening of the central channel to samadhi attainments, which is why your channels must fully open from spiritual cultivation before you can attain spiritual enlightenment. All these things therefore refer to what happens inside the body with its chi, chakras and channels, but no more.

You certainly must open the central channel on the spiritual trail, a feat emphasized time and again in the spiritual schools and accomplished by all successful spiritual cultivators such as Hercules. It is so hard to get this far that some authors retelling the story of the Twelve Labors amplified the importance of the feat by having Hercules split a mountain in two rather than simply establish two pillars. Either way, in real life these mountains became known as the Gates or Pillars of Hercules. They symbolize the two opposing chi masses of the body which are now clearly distinguished at this stage of cultivation.

Religions have all sorts of spiritual stories that people readily misinterpret with purely secular meanings, rather than correctly understanding their true cultivation connotations. They often dismiss spiritual instructional stories outright as just plain nonsense. If we recall the story of the Yellow Emperor of China, it is said that he had thousands of concubines and that at the end of his life he ascended into heaven taking all his concubines with him. How can anyone do that? It's impossible, so on face value the story is just as ridiculous as angels climbing up and down ladders to heaven.

However, if you start cultivating some of these gong-fu stages yourself, you soon realize that the story has a cultivation meaning just as does the story of Jacob's dream in the Old Testament. It means that the Yellow Emperor (who we know was an individual who attained the Tao and became the subsequent founder of Chinese culture[82]) eventually transformed all the chakras and chi channels in his body. These were

---

[82] Many of the greatest cultivators became the founders of spiritual cultures. In fact, the Buddhas and Bodhisattvas who have succeeded in the past incarnate time and again, when the time is appropriate and the opportunities present, to do so or accomplish other great feats for the cultural impetus of mankind. We all know the names of sports stars, actors, singers, rich men, politicians and so on, but in time they fade and the only names we remember are the sages who have helped found deep culture.

represented in his legend by his many wives or concubines, since they were yin, and because of that accomplishment, he was able to accomplish the sambhogakaya reward body and become an immortal who "ascended," thus taking them with him.

This is also why Krishna is said to have been the lord of eight queens[83] and wedded to 16,000 *gopikas* (cowherdesses) as well. Why and how could Krishna marry 16,000 women? If you keep cultivating, then regardless of your religious tradition your chi will transform and countless thousands of channels and chakras in your body - represented in both these stories as concubines or wives who must listen to you - will open and purify. This happened to Jacob, the Yellow Emperor, and thousands of other prior practitioners who cultivated hard enough. It can happen to you, too, regardless of your school, religion or tradition. If someone maintains that it cannot happen, then what is the point of religion and cultivation? In fact, it must happen if you cultivate hard enough.

People misinterpret these stories and immediately dismiss them at face value because they don't understand the spiritual cultivation lessons embedded within them. The Bible reports of practitioners who attained similar achievements, such as Enoch and Melchizedek who also "ascended," but even here people similarly have no clue as to the meaning of these attainments. This is because the "experts" who try to interpret matters lack any deep cultivation knowledge and practice. Hence the blind usually end up leading the blind in religion, and entire traditions eventually become controlled by well meaning individuals who lack the requisite knowledge, wisdom, and attainments to really be able to help anybody. The accomplishment of Enoch and Melchizedek is the simply stage of an Arhat's achievement, if not more.

When you totally transform your body on the spiritual trail we can say all your channels and chakras open, all your chi is transformed, all those wives become yours or "become obedient," all that land becomes yours, the land becomes pacified or reaches a state of harmony, or you will take all those things with you when you "ascend." There are lots of different literary ways to symbolize the same accomplishment of attaining the sambhogakaya, or reward body.

You can only reach this stage after passing through all of the initial gong-fu recounted in Hercules' Twelve Labors and then progressing on further. What we are studying in these labors constitutes the earliest stages of physical transformation on the path, the "baby parts" before

[83] Representing the eight major petals of the heart chakra.

the samadhi and enlightenment accomplishments of cultivation. As my teacher stated, these tantric Vajrayana stages only deal with physical body purification and are not the real heart of the matter. As Confucius mentioned in reviewing his life, there are many years of cultivation necessary before a high stage of achievement, and so these are just the baby steps.

Now this is actually a good place to introduce a particular tantric method, also related to this discussion, which is sometimes used to help open up the chakras and chi channels around this time. This method describes a phenomenon which might actually occur to you around this stage, depending on your preparatory cultivation practices and merit, and so I also want to mention it to help you avoid confusion should it occur.

In Tibetan Buddhism, as a practice technique a man is sometimes taught to visualize karmamudra dakinis, which are beautiful young females you hold in imagined sexual embrace, at a certain stage of the path. Actually, for the real karmamudra practice, the technique is a witnessing practice "guided by dakinis" where you are shown beautiful women in erotic fashion simply to get your yang chi to arise, as that is what usually happens when there are thoughts of sexual conduct. One of the purposes behind this type of technique is to help your vital energies arise and flood the chi channels and one must forego attachments during the process and obey the instructions given. When yang chi rises, devas who assist the cultivation process can help you further open up certain chakras and chi channel circulations and other things as well. In lieu of an actual sexual partner, these mental viewings to help raise your vital energies serve as a substitute.

The arising of sexual desire, which usually involves strong emotional attachment, and the sexual bliss felt in the body (as your chi floods all the channels and cells), both require that you let go so you do not attach to thoughts or the sensations. In the tantric schools, clinging or not clinging means the difference between success and failure for this dangerous path. There are countless reasons we've gone into as to why ordinary people are not qualified for this, and why they never even hear these clear explanations. This is why it requires a high stage of cultivation maturity to be introduced to such techniques by deities or enlightened masters. In Hindu pictures of multiple chakras within the body, one sometimes sees a pair of husband and wife deities residing at the chakra locations, hinting at the pumping sensation felt when chi is pouring through those locales during some of these stages of chi channel transformation. This also refers to the sensations you will feel at certain chakras or in certain channels when progress is made along these lines, which you might also compare to the wiggling pumping motion of a fish's tail. As one might surmise, it is extremely difficult to transform the dense human body which is why all sorts of techniques have been developed for those who truly qualify and have the right vows. If practitioners don't have the right view of emptiness, however, none of these various techniques will work. The testings one receives during the process - such as in the stories of Abraham, Naropa, Yeshe Tsogyel and others - only hint at a small portion of the process while leaving out much that the general public could not understand.

Ordinary people during the course of lovemaking can sometimes get their yang chi to ascend their *du-mai* chi channel if they practice correctly, which is the basis of sexual yoga or sexual tantra to help open up the channels and initiate the opening of the root chakra.[84] This can help transform the body if there is no attachment to lust or the bliss that arises during sex. However, if a man loses his chi or *jing* during the process due to ejaculation (orgasm), the process usually comes to a halt. This is yet another reason why it is beneficial for men to learn non-ejaculatory sexual intercourse as a life skill, for the skill has many benefits.

At some points during sexual intercourse, it is beneficial if both parties pause their vigorous activities and practice relaxation together with detachment, letting the physical bliss that arises (due to the circulation of chi stimulated by sex) transform their bodies while they remain empty and don't attach to the sensations. You stimulate your chi into moving through sex, and then always let go of the bliss that arises due to the chi

---

[84] This refers to Hercules' first labor of conquering the Nemean lion. In all cultivation schools you use various spiritual practices or exercises as if they were a match meant to light a flame. Once you've gotten the flame lit, which means that you can initiate and then feel the rotation of the chi revolving through the channels because the yang chi has been stirred into awakening and its circulation has been opened, you forget about (stop using) the technique and continue to cultivate emptiness from then on. You just let everything go after a sufficient point of arousal and then let the chi circulation rotate without interference. It will produce wonderful feelings during the process of rotation, but you should not hold on to that bliss but just let it transform the body. This is also the proper way to proceed in sexual relations. Techniques such as pranayama, sexual yoga, mantra, vipassana and so forth are all used basically to get the Herculean series of physical transformations kick started, but of course this only refers to the physical purification aspect of the path. This is not actually spiritual cultivation in itself, but just cultivating the physical nature of the body. Real spiritual cultivation involves practicing virtue, good deeds, broadening one's wisdom and searching for one's original nature via a purification of consciousness that maintains witnessing awareness and insight, but without attachment.

flow. The process is similar in analogy to using a gas powered chainsaw, where you pull and pull at the zip cord until the motor starts. After the motor starts running, you don't need to tug at the cord any longer but must simply hold the device carefully. Once started, the saw blades also rotate in an oval pattern which is similar to the shape of the *du-mai* and *jen-mai* microcosmic circulation. Thus, the intent of using sexual relations to assist your cultivation is to do so in a way that attempts to get the chi circulation to start flowing but which doesn't employ a lot of energy that tires you and your partner out. To lose energy is incorrect. To try to absorb energy from your partner is also incorrect. Strange sexual acrobatics that use up energy are incorrect.

Just as in handling a chainsaw, this is a dangerous technique many practitioners might equate sex with cultivation. You can certainly use sex to assist your cultivation, but you should never pursue sexual enjoyments in the name of cultivation because then you are only deceiving yourself and others; sexual relations are in no way, shape or form the spiritual path. There are so many ways to cheat oneself or others and go astray, which is why the first rule on the Mahayana path is about sexual discipline.

During intercourse, it is not as detrimental for a woman to experience an orgasm as it is for a man to ejaculate his semen. A man will tend to lose much more energy than a woman and since a woman's body is designed to absorb his energies, this means it can somewhat reabsorb many of the energies she herself loses, if any, during orgasm, too. Furthermore, her body is designed in such a way that her energies respond to a man's sexual stimulations, and this usually means rising energies rather than depletion. The woman has a natural advantage, but a man does not since his normal response is energy loss. With such advantages, it is only a patient woman who might help a man learn how to build up his staying power and master the natural prolongation of tantric sex which does not involve forceful restraint.

This is not just non-ejaculatory sex, but entails learning how to pause before orgasm, stopping over and over again until a man can learn how to do this naturally. Partners therefore often turn to various counted thrusting methods during sex, such as "nine short thrusts and one long thrust," as an initial means to desensitize the man from ejaculating too early. By this technique a man can more easily learn how to pause when he feels he is nearing orgasm. However, this is particularly difficult to bear for a woman with closed chi channels if the man has stimulated her too much.

Because the chi flow is not smooth, ordinary women usually cannot detach from feeling an urgent need for strong continued thrusting or wild, unpredictable stimulation. A man therefore needs an understanding partner to match him if he wants to learn this technique but because most women are not cultivators, and therefore cannot detach from the orgasmic body sensations which would easily allow this, it is hard for men to learn. In the beginning period when two partners are first learning this method and how to harmoniously respond to each other, it is important for the man not to overly stimulate his own sensitive spots because that might immediately lead to ejaculation. An ordinary woman's strong desire for uninterrupted stroking and thrusting often makes this difficult. To help her partner, a woman must learn how to detach from her own needs for a short while as she becomes the man's teacher and assists him to take the pauses necessary that will help him avoid ejaculation and recharge his energies. This will be to their greater mutual benefit in the long run, and usually helps to deepen the bond between partners and prolong the session of lovemaking. Usually woman who practice cultivation, because their channels are already somewhat open, are the only ones who can handle this without much trouble.

In terms of cultivation, for a man the saying runs, "With no water in the boiler there's no steam in the pipes." In other words, if a man loses too much of his *jing* due to ejaculation then there won't be enough chi available to open up his channels, and his health will suffer as well. Many men actually suffer from depression because they lose too much semen. Sexual dissipation can hurt the waist, eyes (cause floaters), knees, hearing, or make you sleepy, unclear or forgetful. While some say women actually gain from orgasm, it is also true that multiple orgasms in a short time period, with the situation repeated over and over again, are energetically degenerative and will deplete her chi as well.

Thus goes the mundane realm of lovemaking, or ordinary sexual yoga. During the practice of karmamudra yoga, if you have an enlightened master then actual devas themselves might become your teachers and instruct you to do all sorts of inexplicable things such as offer certain colored lights or particular body movements in your imagination. Just follow the instructions and do as you are told, applying wisdom as required. If you practice correctly because you can let go during the process, mentally you will see many different things that are dependent upon your background and training, and meant to guide you. In Vajrayana and the Hindu tantric yoga schools it's said you might see the heads of the envisioned dakinis dropping off, their bodies may disappear, and they might dance, twirl, rotate in a spin[85] and so forth.

All sorts of things are possible including seeing dead bodies and all sorts of unmentionables. You might see your own body turn into a skeleton, and you might see all sorts of other happy or frightening visions, too. That is why tantra is a dangerous path only undertaken under the watchful eye of an enlightened master, and the student must possess a sound mind and stable mentality. What is the actual meaning of what you see? Of course your chi is transforming and channel complexes are opening during this period but you will never really know what's going on or why, or know what to expect next or how long things will last. This confusion and ignorance on your part are a necessary part of the process for you to be able to make progress.

Sometimes a vision is part of a teaching lesson. Sometimes it is used to cause you to rest. Sometimes it is designed to distract you from clinging to the body's chi (the body consciousness) at a certain moment when you are found to be clinging. You must learn how to disengage from the sensations that occur during gong-fu transformations, but the habit of clinging to physical sensations and taking the body as the self is difficult to break. The task of learning how to detach from the form, sensation and consciousness skandhas – which are the consciousness sheaths (koshas) of Hinduism - is extremely difficult for spiritual practitioners. You need every help and reminder along the way that this is what you should be doing rather than fall into a fascination with internal visions that lead nowhere.

Even after the body is in much better shape because its chi channels have all opened and chi flow has become smooth, if you don't continue to cultivate detachment from the sticky adherent tendency of clinging to consciousness, yet let it function without suppression, it will still be impossible to attain the Tao despite all these attainments. If you attain the Tao by detaching from your body and mind by virtue of your high prajna wisdom, as some Arhats do, then the task of enlightenment is easily accomplished and one can readily achieve liberation. But for full enlightenment one must continue to cultivate body and mind, nirmanakaya and sambhogakaya. Just to recognize one's fundamental face, the dharmakaya, is not enough. There is much more cultivation work to

---

[85] Many of these visages are meant to distract your attention from tight holding, and once again help you to let go while your strong chi vitality is pumping to open up channels. A twist can be as effective as the sword of Manjushri in cutting off your tendency to cling to consciousness.

be performed for the task of enlightenment to be termed complete. Then again no Bodhisattva ever thinks their cultivation finished because all of consciousness (manifesting itself as apparent sentient beings) has yet to be transformed, or liberated, from the false cloud of delusion caused by clinging to the functioning of the mind.

Hence for various reasons that will never be explained to you if you are gifted with overt assistance from higher spiritual beings in opening your chi channels (an *abhisheka* or empowerment), all sorts of distractions will be created during the long period of transformation (including internal dialogues that never amount to anything) simply to test the channels, help move the chi, help the practitioner draw their attention away from (detach from) chi sensations, test their ability to separate thinking and conception from the body, and more. Some of these "tests" involve physical events in the outside world, such as in the case of Naropa or Abraham, and some will be entirely internal. All sorts of tricks will be used on a practitioner at these stages, and they will be placed in all sorts of difficult situations or presented with challenges, in order to simply help them make further progress in transforming their chi and channels. It is impossible for you to specify any set pattern or model to the method, or correctly anticipate what is to happen next. For this sort of help in transforming the physical body's chi and channels, all you can expect is chaos and misunderstanding on your part.

Everyone's problems are different, so there is no set or general pattern as to what you will experience along these lines. You might have a particular problem with sexual desire, another person has a big problem with greediness, another person is verbally condescending or prone to anger ... everyone has different problems that have predominated in their life (forming default neural pathways, so to speak, that must be corrected), and of course everyone has a certain number of basic problems involving sex, money, power, greed, status, lying, killing, anger, food, sleep and so on. Everyone has a different state of chi channel purification and openings dependent upon how much cultivation work they previously performed to that point.

The *abhisheka* Bodhisattvas assisting the process know what experiences to put you through, based on whatever problems you have and channels they are aiming to help open, and you should just follow their indications - or ignore them because of your wisdom. As to which is right, you'll have to find out because you'll be thrown into mental quandaries where you might never know what to do for sure. All of that is part of the process and is absolutely necessary for the assistance. As particular chakra or chi channel systems open, physically you will immediately feel definite energy changes within your body including the eventual rotation of the chi within the back-to-front channel orbit.

You will go through many testings, trials, tribulations and much confusion if you get this type of Bodhisattva assistance for purifying the chakras and channels, a process that continues for years although others will remain totally unaware of what is happening. Some tantric masters report first seeing a hag that initially instructed them on the tantric path, others a Bodhisattva, yet others a deity. Everyone's case is different, so whatever you encounter is just an expedient designed to work for your particular mentality. You cannot set your expectations based on what other people have experienced and so you cannot rely on ancient texts in this regard. Furthermore, you will never be able to decipher what is happening as you receive this aid to help transform your body, or understand why you are being put through all sorts of various difficult mental situations. But all your channels must become opened and purified. It is impossible for you to anticipate what will be asked of you to help open your channels, and devas don't want you to understand for many reasons. It is just a process for helping to open up chi channels and nothing ultimately significant you should attach to. People would not believe the explanation of these phenomena if they were provided so masters keep silent on this as a matter of discipline, which best preserves its maximum effectiveness.

On this line of thought, the ordinary people of the world who lack sufficient virtue and wisdom simply cannot be introduced to sexual cultivation practices but would fall into lust and perversion, and then mistakenly propagate this as the spiritual path. Throughout history this has happened time and again. It is an unfortunate fact that many people who are attracted to spiritual cultivation are sometimes extremists or mentally unbalanced, so this is not material that can openly propagated because it would lead to societal decline. It is certainly not a teaching made available to those without wisdom, virtue, and years of deep cultivation study and practice who have been tested. Even if you have those qualifications, to find a qualified partner for this type of practice (with the requisite healthy body, gong-fu, knowledge of cultivation and commitment to dharma) is nearly impossible.[86]

---

[86] As an example, according to traditional tantric teachings a female consort should possess several special characteristics. She must come from a good family so that she has been edu-

Within this type of heavenly assistance, you will be mentally tossed this way and that, and thrown off balance in every way, so that devas can determine which chi routes are blocked and need to be opened. Slowly you will become able to reach higher stages of emptiness attainments, and you will temporarily bump into all sorts of samadhi semblance states along the way. You might see all sorts of visions as well. All sorts of memories and urges will also be stirred into coming up that are linked to chi routes that need to become opened and purified. Tibetan Buddhism calls this the untying of knots in the channels, and there are reactions in consciousness during the process. Going through this whole process is the true tantric cultivation rather than the sexual antics you read about in books, but without merit and wisdom you simply cannot have these experiences. If you think you can just read the Bible, Talmud, Koran, Buddhist scriptures, Taoist scriptures, Vajrayana texts or some other holy books and then receive this sort of help without ever cultivating or performing lots of merit and preliminary meditation work, you are just deceiving yourself.

In Tibetan and Hindu instructional pictures, some dakinis are shown wearing garlands of severed heads, standing on dead bodies atop a chakra, and holding swords, axes, tridents, pokers, staffs, arrows, phurbas, vajras, curved knives or choppers to symbolize the rigorous force of kundalini cutting away or poking away at the blockages within your chi channels and chakra systems. All sorts of schools use these same images, which is

---

cated and has been taught virtuous ways. She must be good natured, intelligent, friendly, respectful, clean living and not promiscuous. Some traditions say her parentage, beauty and behavior must be high enough that she could be selected to be a queen or the chief consort of a king. That beauty will reflect countless past life merits including somewhat flexible channels and the smooth flowing of her chi. She must also be young enough that her body is still healthy and her channels still relatively flexible. She must be familiar with the dharma, meditation and committed to spiritual cultivation. And she should have a reddish mark at either the position of the third eye on the forehead, on the throat, or between the breasts. This signifies that she opened up the third eye, throat or heart chakra from past life cultivation efforts. If too mature then most of her channels would already be closed unless she was an ardent meditation practitioner. As my teacher said, it is nearly impossible for even a Buddha, who has great merit, to find someone with such qualifications. For women it is just as difficult to find an appropriately qualified male partner with good chi and channels who can help her. An apple may look crisp on the outside, but once bitten you know whether it is rotten inside. Thus the outward appearance, while it reflects one's merits, is not as important for partners as is the state of their chi and channels. This is why there is a famous story of a Taoist master who moved in with a pox marked woman also scarred from hot oil burns, for her chi and channels were the only ones that could help him. Those qualified for this method have difficulties finding one another, knowing one another they might not have the karma for sexual relations, and even then they might not know the right techniques of sexual cultivation, or can simply fail to be a good match for one another. Even for the qualified, it is not easy to find a partner who can match you for this technique.

why pictures of the Meso-American deity Quetzalcoatl, who represents kundalini, show a snake's head poking through a hole surrounded by feathers that denote the chi channels.

You can find pictures of dakinis or Buddhas, such as red Vajrayogini, dancing in circles on chakras that represent sexual yang chi techniques related to this instructional mechanism. It takes years of prior pranayama practice, anapana, the white skeleton visualization technique (where you strip off your flesh and offer it away), virtuous living, charitable offerings and other preparatory practices before you might possibly encounter such intensified practices. Pictures of Buddhas in sexual bliss with their consorts often exemplify some other versions of the technique, and sometimes they just represent the harmony between the yin chi and yang chi of the body which should be the natural outcome of cultivation practice. In such pictures there is a natural harmony between the two sexes, which complement one another, but no overt sexual desire.

Whenever you see a male and female in a cultivation picture it often represents the yin and yang chi of the body, or the left and right channels, or front and back channels that must open in a great uninterrupted circulation due to cultivation efforts. Sometimes the duo in sexual embrace represents the pumping action of chi through a specific chakra. Most often, as stated, it represents the chi flow of the microcosmic circulation that connects the *du-mai* with the *jen-mai*, which is why a man and woman are shown in sexual embrace to represent the pumping action felt below. Only an enlightened master will know which interpretation is correct.

The tantric pictures of Buddhas in sexual embrace often refer to the pumping action of the lower chakras which drives chi upwards. This is why the couples are always shown in sitting meditation postures with erect spines rather than in the reclining positions normally used for sex. The pictures have nothing to do with sex but represent a sensation of pumping or squeezing felt most often at the sacral sex chakra as the chi is proceeding upwards. You will definitely tend to feel this pumping during the purification stages of the spiritual path, but it is not something you should become attached to and it disappears as channels are opened and obstructions clear. Once past those initial stages, your chi flow becomes so smooth and regular so that you can forget your body entirely. That's when you can even stop feeling the chi energies in the head called "brain breathing." At the highest stages of an Arhat, the body seems non-existent because of all the transformations it has experienced that purify it. Many

Arhats go into secluded retreat[87] as they go through these transformations so as not to be bothered with the duties of the world and to be able to complete them in peace. Some who achieve liberation choose not to specifically cultivate them with intent, but just let the changes proceed while they attend to worldly affairs.

By letting go of these chi sensations you will allow the body to transform naturally and you can then finally realize a true stage of emptiness by forgetting the existence of the transformed body. However, as an ingrained habit you most certainly are always pushing the chi in your head around this way or that using your thoughts. Once that internal chi flow calms down and becomes smooth, you can stop clinging to those sensations that define the limits of the body. Realizing that the world you see is only your mind, at that point you will be able to let go and cultivate samadhi.

Cultivation is primarily about the mind rather than the body, so physical things are not emphasized on the path because they often lead practitioners astray. Mental cultivation is really the path – to realize that there is no body - and the target of mental cultivation is to initially attain some quiet, peaceful, empty state of mind … and then proceed onwards from there. This is why dakinis are often shown holding an empty skull cup in their hands. It represents the need to let go of the body and need to cultivate an empty mind on the path. An empty skull represents a head free from thought since it is both empty and turned upside down.

Cultivating the natural mind of non-attachment, which we say is empty because it does not hold on to anything, is the true cultivation way, but it is hard to succeed in being open, empty, liberated and natural unless all your chi channels have opened. That is why many schools teach practitioners a variety of preparatory practices to help your progressively learn how to break the habit of clinging to consciousness so you can let go. In terms of the sexual cultivation practices we have been discussing, the empty skull and skeleton pictures you see in Vajrayana clearly indicate that the white skeleton visualization practice is *a necessary precondition* for this sort of technique, as is pranayama practice.

---

[87] You can often read stories of how severe the asceticism can be at this stage, but even more difficult is to remain in the world living a normal life and helping others as the process goes on. As my master often said, this is even more difficult than solitary retreats involving great deprivation, and I believe he is correct. To decide to teach in public, and suffer the inevitable onslaughts from revealing the dharma, also constitutes a great sacrifice as well yet that is the cost of offering. If you say nothing then no one can be helped. If you tell the truth then the ignorant or misinformed will find offense and attack. Hence case after case show the ignorant persecuting the enlightened as well as individuals, especially women, who choose to cultivate.

Naturally the technique of imagined sexual congress is an advanced chi cultivation practice for the path and can only be used by those with an enlightened master and the past karmic connections.[88] Otherwise, everyone watching internet porn or opening a Playboy magazine would say they are spiritually cultivating. Furthermore, this technique cannot be practiced unless you have a very thorough grounding in cultivation theory and study, and have already reached a definite stage of emptiness, non-ego and chi channel purification. This entails years of cultivation effort. Beginning practitioners who have not opened their *sushumna* or other meridians will not even encounter this technique. Of course they will encounter their own sexual energies on the yogic path because they are fundamental energies of the body that begin to become purified on the road of cultivation.

When all the chakras and channels of the body are opened, then as in the story of Krishna or the Yellow Emperor, they are often referred to as obedient wives because your chi has been completely transformed. Some schools instruct practitioners to visualize mandalas, flowers, ancient letters or flames instead of sexual consorts to help open the chakras and channels, and there are many other alternative visualization techniques as well. While it is said that both the kundalini yoga and sexual cultivation teachings came to humans as dharma gifts from the devas of the Desire Realm heavens, many techniques have been invented by human masters who taught them to their students in hopes of their usefulness. You never know which practices might be the most helpful to your own cultivation, so it is proper to try various meditation techniques from the many available to determine their usefulness. However, as a practitioner it is also best to stick to the methods that have traditionally and historically produced the most successes rather than strange esoteric techniques that are colorful but rarely cited.

The legend of Huangdi, the Yellow Emperor of China, whose story suggests that he also succeeded via the tantric cultivation of his body, is fascinating and contains just as many cultivation teachings as Hercules' story. There are several books attributed to Huangdi, such as the *Yellow Emperor's Classic of Internal Medicine* and the *Plain Girl Sutra*. The *Plain Girl Sutra* teaches couples how to have proper sexual relations and how to use sex to heal the body. With sexual relations so easily entered

---

[88] If the motivation for using the technique involves lust you cannot use sexual desire in the path. This is why only advanced adepts, with genuine cultivation attainments, ever encounter such practices.

into nowadays, this is something human beings need to learn. Both of these books are important for cultivators to study, and teachings of an equivalent quality are not found in other cultivation traditions despite dozens of "sexual cultivation" texts in the market from Persia, India and now America. Studying them would be very useful and it's a pity that people in the world don't know too much about them. We still do not have good English translations of these Chinese texts that bring out their full flavor and importance.

Hercules is not going to bed with any women in these labors, so we can surmise that he is not using this type of tantric technique. From the legend's details it is pretty clear that he is using standard cultivation methods to attain some degree of no-thought or empty mind. This labor tells us that Hercules erects two pillars (or splits a mountain into two) which definitely means that he can finally discriminate the yin chi from the yang chi in his body. When that happens, a far left and right chi channel on opposite sides of the body start to be clearly, physically felt and oscillate in turn, which we have already covered.

The discrimination of two chi channels is something we'll see time and again in this story. For instance, a two-headed hound named Orthus, begotten by Typhon on Echidna, was the watch-dog of Geryon's cattle in this story. This two-headed dog represents the connection point between the front and back channels or the left and right channels. In the Labors of Hercules, dogs are always used to represent the conjunction point of multiple channels, and the only question is which ones.

The root chakra at the perineum is always represented as having four petals because the left and right channels connect here and the front and back channels do also. The space chakra at the top of the head is also said to have four petals, too. Though we cannot know for certain, the probability is that Orthus represents the lower interface between the front and back channels.

In addition to finally being able to differentiate the yin chi from the yang chi within his body, the whole Tenth Labor of Hercules is about the fact that Hercules is also able to get the chi flowing freely in the circular orbit of the front and back channels and up the *sushumna* central channel. This is a necessity for the yin and yang energies to finally manifest in this way. Looking down at the body from above, it's as if he opens the compass points in the northern, southern, eastern and western directions. What happens when he first accomplishes this full circulation is that irregularity eventually disappears in the chi circulatory flow for these channels. The chi eventually assumes a smooth circulation through the macrocosmic and microcosmic chi orbits, and there is a fuller opening of the front *jen-mai* channel, too.

In short, by this labor Hercules has finally achieved most of the initial foundation of the physical fruit of the Tao. His achievement is not the Tao but just a good foundation for the higher attainments. The whole process of transforming the body usually takes some ten to twelve years to accomplish after the opening of the *sushumna*, so there is a long way to go after the completion of the Twelve Labors. When we talk of Zen enlightenment or the stages of Zen experience recorded in many record books, these are usually only approached after many more years of hard work at cultivation.

Taoism says it takes about three years to experience the transformation of *shen* to emptiness and the purification of consciousness to the extent that you can let go of the sensation skandha and stop clinging to the body to attain samadhi. Taoism says it takes another nine years of "facing the wall" to forget mind and body entirely to return to the Tao and achieve great enlightenment. This represents around twelve years of cultivation. Confucius measured his progress in decades.

As to realizing the Tao itself, which we call attaining the dharmakaya or self-realization, it is purely a mental attainment and not a physical chi, chakra or channel attainment. Purifying the body simply builds a better foundation for cultivation and spiritual attainments. It allows you to attain samadhi easier, and proficiency at the mental purity of samadhi prepares you for being able to finally realize enlightenment, i.e. realize the dharmakaya. Once you achieve the Tao, however, you should also complete the cultivation of all three Buddha bodies, which include the sambhogakaya and nirmanakaya as well. Many who achieve liberation do not decide to become Buddhas or Bodhisattvas and cultivate all three.

This stage of the Tenth Labor is so important that we should risk repetition and hammer home some of the points again because you won't find them anywhere in print. The repetition will help you see how everything fits together. When you reach the stage where the left and right chi channels become discriminated, you'll often start to feel the chi oscillate between two fairly wide channels on the left and right sides of the body.

Medieval European alchemy represents this stage by the picture of a human with two heads, both male and female. As we discussed earlier, the yin and yang channels, represented as female and male heads in western alchemical texts, become the two horns of Isis in the Egyptian spiritual tradition and the extra two faces on the sides of three-faced Buddhas (the central face representing the *sushumna*) in Asia. In Hinduism the accomplishment of opening and purifying these channel flows is also often represented by a beautiful three-faced being.

The problem with such pictures is that people fall into religion and superstition when viewing them without understanding that they simply represent a stage of cultivation accomplishment. Otherwise, what is a spiritual being going to do with horns on their head or all these extra faces?

All sorts of cultures have beautiful pictures of a wide variety of heavenly beings, protector gods, deities, gods and goddesses who have succeeded in these attainments. The goddess Hecate in Greek mythology, who is also often shown with three faces, is an example of another enlightened woman who accomplished this feat. Her two extra faces do not represent stages of life, but the fact that she opened up her left and right channels which can be symbolized by an older and younger body. The opening of those channels is used to suggest that she attained the Tao. Cultivation schools shine the spotlight on the left and right channel openings because it's the easiest symbol by which to summarily denote the achievement of the whole set of channel openings. Also, it is one of the most memorable of the spiritual achievements, and therefore a highly recognizable signpost for practitioners who get this far in their own attainments. You can readily feel the chi rocking back and forth between these two channels when they open, you can feel the width of these channels, and you can feel the entire length of these channels themselves.

Speaking of these symbols, when you see various items in the hands of accomplished Buddhas or deities, they usually represent various aspects of spiritual cultivation, too. For instance the axes in the hand of Dictynna, Goddess of Crete, represent the fact that kundalini can cut through any channel obstruction in the body. The fact she is dressed in nets represents the resting phase of kundalini in the root chakra, the same phenomenon being represented by a coiled snake with scales[89] in Indian symbolism.

Spiritual masters from different lands often represent the same phenomenon a bit differently in order to better connect with their cultures and make it easier for individuals in their lineages to recognize

---

[89] The snake scales, usually that of a cobra, are equivalent to the pattern of the nets if they were impressed upon the skin.

that particular stage of attainment when they reach it. While they may represent things differently, however, accomplished masters across traditions refer to the same phenomena time and time again because everyone who cultivates sufficiently ends up experiencing the same phenomena. Whether or not a master emphasizes them or even tells discusses them is an entirely different issue in itself, but since that's what our story is about, that is our particular focus.

As we have stated, the three-pronged trident of Shiva, also held by many other religious figures such as Poseidon (Neptune), represents the ascent of kundalini up the *sushumna* from the point where the central channel meets the left and right channels below. It takes a lot of cultivation work to open that passageway but Hercules already achieved this when he cleansed the Aegean stables in the Fifth Labor. The *Six Yogas of Naropa* emphasizes various cultivation techniques to open this particular interface.

Pictures of Quetzalcoatl, a Mesoamerican deity also known as the "feathered serpent," sometimes show a snake's head surrounded by a ring of feathers that represent kundalini energy piercing through a chakra. The feathers symbolize the spokes, petals or branches of the chi channels extending outward from the pierced chakra. With Isis it is the feathers of her wings which represent all the opened chi channels of her body. In each case, the symbols used will vary by culture but they still refer to the same non-denominational stages of the spiritual path.

Statues of Diana of Epheseus (the Greek goddess Artemis) show her wearing garments adorned with yang chi animals to symbolize that kundalini energies have fully opened up her set of chi channels, too. Her unique headdress represents the opening of her crown chakra while its left and right veils represent the left and right channels. Her multiple breasts, like the feathers of Isis, represent the many opened channels and chakras of the body with their various chi flows and distributions.

A mother's breast milk is nurturance and sustenance for a baby, and thus breasts were chosen to symbolize her opened chakras and channels because she is a great mother for her people. Out of humility women cover their breasts but when displayed like this they are a means of teaching and represent offering. Sometimes Medicine Buddhas are shown holding bowls of multi-colored medicine pills in their hands and while different, this has some similar, overlapping connotations.

Artemis/Diana symbolically displays the internals of her beautified, accomplished sambhogakaya as a compassionate offering to help motivate human beings to achieve the Tao and be as compassionate as she is. She represents the Mahayana way of offering oneself to help others just as any great mother would. You should know that both men and women can succeed on the cultivation path from her example. Women who succeed often choose to become protectors of peoples, cultures, nations, and traditions[90] just as men do, which is amply illustrated by the many goddesses of Indian tradition who became "great mothers." This is one of the major avenues of the Bodhisattva way for women who succeed. Artemis/Diana represents not a deity but a woman who succeeded and subsequently became a guide and protector of cultivation, people and culture. She is another example of the compassionate Mahayana way.

Antipater of Sidon, who compiled a list of the Seven Wonders of the Ancient World, often called the Temple of Artemis the most brilliant of all the seven wonders. We might think of it as a testament to the excellence of the Mahayana road of universal compassion represented by Artemis' status as a "great mother." The highest achievement in spiritual cultivation is Buddhahood, which does not just entail perfect self-realization but the commitment to help all beings in the universe, for they are really just yourself. Buddhahood means serving as a great mother, father or protector who dispenses infinite compassionate action on behalf of all beings, the foremost of which is leading them to enlightenment. We may honor the physical accomplishments of heroes such as Hercules, but the spiritual path all comes down to your exercise of compassionate behavior to help others in many different ways, the foremost being leading them to self-realization. Since enlightenment enables you to jump out of the realm of suffering forever, the gift of dharma (enlightenment) teachings and instruction is inarguably the highest of all possible offerings.

Naturally, enlightened beings or heavenly beings don't have bodies that look like Artemis of Ephesus. They don't necessarily have multiple heads, arms or the other unusual features of the beautified bodies presented in various religions. However, out of their kindness and compassion the enlightened Buddhas often project fanciful forms like this as a type of teaching method for learners, and these too are nirmanakaya projections or emanations. They are only meant to represent the beautified, purified sambhogakaya.

The "*vishvarupa*" of Hinduism, such as the transfiguration *vishvarupa* (universal form) of Krishna shown to Arjuna on the battle field of

---

[90] Athena was the patron goddess of Athens and many other Greek cities while Isis was the protector of Egypt.

Kurukshetra, is another example of a sambhogakaya representation. Enlightened beings hope in exhibiting these beautified forms that people will in turn be inspired to cultivate. They therefore use beautified bodies as a form of teaching in dreams, visions, etc. in order to inspire respect for cultivation teachings, motivate people to help preserve the spiritual teachings, and encourage spiritual practitioners to work hard to make further progress.

The achievement of the sambhogakaya represented in these depictions is the highest state of physical excellence one can possibly achieve as a human being, but it only has importance if you are devoted to helping all beings. Otherwise, why cultivate a body of the most purified form of the five elements, "akin to light," that is almost endless? You can only cultivate the sambhogakaya if you never take or hold on to any body, form, or appearance as the self, as the Tao, or as the accomplishment of the Tao. As Shakyamuni Buddha said in the *Diamond Sutra*, "If you seek me in form or sound you will never realize the original nature."

Even a purified reward body is as effervescent as a dewdrop, lightning flash, bubble, dream or phantasm. It is not the true reward body of the Tao because the original nature itself is the true sambhogakaya, so one must never get attached to any type of physical or purified chi body. As the Sixth Patriarch of Zen said, the real sambhogakaya is the original nature itself. You must never fall into the belief that there is such a thing as a permanent, eternal physical body.

The ancient Greeks honored Artemis/Diana's cultivation by having her figure struck on coins showing her either with a staff of entwined serpents (which clearly represent the rising kundalini energy) or the *ouroboros* eternal serpent with its tail in its mouth (which represents the connected orbit of the front and back chi channels). Since the *ouroboros* represents the connected circular orbit of the front and back chi channels linked together, namely the hookup between the *du-mai* and the *jen-mai* chi channels,[91] clearly Artemis/Diana is connected with the path of spiritual cultivation. All the schools describe this orbit in some way because you always eventually feel it at the lowest stages of the path.

If you also wonder why Artemis is featured so prominently in the labors of Hercules, it is because she is the goddess of the hunt, which often represents cultivation. The activity of hunting, or stalking game, is the unique Greek way of representing the striving for spiritual

---

[91] See Emblem XIV in the *Atalanta Fugiens* of Michael Maier. Also, the Leviathan of Vast Face in Jewish Kabbalah theory, represented by a snake swallowing its own tail, is a similar image.

progress in an activity based culture.[92] Hunting is a pursuit that requires patience, and the path of cultivation is all about committed effort with patient endurance. Hunting is typically a male occupation, but Artemis represents the processes and stages of the spiritual path since it entails the transformation of both yin and yang which a female, doing a man's activities, clearly represents. The ancients proved through their art and literature that they knew countless cultivation details because, as stated, they are non-denominational phenomena for all spiritual practitioners.

The ancients were not so ignorant as to be oblivious to the road of spiritual cultivation as we are today. Today we label many ancient peoples as pagan, but that does not mean that spiritual cultivation was non-existent, or that people were not subject to codes of conduct, that virtue was not prized and ethics were absent. It is because so many people achieved some stage of attainment that so many dissimilar cultures have vested their cultural figures with symbols of these same stages of gong-fu.

If you just rest your mind and cultivate an empty mind by letting go, you too will definitely attain the spiritual path and its fruits regardless of your tradition, so nothing could be more non-denominational than this. Spiritual attainments are a totally natural, non-artificial by-product of the process of abandoning mental clinging, a habit so ingrained that you do not even know you are doing it. The labors of Hercules are simply the western representation of the sequential gong-fu stages that occur along the spiritual path, the cultivation challenges one meets along the way, and some of the methods for overcoming the difficulties encountered.

Go east, go west and the spiritual path, process and gong-fu attainments are the same. Even the spiritual practices people use across religions are usually the same essential exercises tweaked a little differently in opposing traditions. That's what we find in the Twelve Labors of Hercules.

Over the last two thousand years we have lost this basic understanding of the spiritual, physical and mental transformations involved within the process of spiritual striving, something I am trying to help restore by transmitting all this material to you. We have chucked all the real stuff that works aside, and instead pursue academic knowledge, ceremonies of religious worship, disciplinary rules (Sharia law, Talmudic codes, etc.) of purity and other roads that we think will liberate us, but which will not

---

[92] Artemis is often shown carrying a bow and arrows to represent the spine and central chi channel, or with the javelin which, like the trident of Shiva, represents the activity of chi poking through the channels.

lead to any higher spiritual attainments at all. Nothing. Nada. Zippo. Nevertheless, search within even the orthodox religions and you will find many of the basic cultivation teachings we have gone over as well as the same common principles and techniques of spiritual practice.

It *has to be* that way, but it is up to you to throw aside the ignorance and discover this for yourself. The discovery all depends upon your wisdom and merit. Whatever you do, you have to start devoting yourself to true spiritual cultivation practice to achieve anything along these lines in life. The universe is endless, and if you don't start now you will most probably be lost next life as well, and who can say that your next life (or lives) will be better than this one? It is better to start cultivating when one knows the purpose and techniques. Never lose your chance when it comes to spiritual cultivation.

As a society we have in many ways turned the compass upside down and have been headed in the wrong direction, but we can still turn around and start heading in the right direction once again. It just starts with learning how to let go and relax the mind, and there is nothing, absolutely nothing denominational or evil about this sort of meditation practice. If something happens because you learn how to rest the mind and let go of clinging to consciousness, it would take a twisted individual to somehow turn the results into something evil, misleading or unnatural. From the attainment of being natural achieved by abandoning all the invisible habits of mental clinging, all sorts of spiritual results will follow. This is the pathway for "finding God," which is the objective of both eastern and western religions.

The problem today is that people don't know how to relax anymore so that their mental afflictions can die down. With the world becoming ever speedier and complex, the true spiritual pathway is getting buried under more and more sand. Our minds are becoming burdened with stresses and anxieties unknown to ancient ways of life. The simple truth remains: religion will not save you in this new environment if it simply means participation in rules of discipline, rituals, ceremonial worship and study. You must devote yourself to what Christianity calls the process of "deification," "divinization" or "theosis," which are the Christian terms for the practice of spiritual cultivation to "become one with the Father." Even Christianity recognizes the need for genuine spiritual striving past basic church attendance, and yet this basic fact has become buried underneath the dogmas of over 33,000 different Christian denominations.[93] Nevertheless I must tell you that the ultimate that a human being can achieve in this lifetime is accomplished through a path of proper spiritual practice.

Male or female, you can reach all the stages of spiritual accomplishment Hercules has thus far experienced if you start to devote yourself to meditation practice. It's not beyond you and can be attained in one life, or at most three lives for those who are slow going. For the highest spiritual accomplishment possible as a human, or for the highest possible human excellence, you need to cultivate your mind and your behavior. Only the cultivation of a mind of clear awareness that knows thoughts but which does not cling to them enables you to achieve this. The phenomena within your consciousness are ephemeral and transitory, so why are you clinging to them every moment? When you let go of holding on to consciousness (such as body sensations) your chi will change, your energy channels will open, your mind will open and purify, and you will finally be on the path to the spiritual progress which religious participation is supposed to be about.

The general public remains quite ignorant as to the true path of spiritual practice and all the accompanying physical gong-fu on the spiritual trail which we are describing. Rather, the public mostly engages in religious ceremonies, rituals, and activities that really won't earn anyone a high stage of spiritual attainment. However, the actual way is simple: all you must do is rest the mind from clinging to the experiences of the body and mind; the real you has no body. Thus this practice is the most natural, non-sectarian, non-artificial, non-evil, logical, and virtuous activity possible. Start practicing it and you are on your way. This teaching is even in the Bible in various places,[94] yet people still don't realize the teaching or practice it! All synagogues, temples, mosques and churches should be teaching meditation and the stages of achievement, but no one is doing so.

When you relax the mind by letting thoughts come and go without clinging, you will find eventual peace and still be at maximum effectiveness for dealing with the world. You will perfectly adapt to everything and every place, every situation and circumstance. You can perform every activity quite well without identifying with them and imagining you are

---

[93] Barrett's *World Christian Encyclopedia*, published by Oxford University Press, counts over 33,830 different Christian denominations. It also identifies over 10,000 distinct religions, of which 150 have one million or more followers. For brevity's sake, in this book we only concentrate on examples from the largest and most well known religions.

[94] Just a few examples being Psalm 46:10, Psalm 37:7, Psalm 131:2, Psalm 65:2, and Psalm 62:1.

the doer. You will abandon worries, stress and vexing passions, and you will finally attain purity. You will experience that *and* you will still attain your maximum capability for functioning in the world fulfilling your duties or performing whatever you choose to take as your calling. Your effectiveness will not decrease but will increase just as taking a holiday vacation ends up refreshing and empowering you. In actual fact your capability for accomplishing tasks increases and your wisdom expands the more that you spiritually cultivate, enabling you to accomplish virtually whatever you like.

My own teacher built the first private railway in China with virtually no money in his hands, and accomplished countless other great deeds in the fields of politics, business, and education because of his cultivation. Enlightened Confucius was a skilled administrator and politician who helped eliminate major troubles in every capacity for which he was employed. Both Kuan Tzu and Zhuge Liang attained the Tao and became Chinese prime ministers who accomplished great things for their country, so much so that their names are still widely known today. I could list countless other individuals who succeeded in cultivation and whose worldly record and influence proves that you never become useless by adopting the cultivation way.[95] It empowers you. It increases your capability. Your wisdom and capabilities grow beyond that of normal men. All men and women who truly wish to be great should cultivate. It is the one thing you should do in life regardless of your station or calling.

[95] As just a very few additional examples from my own teacher's case, he got China and Taiwan to meet in secret on unification talks, saved the cultivation schools of Taoism, Confucianism and Buddhism from China's Cultural Revolution by bringing them to Taiwan to preserve them, corrected many errors of interpretation that had crept in over the years, and then helped return them to Communist China through the publication of millions of books (an accomplishment on par with Tsong Khapa's), solved endless strategy problems for businessmen, gave out numerous bottles of medicine to students and visitors with specific problems, provided countless university presidents with ideas on new departments to be opened and strategies for growing their institutions, and untiringly counseled high level government and military officials on large scale geopolitical and internal development strategies and other difficult matters too numerous to recount. There were countless instances where he would tell someone to do something right away that, if they immediately listened to him (though the act might have been difficult), ended up saving their life (or business or wealth, etc.) from some unforeseen catastrophe that would strike in a few days time. I cannot even begin to go into all the accomplishments of this man who, because he attained the Tao, also knows how to hide from the limelight and remain invisible despite his contributions. It is hard to imagine how much more effective he would have been had he had money or power in his hands. People think those who become enlightened fall into the category of useless religious people or individuals who accomplish nothing for the world, but this is not so. As I have tried to show you, the enlightened become extremely active and the ultimate protectors of nations, cultures, peoples and spiritual cultivation teachings.

Everything you want can be obtained or accomplished through the route of true spiritual cultivation. You do not have to be a monk or even be "religious" to succeed on the path but can simply continue following whatever you want to do. So what are you waiting for? What teachings are you missing? What's preventing you from getting started? I've told you everything. You simply need to start learning how to rest the mind, and that means practicing meditation. There are lots of cultivation techniques you can try, from mantra and visualization practice to watching your mind and so forth. Nearly all the religions have these methods, which should prompt you to reason out the why! Once you start practicing meditation and make progress you will start to experience all these sequences of chi and channel transformations.

If you learn how to just rest the mind, you will put yourself "in tune with God," and all that should transpire, as the epitome of perfection, will do so quite naturally. This is the natural basis of the spiritual path enshrined within genuine religions. It is the most natural, non-sectarian practice there is, something not opposed by any religion and something that cannot in any way be classified as "evil," "pagan," "agnostic" or any of the other derogatory things that religious professionals usually throw at something when they fear the loss of their power, prestige, followers and money flows. We are simply revealing some of the major gong-fu stages of the spiritual advancement process for beginners, and the records show that these same phenomena happen to the accomplished members of all religions. Spiritual gong-fu is just part of the all important science of human beings, but it is funny that no one is studying it and making the connections.

While we have been discussing the physical gong-fu of the path, you must be told that the detailed explanations for the stages of mental purification during the journey can be found in Buddhism and many other eastern cultivation schools. The eastern schools offer the best directions on this aspect because it is hard to find clear teachings on these matters within the western orthodox religions,[96] and yet they contain relevant teachings as well. All genuine schools contain teachings on mental purification and noble human behavior, for this is a non-denominational outcome of the path, too.

---

[96] You might, for instance, find many of the gong-fu phenomena that fall out of the spiritual cultivation path catalogued in Roman Catholic encyclopedias, which thus recognize their existence, but you won't find explanations behind the phenomena or details on how to cultivate them or pass through them to progress to the next stages of accomplishment.

There are many possible rewards for spiritual practice, but two are most often cited in particular: going to heaven as an intermediate step of spiritual progress, or attaining the Tao where you jump out of everything and can then select wherever you want to go and whatever you want to do in subsequent incarnations.

There is no state of ultimate physical rest in the universe, and karma rules all our comings and goings until you reach a stage where the mind transcends karma. In finding one's underlying pristine awareness that is not bound by consciousness, one's mind is no longer controlled by the promptings of consciousness. This is why enlightened Zen masters can find outrageously successful solutions to incredibly difficult situational dilemmas – their minds are free of the ties of consciousness and can react to the necessities of the moment by going outside of normal conventions. An ordinary mind, however, is attached to the thoughts of consciousness and therefore bound by karma. All karmic states are impermanent, having a beginning and an end.

Thus while there are many teachings targeting a heavenly rebirth (since it is the low end goal of most religious instruction), back down again you will eventually come after your heavenly merit is all used up. Then where will you be? In fact, because of reincarnation you will endlessly bob up and down over and over again, through incarnation after incarnation, until you finally decide enough is enough and you want to put an end to all the suffering by attaining the Tao. It's like the habit of smoking where you may want to quit but you won't actually stop until you *really* want to quit and then choose to make the effort.

It's at that decision point, where you finally start taking the crucial steps to become liberated, that the Buddhas, Bodhisattvas and heavenly beings can finally help you the most with your spiritual progress. You have to make the decision to spiritually cultivate and show your commitment through practice. Then help will come, deep help will come.

To say that "the Buddhas will help you" has nothing to do with Buddhism because the saying just means that *enlightened* beings will help you. "Buddha" has nothing to do with Buddhism but is simply a short word to indicate anyone who attains the spiritual accomplishment of enlightenment. If you are Jewish and become enlightened you are called a Buddha, if you are Muslim and reach self-realization we say you become a Buddha. While I like using the single word "Buddha," you should not take this in a religious way and get hung up on names or religions on the road of spiritual cultivation. It's just short hand for saying "enlightened being" all the time. Hence, just look for the proper cultivation teachings, wherever they may be found, for all spiritual roads collect pollution after a long time. You should always benchmark and select the best from whatever schools are available, and that's why I commonly use this term.

Spiritual cultivation teachings of some type are always available in the world, but not necessarily the high Consciousness-Only teachings or gong-fu explanations we have been discussing. There is a general rule for most things that the "bad drives out the good" over time and matters drop to the lowest common denominators, so the highest teachings are usually lost or destroyed due to the bad karma of human beings. Shakyamuni Buddha, for instance, prophesied that his own teachings would quickly deteriorate in India because the karma and wisdom of the people was simply insufficient to maintain them. Buddhism in India was only embraced by the highest and most intelligent portion of the populace, and therefore was destined to die out. The public always just prefers rules for living and ceremonies or prayers that might allow them to calm their minds or get what they want.

Everything phenomenal is destined to pass away, so it is no surprise that nations, cultures, races and even religions have all been destroyed and disappeared throughout history. Shelley's famous poem of Ozymandias reminds us clearly of this inevitable fate of impermanence, which Taoism calls "transformation" and the *I-Ching* calls "change."[97] That is the definite outcome of all things in a relative world of impermanence. Christianity, Judaism, Islam, Taoism, Buddhism … despite their popularity now they will all disappear in time and other religions will rise to replace them. No one can promise you that correct spiritual teachings will always be available to you in future lives, especially if you waste your chances to cultivate now and establish a positive karmic relationship with a bona

---

[97] I met a traveller from an antique land
Who said: Two vast and trunkless legs of stone
Stand in the desert. Near them, on the sand,
Half sunk, a shattered visage lies, whose frown
And wrinkled lip, and sneer of cold command
Tell that its sculptor well those passions read
Which yet survive, stamped on these lifeless things,
The hand that mocked them and the heart that fed.
And on the pedestal these words appear:
`My name is Ozymandias, King of Kings:
Look on my works, ye mighty, and despair!'
Nothing beside remains. Round the decay
Of that colossal wreck, boundless and bare,
The lone and level sands stretch far away".

fide path and practices. One should always seize any chances to support the teachers, practitioners and roads of genuine cultivation practice, wherever they may be, because this, too, will help contribute to your ultimate success.

Do not lose your chance to cultivate, establish a relationship with real spiritual teachings, or support genuine cultivation teachings and help to re-establish them so that they are here for others *and you* on your return. That is establishing real merit for the universe. As the *Diamond Sutra* says, to personally practice, promote, transmit, support, and re-establish true cultivation teachings for the Tao earns more merit than almost anything else you can possibly do in the universe other than achieve the Tao yourself. True spiritual cultivation is the road to the true bliss promised by all religious scriptures because it is by cultivation that you reach the ultimate Source of *all* spiritual paths and jump out of the false phenomenal realm of suffering. Someone must tell you about the Supreme Reality and the way that leads to it, but are you supporting that? What are you actually supporting?

Now, since we are talking about the phenomenal differentiation of yin chi and yang chi in this labor, when you start cultivating you may sometimes feel the yin chi or yang chi of your body for a few moments, and thereby get confused. Feeling the yin chi of the body, a person may feel more feminine even if they are a man. Feeling the yang chi, a woman sometimes feels more masculine. This even happens to ordinary people in society who do not cultivate at all but whose minds are a bit emptier, "looser" or quieter than others. For the physical nature, hormones play a part in this as well.

This is a natural phenomenon due to chi, but those feelings sometimes confuse people. All you are doing is momentarily feeling the yin chi or yang chi of the body when the two become differentiated from one another. You are not actually turning into a member of the opposite sex, or one who has such inclinations. You should not run with the feeling but just understand why it is happening, let go, and it will transform as the chi continues to purify and relevant channels open. On the path of cultivation you will sometimes feel the full mass of yin chi or yang chi like this.

In another story about Hercules, but not part of the Twelve Labors, there is actually a short lesson on this phenomenon. In that story Hercules inadvertently kills a man and as punishment is sold as a slave to a Queen Omphale. During this time, Omphale wore his Nemean lion skin and carried his olive-wood club while Hercules was forced to wear women's clothes and do women's work. Obviously, the positions of yin and yang are being switched in the story.[98] Hercules even had to hold a basket of wool while Omphale and her maidens spun it into yarn (representing work on the chi channels). After his time was done, Hercules was eventually freed and Omphale married him, showing the eventual balancing of the yin and yang energies once again.

This tale refers to the balancing of yin and yang chi in the body where the two energies even switch positions for a short while. Hercules wore women's clothing to show there comes a period in cultivation when the body's yin chi is felt everywhere for a short time and predominates over the yang. All the chi channels dealing with yin energies open and it is yin energy that you feel when that flooding occurs.

Naturally this type of feeling only lasts for a few minutes rather than a year, but like all transformative stages it is so striking and out of the ordinary that you definitely notice it. Such things happen briefly on the cultivation trail for people who really cultivate their bodies on a deep level, but the experience is beyond the reach of ordinary cultivators. In any case, after going through this type of experience, you will quickly become in balance once again.

This necessary balancing of the yin and yang energies within the body is why the very earliest original form of Esoteric Buddhism showed pictures of male Buddhas together with their female consorts, but

---

[98] This simply means that all the chi channels open, and that both yin and yang chi purify. For instance, we sometimes hear a woman say today she "discovered her sexuality" after letting go during sex to a degree she never could previously. The right type of letting go or surrendering without losing energy (a form of emptiness cultivation), while the yang chi is rising due to the stimulation of sexual activities, often provides a small opportunity for the chi channels to open. During the changes experienced as her channels open and the chi spreads out, she might anxiously wonder "what's happening to me?" because of all the powerful feelings that arise. One often "feels alive for the first time" as new virility routes and chi circulations start opening. In sports this is also sometimes experienced as well when there is a true surrendering or letting go as the body's energies are pumping, and so some athletes try to find themselves through sport and recapture that feeling of "flow" but can only at best open up minor channels within the body. As closed or shunted chi channels open, an individual will always begin to feel virility and vitality in new areas of the body. As one's chi changes and channels open then one's consciousness will also transform. With the right type of meditation practice to keep the process going, one's "mind will open" accordingly as the chi purification progresses. One becomes more alive as well as more open, caring, and accepting of events and others. The personality "warms" or softens. This can happen to a small degree for some people through sex or athletics performed in the right way but the most profound and deepest changes can only be accomplished by cultivating meditation, the results of which are seen in the Twelve Labors. Know for sure that sex is absolutely not the pathway to the Tao, but in following the correct virtue and wisdom principles, sexual relations can serve as an assist rather than a detriment to one's spiritual efforts.

without engaging in sexual relations. They simply sat next to one another in harmony. The principle to understand is that the yin and yang energies of the body must eventually harmonize in a natural way by becoming balanced, but as this labor points out, there is a short time where you will feel that they sometimes oscillate in the channels or manifest as full body experiences while the chi, chakras and channels are being purified. During the purification of the channels a person will undergo many emotional experiences, and so as not to be bothered or interrupted with worldly concerns, many masters go into retreat when they are at such stages of physical and mental transformation.

It takes a long time to transform your chi, chakras and channels, just as it takes a long time to lose weight or do something difficult like change the typical thought patterns or traditions of a nation. It cannot be done overnight. To assist the process at certain stages, in some schools of Tibetan Vajrayana and Hindu tantra, men are sometimes told by an enlightened Esoteric master to visualize becoming a female Buddha like Vajrayogini while women are sometimes instructed to visualize becoming a male Buddha. This is just a chi practice and only used for a short while. At other times, to help get over sexual desire and a natural tendency to focus on the lower regions when it arises, they might be taught to envision a Buddha and consort having intercourse over the crown of their head.

These practices are all just expedient means, medicines to cure temporarily illnesses. They are used for just a short while until the situation passes. They are used as a way to engender concentration or help open up certain chi channels, and are not to be taken as some sort of physical transmutation. It is like holding a special yoga pose for a short while to help therapeutically stretch or open a muscle. There are all sorts of practices like this, which masters have developed to help people balance their bodies and transform their energies, but those methods are not to be clung to. For instance, the Hindu sage Ramakrishna performed a different sort of tantric practice by imitating a female for a short while, as recommended in some tantric literature, to see what it would do for his chi and channel transformation.

Spiritual masters – and most often those without teachers themselves - often test cultivation practices that have been written about in ancient texts to verify them like this. My master, as an example, would practice all sorts of samadhi just to see the end result and compare it with ancient scriptures. For instance, at one time he cultivated the samadhi of non-knowing ignorance for a few weeks just to see what the effect really would be.

As to Ramakrishna, he cultivated dozens and dozens of different Indian tantric techniques. Some "scholars" mistakenly took Ramakrishna's yin cultivation as a form of homoeroticism because they lacked sufficient cultivation knowledge and gong-fu, misunderstanding the fact that Ramakrishna performed dozens of different tantric practices to see their effect on his body. Masters often try different techniques in different lives, and this might have been a case of investigating the effectiveness of techniques other than sexual practice for helping to quickly transform the human body's chi and channels. Even the life story of the celibate sage Shankaracharya hinted at this possibility at using sex in cultivation matters, but most enlightened individuals (and certainly monks and nuns) wisely avoid this route because of all the dangers, troubles and complications. Buddhas and Bodhisattvas are always trying to invent new techniques to help human beings pass certain difficult stages in their cultivation because the human body is such a deterrent to the path. It is just like Mahatma Gandhi's practice of trying out different diets to see their effect on his body. Great masters often test ancient teachings like this to see what is right and what is wrong because not everything passed down from the past, especially in cultivation matters, is valid.

This is one of the reasons we have so many strange dogmas passed down within cultures and religions; no one has bothered to verify them to correct them. Even when corrected, many will still cling to the past because ignorant people are often afraid to kill off ancient traditions even when they are harmful or wrong. Hence, the dust collects on everything after a while, and practices that should have been abandoned ages ago are maintained in societies even though harmful, incorrect, ignorant, or just outdated.

Bodhisattvas who practice medicine often try herbs out on themselves to see their effects, as another example, and in this way they can learn what the herbs do and which ones can help people in which manner. You must always be careful with such techniques and employ your wisdom to the maximum because many individuals in the past who tested medicinal substances on themselves have died because of accidental poisoning. Just because you have samadhi does not mean you will not die from poison! Cultivation is all about science and wisdom. It is not about stupidity or superstition or blindly following others and tossing logic or safety out the window.

Many masters try a variety of practices once they have reached a certain level in their cultivation because they want to know what certain practices are like, what they will do, and whether they can or cannot help cultivation students. You cannot trust all the reports in ancient books but have to sieve the information through wisdom, personal experience and self-authentication. Shakyamuni Buddha even said so himself, saying "Don't believe me but just test everything I say, and then decide." If most religions went by that scoring system then countless cherished religious dogmas would certainly fail the test.

If you don't try things out for yourself, sometimes you just cannot know the ins or outs of a particular samadhi or cultivation technique and what it will actually do for you. Scholars and religious functionaries, who we most often turn to, don't understand any of these cultivation topics because they lack the necessary learning and spiritual gong-fu themselves, so why they feel qualified to even comment and why people listen to them is beyond me. All they ever seem to do, despite brilliant intellects, is make major mistakes that thwart the ability for ordinary people to succeed on the path. It is like selecting a diet that is personally best for you. The fact is that many different types of diet abound, but because of genetic individuality and your own personal habits you'll have to test them to determine which one will best work for you.

It takes time to reach a state of balance between the yin and yang energies in your body. This always eventually happens because your real mind is neither male nor female, and it does not cling to any type of energy. All those things are ultimately fictitious. The mind is neither male nor female, just as the original nature is neither yin nor yang but beyond all phenomenal forms, attributes and characteristics. In cultivation you must trace your consciousness, or ordinary mind, back to this attributeless source which is beyond consciousness and all characteristics whatsoever. That is the underlying Supreme Reality.

You cannot say that the enlightened Buddha Kuan Yin (Avalokitesvara), for instance, is definitively either male or female because Kuan Yin can appear in any form as required to help sentient beings. We simply have the fact that living beings are born into a particular gender simply due to karma, and after one or more lives their gender may change as will their race, country, religion and so forth. People hold tightly to their present religious views not recognizing that they are ultimately destined to change, and the new religion you will eventually inherit is just another set of views you will defend most fiercely until you are born into a different tradition once again. As to your own gender in this life, trying to manifest oneself as the opposite gender produces an unnatural imbalance in your chi, and certainly difficulties in real life and cultivation.

It does not matter what gender you start with in this life. Both male and female can succeed at enlightenment just as we have seen. In terms of reincarnation, your gender is simply a phenomenon you inherit due to karma so it's not an absolute phenomenon. Your gender changes all the time and therefore the male or female body you have during this life is your present starting point for spiritual success, so go for it rather than "wait for better circumstances." There is no better time to start than now, and each gender has certain advantages. Gender changes all the time throughout incarnations as does your country, race, and religion, so don't mistake that as an obstacle to the Path. Therefore you should not get attached to either the yin chi or yang chi when it manifests in your body but just ignore the sensations and let them pass since they are not the real you.

Don't over-emphasize one sensation or another that arises in your body. Just be natural, which means abiding in the natural mind, which is empty, and ignore what is not you. What comes comes and what goes goes and you simply should react as is natural without being attached.

The big problem for most cultivators is that they are always attaching to the body consciousness, which is made up of the feelings and sensations of the body. We anchor ourselves to the body sensations and mistakenly say, "This is me." We identify with the body and take it as our self whereas the physical sensations we feel are just the body energies reacting from some type of contact. Your mind simply experiences that sensory input and you mistakenly take it as the basis of a self. You form this idea that you are the body, and then a memory that you are the body, and constantly attach to this memory. The real you, however, transcends the mind which knows these sensations, and the body.

We constantly push play with the chi in our head, pushing it around with our thoughts, and also attach to all sorts of body sensations throughout the day. Once you detach from the body you can realize that you don't need to do this and in fact, it gains you nothing. Space, the universe, thoughts, appearances … all things appear within your mind, because of your mind. To you they are just consciousness. Everything you experience is just your mind – you are experiencing your consciousness. What you see, smell, taste, feel, hear and think is all consciousness. You can only experience consciousness and nothing else. As to the sense organs that are constantly stimulating consciousness and providing it with input, there is a universal pristine awareness that seemingly appropriates the body, shining through its sense organs to make sensory consciousness possible. That one single consciousness manifests itself as the "I-thought" within the individual and projects itself through the senses to make seeing, smelling, hearing and so on possible. Because of the body and the mistake of clinging, you ignorantly mistake existence as something individualized, but there really is no such thing as a separate being, ego, personality or life in the universe because this pristine base awareness is one unity. What gets liberated through spiritual cultivation is the consciousness, because there is no entity. The idea of a truly existing separate individual or self is false because it is just this one awareness that is operating through the vehicles of all bodies, and the idea of the self is a fiction brought about by wrongly identifying with the body and "I-thought" that arise because of it. Consciousness gets tied up in ignorance and imagines a self.

In cultivation you must find that pristine awareness that is always there as a bedrock. It is one homogenous whole that is aware of all that is and not limited to consciousness. Therefore you should just let things appear and disappear, arise and depart in your mind without holding because it's that stationary, foundational essence you want to find. Other things just arise and disappear all the time in your mind, so these non-stationary objects aren't the real you and don't represent true reality. They represent a dream world held together by laws of interdependence (cause and effect), and everything within this dream world, though arising on the basis of certain rules of cause and effect, is momentary and ungraspable. Mind exists and lets you experience a world because there is an underlying clear basis of awareness, which is like a void (not empty space, but an absence of everything) that is empty of all characteristics, and yet it gives birth to thoughts and images. Those images are appearances within it, and so they are one with its essential nature. Those appearances don't truly exist for even a fractional Planck second, but are simply empty appearances, like the images in a mirror that lack any true substance, and held together by cause and effect. It is through cultivation that you can ultimately find this underlying clear basis that is self-so, uncaused, pure, real and changeless, which makes it eternal.

In Zen this pristine awareness is still considered a guest rather than the ultimate Host (meaning that the self-illumination of the Host is an attribute of the Host one should not cling to, though of course identical with the Host), and so we say that the ultimate Host is unknowable. In that original state there is no experience, so you can only be That without experiencing That. In that state of One, there is awareness that is not aware of its awareness, and hence there is no subject or object, birth or death, thought or experience. Since there is no subject and object there is no witnessing as an entity. It is a no-knowing state. You can be It, but not know It with the awareness that is its function. In the state of manifestation, however, apparent knowers seem to appear, but the "I" that they use all relates back to the One Self without their realization. The One True Self is everybody's same True Self. There are, in actuality, no individual doers. One undifferentiated consciousness assumes all the roles of the supposedly independent doers or experiencers in one great big dream play.

Because you are beyond consciousness you cannot say what you are, yet you are … and yet what you are is undefined. The real self is beyond the witness, but to realize it one must first realize the state of pure witnessing that is inherent in all spiritual practice. You must first discover that you are the changeless witness of the river of consciousness that flows by, which always transforms but never changes or alters the pure witnessing in any way. Your own changelessness is so obvious you don't even notice it but get blinded by the ignorance of clinging to the endless stream of pictures that arise. To first find that pure state of witnessing you must engage in the cessation-observation practice of meditation that allows you to reach quiet mental states where awareness (witnessing) still fully shines until you can recognize the witnessing itself. Then the next step is to transcend this, too.

That is the spiritual path – tracing witness-consciousness or conventional beingness ("I-amness") back to its ultimate source - but using meditation to do so. Without the purity of clear awareness produced through meditative practice you will end up clinging to the very thing that screens the realization, namely thought. You absolutely need meditation to purify the mind and transform the body so that you can make the breakthrough to complete the investigation. Meditation is true spiritual practice, true puja, true religious participation, true self-improvement, true self-actualization.

The spiritual path must definitely apply equally to both sexes or it would not be a true path. Instead, it would be an artificial invention. All sorts of things arise when you cultivate. For instance, just as we have been discussing, ordinary people who don't meditate but who have a relatively quiet mind can sometimes feel the difference between yin and yang chi in their body and might mistakenly grab onto one rather than the other. They can get confused by this and go astray. Cultivation helps people become balanced because it teaches them never to drop into transient phenomena which are all destined to depart. Feelings like this, no matter how much you try to hold them, are as effervescent as the wind, which no one can grasp. Therefore, don't get confused by the chi winds which arise during cultivation!

Karma determines the manifestation of any particular phenomenon in the universe that arises like this, both spiritual cultivation phenomena and mundane phenomena. For instance, if you have the karma to be persecuted you'll land in a race, sex, class, country, religion or time period – whatever the appropriate situation is - where you'll be persecuted because of your own past persecutions of others. If your karma is to become rich, circumstances will arise wherein you become rich. All phenomena arise because of the cause and effect of karma that connect absolutely everything in one giant web. All recompense, good and bad, is due to a combination of your past behavior and present behavior so vow to change your behavior when bad karma arises, do so, and move on.

When the time is appropriate to experience bad karma or experience good karma, the appropriate conditions will always occur, and afterwards the situation will change once again. Everything passes so there is nothing you can grasp or count on to last forever. Your mind stream always has been and always will be an endless rushing river of change, so to experience better futures you must cultivate virtue, merit, purity and good behavior. For better futures you must try to improve the world and your own behavior.

If you have the karma to enjoy riches in life then you'll be rich for as long as that merit lasts. If you have the karma to be beautiful or handsome, healthy, famous or anything else, the condition will last as long as the karma lasts.[99] Conditions are constantly changing; there is

---

[99] For instance, it is easy to produce the karma to enjoy fame or riches from acting or singing. Those who are now famous for their entertainment talents have freely offered their performances in many past lives. Because of that offering the karmic return is not only entertainment skills in this life, which still require time and training to develop, but also the fact that people will tend to like their personality and/or performances. The past offerings that have earned good karma are what differentiate the career success. One's success or popularity in such fields is not entirely due to the personal efforts of this present life. The success is due to offerings made in previous lives which factor into the resultant popularity and success in this one. Hence, it is very easy to plant the seeds of wealth, fame, fortune or other enjoyments for

nothing fixed you can rely on in the phenomenal universe. Life always brings change and suffering. The transient realm of manifestation is defined by suffering. Therefore, the only important thing in life is to look for what's truly constant, permanent and eternal, which is your unchanging original self beyond the suffering and affliction. To seek that ultimate one, the fundamental Source or True Self, is the path of spiritual cultivation practice, which naturally involves purifying your mind and behavior as stated. If you do not find the Source in this lifetime, at least you should be making efforts to help all other beings and relieve their sufferings since, in the truest sense, they are essentially you. This is why Buddhas devote themselves to saving all beings. Thus it is amazing the number of people in the world who have reached the heights of a career collecting money, fame, power and all sorts of toys, and yet who have not done one thing for the people, which are themselves. The spiritual road is also the road of compassionately acting for others, since they too are the one Self, but those furthest from the Tao revolve in selfishness and rely on distinctions and therefore do not understand this.

What are sentient beings? For instance, what are people, animals, ghosts or deities? There is just one single impersonal consciousness that just appears to be divided into what we call "sentient beings" by virtue of false imaginings, or the ignorance of consciousness. One original self-illuminated beingness actually stands behind the roles of all sentient beings. Just as the manifested arises out of the unmanifested, the state in which you were before you develop the thought "I am" as a sentient entity is actually your real nature, that underlying Self always there. That is what you are. It is pure, eternal, never changes, and free of suffering.

Essentially it is the spiritual path of cultivation practice which can help you find your unchanging, permanent, blissful original nature that gives rise to awareness, and thus can be called the Self or True Mind. If you succeed at enlightenment or self-realization, then regardless of your sexual gender, culture, country, race, religion or any other classification scheme, you can finally jump out of this endless flow of tribulation. Bad stuff will still happen as karma works out, but one is not affected by it. Furthermore, spiritual cultivation enables you to jump out of everything and thereby exert some control over matters, or change something bad

---

a future life just by offering. However, the hardest karmic wealth to gain is that of wisdom, which requires both cultivation effort and study. In other words, it is easy to be born rich in your next life just by offering a lot this life. But no amount of money, skill or talent will help you succeed in spiritual cultivation other than efforts at spiritual cultivation and the support of spiritual cultivation.

for the better. Religion does not enable you to do this. Spiritual practice does. The only people who can truly help the world are those who cultivate to transcend it, and those are the enlightened few who achieved the Tao through cultivation practice. To find an enlightened master takes many lives of merit and cultivation. It is a rare opportunity, and also a great responsibility on your part, too.

Male or female, yin or yang, you absolutely must learn how to spiritually cultivate during the course of this life. And when you experience the feelings or sensations of yin or yang chi or the channels or chakras along this route, you must learn how detach from them because they are not you, and you are not the body either. They are not the important thing. One must not get confused by any feelings of yin chi or yang chi, or lights, sounds, colors, visions, visitations, superpowers, memories, thoughts or anything else that might appear during the course of spiritual practice and your progress. To do so and mentally cling in any way is to become imbalanced.

You must dis-identify from the body and let go of all physical sensations in cultivation. Be aware of them, but let go of sensations such as itching, coolness, warmth, heaviness, lightness, shaking, hardness, softness, and any of the rippling, crawling, sinking, floating, flooding, moving feelings of chi flow in the body that you are destined to experience on the path.[100] Let go of any smells, colors, sounds, forms, thoughts, emotions, sensations, appearances, … every thing and every type of phenomenon. Then you can start to make true spiritual progress and your real yang chi can arise, you can open your *sushumna* central channel, your chakras will unfold, your chi will purify, and you will attain the clinging-free states of empty mind called samadhi that are characterized by stainless awareness and spiritual freedom.

Samadhi states are not the Tao, but they are a good stepping stone on the path to the Tao, which means enlightened self-realization. Most of the genuine spiritual schools teach you to cultivate samadhi states of spiritual attainment but the followers of these religions don't know it.

---

[100] Both Buddhism and Taoism have cataloged all of the different types of sensations that readily arise on the cultivation path. As a common event, people cultivate meditation and often start to feel various energies in their bodies. As the chi energies work through opening up blocked channels, some practitioners might start experiencing various sensations and think they are doing something wrong. Meditation never causes sickness or illness in the body. Never. This is always a wrong interpretation. However, the energies released because of meditation often reveal latent illnesses deep within the body that, once discovered, often produce painful reactions as they heal. When the chi channels to an area of sickness or damage are finally opened, then pain might be experienced but healing is the result.

The actual spiritual path is always about realizing your mind, but that objective becomes lost under all sorts of other artificial imperatives.

The point is, if your mind is more empty or quiet, which means you tend to hold on to thoughts less than others, your yin and yang chi will tend to naturally become differentiated. Therefore you might naturally encounter feelings like this. Do not drop into them. Do not cling. That is not the right way to cultivate.

The cardinal rule of cultivation at each and every stage, regardless of the phenomena that arise and how fascinating or blissful they might be, is "emptiness all the way," "let go, let go," "neti, neti," these phenomena are not the Tao. To cultivate such a mind is called cultivating the mind of detachment. You do everything you must, but you don't cling. You are fully engaged in the world, but because you don't hold things too tightly you can laugh at yourself and others while doing everything proper and necessary in all your activities. A situation passes and then you're on to the next one. Life is easier, and you're that much more effective.

Detach from whatever mentally arises in life – because all the things you experience are just mental phenomena that won't stay anyway - and not only your mind but your body will transform to their highest natural state of perfection. That natural state of perfection involves your body's healthiest, highest, most purified physical form – the sambhogakaya. Just as eating a different diet will transform your body, correcting your mental habits will cause your body to transform as well. Your body is actually energy - or alternatively consciousness - and now by regaining natural mind you are allowing your body to regain its natural self. However, this is not the Tao. To attain the Tao you have to discover the root source of body and mind, matter and consciousness. That fundamental essence is what never changes, and *That* blissful, eternal, changeless purity is your true self, or True Self. Since everything arises from That One, it is also called the Source. Because it gives rise to mind and consciousness, it is also called Buddha-nature.

What fundamentally *is* – the fundamental original essence - always was and always will be. This fundamental nature that gives rise to our beingness ("I Am-ness") never varies. That fundamental essence is *what you ultimately are* and it is what gives birth to ever changing effervescent consciousness, which is fundamentally empty of any true reality. This fundamental essence has awareness or consciousness as one of its infinite functions. On the road of spiritual practice one finds that only consciousness – the pristine awareness - can be said to "be" but not its transformations. In reality there is only one state and when distorted by self-identification it is called a "person." When afflicted with the sense of being it is called the witness, but when without attributes (pure, eternal, limitless) it is called the Supreme.

You are ultimately the original nature, God, Brahman, Ein Sof, Buddha-nature, Allah, Parabrahman, fundamental essence, dharmakaya, Supreme or however you wish to call the Source. That is your true essence or True Self. If you trace consciousness back to its ultimate roots you will discover this, and you can only accomplish this on the path of spiritual practice. Science cannot discover this ultimate source, but you can.

That is how you become "one with the Father." You must turn around to find the source of all this manifestation, and that is the spiritual path of cultivation that starts off with meditation and involves all these purifications of your chi and consciousness. Without that purification, the task of discovering the True Self is impossible. The most you can otherwise experience is to accidentally bump into various purified experiential realms that you might mistake for the ultimate. When you finally discover the Ultimate Truth because of your spiritual practice, you can finally become the same as Jesus and many other realized sages who announced, "The Source and I are one." It's not the situation of "an individual who becomes the Source," because there is no such thing as a truly existing self or individual or sentient being in the entire cosmos. You wake up and discover what you always were; ignorance drops away and you realize what you truly are.

Upon enlightenment you actually don't obtain anything because the real you, or True Self, has always been there; you cannot obtain something you already are. You simply let go of ignorance to realize It. In fact, realization is already there because you can never be really ignorant of the Self; everyone is already realizing the Self. You are fundamentally enlightened already but must simply let go of the stains and contaminations you cling to that shield this. You just awaken to ultimately realize that you are essentially this one original nature and come to recognize that your mind, like all other phenomena in the universe, is just one of its myriad functions or manifestations. It is really just functioning wisdom, functioning knowing. You may think you are a separate mind but consciousness is actually one undivided whole. Individual minds are like waves on one ocean of consciousness that has no divisions. Consciousness is all one whole that expresses itself in different shapes and forms we call beings, and from the standpoint of the Absolute they don't exist. Hearing this tends to frighten some people, which is why most religions just offer out partial truths to help lead people up step by step until they can accept the great dharma truths of existence.

The presence of a false ego, constructed by habit energies of clinging to the false body and consciousness, makes you think you are a separate entity and that *all this* is not you. But all this *is* you because you are that ultimate nature. Everything you are experiencing is only consciousness because that is the only thing you can ever experience – your mind or consciousness - so you are always only experiencing your mind. But that consciousness is part of an undivided whole which you can discover as you learn how to let go of consciousness itself.

There is nothing separate about you because you are part of the entire tableau of manifestation; all of the universe, absolutely everything participates in your own manifestation. This is the meaning of oneness. Search for a real, independently existing "I" within this All and you won't ever be able to find anything fixed, substantial, separate or permanent. The ego is just a group of thought notions you cling to and mistakenly take as real, and if you read various scriptures or sutras you can find out how this all came about. You spend your whole life working hard trying to achieve something in life because of a sense of "me" or "mine," but the "I"-notion is merely a functioning without a real, substantial, independent entity behind it. It is not the case of a real independent individual that has consciousness but that consciousness assumes innumerable forms, like the moon's image that is seen reflected in a million puddles.[101] Even the whole of consciousness is not yet the absolute nature, but just another function of the original nature – an empty appearance that arises out of its essence.

What is your true unchanging self beneath all this experience? That's what you have to search for and discover on the path of spiritual cultivation, for that original essence underlies the consciousness of all beings. We can say "all beings" but that's just a false terminology once again since there is no such thing as a separate independent self or being anywhere in existence. It's just one mass of consciousness, which is why

---

[101] One alone exists, and while it seems to be experiencing itself in countless sentient beings, in truth they do not exist because everything is the Self, your own Self, the absolute fundamental nature. What we call individual sentient beings, souls, entities and so forth are only apparent divisions within the One Self. We think we are truly self-so individual beings, but that one underlying awareness is operating through all beings which, by virtue of the body, have seemingly separate consciousness that we assume is the self whereas it is a false self and not the real Self.

Buddha, who has reached the state transcending consciousness, said in the *Diamond Sutra* that he knows the minds of all beings.[102]

After enlightenment, by shifting the focus of attention the enlightened can experience the consciousness of whatever is the object of attention, and thus become the inner witness of the thing. Since one can be the subject and object of experience, we say there is no difference between subject and object. You can also say one transcends subject and object, is nether subject nor object, or both. The idea of being a separate entity originates from ignorantly grasping on to parts of this whole and calling them a self. You carve out a singular appearance from an infinite tableau of appearances and attach to it, calling it a self. This is because of ignorance, because of a bundle of habits energies of mental clinging that have obscured the Truth. You do not own consciousness; it is not your personal property. The entire cosmos arises out of one absolute

---

[102] This also why an enlightened master can hear those who call upon his or her name for help, and why fully enlightened Buddhas can hear anyone who recites their mantras, thereby becoming able to respond. Despite calls for help, however, sometimes your karma is so thick and your merit so small that very little can be done in the moment, but whatever help can be performed is offered by Buddhas who have vowed to compassionately intervene in the affairs of all. Constantly reciting the mantra of a fully enlightened Buddha is like using a computer password to make contact and gain access to their enlightening power. This is yet another reason why mantra recitation works although ordinary people speculate it is simply due to the powers of vibration. Once you reach the base of awareness that transcends all consciousness, all consciousness is available to you. Thus as a Buddha you can hear and respond to calls for help to the extent that the present karma can be affected; sometimes a knot takes a long time to untangle, and karma that is owed must always be experienced, but not necessarily in the form that first arrives. The compassionate responses of Buddhas and Bodhisattvas are nirmanakaya, also known as emanation or projection bodies, within the overall single body of consciousness. Since there is actually only one consciousness, the memories of consciousness can be known for countless eons past; how far past you can see is a function of your stage of cultivation. And because of the interdependent laws of cause and effect that determine all future situations, such as the inviolable cause and effect laws of physics, the future actually *exists in the now*. Therefore many future events can also be known, and therefore also changed, if the right efforts are made in the right directions. That's why spiritual masters should be consulted and heeded when someone wishes to change the fates of individuals, society, nations or anything! Buddhas support all virtuous activities with their help, but you must make an effort yourself. At one with the unpredicated original nature that is free of all causes and conditions, the appropriate responses can be determined that will change sections within the form of the whole that is itself constantly undergoing ceaseless transformations, and producing the karma of individual situations. Since no event is a single event but linked to everything else in existence, and because all of the "pieces" of reality are constantly pounding it on all sides to have all sorts of desires satisfied whose solutions interact with one another, strong determined efforts in a certain direction are often needed to change fated karmic events, and hence in reality nothing is actually fated. What you experience as karma is what you have participated in producing by both action and inaction. Some karma is so thick because of the compendium of prior causes that it is extremely difficult to change, and hence from a practical standpoint we can say it is fated. In other cases you must mantra for help while consistently working in the right direction until conditions unwind enough for your desired fortune to come about.

supporting nature, and you are just a tiny part of the total effervescent manifestation, which includes *all* consciousness. You and I are not two but the same absolute oneness. We are the same fundamental face. All of the manifestation (the universe) that arises is actually just Consciousness, or One Mind, and what appears is basically just an illusion. Because of your unity with the absolute nature, upon realization you can say that all manifestation is your expression because it is not different from what you are in your unicity. While you are consciousness only in manifestation, what you truly are is prior to consciousness itself which is pure awareness, the fundamental substrate, the absolute original nature, the empty essence which has the nature of empty awareness.

It is through spiritual practice that you can eventually break away from attaching to the false world you have created from your imagined ego, a small cocoon you have spun for yourself while rejecting the Real. False thoughts and the habit energies of clinging from endless lives have caused you to give up the natural freedom from pain and suffering that is your beingness. If you detach from the passing scenery you will regain the bliss of the Self and knowledge of what you really are. Through spiritual practice, starting with meditation, you detach from the notion of being a self, which is called ignorance, and from other thoughts to discover the foundational original nature from which everything originates. It is pure, permanent, unchanging, blissful, Real. When you recognize the primordial basis, the fundamental essence, God, Tao, Buddha-nature, Allah, Brahman, etc. you truly become liberated. All other deeds or events in the universe are just transient accomplishments of inferior unreal merit. This accomplishment is the only real merit, the accomplishment of recognizing one's self, of coming home.

On the road of spiritual cultivation, you "return home" by recognizing the source essence. First you detach from your own mind and consciousness and then strive to realize the source of consciousness, which is ultimately the original nature. As you proceed along this path of detaching from the false realm of consciousness, your mind becomes purified and as mind (consciousness) becomes purified the chi of the body becomes purified. This means that as wandering thoughts drop out you will start to experience a peaceful, blissful, nakedly empty mind. Therefore the chi of your body will become purified as this happens because chi and consciousness are linked. As your chi becomes purified, your body will undergo transitions or purifications, too, for the body is ultimately solidified chi or energy. That is why it undergoes transformational changes during the process of cultivation, and why you experience all sorts of gong-fu through the process. As it purifies it becomes healthier by shedding illness and aging, becoming the best it can be.

The separation of yin and yang chi in this labor is just on of these transformations. As mentioned, western alchemy often represents this stage of the chi becoming separated, differentiated or "clarified" by a single body with both male and female heads. At a higher stage of transformation represented by a rebis (a male body with two heads), it means you can finally achieve a transformation body.[103]

The nirmanakaya attainment, or third body of enlightenment, means that you have mastered the functioning of the original nature. Nirmanakaya "bodies" are active projections of consciousness in the whole realm of consciousness. Since the projections, movements or functions of consciousness can take any form, nirmanakaya can be physical bodies, physical forms, energies or even thoughts. A sudden brilliant thought for how to save yourself in a difficult situation, for instance, can be a nirmanakaya emanation that arises because of your merit and you'd never ever know the source, thinking the thought entirely your own (which it is since everything is you).

Shakyamuni Buddha discussed the capabilities of Buddhahood in many sutras, but he also mentions that the capabilities of enlightenment, such as nirmanakaya projections, are so astounding that he would not reveal all of them for fear that people would then fail to believe his basic teachings. Once you transcend consciousness, however, you can do almost anything within consciousness if you set your mind to it, and this is how Buddhas and Bodhisattvas accomplish their vows. But as stated, Buddha always talked about proving for yourself everything he taught, so you will have to reach this stage of attainment to verify his claims. The tales

---

[103] Called a *hua-shen* in Chinese, or nirmanakaya projection body in Buddhism. This is also called an emanation body. To fully master the production and use of transformation bodies, which represent actions in the realm of consciousness (since actions produce transformations), is one of the requirements for complete and perfect Buddhahood. You can read the accounts in the Buddhist sutras of past Buddhas and the countless emanation bodies they have generated and continue to generate to fulfill their endless vows to help enlighten all beings and save them from sufferings and disasters. The universe lasts forever and there is no ultimate state of rest for mass consciousness. Therefore, while they have achieved liberation and are free from the effects of consciousness, they have made endless vows to undertake all sorts of helpful actions for the realm of consciousness, the utmost of which is protecting the dharma and bringing all parts of consciousness (all beings) to enlightenment. Sometimes a single helpful thought is a transformation body, but whether or not you heed it is a function of your wisdom and merit. If your mind is clouded from too much desire and attachment, which reflects a lack of merit since it means a great deal of ignorance screens the source, you might not even notice the helpful influence.

of Hercules' Twelve Labors just go to show that all the transformative gong-fu talked about by Shakyamuni do indeed occur, and have been recognized by countless other traditions, too!

To become fully enlightened you must cultivate the dharmakaya (Truth body), which means you must come to realize your fundamental nature. You must also cultivate the sambhogakaya reward body of purity. Lastly, you must attain the nirmanakaya or ability to project compassionate intent as a functioning in all the realms of consciousness.

The full description of these three tasks, that together represent the attainment of one hundred percent "perfect and complete enlightenment," is beyond this text. Only a handful of people have accomplished this since Shakyamuni's day. We can only go over the labors of Hercules and show how these initial physical and subtle body accomplishments from spiritual practice are reflected in countless other traditions. Anyone who spiritually cultivates sufficiently goes through these transformations of the outer physical and inner subtle bodies. As to how far you proceed after the twelve stages it is all up to you and your efforts. These Twelve Labors simply represent the laying of the foundation for higher attainments on the path.

These spiritual stages are very hard to attain. Individuals who attain them and then go beyond, and who then devote themselves to humanity become the greatest of cultural heroes if they choose to follow the Mahayana Bodhisattva way. The stages of the spiritual path are non-denominational, but many cultures and religions do not recount these highest of possible attainments because few have achieved them. But this is the ultimate one can achieve in a human life.

In this historic time of colliding religions and cultures, it is finally time for all this information to become clear, common knowledge. Otherwise, humanity will remain confused about the difference between religion and spiritual cultivation, and will become lost in a world of technology, science and materialism that does not recognize spiritual cultivation at all or even the value of human life. Hence, we must start on this road by revealing the spiritual path through the Twelve Labors of Hercules.

If you open all your chakras and channels and transform your yin chi into yang chi, you are on your way to attaining the sambhogakaya. That accomplishment is why the Yellow Emperor Huangdi can take all his 3,000 concubines (a figurative number to represent all your chakras and chi channels) with him into heaven, for he reached a very high stage of the Tao. Yes, he died like everyone else, but he completed the purification of his inner subtle body to the highest extent possible which is only possible after attaining spiritual enlightenment.

After someone dies who has made inroads into transforming their physical body due to their spiritual cultivation, such as St. Francis of Assisi, Saint Bernadette of Lourdes or master Tsong Khapa of Tibet, it often will not decay. Rather, it can maintain a state of "incorruptibility" after death and in Tsong Khapa's case, even the blood can remain in a jellified form after hundreds of years.[104] Some masters, whose deceased bodies are burned, will leave behind colorful pebble-like relics called *sariras*, and some can even transform their dying body into light while leaving behind bits of hair or fingernails. The bodies of Kabir, Bodhidharma and Jesus could not be found after they died because of a certain stage of attainment they wished to demonstrate. A similar disappearance is reported of the Marathi poet saint Tukaram. All sorts of stages are possible after the body has been transformed long enough and deep enough, and the Buddhist scriptures and other schools record many such possibilities.

There are a wide variety of transformation stages available dependent upon the stage of cultivation you attain. Everything is essentially consciousness in manifestation, and by cultivating consciousness back to its original purity one can take chi, or energy, along with it. Since *jing* becomes transformed to chi on the spiritual road, these transformations of the *jing*-based human body might be infrequent, but not impossible. Your chi becomes transformed and then your blood, your arteries and nerve and chi channels, your muscles, bone marrow, tendons and sinews, bones, and then hair. This sequence alone takes over nine years of cultivation effort at high stages.

The purification of his chi and the opening of his channels is why Jacob in his dream is given all the land in every direction; the land in every direction refers to all the transformed chi and channels in his body. The need to transform your inner subtle body on the road of cultivation is why the tale of Jason and the Argonauts is all about retrieving the golden fleece. The fleece is an already transformed yang chi and chakra-channel system within the human body, and Jason aims to obtain it. The burning bush of Moses also represents the transformed chakra-channel system within the human body lit up by the brilliant chi energy.

This stage of purification is what you must start to cultivate through a spiritual life. If you just attend services at a mosque, temple, church or synagogue it just is not going to do it. Many people literally believe there

---

[104] Due to his purification of the body's water element.

was an actual burning bush that spoke to Moses, but if so, why aren't there burning bushes everywhere speaking to people? One must rely on wisdom to separate the symbolic from the actual, and the true from the false yet when it comes to the Bible, most people cannot do this. They turn everything over to mystical causes or superstitious explanations and thereby cannot interpret things correctly.

Because people cling to the stories within the Bible and interpret them in literal fashion like this, you can understand how difficult it must be to teach all sorts of higher spiritual topics to the ignorant or uneducated lacking in wisdom or spiritual attainments. Moses described the purification of the body's chi and channels in an allegorical fashion fit for his culture because it happens to all people on the road of cultivation. Buddha, for instance, called that internal network of channels and chakras within us a "wish fulfilling tree," and remarked that there are other structures for beings in different parts of the universe.[105]

Basically the physical body must transform on the road of spiritual practice. If it does not, you are not practicing correctly or hard enough.

In actual fact the physical body can become so transformed that, according to the Buddhist sutras, it can become like a little world where countless other Bodhisattvas can cultivate in purity. Chinese Taoism and Hinduism also hint at such capabilities. A single pore of a Bodhisattva, it is said in the Buddhist sutras, can contain countless sentient beings who are cultivating. Such high level teachings strain the belief of devoted cultivation practitioners, not to mention ordinary people, until one actually sees and then comprehends such gong-fu stages for themselves. I was lucky enough that my own teacher once showed me such an accomplishment so that I finally understood what the sutras were talking about in this respect.

The *real* accomplishment in spiritual cultivation is to realize your original nature, and so all these stages of purification are still just secondary attainments on the spiritual road just as are miraculous

---

[105] Being very scientific, and able to speak directly without need of symbols because he had students with high wisdom and samadhi attainments, Shakyamuni Buddha discussed all sorts of topics like this. Some topics included how life appeared in this world and became divided into two sexes, including many details left out from the simple symbolic story of Genesis. He also spoke about life in different regions of the cosmos. He spoke about solar systems of planets and how multiple solar systems combined into larger aggregates all the way up to galaxies having the exact same spiral, cup or disc shapes we recognize today. Most religions usually present symbols and allegories to help teach people and lead them upwards, but people without wisdom or attainments grab at these expedient teachings and mistake these stories for absolute truths.

superpowers. However, stories like the Labors of Hercules help motivate people to practice so that they can finally jump out of the realm of *samsara*, and explain some of the landmarks of the spiritual path you are likely to encounter on your journey. Not only will you experience many of these phenomena yourself when you cultivate, but because the western traditions like material things rather than the consciousness descriptions preferred in the East, these stories can help inspire individuals to cultivate. But remember that we are looking at just part of the equation here on the spiritual journey – the physical or existence side of the journey – and we are only dealing with the introductory phases as well.

The spiritual path can be explained from either the aspect of existence or emptiness. This dualistic approach is a combination known as Yogacara-Madhyamika, or the Consciousness-Only school, and we are focusing on just the Yogacara or yoga side of the attainments while ignoring the Madhyamika side that explains consciousness and its inherent emptiness. Both sides are needed to explain the path because no one symbol, school or approach usually explains everything on the spiritual road.

There is a tremendous benefit to having lots of stories, symbols and teachings to explain different aspects of the spiritual path and the typical events and challenges encountered along the way. In our case, we might seem to be over-emphasizing the physical side of the path, but once again that is simply because this is all that we are given in Hercules' Twelve Labors. To counter this wrong sort of emphasis I have added Consciousness-Only teachings wherever possible, but it certainly is not enough.

If we were using a different book to guide our discussion - such as the *Brahma Sutra, Lotus Sutra, Diamond Sutra, Chuang Tzu,* Koran or Bible - we would be discussing entirely different topics altogether, but those discussions will have to wait for other opportunities. So do not get confused and think that the physical transformation side of the journey is what you should be emphasizing. People simply need direction for that aspect of the path, and this story is designed to supply that very guidance. The first priority is to attain the right view and start cultivating meditation to realize who and what you essentially are. You are not creating anything new or making anything up but simply discovering the Truth that all sorts of false dogmas and beliefs try to hide.

Hercules' story describes some of the major signposts of physical gong-fu that you often encounter along the royal road of cultivation. It does not contain all the important points but speaking frankly, the

Greeks seem to have put together a clearer description of the gong-fu steps and stages than anything found in the East. It is incredible to discover that one of the most advanced descriptions of the gong-fu stages of the spiritual path came from the West rather than from India, China, Tibet or some other Asian locale. Most of the deep teachings on these matters definitely come from eastern sources. The Twelve Labors are not only excellent in this aspect, but they provide a basis from which to launch into explanations of related topics you are unlikely to hear about despite years of spiritual study.

For instance, while we are speaking of yang chi and the physical body, it is important to remember that just because Hercules was exceedingly strong this does not mean you should be using strong force in your cultivation. Clinging to your chi is one of the most common mistakes people make when they start to use forceful techniques on the cultivation path. You will often see martial artists mistakenly taking this route because they try to cultivate yang chi "for more power" behind their movements. They consequently interrupt the natural chi flow of their bodies by trying to hold on to chi, and consequently it cannot become purified. When you see a martial artist with a darkened countenance, you have often found someone who does not know how to truly let go and cultivate the empty mind that signifies a master of gong-fu. They are typically using too much force in their martial arts.

This type of cultivation is wrong, wrong, wrong. It's even said that the asuras in heaven – which are the titans of Greek mythology, jötnar of Norse mythology, the angry gods of Buddhism and demi-gods in general etc. - are not as good looking as the higher devas because they cultivate in a similar clinging manner. They never learn to truly let go of their emotions and so their chi and consciousness cannot fully purify because of their clinging. Accordingly, it is said that their countenance is not as attractive as that of the higher heavenly devas.

The way to the highest heavens, or to perfect enlightenment if it is not the heavens you seek, is to cultivate an empty mind of not clinging so that consciousness can purify, and through that purity one can recognize the source. Purified consciousness, a mind of purity, is always empty yet ready to give birth to thoughts. When thoughts arise, one does not stick to them but simply acts as is appropriate without clinging. That is true spiritual cultivation and religions offer countless ways to help you get started with this.

The sequence of unfolding on the true spiritual cultivation path, from purifying the mind by non-clinging (which is accomplished by learning meditation), essentially looks like this:

- The wandering monkey mind of thoughts dies down. The mind becomes purified, or more silent and peaceful, because it empties of wandering thoughts. It reaches a stage called emptiness, cessation or quiescence.
- Yang chi in the body arises because this state of quiet means that thoughts no longer interfere with or block natural chi flows that should be there. The physical body transforms in response to the increased chi circulation and chi channels and chakras open that represent a stage of physical purification.
- You subsequently attain mental peace, feelings of bliss and joy, and various manifestations of physical gong-fu as the process continues and deepens.
- You can finally cultivate samadhi states and then realize the Tao

In the Hesychast and Eastern Orthodox Christian path this process of attainment is called Purification, Illumination, and then Divinization (*Catharsis, Theoria, Theosis*). Practitioners in this school rely on mantra practice – a constant repetition of the Prayer of the Heart to get the process kick started – to quiet the mind and then go through all the same stages we have been discussing. In the western schools the arising of kundalini becomes the "fire of separation," *incendium amoris*, or the "divine love that burns" but it is all the same process of purification suffered through the path. People are just taking the same phenomena and calling them by different names, and because of that religious covering people get lost and confused.

The Tao is your original nature and has always been here. You are not creating anything new on the road of cultivation but simply trying to realize It, the underlying absolute state that is always present, pure, beginningless and eternal. That is the True Self. You are simply trying to discover what has always been your True Self and when you achieve this, you have achieved the divinization spoken of within Christianity.

Your True Self is not some beautified form of purified chi or light or anything like that. It is empty of all phenomenal forms, attributes and characteristics, which is why we say it is like a void. It is there prior to the arising of consciousness, it is there before you were born.

Whether consciousness is there or not It is not tainted by anything, and thus being unconditioned we say It is formless and without marks, signs, attributes or characteristics. It is the source of all reality. It is like space in the following sense. Space is there whether darkness or light is there; the absolute state prior to consciousness is always there permanently as the bedrock within which there is arising. Your mind is discontinuous because of dreamless sleep, coma, and stages of no thinking, and yet there must be something continuous to register that discontinuity upon leaving those states. There cannot be a break in your being. Some type of base consciousness or pure awareness must exist even while you sleep. There must be a base of pure consciousness for all experiences, including sleeping. That clear base must lack thoughts and be free of pleasure or pain. There must be some kind of clear awareness always there behind conscious and unconscious states. When awake you know being-ness, consciousness, I-am-ness, mind or however you wish to word it, but when unawake and unconscious you are simply your original state. That pure self-nature is awareness but it is empty of content, and yet that pure awareness, always there, bodyless, without content or attributes, is what you always are. It is your true identity.

In Zen and several other spiritual schools they say you must search to discover your "fundamental face," which means the original nature or absolute that has the nature of awareness or illumination, and that fundamental essence must be the same for everyone otherwise it wouldn't be fundamental or absolute. If you really realize the truly formless One then it must be the same emptiness or formlessness reached by other sages from different religions if they, too, truly reached it. Religious membership has nothing to do with the achievement, or awakening. Whatever is changeless must truly be one with whatever else is changeless. There cannot be several pure, eternal, changeless original natures. All the fighting that occurs between religions is therefore usually about things other than matters of religion because this is what all beings ultimately reach as the highest and clearest on the road of religion and spiritual practice.

After a state of "no thought" or non-thinking, such as deep sleep, you can awaken to consciousness again only because there is a constant substratum present. That substrate is called the alaya consciousness in Buddhism, which is the underlying state of base consciousness that gives birth to both mind and matter. The absolute nature is the substratum or foundation of everything known, and thus is called the original essence even though the word "essence" usually represents a substance or thing and the original nature is not a thing. It is the absolute state because it comes before everything and never changes, so it is beginningless and endless, permanent, pure and eternal. It has, as one of its capabilities or functions, primordial fundamental unconstructed non-moving awareness that knows consciousness.

Personal consciousness, on the other hand, is always flowing. It is inconstant and ungraspable like a dream, mirage or hallucination and therefore is not real. Your chi is always changing, your consciousness is always changing, and your physical body is always changing. It just happens that in cultivating to attain self-realization and realize the Tao that your phenomenal body, which is not the real you, will transform as consciousness purifies – because of the connection between chi and body-mind - so that it no longer presents an obstacle that impedes your realization. You must transcend both the body and mind to find the ultimate source of the body and mind. If the body is not transformed then it is hard to ignore the body, and so it does transform on the royal road of spiritual cultivation.

On the road of cultivation, there are lots of ways that the form schools, which emphasize the cultivation of the physical body, try to open the *sushumna* central channel using quite active cultivation techniques. They typically combine emptiness meditation with pranayama, mantra, prayers, visualizations, physical exercises, the practice of making offerings, and other cultivation methods. If you follow your breathing through a practice such as anapana you can achieve much of what these practices attempt to accomplish. If you just let go – the process called emptiness meditation that enables you to transcend thoughts and the ego – you don't need to worry about chi channels, chakras, pranayama, mantra, visualizations, *kundalini,* rituals, rules, ceremonies, worship or anything like that. Vedanta, Zen, Mahayana Buddhism, the original Taoism and Mahamudra stress this direct method of self-realization, but few actually practice it.

While many of the methods used in the form schools are forceful techniques, you must understand that their only purpose is just to get the cultivation process of chi purification kick started, like the striking of a match to light a flame or the kicking of a motorcycle pedal to start the engine. Once you've gotten the fire lit, there's no reason to hold on to the match anymore. If you continue clinging to the flame then it will burn you, so you should stop using any forceful practice technique once you've got your chi circulations going.

You don't carry a raft with you after you use it to cross a river. You leave it at the river bank once you've gotten to the other side. Once the kundalini arises, you are basically on your way if you maintain a practice schedule of emptiness meditation and do not carelessly lose your sexual energies that deplete its force. Once the process is started, you must not overly focus on the body but simply maintain an empty mind of non-attachment through meditation along with sexual discipline. Then it will work to open up the channel knots and clear them of obstructions, and there's nothing you need do but simply note the process.

One of the many mistakes most form school (body cultivation) practitioners almost always make, is that they keep holding on to body-emphasis practices well past their usefulness, and tend to cultivate the body too much in general. That focus actually tends to impede their cultivation progress, which is why nothing ever happens. Remember that you might need some force to kick-start a motorcycle engine into starting, but afterwards you don't need to hit the pedal again because the motor just keeps running on its own. Body cultivation is the same way in that you don't have to keep using most tantric body techniques after the chi channels open and the chi finally gets moving. The methods are just used to get you started.

Now speaking of crossing a river there is a similar passage in this labor. Prior to meeting Erythia and Geryon in this Tenth Labor, part of the journey requires that Hercules cross the Libyan desert. Hercules becomes so frustrated at the unbearable heat during the crossing, which refers to the heat of the kundalini at this stage, that he shoots an arrow at Helios, the Sun in complaint.

The kundalini energy is so hot and drying to the body at this stage of transition that it will even parch your lips even though your room is cool and pleasant. You'll find your lips dry and cracked and wonder where that came from. You won't be sick or feel sick during this phase but will find yourself hot and parched, which also happens when you go through the Big Knife Wind as well. However, you should not drink cold liquids at this stage because it would interrupt the chi in the body. Just drink room temperature water, hot water or hot beverages like herbal tea. This is such an important health principle for your entire life, and for success in spiritual training, that I should discuss it a little more.

Any Chinese medical doctor will tell you that drinking ice-cold water is hazardous to the long term health of your stomach. Your body internally operates at around 98.6 degrees (37 degrees Celsius). Drinking cold beverages hurts those warm stomach cells because of the extreme difference in temperature you expose them to when you suddenly ingest cold liquids. The vast difference in temperature is like pouring boiling water over a frozen automobile window during winter time. What happens? The window immediately cracks and shatters. Knowing this, imagine what that great difference in temperatures is doing to your stomach every time you drink ice-cold liquids. It is definitely weakening the stomach lining even though modern science has not discovered this yet.

You may not feel the effect of drinking ice-cold liquids when you are young, but the cumulative habit of drinking cold liquids slowly weakens the stomach lining as you get older and provides an entry way to both disease and accelerated aging for the body. It's like bending a metal paper clip backwards and forwards hundreds and hundreds of times. You can only do this for so long before the metal clip eventually breaks without warning. It suddenly snaps at its weakest point even though it's made of metal. Drinking very cold liquids is also a type of repeated abuse that similarly harms the stomach but the vitality of youth tends to hide the effects until you get older, and that's when they finally appear.

Western science doesn't yet have this teaching on cold beverages, but who said western science understands everything? What it thinks it knows today is corrected again years later. It does not even recognize the existence of chi and certainly says nothing about whatever affects it. It offers very little understanding of the connection between sexual dissipation and cultivation either. And in terms of sexual dissipation and cold fluids, one should never drink cold fluids during or immediately after sexual relations because this will hurt the body, and sexual partners should not expose themselves to air conditioning air flows or cold drafts during sexual intercourse either. If you feel uncomfortable the next day after sex the previous night, it is almost always because of incorrect technique or because you caught a "wind invasion" cold during the process.

If you always expect western science or western medicine to have the answers for your cultivation experiences, you will be very sorry because it lacks an understanding for numerous topics, and cultivation is at the top of this list. Scientists would even deny that the miraculous stories of many spiritual greats were ever true, and thus many say they never happened. If demonstrated today, scientists would try to invent all sorts of modern explanations rather than acknowledge cultivation once again.[106] The knowledge base of science is just not large enough yet for it to encompass spiritual cultivation. People often take scientific viewpoints as "facts" but please remember that what science pronounces definitive today is often overturned tomorrow.

In life you must familiarize yourself with a large variety of information and teachings, see what makes sense, and adopt those that are beneficial into your life. This is called the practice of "benchmarking," or taking the best from wherever you find it, and it should be applied to the field of spiritual cultivation practice, too. It is also called wisdom because it's a smart thing to do. You should combine a lot of different disciplines if you really want to fully understand the cultivation path. You don't have to analyze things and say "this method came from that school and this method from another school." As long as it is a virtuous vehicle in line with the proper principles of cultivation, forget the nitpicking scholars and just use what works.

Continuing with our story about the crossing of the desert, the Tenth Labor says that Helios, admiring Hercules' courage for his efforts, loaned the hero his own golden cup which enabled Hercules to sail across the sea. This golden cup probably represents a little bud at the top of the head beneath the crown where the front and back channels join together with the *sushumna*. This little bud is sometimes represented as a cup, goblet or small flower depending upon the cultivation school.

When Helios gives Hercules the golden cup used for traversing night and day, this means that Hercules finally achieved the microcosmic rotation of the *du-mai* and *jen-mai* chi channels. This is the *ouroboros* chi circulation that runs up the back and down the front of the body in a continuous looping orbit. The Chinese Taoists call this the River Chariot rotation, and the Jewish call this the "way of the chariot" as well because when it first opens it feels as if a little ball or wheel is traversing the opened orbit. The feeling reminds you of a little water wave (like what surfers ride on) that originates from the perineum, travels up the *du-mai*

---

[106] And magician entertainers, desiring publicity, would fallaciously claim they could duplicate the same phenomena. When it comes to genuine cultivation teachings, it seems they always come under attack, and their teachers as well. There are endless ways, through ignorance or on purpose, by which people create terribly bad karma by trying to harm the dharma or its teachers.

chi channel in the spine to the head, and then proceeds downwards the front of the body to the perineum once again.

The wave of chi initially feels strongest near the lower spine as it goes up towards the head, but loses its fullness, evening out so to speak, as it reaches the head and then descends. The rotation is unmistakable, and feels a bit viscous at first until it smoothens out after many rotations.[107] The Vajrayana school of Tibetan Buddhism that developed in part with materials from the yoga traditions of India, segments the spiritual path into a generation and completion stage and says the completion stage begins when the chi enters and clears the central channel. This is what happens in the Fifth Labor of Hercules. However, Chinese Taoism pays special significance to the initiation of this microcosmic circulation, also known as the River Chariot rotation up the *du-mai* and down the *jen-mai* within the body, or "small heavenly circulation." Perhaps this would be a better signpost or road marker since it already entails the opening of the *sushumna* and initiation of a chi circulation that can continue on independently if you maintain practice.

This is something you actually feel for yourself without any chance of illusion, which is why it is also described within the Bible, whereas you can only know that the chi has entered the central channel in tantric Buddhism due to visionary marks or signs provided by compassionate Bodhisattva dharma protectors. The circular nature of this orbit is why it is often favorably compared to the orbits of the planets in many spiritual traditions. The singular front and back circulation is called the microcosmic circulation, and is also often compared to the passing of the sun through night and day. When you add in all the other chi channel circulations, the entire body of different pathways is like the orbit of many different planets in a solar system. Thus this larger set of circulations is

---

[107] When it first occurred it made me think of a little pearl rolling around in a gritty iridescent shell that eventually becomes smoother from all the rotations. I remember writing in my diary, "The bliss is subtle. Beauty flows to the limbs, round and perfect. Rolling undulations of pleasure, the experience is like thunder ... there are no sounds, but it reminds me of thunder. It's like a tiny pearl that rolls around in a mother of pearl shell. The chi reminds me of the warm yang feeling from high quality pure white jade or a woman's creamy white complexion. That's the only way I can describe it." Also,
Soft, round, full
The worries of the past fall away.
Beauty flows to the limbs,
The body seems as if not there.
A fine clear wine cannot in any way compare,
I want to give it to everyone,
But how can I share it with you?
Better just to leave it alone.

called the macrocosmic circulation or grand circulation, which compares man to the cosmos (Heaven, or the great universe) because he has many different planetary orbits within. This is how man becomes a microcosm of the macrocosm.

If you succeed in initiating the microcosmic circulation after all this cultivation practice, it is like striking a match to light a flame that will continue to burn (circulate) on its own if you don't make a mistake and lose it. It is easy to lose this circulation - which transforms the body in ever greater degree as it proceeds - through sexual dissipation and lack of cultivation practice. The entire point of Vajrayana practices such as the Kalachakra, Guhyasamaja, Heruka Chakrasamavara, Vajrayogini, Yamantaka, Zhunti[108] and other tantras is to arrive at this exact stage where the back to front *du-mai* and *jen-mai* chi circulation has started rotating. All of Shingon practice is designed to get you to this initiatory stage of physical transformation on the road to enlightenment. The entire purpose of yoga practices in the *Hatha Yoga Pradipika*, *Patanjali's Sutras*, *Gheranda Samhita*, Shiva Samhita, *Brhadyogiyajnavalkyasmrti*, *Hathatatvakaumudi*, and *Vyasa's Yoga*, among others, is to reach this stage in physical transformations that in time, can produce a foundation upon which you eventually attain samadhi and the Tao. The whole point of entire corpus of Taoist spiritual exercises – qi-gong breathing exercises, inner watching, Big Dipper visualization practices, medicinal ingestions, etc. - is to enable you to reach this stage where the microcosmic circulation finally starts rotating. An incredible amount of cleansing has to go on prior to reaching this stage in order for it to occur. All the emptiness meditations within the *Vijnanabhairava* of Kashmir Shaivism will produce this stage if practiced correctly and long enough. If one understands the message of the *Yoga Vasistha* they will also be able to drop the false mind of consciousness and attain this on the way to realizing the Tao. The whole point of spiritual exercises and ardent

---

[108] Many in the Esoteric School of Buddhism do not realize that the Zhunti sadhana, the body impurity white skeleton visualization technique, or Shingon Matrix and Diamond World Mandalas, are also essentially tantras. So is the Shri Yantra (Chakra) Mandala from Hinduism. They simply serve as an object of focus for stable visualization practice. The objective of these practices is for you to develop a stable state of concentration where the mind remains steady in visualization and does not wander, so miscellaneous thoughts are thereby kept away. After one attains some degree of mental stability, they should release their hold on the mental image to experience a degree of emptiness or empty mind. Practicing these tantras does not require secrecy or any empowerments of any type. They are open and free and can be practiced without any restrictions or necessary initiations (empowerments). You can find out more information on how to practice the Zhunti Visualization or White Skeleton Visualization on the internet.

prayers recited round the clock in Judaism, Islam and Christianity is to reach this "circular" stage of transformation, cited in the Bible, which proceeds automatically after initiated, deepening to new levels as time goes by as long as the practitioner does not lose it through carelessness.

If you are looking for a common stage which all schools know, it is this rudimentary commencing of the *ouroborus* circulation. In my personal opinion, it is better to emphasize when this rotation begins and starts to independently circulate on its own than to call the entry of the chi into the central channel the start of the completion phase. Some may not know what progress they have achieved along those lines, but the initiation of this circulation is unmistakable and not subject to illusion. Only after a long time past this stage can one achieve the various superpowers attributed to spiritual adepts, which of course are achieved by practitioners in all traditions who pass these stages. This is laying the physical foundation for the Tao of the sambhogakaya, and if one reaches this far they will most probably have seen the Tao and realized the truth of non-ego or selflessness we call "empty mind." They'll have had some experience of the meaning of "emptiness."

It will take many years for the majority of chi channels to open and transform through such rotations - about ten to twelve years - and one must learn how to keep the process going by continually cultivating emptiness and discipline during this period rather than focusing on the physical body. You work so hard to get this rotation started, and then you let it go and ignore it while it proceeds on its own. After it initiates, you should not focus so much on the body anymore because you've used your match to light the candle, and so that match isn't needed anymore. Only emptiness cultivation can from that point onwards quicken the pace of the transformation in the sense that not cultivating thought free meditation will slow it down.

In time, all sorts of different chi pathways will eventually open that are not described in texts, for cultivation texts commonly say there are 72,000 different channels or more within the body, and all sorts of experience not mentioned will continue to occur. For instance, when the chi goes through different regions of the body opening up channels, various memories may arise due to the connection between chi and consciousness. These may be either good or bad experiences, positive or negative emotions may also come up, and one is sure to pass through the full spectrum of emotions and habitual behavior energies in time. Sometimes one will even start imagining inhibited behaviors seemingly without cause because certain channels start to open whose chi circulations have been shunted elsewhere. Remember that chi and consciousness are linked, so that when chi flows are opened there will be reflections in consciousness as well.

You must be clear that no one is ever given license to misbehave or engage in immoral acts on the cultivation path during these transformations. Therefore one must always cautiously proceed with wisdom as this process of chi transformation, consciousness purification and channel opening proceeds. One must realize that because of our parentage, race, gender, country and religions and so on we grow up with and adopt all sorts of customs and traditions. Most people become rigidly adherents to these rules as life unfolds, especially if they are overly religious or pious. Wishing to be virtuous, they end up trying to follow religious rules to the letter, such as Talmudic or Sharira codes that we are taught are inviolable rules or regulations from Heaven, in a ridiculously overly strict and inflexible fashion. They are just human conventions. A great individual knows there are always allowable exceptions to these humanly invented rules of discipline, which are only meant to guide in the first place, however in breaking the rules of repressive societies and regimes there are always karmic consequences unless one is wise enough to skirt around them. This is why for someone to succeed wisdom should always be their constant companion on the spiritual path.

Actually, no such rules and regulations exist in the absolute nature; all these rules are made by men and we train to hold ourselves tightly in a straightjacket of such artificial restrictions. The enlightened mind, however, is free of all restrictions and just acts naturally with compassion and virtue as is appropriate to any situation. Like Socrates who refused to escort men to jail when he knew it was not right, or the clerks in the *Tale of Two Cities* who started to eat the names of individuals destined for the guillotine, you neither do what is wrong or stop from doing what is right regardless of what religion and society say. If the donkey falls into a ditch on the Sabbath, of course you should work to pull it out. It's common sense. A realized man is well behaved but follows the laws of his real self, not those of society when they differ. As Socrates and other spiritual greats have demonstrated, they are not flippantly disorderly or disobedient but will break laws according to what is correct or necessary from circumstances. It is foolish people who cling to rules and regulations in general, and who take them as the spiritual path. Buddhism has identified this fault as one of the five great errant perspectives in spiritual practice.

What were created by sages and ordinary men as expedient guidelines to help society we unfortunately end up taking as absolutes over time in religion, and we force ourselves into following man made constructions when wisdom is the best guide to all situations. Holding too tightly to artificial rules using the force of will creates restrictions and knots in our channels that must open. It is not that one should ignore those guidelines unless, of course, they are out-dated, should be discarded or were errant in the first place. Rather, the point is that the way in which we conduct our minds creates the knots and obstructions in our channels in the first place, especially when it comes to artificial inhibitions we force upon ourselves. If our mind is empty, following wise restraints is just a normal thing whereas if we must force artificial restrictions upon ourselves, we do not solve the underlying problems and the impulses will still arise in subsequent lives, although amplified. Only a person who clears their channels can proceed in life without such restrictions and still remain in harmony with the Tao and society. They are perfectly orderly and law abiding, to say the least, but also free to act in the manner necessary for all situations even if those actions go against conventions.

Naturally it is best if we simply learned how not to do what is harmful while remaining detached. It is always best to live by science and wisdom to guide our behavior and our interactions with people and phenomena, but people cling and that mental pressure is like the body dent which develops on a sleeping mattress you nightly lay upon. Similarly, if you wear tight shoes then your toes will tend to become misshapen over time, and cultivation is like a medicine that restores normal toe spread. So as those closed off channels open, imaginations of those inhibited behaviors may cross the mind as one's whole body transforms and one becomes free of the crimped restrictions.

Your wisdom also starts arising at this time because you recognize societal and religious codes are all created by man, and recognize that you should act naturally in a situation according to wisdom even if your behavior goes against traditional customs. This is the enlightened mind of wisdom and compassion which does not hold to rules and regulations but acts as is appropriate in the universe. Do not interpret this as meaning anything goes, for the sage preserves a straightforward relationship to government and societal conventions whenever it is proper.

Karma always has consequences you cannot escape, and the path is one of virtue, ethics and compassion to the end. Therefore there is no license to lie, kill, steal, cheat, and so forth as these shunted channels are finally opened. I am only describing for practitioners who reach this far the actual meaning of tantric lineages involving eating meat, drinking liquor, sexual relations, and breaking dietary or other prohibitions when they have been prohibited in those societies. Some tantric lineages say there are no restrictions to indicate this, but that does not mean that anything goes or that karma will not follow your actions and behavior. Thus we find that in Hinayana Buddhism the first rule is that one should not kill whereas in Mahayana Buddhism the first rule is not to become errant regarding sexual behavior. For all disciplinary rules there are always exceptions, but for every exception there are karmic consequences just as there are for any acts you undertake.

One must never engage in harmful or immoral activities, so when the channels associated with such crimped restrictions start to open, now you will understand why you will go through various emotionally trying situations. One always cultivates an open, empty mind that accords with all beings and situations in virtuous ways. One simply acts with wisdom and compassion according to the situation and not in reference to artificial rules of society or religion. This is the true cultivation path.

About two or three days after the initial opening of this complete circular chi circulation of the River Chariot, or *ouroboros,* you won't feel the rotation any longer. This means that the major obstructions and blockages within this circulatory orbit have been removed. For life in general, when the chi flow becomes smooth in the channels it's because there are no longer any obstacles to the flow. At that point you will forget the body; you won't even be aware of it any longer and therefore you will experience a sense of bliss or well-being and feel happy; otherwise, you feel unwell and unhappy. This is another reason why cultivation is a cure to both mental and physical ills. These chi flow rotations when opened, by removing impurities from the body, also eliminate illness and the obstructions preventing a long and healthy life.

In the story Hercules kills the two-headed dog Orthus, at the root chakra below, which enables him to open up this very special circulation. In addition to killing Orthus with his club, in the story Hercules also kills the herdsman of the cattle, Eurytion, who probably refers to one of the chakra gates along the *du-mai,* such as the jade pillow at the back of the head.[109] The herdsman Eurytion could represent many things in this story, so it would be dangerous to assert that he represents any phenomenon in particular.[110] The best we can say is that he represents something along the *du-mai* and *jen-mai* which opens in this labor.

The night and day aspect of the story certainly represents the rotation of chi in the circular River Chariot circulation through the *du-mai* and *jen-mai* back and front energy channels. In countless cultivation schools the rotation of chi in the body is compared to the rising and setting of the sun, and so it's no surprise that the Greeks used this symbol of Helios and his golden cup for this circular chi rotation. What it all means is that Hercules finally achieves (and clearly feels) the unobstructed chi circulation of the *du-mai* and *jen-mai* channels in this Tenth Labor.

According to Taoism and every other cultivation school that recognizes its existence, after you initiate this rotation you must not lose it through sexual excess. You must maintain it by continuing to cultivate an empty mind along with practicing sexual discipline. Once you get this rotation started, which is initially accompanied by a wondrous feeling of purity and "roundness," the body's chi, channels and chakras will start transforming on their own without the necessity for any more specific steps at physical cultivation other than thought-free meditation. A long period of practice is still required after this opening, but it is a grand milestone achievement nonetheless.

Hercules eventually uses the golden cup of Helios to reach Erytheia. There he kills the herdsman Eurytion and then finally conquers Geryon, which means he finally can get chi flowing smoothly through the *du-mai* and *jen-mai* and then the *sushumna* and all the major *sushumna* chakra circulations, too. He can do that because he also opens the left and right channels, represented by the two pillars that he previously set up. As stated, these are the same two pillars, Boaz and Joachim, mentioned in the Jewish biblical account of the building of the Temple of Solomon.

---

[109] Taoism points out that there are three gates in the *du-mai* where your chi often feels blocked during the earliest stages of cultivation. These are the tailbone gate at the coccyx, dorsal gate in the spine near the shoulder blades, and jade pillow in the back of the head near where the top of the spine meets the skull.

[110] Eurytion was the son of Ares, who represents masculine yang chi, and the Hesperid Erytheia. He was born next to a river in the hollow of a rock, which suggests the skull. These clues taken together suggest a feature within the head such as a chakra along the route of the macrocosmic circulation. An obvious candidate at the back of the head is the "jade pillow gate" of Taoism, which is an especially fine fit since Eurytion was a giant (meaning tall).

Hence Hercules has, in effect, opened up his front, back, left, right and central channels within his body.

Hercules can now differentiate between the yin and yang chi of his body because the left and right channels are fully opened, he can feel the chi circulation through the front and back channels start revolving, the chi flow from the root chakra upwards on through the *sushumna*'s major chakras (belly, heart and throat) commences,[111] and he experiences all this along with the heat of the kundalini or rising yang chi. His results are what true emptiness cultivation allows you to accomplish. It is only when you are able to give up holding on to consciousness that you will enable it to naturally purify the body. This is how you ultimately succeed on the spiritual path.

It is important to stress again that you simply *must* attain control over sexual urges at this stage to pass through it. Don't give in. If you fail at maintaining discipline, forget about the lapse and try again. Try as many times as required during the whole path of cultivation and you will eventually succeed. Cultivation does not mean that you cannot have sex on the path, unless you are a monk who has taken the vows of celibacy, but that one should try as much as possible not to lose their sexual energies, and hopefully not at all. Everyone thinks that cultivation means no sex ever but this shows they certainly misunderstand the teachings as well as the principles of proper sexual relations.

In any case, one of the key skills men should learn to master in life is how to engage in sexual relations without ejaculation, which helps both parties tremendously. This skill will put you way ahead in the game of life even if you don't spiritually cultivate. The discipline of being able to maintain chastity, accomplished by cultivating emptiness and detachment, is just as important to learn. Sexual desire can become so intense when the yang chi rises that it's almost unbearable, but through the meditative practice of letting go brought into regular life you can develop the ability to ignore the discomfort you feel as your chi opens your energy channels. Whether or not you give in to sexual desires, or let go of those impulses and let those energies work to open up your channels, depends on how much you really want to succeed at your practice. The key is that you must learn how to ignore the sensations through *emptiness detachment* even though the volume of discomfort rises as chi channels begin to open.

---

[111] See Emblem XVII in the *Atalanta Fugiens* of Michael Maier.

After killing Geryon, Hercules starts back with the cattle, which represent his yang chi, but he has trouble keeping them together. This would be expected because now that the full channel circulations have been opened the chi will run through these newly accessible orbits and start clearing out any obstructions. However, this will not happen in any regular, orderly, smooth sort of fashion. When you initially open up a channel, the chi circulations in the body have to adjust themselves, and this process of equilibrium seeking adjustment can sometimes cause you to temporarily experience unusual chi flows and energies.

This is another reason why Taoism calls kundalini the "clumsy" fire. Chi does not circulate clumsily, but just appears to run here and there without pattern as it tries to reach a state of internal balance within the body. Just as the waves on a lake will rock back and forth everywhere until the waters finally reach a peaceful equilibrium, the body must go through adjustments here and there as certain channel sections adjust to allow a wider circulation of energies. In spiritual cultivation you will always experience this type of process at higher and higher stages, and at levels of more refined chi, over and over again.

In this labor, two sons of Poseidon try to steal some cattle from Hercules as he leads them home, and Hercules kills them, too. This part of the story refers to an opening of some minor part of the channel orbits, and because of the Poseidon parentage most likely deals with the lower trunk of the body. It might refer to the opening of the *jen-mai's* subsidiary channels near the sexual organs but the exact meridian identification is not something definitive.

People always think they fully open the *jen-mai* after the macrocosmic orbit and the "eight extra meridians" seem to open, but opening the *jen-mai* fully and completely down to the sexual organs on through to the root chakra is not that simple. There are many stages to this process and the description is kept secret. In that region, some of the chi seems to flow upwards or backwards rather than downwards. The process can also briefly produce sharp shooting pains up the front of the body starting in that region, and it takes a long time to open this area fully.

Remember that the opening of the larger channels in a circulation does not mean that all the smaller channels within that circuit completely open at the same time. It takes time to fully open a chi channel circulatory set of meridians. Therefore when yet another bull escapes in the story and Hercules must wrestle to get it back, it simply means yet another part of the overall circulatory pathway starts to open and the chi flows in that direction. Wandering here, wandering there, the chi will flow in any direction required when seeking full equilibrium.

For all these minor events, it's not really important to know which particular channels or regions are opening. As stated, the process of fully opening all the channels will take years past the completion of Hercules' labors. The only things you can understand are the general principles of the process, as we are describing, and the initial openings of the major channels since the events are so strikingly unmistakable and memorable.

You don't have to know which of the smaller chi channel circuits specifically open on the road of cultivation just as you don't need to know anything about chakras or what to do with them. The opening of all the chi channels – wherever they are and whatever they are supposed to do as their function – simply happens when you cultivate, and you don't have to know or do anything about it. You are simply lucky to have this information so you don't worry, that's all. You don't even have to know there is a front, back, left, right or even *sushumna* channel either, although their existence becomes readily apparent as your gong-fu naturally progress. You don't need to know the direction of any chi circulations either, how many chakras there are, how many spokes (petals) each has, and what sounds or colors might represent them. All that information is useless.

You don't need to know any of this sort of information, which is why you don't find it taught in the highest spiritual schools. In fact, you don't need to know anything like this at all. Let me say it again: *you do not need to know any of this at all, and that is why the highest cultivation schools, such as Zen, do not teach this!* Just practice cultivating an empty mind, letting go, and what is supposed to occur as a transformative process of purification will all happen naturally. It's just the body going through a series of transformations wherein its five elements become purified. This is why Shakyamuni Buddha lumped all these events together and labeled them the purification of the body's five elements, telling practitioners such things would happen but that they should just ignore them.

All the genuine Christian, Jewish and Muslim saints of the past succeeded without any knowledge of this information, so this is proof once again that you need not study it or know it. On the other hand, you can find some of this information within these traditions. Furthermore, if you really do want to study these matters – because a true cultivation aspirant vows to learn all dharmas – you might want to look into the Indian Nath yoga tradition of Gorakhnath and its materials. Regardless of the source, however, one should not put too much trust in descriptions of chakras and their colors because they are usually not the truth but just expedient means for special visualization techniques.

You *do* need to know how to let go of thoughts and attain a mind relatively free of discriminative thoughts (empty mind) on the cultivation trail. This is the important thing you must strive to learn through meditation. This is what spiritual practice is all about, so it is proper to learn various meditation practices to help cultivate that objective. When you achieve an empty mind it enables all these chi flows to start circulating naturally without any obstructions or deviations caused by the interference of mental habits. This is what enables you to experience all these things in the first place.

In the truest form of spiritual cultivation, one simply lets their chi flow freely[112] and it will eventually clear all obstructions and assume the correct circulation within your body. You don't need to guide the process because in fact you simply cannot – you don't know where it needs to go or what has to happen, so just ignore it just as you ignore the fact that your body is becoming more developed as you grow up. You don't guide *that* process and you don't need to guide this process either. Even so, this is a mistake most Taoists continually make because they misinterpret old texts.

In this story, the herding of the cattle might make it seem that Hercules chooses the avenue of trying to lead the chi through different chakras and channels, but that is also mistaken. Hercules never tries to specifically lead the chi in any particular direction; the cattle go where they like. The "herding" of the cattle simply means that he opens yet

---

[112] In Christianity, monks and nuns would practice "offering everything over to God" and letting God handle all their mental problems so that they could accomplish this. By turning everything over to God (or submitting to the fate of Allah, as said in Islam), they could let go. They could ignore thoughts, body sensations and quickly pass through these stages without attachment to thereby quickly attain the Tao. Spiritual practice is as simple as that. Surrendering means to let go. You skillfully use whatever mental trick will help you let go of clinging to thoughts until your channels open and you become naturally free at every moment. At that point there will be no tricks or methods necessary any longer because you will reach a true stage of continuous "no-effort." The problem in spiritual practice is that no one knows how to "let go" and be natural or effortless at the start because we are always constantly holding tightly to consciousness, and do not even recognize we are doing so. It is an invisible habit that we do not even know we are engaged in because the habit runs so deep, and releasing it gives us energy. We use a lot of energy in clinging to thoughts, but don't know we are doing so because we have become so used to the effort. Spiritual practice, in effect, comes down to figuring out what it means to truly detach, let go and be natural. What is wrong with being natural? Nothing at all. But few can do it to reach their genuine state.

another part of his full chi flow circulation and that the chi simply wanders through it.

In the story Hera eventually sends a gadfly to sting the cattle as Hercules is herding them back home. This stinging gadfly means that mental afflictions will arise and greatly disturb your peace at this stage of attainment. Chi currents will tend to go astray. Mental afflictions, such as sudden thoughts of anger, hate, violence or other urges, will also arise and disturb your emotions to no end after all these channels open. If you are getting help from dakinis or daki (devas), you may even be put through lots of emotional stress at this point as they "test the circuits" to determine which chi channels they still have to work to help open next.

Strong sexual desire is also a stinging mental affliction, too, and it will certainly arise at this stage of strong yang chi. You should realize by now that whenever there is strong yang chi there is usually strong sexual desire until it has been purified. Additionally, mental afflictions will arise when errant chi winds arise in the body because chi and consciousness are linked. Thought-free meditation is really the best way to deal with these problems whenever they arise, and that's how you should deal with them in this labor. Desires arise, but you don't pay them any attention. You don't block them, but you let go of them without acting on them and they will naturally pass as the channels clear.

When you suffer these kinds of afflictions, or frequently experience the same type of mental ailment over and over again, it often means there is a constriction, knot, obstruction or blockage in a set of channel chi flows. Of course, sometimes mental afflictions can arise as the result of the diet or living circumstances. If they occur frequently or repeatedly as a feature of your personality, they might not represent learned behaviors but might indicate deep seated habit energies in the alaya consciousness[113] that must be transformed.

---

[113] The "alaya consciousness" is a term from Buddhism describing the foundational base nature of consciousness. For instance, while awake we say you are conscious. When asleep you may dream, which is yet another form, type or transformation of consciousness. Sometimes during sleep there is no mentation at all, and yet when you awake your ordinary consciousness resumes again. We don't say you were not existent during sleep even though normal consciousness seemingly disappeared. You were simply unconscious, so do not remember what happened. Because you do not remember it is does not mean that awareness was not still functioning. What makes it possible for existence to stay constant through all these states is the presence of a base state of clear consciousness, a primordial continuum that underlies all other states of consciousness that might experience interruption. It is like the deepest ocean water which experiences a surging of ocean waves on its surface. All the waves on the surface seem separate from one another but are actually transformations of the same basic

Buddhism calls these energetic predispositions that can suddenly turn into thoughts or behavior the "seeds of the alaya consciousness," and the seeds of the alaya consciousness produce obstructions in the chakras and channels just as our genes, body shape, and fortune come from karmic seeds as well. Typically such things manifest externally to the world as imperfections in our bodies and behavioral patterns. Some errant behavioral tendencies are learned, some are inherited, and some come from past life tendencies, which is why the heart of spiritual cultivation in the end boils down to transforming your mind and behavior.

Since everything has to be transformed through purification on the road of spiritual practice – including your chi (energy), physical body, habits, consciousness (mind) and karma - cultivation is the right way to accomplish all this through just one avenue of practice rather than through a hundred different vehicles and disciplines. The seeds of habit energies work to produce your karma, including such big issues as your race, gender, religion, parentage, country of birth and so on. They also work to produce your habits, personality and behavioral predispositions. They even contribute to the particular obstructions you have in your chakras and channels. It is through spiritual cultivation, rather than through visits to a psychologist or psychiatrist, that you can transform all these things and start to gain some mastery over them.

The point is that in addition to purifying the body, cultivation is a process of transforming deep seated energies of consciousness that turn into repeated mental and physical behaviors. It is all connected; a body in poor physical condition produces errant chi flows and thus bad states of mind. In turn, bad mental states create errant chi flows that harm your body, not to mention your relationships and efforts to accomplish things in the world. Because cultivation directly transforms your chi and consciousness, the results of psychology or psychiatry don't hold a candle to the possible therapeutic results that can be gained from deep spiritual cultivation.

Psychoanalysis doesn't help purify either the mind or body but meditation does because it transforms the underlying chi flows that are connected with the body and consciousness. To rid yourself of a symptom, attack the cause and work on the root! If you are sick, in some instances meditation might even open the chi channels to the diseased organ systems and produce a spontaneous remission or alleviation of the

---

ocean water, or base consciousness. The transformations of consciousness we experience are all transformations of the same base state ground consciousness, or alaya.

condition. What psychologist or psychoanalyst can help you do that? For this next hundred years, to maintain their sanity and live balanced lives people will have to increasingly turn to the road of meditation.[114]

The road of spiritual cultivation does indeed involve transforming this impure physical body of ours that we receive as a karmic inheritance, but it is all about transforming the mind and behavior as the foremost target. As in Confucianism and Christianity, the Mahayana path of cultivation is not focused on cultivating the body because that sort of transformation comes along for the ride. Hence it is not emphasized so that practitioners concentrate on the important thing. The spiritual path is ultimately about knowing your mind, and while cultivating your mind and behavior you let the body transform in the process. If you switch the focus you usually will go astray.

Because of the stinging gadfly, the herd of cattle which Hercules is leading back to Greece does go astray and becomes scattered far and wide. This means your chi will run everywhere during this stage of attainment because countless new channels have opened. Furthermore, wandering thoughts and afflictions are still arising to pull you this way and that. In fact, as new channels open some deep mental afflictions - sometimes painful and bothersome - will often become revealed at this stage whose underlying habit energies will not be so easy to eliminate. This is because even if you succeed in silencing your wandering thoughts, it still takes time to purify all the habit energies of consciousness that have built up over countless lives and which are connected to particular chi flows. They can only be purified slowly over time, just as it takes time to master any stage of cultivation gong-fu.

As you cultivate the Tao, the rule is that spiritual gong-fu only matures step-by-step. It never transpires all at once but evolves slowly, and what does happen is something you are always ready for because it occurs according to the body's own schedule. Even if you became enlightened this very instant, it would still take time for your body to completely

---

[114] One of the many famous predictions for this century that my teacher made many years ago is that mental illness will increase like a plague and become a bigger worry than the threat of cancer. Several factors could account for this. Our poor diets are lacking in nutritional content and are causing us to consume incredible levels of dangerous pesticides, chemicals and pollutants we cannot eliminate from our systems, which are internally building up to unmanageable levels. We are also being exposed to increasing levels of radio waves and electromagnetic pollution that are bombarding our cells and jostling their cellular receptors. The stressful pace of life is ever increasing in the external world, and along with it people are experiencing higher levels of anxiety, depression, insomnia and other mental illnesses. These are just the tip of the negative conditions on the rise.

transform. People often think that if you attained enlightenment you would instantly have superpowers such as being able to fly through the air, but that is not so. Even after opening up his *sushumna* channel and transforming his chi, channels and chakras, Hercules still has no superpowers and won't for many years unless he continues cultivating to attain samadhi. While such abilities as flying are indeed possible if you cultivate them,[115] they only become possible after you have sufficiently transformed mind and body, and that takes time. Some masters don't even bother to cultivate such abilities, and are satisfied with just becoming liberated.

This time requirement for cultivation progress is why the stage of True Cultivation Practice (the fourth of the five larger stages of the spiritual path) is a slow phase of transforming your behavior, dissolving deep mental afflictions and unwinding mental knots all in addition to letting the body purify. Because this takes time and the experience is easier to maintain at full strength when you are not bothered during this period, many masters go into retreat after their awakening in order to devote themselves fully to these transformations.

Remember that whenever your mind changes then your body will transform in response. Your physical chi always responds to your mind, such as when you become frightened or experience a feeling such as love. In spiritual practice the primary emphasis is on cultivating the mind rather than body, and on letting go of consciousness so that it empties or purifies. In return, your chi will purify and your energy channels will open. Because of the fact that your mind becomes more purified, a portion of your chi energies will always end up transforming your physical body without any need of your attention. The phenomena that arise in response constitute the labors of Hercules.

Chi and consciousness are linked, and since chi is your life force then your chi and your body are linked. Because of these inherent connections, you can ultimately attain the reward body of physical purification just by cultivating a purity of mind and behavior. Yes, the spiritual cultivation path can be that simple. This is why Confucius taught people to cultivate a straightforward mind by always watching or witnessing your thoughts with mindfulness and then correcting yourself. The real thing that knows the comings and goings of consciousness, the real thing that witnesses is you, what you are -- your true nature.

---

[115] Such as in the cases of Milarepa, Padre Pio, Lu Chun Yang, and various yogis who cultivated their internal energies accordingly.

Through the path of witnessing, also called mindfulness or vipassana or remembrance, one can eventually realize this. When you do not get involved with the flow of the mind - meaning the thought process or flow of internal dialogue – then you are not the mind. In witnessing you transcend it. When you are in a position to observe the mind (witness it) you are other than the mind. You are apart from thought. That is why the practice of witnessing is the primary road of cultivation and eventually leads you to the source. Only witnessing without clinging enables you to detach from consciousness, or give up the association with consciousness and the body.

When you read of the (invisible) tongues of flame experienced by the Apostles in the New Testament, this is also a well known stage of cultivation mentioned by multiple schools that can be achieved through such simple practice. It refers to an extremely rudimentary stage of emptiness that naturally occurs to individuals of virtue.[116] It is only when you meditate that you can reach much higher stages of spiritual attainment. Without meditation today, people simply cannot truly cultivate an empty mind of purity – a straightforward, non-crooked mind of virtue - that does not hold on to thoughts.

What does the sambhogakaya reward body of physical purity actually represent? Typically people only talk about the esoteric aspect of the sambhogakaya, which is an apparitional beautified body of ultra-purified chi or the most purified essences of the five elements. It is not an astral body, though some think of it in that way. Some say it is akin to light simply because we don't really have better terms from our world for describing it. Only sages can see it.

In any case, to attain the sambhogakaya your coarse physical body must become transformed during the process of cultivation. It's not that you attain a separate astral-like body of purified chi, but that this physical body itself must transform, too, through a process of purification. If your physical body transforms, which is essentially also a process of transforming away bad human karma, that body in itself becomes a reward body for your cultivation. You should therefore think

---

[116] Usually the "tongues of flame" are first seen on the top of the two shoulders, and then finally on the top of the head so that there are three flames in total. They are just manifestations of chi that occur to people of relatively empty minds who practice virtuous ways, and they can only be seen by people who have opened up their "third eye" chakra. This is a very rudimentary stage of the path, and quickly disappears as you progress. It only indicates that someone is relatively virtuous and a little empty, but is not any significant stage of attainment itself.

of your physical body becoming transformed on the cultivation path as your sambhogakaya. It is not you, but simply a vehicle appropriated by consciousness.

After his death, it is recounted that Shakyamuni Buddha was able to extend his feet outside his coffin when his student Mahakasyapa arrived to say farewell, a fact many people take as proving he indeed had attained the sambhogakaya (because some people following Tibetan Buddhism misunderstand Vajrayana teachings and mistakenly assert that he did not). Therefore, you should not consider the sambhogakaya as anything ultra esoteric other than your physical body becoming younger, more flexible and supple, and disease-free as your energy channels open. This type of notion is more naturalistic and quite in line with scientific thinking.

As you cultivate correctly your chi will transform, your channels will open, your personality will soften, and you will become free of knots and afflictions. These are all the benefits of accomplishing the sambhogakaya. The sambhogakaya represents the opening and purification of all the chi flows within your physical body. It means the five elements of your physical nature are all becoming purified and balanced because your physical human karma has been transformed. The "reward" aspect of the sambhogakaya is to enjoy such a transformed body and beautified or purified chi. With these accomplishments, one can then exhibit many yogic superpowers as the stories of various masters across traditions often illustrate.

On the cosmic scale, a human life is considered a bad karmic existence as compared to a heavenly existence where one enjoys the beautified body and life of a deva. Because the human body you've inherited becomes purified on the road of cultivation, however, this means that you are purifying your human karma on the road of cultivation, which is why you can be reborn in a higher realm. Only cultivation enables you to be reborn in the highest of the spiritual heavens.

Therefore, you must not consider the sambhogakaya as something like a purified astral body without considering what it also entails in terms of accumulating the necessary merit, purifying your karma and the body's physical elements to attain it. Both your physical body *and* your internal chi body become transformed in order to attain the sambhogakaya.[117] These are karmic inheritances that are being transformed. What is the

---

[117] In fact, the Sixth Patriarch of Zen, Hui-neng, said that when you realize your self-nature, that is the real sambhogakaya. This is absolutely correct.

bad karma that is being transformed on the road of cultivation? Mental afflictions and errant habit energies, physical afflictions and mental knots.

Hercules has the basic yang chi accomplishment in this Tenth Labor, but it's not yet flowing smoothly within his body. It runs everywhere opening up new channel orbits that have hitherto been blocked. Now that they are opened, a new balance can eventually be reached and the overall natural, normal circulation of chi energies can finally reassert themselves. In the story, Hercules has to run around Thrace gathering the escaped cows which shows that the yang chi is flowing everywhere in his body now that a fuller circulation has been reached and the previous obstructions cleared.

Only after a long time does his chi circulation become smooth and regular, and the cattle manageable, but this requires a lot of revolutions that Taoism calls the "multiple refinings." The longer it flows through a previously obstructed channel, the more the chi flow will smoothen out. Chinese Taoist texts indicate that it requires a lot of rotations to purify the chi and open finer and finer channels by always citing a large number of chi rotations. You will always read descriptions of "nine," "thirty six," "ninety nine" or other such numbers of revolutions that do not reflect actual counts because there is no such definitive thing. They simply indicate that your chi must go through a large number of circulations which will make you appear younger and more handsome or beautiful as they occur.

In actual fact, the chi must circulate for years through the channels before they are all completely opened and transformed, so the Taoist idea of a fixed number of rotations people mistakenly hold onto is entirely fictitious. The "brain breathing" in the head, which includes feeling the chi sensations within the head channels, is particularly difficult to finally silence.

After he regroups the herd of cattle scattered by the gadfly, Hercules blames these troubles on the river Strymon in Thrace and so he fills the river with rocks to make it unnavigable. In interpreting this part of the story, we must put up a large sign of caution here. Just as you should never hold on to your chi, you should never try to block or cut off any chi channel circulations during cultivation. You never try to cut off circulatory routes for the chi. Therefore you must not interpret any part of the labor in this way. All your chi channels should open and remain opened because they all exist for a reason.[118] Since Hercules suffers

---

[118] Just as all your nerves, lymph channels, veins and arteries exist for their own specific functions.

no harm from filling the river, in this case his actions must represent something else other than closing off a channel, which itself would be like amputating an arm.

It is not that a chi channel is purposefully blocked in the story. Hercules only reduces the chi flow or current of the river Strymon, which also means he reduces the current of thoughts or predispositions in a certain direction. This part of the story probably indicates a reduction in mental afflictions or sexual desire, but as to the specifics, once again we cannot know for sure. In any case, it shows that he is no longer controlled by certain chi flows driving him to do this or that. He has surmounted or transcended those impulses, and this interpretation certainly applies to this stage. The longer you cultivate, the less desires or afflictions will impel you.

While Hercules has cultivated this far and attained some stage of emptiness or non-ego, it does not mean that sexual desire no longer bothers him. However, in all likelihood, as a practical matter in order to be able to get this far, Hercules probably no longer lets his thoughts run wild in this direction. At this stage of cultivation when the chi starts running through the major and minor orbits, sexual desire will initially bother you like a stinging gadfly, and you just have to ignore it even though it might drive you crazy. He reduces the problem by detaching from it, and this is represented by his actions.

Hera's gadfly can basically represent any type of stinging mental affliction, but when your yang chi arises and vitality flows everywhere it is normal for sexual desires to arise in abundance. However, the higher you cultivate the less sexual desire will bother you, and that is how I would personally interpret this part of the story.

All in all, we can say that in this Tenth Labor there was a monster named Geryon, having three human bodies joined at the waist, who owned a herd of beautiful red cattle. Since the root chakra was previously opened, the three-bodied Geryon represents the three chakras above it on the *sushumna* route to the crown chakra – the belly, heart and throat chakras – which now become filled with chi during this labor and whose own channel systems start to open. Geryon's red cattle represent the ascending yang chi of the body which is now coursing through a yet wider set of chi channel circulatory orbits.

In this labor Hercules is able to open more new chi channel circulatory routes branching off the *sushumna*, but only because he first fully opens the left, right, front and back channel circulations, too, which enables his chi to start traversing everywhere without obstruction. Hence, this story not only reveals traditional cultivation teachings but also describes the gong-fu you really do experience at this stage.

Hercules also at first erects the two pillars of Hercules in this labor, or in some versions of the legends it's said he splits the Atlas mountains into two parts. This means he opens the left and right channels on opposite sides of his body and can finally discriminate the yin chi from the yang chi in his body.

The opening of the front and back circulatory orbit, represented by the travels of the golden cup of the sun along its daily revolutions, happens next and the River Chariot rotation now commences. This happens due to the death of the two-headed dog and Eurytion the giant herdsman, which occur along the route of the *du-mai* back channel in the spine, so Hercules achieves the full microcosmic and macrocosmic circulations spoken of in countless cultivation traditions.

Of course, Hercules triumphantly vanquishes the monster Geryon, which takes no time at all after these other accomplishments, and after a long journey homewards, where the cattle initially scatter about but finally become manageable, he eventually brings them back to King Eurystheus.

This all simply means that Hercules' chi circulation finally starts moving regularly and peacefully through all these newly opened meridians. His chi flow eventually becomes balanced, and he in turn transcends many of his mental afflictions from this achievement. In short, he finally opens most of the major chi circulatory routes within the human body – the front, back, left, right and central chi channel systems - and achieves an even better foundation than previous for eventually attaining the Tao.

THE ELEVENTH LABOR:
BRING BACK APPLES FROM THE GARDEN OF THE HESPERIDES

[2.5.11] When the labors had been performed in eight years and a month, Eurystheus ordered Hercules, as an eleventh labor, to fetch golden apples from the Hesperides, for Eurystheus did not acknowledge the labor of the cattle of Augeas nor that of the hydra. These apples were not, as some have said, in Libya, but on Atlas among the Hyperboreans. They were a present from Earth to Zeus after his marriage with Hera, and guarded by an immortal dragon with a hundred heads, offspring of Typhon and Echidna, which spoke with many diverse sorts of voices. The Hesperides guarded the apples as well. So journeying Hercules came to the river Echedorus, where Cycnus, the son of Ares and Pyrene, challenged him to single combat. Ares too engaged him in single combat, but a thunderbolt was hurled between the two combatants, bringing the fighting to an end.

Going on foot through Illyria and hastening to the river Eridanos, Hercules came to the nymphs, the daughters of Zeus and Themis. They revealed the sea god Nereus to him, and Hercules seized him while he slept. Although the god turned himself into all kinds of shapes, the hero bound him and did not release him till he had learned from him where were the apples and the Hesperides. Being informed, he traversed Libya. That country was then ruled by Antaeus, son of Poseidon, who used to kill strangers by forcing them to wrestle. Being forced to wrestle with him, Hercules hugged him, lifted him aloft, broke and killed him. He had to do so because when Antaeus touched earth he became stronger, so some said that he was a son of Earth [Gaia].

After Libya Hercules traversed Egypt. That country was then ruled by Busiris, a son of Poseidon by Lysianassa, daughter of Epaphus. This Busiris used to sacrifice strangers on an altar of Zeus in accordance with a certain oracle. For Egypt was visited with famine for nine years, and Phrasius, a learned seer who had come from Cyprus, said that the famine would cease if they slaughtered a male stranger in honor of Zeus every year. Busiris began by slaughtering the seer himself and continued to slaughter any strangers who landed. So Hercules also was seized and taken to the altars, but he burst his bonds and slew both Busiris and his son Amphidamus.

Passing by Arabia Hercules slew Emathion, son of Tithonus, and journeying through Libya to the outer sea he received the goblet from the Sun [Helios]. And having crossed to the opposite mainland he shot on the Caucasus the eagle, offspring of Echidna and Typhon, that was devouring the liver of Prometheus. He released Prometheus from his torment, after choosing for himself the bond of olive, and to Zeus he presented Chiron, who, though immortal, consented to die in his stead.

Now Prometheus had told Hercules not to go himself after the apples but to send Atlas, first relieving him of the burden of holding the heavens. So when Hercules came to Atlas in the land of the Hyperboreans, he took the advice and relieved Atlas from his burden asking Atlas to fetch the apples for him. But when Atlas had received three apples from the Hesperides, he came to Hercules, and not wishing to support the heavens again said that he would himself carry the apples to Eurystheus, and bade Hercules hold up the sky in his stead. Hercules promised to do so, but succeeded by craft in returning the task to

Atlas instead. For at the advice of Prometheus, he now begged Atlas to hold up the sky till he could arrange a comfortable pad for his head. When Atlas heard that, he laid the apples down on the ground and took the heavens from Hercules. Hercules picked up the apples and simply departed. Some say that he did not get them from Atlas, but that he plucked the apples himself after killing the guardian snake. Hercules brought the apples back to Eurystheus. But he, on receiving them, bestowed them on Hercules, from whom Athena got them and conveyed them back again, for it was not lawful that they should be laid down anywhere.

For his Eleventh Labor, Hercules was assigned the task of stealing the apples of the nymphs known as the Hesperides. These apples had been presented to Zeus from Gaia (Earth) as a wedding gift for his marriage to Hera. Thus we know they represent something within the physical body, born of earth, that deals with the union of yin chi and yang chi. That union is clearly represented by the marriage of Zeus and Hera.

The golden apples were kept in a garden at the northern edge of the world, which in our body means upwards, and they were tended to by the Hesperides. These nymphs were daughters of the titan Atlas who held up the heavens upon his shoulders, and thus we have reference to something in the head once again. Because there are female nymphs constantly attending the garden in the story, we can also surmise that the apples have something to do with transforming the body's yin chi or opening up polluted channels.

The apples were also guarded by an immortal hundred-headed dragon, named Ladon, who was the offspring of Typhon and Echidna. Dragon heads in our story usually refer to chakras, but in this case Ladon is special because he spoke simultaneously with a Babel of tongues. This refers to all the thoughts running around in our heads that eventually quiet down due to spiritual cultivation, and Ladon's many heads refer to all the tiny chi channels in this "garden."

The garden in the story actually represents the chi channels inside the head where we find the thousand-petalled golden crown chakra of the body and many other chakras. In Taoism this area is also referred to as an orchard, and the orchard is said to grow sweet immortal peaches. When the thousand-petalled chakra starts to open, various traditions refer to the process as "eating its fruit" because there are hormonal changes in the body that go along with the melting of the restrictions around its channels.

These hormonal changes produce the sweet saliva mentioned in countless spiritual schools and hence various schools make reference to fruit (such as peaches or dates) or wine at this stage because of their sweetness. In Chinese Taoism the fruit of opening this chakra and swallowing the saliva is usually represented by eating heavenly peaches that banish sickness and bestow immortality.[119] Naturally there are not any such fruits because they simply symbolize this process.

When you reach the initial stages of opening the crown chakra due to these stages of body purification, in vision you might see the dome of a sky with many bright points shining like stars. These bright points are actually the tips of the petals of the crown chakra, and until a higher stage of cultivation is reached the yang chi has not yet run through them completely. What must happen along the course of spiritual cultivation is that the yang chi must push out the yin chi obstructions in all the channels of the body, which means that kundalini must even run through these narrow channels.

When you first start purifying the inner layers of your inner chi body, you'll eventually see the crown chakra after a sufficient number of channel clearings and unwindings. When Hercules is said to wrestle someone during his labors this represents the unwinding of a layer of chi covering the channels; it is being pulled out of the chakras and channels, and then pushed out an orifice. In other words, obstructed channels become unobstructed as the yang chi pokes through them, and this is symbolized by wrestling in the labors because it is often compared with sticky unbindings or unwindings. After completing a full set of unwindings[120] you'll eventually find yourself dealing with the crown chakra, which is dealt with last in each cycle.

In the Esoteric school and in the tantric yoga schools of India, cultivators practice fierce pranayama *kumbhaka* with the hope of eventually forcing yang chi through these tiny channels. They practice holding their breath for as long as possible, while simultaneously relaxing the body as fully as possible, so as to let the chi pass through these channels as much as possible. Pranayama practice is a great technique

---

[119] See Emblem IX in the *Atalanta Fugiens* of Michael Maier to see how a western alchemist represented this sweet saliva.

[120] After a full set of unwindings or untyings is done, you have to rest about a day in order to proceed on to the next set of unwindings.

for health in general and proves quite useful for the speedier attainment of cultivation gong-fu. True emptiness meditation, or anapana practice, will also accomplish the opening of channels as well, but not necessarily as quickly for those who cling. Pranayama practice will indeed definitely help you on the road of spiritual cultivation, and I highly encourage it. In addition to its spiritual purposes, it has been recommended by countless masters for improving one's health and increasing one's longevity.

In many cultivation schools other than yoga or Tibetan Buddhism, practitioners simply cultivate emptiness and in time these channels open spontaneously. Naturally you must practice celibacy during this time for the best results, which simply means you shouldn't lose your semen, *jing*, or "elixir" through sex of any kind. In some schools you can still have sexual relations, but a man must not lose their semen during intercourse. At the stage of the Eleventh Labor, however, we are talking about no sex at all.

Your *jing* must transform into chi on the road of spirituality, but if you lose that *jing* then you won't have sufficient chi to open your channels. The principle is: "If there is no water in the boiler there will be no steam in the pipes," and so it is easy to understand why the loss of *jing* (the water element) means a loss of chi (the wind element, in this case represented by steam). You don't always have to be celibate on the road of cultivation – plenty of married individuals from both genders have succeeded - but you certainly need to be temporarily celibate at the higher stages of gong-fu in order for the chi to open up all the chakras and channels. You should strive to be clear about all this because most people get confused. Celibacy is not a commandment, moral issue, ethical issue or spiritual issue but an energetic issue that ties in with mental issues; you do not want to be losing your energy on the path if you want to succeed.

In any case, one has to get to the stage where your yang chi (rather than yin chi) is running through these tiny channels[121] due to your cultivation efforts and then they will start to warm up. After this starts to happen, a type of golden brown liquid, which appears like golden honey, will seem to melt from around the crown chakra channels and drip down. As previously explained, for everyone the vision of what they see will appear a little different.

Taoism often describes the opening of the head chakra channels in fanciful ways but people usually don't connect the underlying process to the descriptions. In Tibetan Buddhism it's said that you need to warm

---

[121] Indians call them "*nadi*."

or heat the channels so that "the bodhicitta can melt" and the channels will open. This basically means that the whole process is accompanied by the heat or warmth of kundalini, and that you become more pliant, flexible and softer through the process. It does not necessarily mean that there is actually a substance that must melt, but it does mean that the purification process of the path, which is within the stage of Warming, will always be accompanied by a warmth you can feel. All you need do, to prove this to yourself, is mantra for a few hours and you will feel your belly eventually get warm from this type of purification process.

Now in the case of the Tibetan ascetic Milarepa, one of the great cultivation heroes of Tibet, it is related in one legend that at a certain stage he saw a thousand quivering vaginas in the sky which were demons coming to attack him with temptation and destroy his cultivation. To pass this stage by "banishing" the demons, Milarepa simply mentally generated a thousand penises to satisfy the vaginas, and then they disappeared. This story disguised the thousand petal tips of the crown chakra in a memorable way and revealed yet another technique sometimes used to open up the chi channels which one often encounters at this time. Using imaginary visualization of sexual relations to raise your yang chi to help open the channels, while not losing any semen, is called karmamudra practice. Only an enlightened master has enough wisdom to watch over this sort of practice and devas will also have to come and instruct those introduced to it.

Both the schools of kundalini yoga and sexual cultivation practices are said to have come to human beings from the higher Desire Realm devas. Hence they are somewhat related. Karmamudra sexual imagination falls into the school of sexual cultivation techniques, but this is not a method of cultivation that can be used by all. The enlightened Tibetan Master Tsong Khapa and many Hindu masters have strictly forbid it, for good reason, because ordinary people are not qualified to follow it and its dissemination usually leads to destructive tendencies and disorder in societies. After five previous enlightened incarnations, only then did the Sixth Dalai Lama finally use sexual cultivation to help fully open his channels and transform his body at the appropriate time. His advisors were all against his announcement that he wanted to use this technique until he took them to the wall of the Potala Palace and he began to urinate off the wall. Before the urine could hit the ground he withdraw it back into his body. Only after seeing this did they finally cease their objections for he had clearly proved his gong-fu and qualifications. Shakyamuni

Buddha wisely forbid this type of practice even to his greatest students, who were the most qualified people you might find, and many Hindu masters have warned of the dangers of the "left hand" schools as well.

If sexual cultivation became widely publicized and accepted as a spiritual practice, history shows people would say they are cultivating when simply pursuing sexual partners and sexual gratification. When sexual gratification outside of wedlock has been given license through the blessing of a spiritual title, it has produced nothing but disorder and suffering throughout history. When standards of propriety are socially abandoned and promiscuity rises, people tend to hurt both themselves and others. Nevertheless, sexual license is so prevalent today that some words should be said to help partners uplift their efforts, which otherwise amount to very little in terms of spiritual assistance.

What ordinary individuals can do to improve their normal love life is read the Yellow Emperor's *Plain Girl Sutra*.[122] Men, who are at the most risk for energy loss from sex, must in particular learn to hold back from ejaculation during sexual relations, but without a forceful restraint which would impede the chi flow as well. This requires a lot of starting and stopping when they are first learning ejaculation control. Women need not worry about any potential loss of energy through orgasm, but a woman cannot be helped much if her partner continually loses his energies. She does not give anything up if she helps her male partner learn the difficult yoga – for this is yoga, not spiritual cultivation - of how to engage with her in deep lovemaking without ejaculation. By first mastering various stroking techniques that enable a man to pause and retain his staying power, and which refrain from overly sensitive movements in the early stages of learning, partners usually find much greater sexual pleasure in their relationship, and sometimes even small changes in their chi and channels. But of course this cannot happen instantly or overnight. The method is challenging to learn and requires cooperation between the lovers. Its discussion is not to promote more sex nor is it an encouragement of sexual indulgence, fantasies or sexual escapades. The point is that sex does not have to be the enemy of spiritual cultivation for lay practitioners. With some knowledge our sexual activities can be brought more in line with our spiritual aspirations and moved to a higher level of manifestation.

---

[122] Some other books include Jolan Chang's *The Tao of Love and Sex*, Dr. Stephen Chang's *The Tao of Sexology*, Doug Wile's *Art of the Bedchamber*, and Yogani's *Tantra: Discovering the Power of Pre-Orgasmic Sex*. The "valley orgasm," Kegel exercises, and other methods are part of the learning discussion.

Passion can be used for a higher purpose, though of course the highest purposes cannot be achieved without also mastering emptiness meditation, pranayama, and the skeleton technique. This is clearly shown in Tibetan *thangkas* where a deity is seen holding arrows and standing on skeletons or dead bodies, and draped with severed skulls representing emptiness or no-ego. However, even if couples do not wish to use sex as part of their spiritual life, it is in the best interest of both partners for a man to continue to improve his staying power, which requires a sometimes difficult to achieve cooperation from both partners. For couples who choose to learn this, the man in particular must practice correctly so as not to damage his bladder, prostate, kidneys or urinary tract. The male practice of pressing the perineum inward to block the uretha before sexual discharge, in order to mechanically stop the exit of semen from the body, hurts many men. One Chinese surgeon in New York also reported to me that a common male practice of hanging weights from the penis results in countless emergency surgeries each year to repair torn ligaments in the male sexual organ. Men must be careful as to what they try to learn in this area of techniques, for not all is correct.

The trick in sexual cultivation is to eventually learn how to kick start the chi into rolling within the *du-mai* back channel, but without tiring oneself or losing energy through excessive physical exertion or by ejaculation-orgasm, which usually brings the process to a standstill for awhile. This cannot be learned in one day, and most people usually cannot find a suitable partner to match them for the practice as they must learn to work together to stay in front of orgasm for a long while. If neither partner is not a meditation practitioner, the highest levels of the technique cannot be mastered. Once the chi in the *du-mai* starts moving and rises to the head (after which it will descend down the *jen-mai*), sexual partners should rest, enjoying the physical bliss but without attaching the sensations. They should not try to blank out to suppress the mind to "experience emptiness," but should just drop their attachments to their physical and emotional responses, let them arise, and also let them depart without any clinging interference. Experiences that arise cannot stay, and holding on to them will not prolong them or increase the enjoyment. The partners should let go and thus will then experience a transformation of the normal energies that are stimulated during sex. While not the true chi of cultivation, those energies will still help the partners to open their channels a little. Only meditation can truly open the channels, but this is definitely a useful assist. Another warning is that partners must not try to move or absorb the energies or substances of the other during sexual intercourse (such as in *vajroli mudra*), as these are also harmful mistaken techniques.

It takes time for the chi to descend in the body after it reaches the head, and that time varies by individuals. It ranges from a short while for those who cultivate to a longer while for those who do not. For the chi to descend down your front channels to complete a full orbital circulation along this pathway, one must learn how to let go of the feelings of bliss which arise as it fills the channels, and refrain from clinging. Of course one must also learn how to produce this physical chi-born bliss through the correct form of sexual technique. Each partner will eventually learn what they have to do to preserve the chi circulation inside them, and after a while will learn what stimulatory methods will help their partner as well without producing ejaculation or orgasm, which usually brings the process to a halt.

For the man's situation, he should never attempt to withhold his ejaculation by using too much forceful restraint or by pressing acupuncture points in the perineum (or other strange techniques) that would back up the physical body's normal channel flows, as this always results in all sorts of health problems, especially to the prostate, kidney and bladder. Lacking the proper know-how, most men never master non-ejaculatory sexual yoga (as this is not truly sexual cultivation unless one of the partners is qualified) without producing eventual health problems. It is better for them to learn how to adjust their breathing and stop their sexual movements when they feel ejaculation is near, in order to get a beginner's handle on the proper technique. Men typically don't know how to practice non-ejaculatory sexual yoga correctly or don't put in sufficient practice effort to learn the proper methods. Even after finding a suitable partner, the relationship requires an adjustment time for mastering the technique (that applies to both men and women) because partners need to learn each other's responses and because the sexual organs may not be a good match for one another. It is easy to be born rich or good looking, but requires much more merit to be born with sexual organs perfectly suited for this technique.

Women have a similar difficulty to men in finding partners who are qualified for this technique, who do not ejaculate too frequently, and who do not rush through the act of sexual intercourse or prior stimulation that helps prepare their entry. The correct technique is not a matter of penile thrusting in exotic positions, though this often helps touch hard-to-reach spots within the woman's vagina. Rather, the correct technique is typically of various deep and shallow thrusting rhythms from different angles to prepare the woman, and deep penetration to touch the woman's vagina in the appropriate spots that bring about responses that will both excite her and move her chi. For this technique the woman's orgasm is not required; it is not essential that it be avoided, and it certainly will from time to time occur. The vagina is designed to reabsorb any energies and secretions it releases, including the energies of the man, so a woman is less limited than men when it comes to correctly practicing this technique. Women can more easily start again at this cultivation technique after an orgasm and therefore should not worry about preventing it at all.

Some people think these techniques are going against nature, but it is perfectly natural that a certain type of sexual bliss has been found to be helpful for opening the channels. It requires that you learn how to stimulate and let go of physical bliss while cultivating it to a fullness in a harmonious way. But you must not call this spiritual cultivation because you cannot destroy delusion and attain enlightenment with your lower torso. However, this will certainly help to open your chi channels and harmonize your emotions. If both partners can learn how to help one another adjust their bodies to a state of comfort using sex, which adjusts the body's energies, this insight can help most loving relationships. The search for a lasting sexual high or extreme peak that brings peace or fulfillment or enlightenment or whatever is unachievable. However, achieving a comfort or bliss that lasts a very long period - because the chi flow has become smooth, harmonized and regular - is an accomplishment indeed, and part of what sex should be used for within a relationship. Once again this is not true sexual cultivation, but simply sexual relations for physical health that in turn may help your cultivation efforts. I am only reporting what I have been told through esoteric sources.

If both parties can reach a state of physical bliss where they can forget the body and just feel the bliss without attachment so that the chi can roll and body can transform, that's really accomplishing something in terms of chi and channel practice. That's one simple example technique. They can try again as many times as they have energy but must not fall into the attachments of lust or deplete their energies. Their chi should spread throughout their channels and not be lost through crazy physical exertions and sexual antics like you see in the porn movies of today. The sexual yoga portrayed today concentrates on almost everything else except the place where the man's chi channels in the penis can touch a woman's chakra channels inside her vagina, and thus stimulate the circulation of chi upwards and throughout the meridians of both partners. If one's chi can eventually reach a state of blissful harmony and balance, such that you can detach from it and let it go, that's the most you can hope from this practice though of course it indicates that the channels are being transformed.

As a method for attaining enlightenment, you must forget any notions that the vehicle of sex will help you along those lines. But when done in the proper fashion, sex can certainly help transform the body, open one's channels, and harmonize the spirits. The open sexuality and promiscuousness of the world has reached the stage where it will not decline, therefore partners should at least know how to use these higher techniques within their proper sexual relations for the greatest possible physical and cultivation benefits. To learn more one can research the Chinese Tao school for relevant teachings, but must be careful not to take the writings of modern teachers as necessarily accurate.

According to the traditional rules of strict Vajrayana, there were only three periods when one could engage in sexual cultivation under the auspices of an enlightened master. One of these situations was only after an individual had cultivated their chi and channels to a very high level, such as after going through all the Herculean transformations, but were still unable to attain samadhi after having tried countless cultivation techniques. It was only after they had tried everything else, and all these other methods had failed, that they might be permitted to try this technique.

Most people are just not qualified for this practice and even if they were, they would not be able to find a suitable partner with purified chi and opened chi channels either. As my teacher always says, even a Buddha could not find a partner in this world. Therefore, there are many alternative ways to help open the body's channels, including those in the head, such as by visualizing a shining golden Buddha (e.g. Amitofo) over the crown. There are also the Hindu ascetic yoga practices of Shiva or Goraknath together with kundalini practice, mantra practice and bottled-wind pranayama for opening the chi channels. The highest method seems to be the direct emptiness-prajna wisdom cultivation emphasized by Shakyamuni; most sages succeed on this path because this road is the most direct for achieving enlightenment and entails the fewest obstructions, detours and mistaken by-paths.

The Tibetan practice of concentrating on colorful mandalas to reach mental stabilization is yet another way to help open the chakras and chi channels once the requisite state of one-pointedness of concentration is reached. Naturally this visualization road only leads to success if the individual is practicing mantra, anapana, and pranayama as well. An interesting note is that Tibetan mandalas often represent chakras and their chi flows, yet most practitioners don't know this.

Another school of mandala visualization practice is found in India in the school of Kashmir Shaivism. The Sri Chakra or Shri Yantra of the Hindu goddess Lakshmi, who represents abundance, is an example of this type of Indian mandala practice called a *yantra* that combines a representation of several different chakras stacked together.[123] You concentrate on visualizing this type of mandala until you reach a stable one-pointed concentration, and then like in the skeleton visualization, you let go of your mental holding to experience mental emptiness.

---

[123] One can often find various Esoteric school pictures of Buddhas with multiple heads stacked atop one another, and these extra heads also represent the chakras on the *sushumna* that are used for visualization practice. These visualization methods are not usually taught to the public because without the right teachings, and not having had a direct experience of the right view of emptiness, students who concentrate on chakras can release all sorts of energy streams within the body and land in all sorts of trouble. Without a tantric yoga or Vajrayana master to guide them, their cultivation then always goes astray. It's like opening a single valve in a complicated hydraulic system which afterwards permits the energy release to flow everywhere even though the piping is not yet rated for that volume of activity. This causes an imbalance in the system. When this awakening prematurely happens before other chi channels have been opened, the student will run from teacher to teacher and book to book searching to understand what occurred and looking for how to handle the hot chi flow until it rebalances. This is why many chaste young men experience painful kundalini awakenings after applying themselves to pranayama yogic practices and meditation. Examples abound with Christian monks who recited the Prayer of the Heart on the heart without doing much other prior cultivation work as a preparation. Because they didn't perform all the preliminary cultivation practices that open many channels slowly, when the yang chi finally awakens it impossibly tries to pry open up all the channels at once, which naturally causes suffering. After things calm down, if they lack knowledge of the Tao and the true cultivation path, such individuals almost always drop into superpowers and go astray. I once met a Taoist practitioner who exemplified this type of catastrophe. He had undertaken a cultivation retreat in the mountains (he picked a mountain with the wrong energies, too), used a variety of strange esoteric techniques to concentrate on the energy centers of his body, and had prematurely unblocked partial chi pathway circulations that subsequently caused him all sorts of troubles. In the Twelve Labors of Hercules the pathways open naturally in the correct sequential order because the cultivation is done over time, and there is always balance despite any minor discomfort due to the process. This Taoist required two years of constant herbal medicine adjustments to help him rebalance his body and relieve some damage he had caused to his digestive system, and as to his spiritual cultivation his efforts had thrown him off track. People always make the mistake in the esoteric schools of incorrect practice techniques or using too much force. Then again, if you know what you are doing and have the right view of dharma and correct cultivation understanding, such methods can be an excellent way to speed your progress. It all depends on your practices, wisdom and merit.

The spiritual schools of the world offer a variety of different cultivation techniques such as this, but they are all based on the same two principles of cessation and witnessing. All cultivation practices depend on these two principles, a topic stressed time and again in the *Sandhinirmocana Sutra*. You reach a state of quiet mind or "cessation" from whatever is your practice technique and then stay aware witnessing or observing your resultant quiet mental state. Eventually the mind becomes so quiet, and witnessing so pure, that with detachment and insight you can attain samadhi and realize the source of awareness.

Because most religions and schools depend on these same two principles of cessation and observation (witnessing), this is why you often find the same basic meditation practices repeated across various traditions. It is because they all depend on these same two principles, and there are only so many new practices you can create that make use of them. In actual fact, while the gong-fu of the path is non-denominational, most all the spiritual schools and religions are to some extent sharing the same basic cultivation techniques as well. While there are some unique tantric body practices that dramatically alter a person's chi and cannot be performed successfully without the watchful presence of a wise master, they still depend on the principles of cessation and witnessing in the end.

The visualization practices on male and female Buddhas found in Esoteric school tantras such as the Chakrasamvara, Guhyasamaja, Vajrabhairava, Vajrayogini, Yamantaka, Heruka, Kalachakra and various others[124] serve a similar focus as mandalas for cultivation practice. You concentrate on an image and thereby keep wandering thoughts away because your mind becomes occupied with a visualization that requires stability. When the mind becomes stable and silent the witnessing continues, and witnessing with a quiet mind can eventually lead to samadhi attainments. Witnessing is natural but holding on to an image is not natural. That holding is cultivating samadhi, which is a type of mental stability. You should eventually release any visualization rather than hold on to it when doing these practices. The method is just a way of eventually achieving one-pointed concentration, and then (from the standpoint of a quieted mind) the ability to clearly introspect and become aware of the source from which the mind springs ... which all the while cultivates your chi and channels in the process.

Tradition says that enlightened dakinis will lead you through many of the higher esoteric techniques we have been discussing if it's appropriate,

---

[124] Either of a single enlightened being, or of a Buddha (enlightened being) and their consort.

but since both male and female heavenly beings can help you with your cultivation it is perhaps better to say "devas," "deities" or "angels" rather than just "dakinis," for that term only refers to female deities. In the wide universe there are always higher Bodhisattvas willing to help others cultivate, meaning us, and this sort of assistance affirms that "Heaven will help those who put in the effort."

You need to have already opened up your *sushumna* central channel via much preliminary work in mantra, anapana, pranayama, skeleton practice, emptiness cultivation and so forth before various tantric visualizations can really be worthwhile. For instance, you can readily find tantric pictures of Buddhas standing on skeletons or wearing severed heads on their bodies. These pictures teach the preliminary necessity for practicing the white skeleton visualization and for attaining the correct view of non-ego prior to achieving such advanced progress. Furthermore, you usually cannot succeed in these techniques without the previous practice of pranayama either.

As a side note, when you look at these tantric pictures you will not only see lotus flowers representing chakras but will often see various instruments in the hands of the Buddhas such as axes, picks, tridents, arrows and so forth. These represent the ability of the yang chi kundalini energies to pierce through the obstructions of the chi channels and chakras as we previously covered. Every tradition seems to recognize the importance of conveying this idea.

Many people are enticed by the various esoteric schools because they offer majestically colorful techniques, such as the tantric pictures of male and female Buddhas together, that appeal to the imagination. But frankly, most practitioners get lost in these schools. My own teacher, who is recognized as an enlightened master of the Vajrayana Esoteric school - as well as Zen, Taoism and Confucianism - says that practitioners on these roads usually represent the most catastrophes in spiritual cultivation. Rather than free people from clinging and superstition, most practitioners wrongly practice these techniques and increase their mental attachments that last across lifetimes. They tend to amplify attachments to the body, the tendency to grasp onto form, and the idea that consciousness should be encapsulated in form.

Wrong, wrong, wrong – all wrong in so many ways. I have traveled through Asia talking to many spiritual practitioners, and I have noticed most people feel proud that they know some "secret esoteric practice" and believe it will speedily win them great spiritual progress. They neglect to realize that spiritual progress is all based on science rather than mystery or superstition and that there are no secrets to spiritual cultivation. There is just the necessity of doing the right things in the right way long enough with consistency, and learning how to become empty or detached so that thoughts can die down. As an example, you can use visualization practice to do this if you know how to stabilize the busy mind and then let go, or you can simply let go and achieve the very same result directly. You can also follow your breath to calm your thoughts. You can mantra until your mind tires and wandering thoughts die down, or you can just witness your thoughts until mentation subsides. The method you use, and success you achieve, all depends upon your wisdom. Shakyamuni's clean prajna way is just as quick and powerful as Vajrayana techniques, and even more so and without any attendant obstacles. Unfortunately, most people don't believe this, but it's true.

The colorful pageantry and esoteric nature of tantric yoga techniques, Taoist visualization or Vajrayana techniques attracts so many people, but most practitioners get trapped in their false thoughts when they tread these roads and forget that they are seeking our true fundamental nature rather than further functions of consciousness. That's why there are far more success stories of individuals who practice pure Zen and Mahayana Buddhism, or Vedanta or Mahamudra, than from the esoteric schools.

This is because such practitioners learn to drop holding on to everything, especially the physical sensations of energy in the body that we habitually come to identify with as part of ourselves, which they are not. They are just the sensations of the body, which is a piece of equipment appropriated by consciousness.

Successful practitioners often learn how to ultimately let go of consciousness, including bodily sensations, through the practice of witnessing meditation, and their chi resultantly purifies because of the non-clinging so that consciousness also in turn further purifies. From that new stage of higher mental purity they continue to let go of grabbing on to the workings of consciousness (thoughts) until they can eventually detach from all the workings of consciousness in total and thereby realize the underlying pure empty awareness that's always there, and then its source which is the source of all awareness and consciousness in all sentient beings.

There is one fundamental source. Because there is one fundamental source underlying all consciousness and awareness, one fundamental or primordial substrate that is the essence of beingness, there is no such true thing as any independent, separate, self-so sentient being because that fundamental essence is All. The truth is that many experiencers – which we call sentient beings - appear in one undivided, indivisible awareness and though they apparently seem separate in memory and perception, they are one in essence. All those uncountable experiencers, which we call "sentient beings," are possible because of that one underlying awareness that is pure, eternal, changeless and the possibility of all experience. It shines underneath all consciousnesses. People get confused on this point, clinging to external religions and dogmas,[125] and get confused by all the roads of practice and transformations of consciousness and changes of the physical body and its energies that happen as they purify. They become fixated on non-essentials and forget the search for their true nature, the source.

The successful practitioners diligently ignore all sorts of spiritual gong-fu and physical sensations that arise on the path knowing well they are not the true source or ultimate objective of their practice, and are destined to pass. They quickly learn how to detach from the body, as they never practice bringing consciousness into the body, nor do they play with the chi, channels and chakras.

In early Taoism, no one made these mistakes either, as Taoism had not yet degenerated into the school we see today in which nearly everyone is trying to open their channels by visualizing macrocosmic and microcosmic orbits while spinning their wind chi this way or that way and clinging to all the sensations. Unfortunately, that just never works. Successful adepts typically have always described that these circulations occur as a result of cultivation practice, but visualizing their occurrence won't make them occur.

You will indeed feel sensations of wind in the body if you practice this way, but that's about all. You certainly won't open the channels, meridian orbits, chakras or transform your generative energies into purified chi. Hercules doesn't seem to be doing this type of visualization practice, but many practitioners take this road and naturally fail. They

[125] A common mistake is to believe the original nature, often called "God," is a personal being that spoke to Moses or Krishna, Mohammed or Christ. The Self, or original nature, is the sole unchanging reality. The original nature is neither being nor non-being, and thus certainly is not a person who talks to people. When teaching common people it is simply skillful expedient means to tell them that there is an ultimate being or creator. This is done in order to tame the ignorant public and lead them to better ways of living. As the enlightened sage Ramana Maharshi said, who comes from the Hindu tradition of countless gods and deities, Iswara, the personal God, is true only from the relative standpoint of those who have not realized the truth through enlightenment. Only the absolute being (original nature) is real, and so even a personal God is unreal. In our spiritual striving we must find the original nature and nothing less.

cling to old books by Taoist adepts who described the chi movements that occurred after they made some progress in meditation, as in the Twelve Labors, and think they should try to imitate those sensations. These readers ignore the highest Taoist masters who actually succeeded in self-realization as a result of practicing non-clinging, and who never mentioned such gong-fu. Just as the Zen school has declined, Taoism has declined as well because of this.

The books from all the schools which advocate non-clinging seem boring, so no one wants to sit down and learn how to truly let go of the mind through simple meditation. Instead, everyone feels excited when they read books with fascinating descriptions of spiritual gong-fu and they want to try this or that exotic practice, thinking its unique nature is what will bring about these unique results. People seem to think they have finally found all sorts of hidden secrets when they read about unusual spiritual practices and the states of gong-fu we have described, but they commonly occur to everyone who transforms the body. In reading about Hercules' adventures you have actually hit the jackpot along these lines but the process of attainment is not anything secret at all, and there is not only one school which reveals these stages and their progression. These results are totally non-sectarian. They don't belong to any one school or tradition because such phenomena will occur to everyone, and are thus part of the science of being human.

After you succeed in seeing the Tao and thus understand the path because you have experientially seen the meaning of emptiness (due to an actual experience of empty mind), only then is it safe to put more emphasis into trying to transform the body. If you try to bring the chi flow gong-fu results of the path into the process of causation, you are not likely to succeed unless you first see the Tao, which means experientially understanding emptiness due to an actual experience of no-thought. You must have *that experience*, which a master can often give to you via transmission, and then match that experience with the theory transmitted in dharma studies. That is why the Fifth Patriarch of Zen said to the younger Sixth Patriarch, "If you do not first see the Tao, then all your cultivation work is in vain."

Whether or not you can ultimately succeed in spiritual practice is not because you like a particular cultivation technique or spiritual school or have any special affinity with them. Success is not guaranteed to you, nor barred to you, as a Jew, Muslim, Christian or member of whatever group or sect you identify with. Rather, success is a function of your understanding, practice method, your commitment at continued effort, your spiritual wisdom, and merit. Just because you become exposed to Esoteric school teachings does not mean they are supreme, or that you will succeed on this path. Although Shakyamuni Buddha had extremely high stage students, he refused to teach many of these Vajrayana topics and instead he lumped all these physical manifestations together and simply called them the *transformation of the body's five elements.* You must take some time to reflect on why he did that. He didn't teach them and, yet, he was able to lead so many people to enlightenment!

Now returning to our Eleventh Labor, to steal the apples from the garden of the Hesperides, Hercules first had to find out where the garden was so that he could get there. To do this, he first had to catch Nereus, a shape-shifting sea god, to learn where the Garden of the Hesperides was located. As Hercules grabbed him tight, Nereus turned himself into all kinds of shapes in an attempt to escape but to no avail. Hercules didn't release the sea god until he got the information he needed.

This refers to a remarkable phenomenon that you might briefly encounter as the layers of chi surrounding the chakras and channels are released during the purification process. Something resembling a living chi "blob" might suddenly appear in a colorful vision like a lucid dream. When you see this chi in your mind, it will seem like a vivid, bright and vibrant living thing; somehow it will instantly respond to your thoughts. It may seem as if it has the capacity to respond to your will; whatever you want it to be, whether you think of a color, shape, form, substance – anything – this type of chi will instantly turn into that.

Think of fire, and it becomes fire; think of emeralds, and it becomes emeralds; think of metal or water, and it seems to become metal or water in the imagination. The experience passes in minutes. It is not actually a real event but just another testing vision given to an individual. The experience demonstrates the pliancy of the mind, the imaginative capabilities of consciousness and what one can accomplish through nirmanakaya capabilities once mastered, but practitioners do not realize it at that moment. This shapeshifting experience is so extraordinary and unlike any other previous visions to this time that, like the shapeshifting Nereus, it is something you will always remember. It actually may occur several times over the course of these labors.

Hercules' story is primarily a tale of the physical gong-fu that happens when you enter into the road of spiritual cultivation and your chi starts transforming your body. The story does not deal too much with consciousness and his mental cultivation, which would have probably have been of little interest to a Greek audience fascinated by miraculous wonders and tales of strength and heroics. Nevertheless the consciousness aspect of the path arises in the story through experiences like this, time and again, because without that purification prerequisite the story cannot even take place.

You already know that one of the world's spiritual schools which heavily emphasizes the physical transformations due to cultivation is the Vajrayana school within Tibetan Buddhism, also known as the Esoteric school of Buddhism. Because of this, for a better understanding of Hercules' story and spiritual cultivation in general we should spend some time on this spiritual tradition. For instance, just as the shapeshifting Nereus could assume any form, in Tibetan Buddhism you often see colorful pictures of various Buddhas in various forms with red, blue, yellow, black, green, white, and gold colored skins along with multiple arms and appendages.

Practitioners in this school are often taught "deity yoga," which is a type of cultivation practice that entails visualizing colorful Buddhas or deities until the meditator attains stabilization and by this accomplishment realizes that the deity and the practitioner are in essence the same. If practiced successfully, the meditator will attain stable one-pointed concentration (mental stabilization), the opening of their chi channels, more pliant visualization capabilities, and hopefully wisdom insights into the true nature of reality – an experience of emptiness. By realizing that one's environment is basically their mind, and by identifying with a visualization, through this route practitioners can abandon the fixed mental habit that reality is something solid "out there."

If you actually succeed in this type of visualization practice, it is said that adepts with divine sight who walk past you in your room may often see you in the form of the Buddha you are visualizing, which means the chi of your body is transforming. However, only someone who meditates on emptiness coupled with one-pointed concentration on the form of the deity can really succeed in the practice.

Success in special techniques like this always requires emptiness meditation along with the knowledge and discipline of the Tao. Many religious groups besides eastern esoteric practitioners, such as the Jesuits, employ visualization methods in their cultivation techniques. However, in practicing visualizations of a provisional imaginary appearance, it is almost impossible to succeed in the practice without knowing the correct principles and cultivating the correct mindset.

One of the great practice techniques for mastering one-pointed, stable concentration like this, which many great scientists and inventors are known to have achieved, is called *kasina* meditation. A common feature of this practice is to learn how to form stable visualizations of different colors, and sometimes one after another. If I were a young man in college who wanted to become a scientist or mathematician, I would definitely be practicing *kasina* meditations because of the great benefits they would bring to my mental capabilities and the ability to achieve mental breakthroughs. Great scientists like Nikola Tesla, Albert Einstein and Richard Feynman could visualize complicated images in their minds, and this practice helps you develop that skill. The meditation section of the *Visuddhimagga*, or *Path of Purification* by Buddhaghosa, explains some of these practices in detail and many more are available in Indian tantric texts on yoga asanas, concentration and pranayama breathing methods.

Traditionally in visualizations the fire element is represented by the color red, the water element by black, the wind element by green or blue, the earth element by yellow or gold, and the space element by white or clearness. Different spiritual schools also use various colors to represent the chi of internal organs such as the heart (red), liver (green), lungs (white), kidneys (black) and so on. Sometimes, you will see these colors while meditating, or in dreams, because your body is trying to tell you that you have a problem in a particular region.

Most esoteric school practitioners don't realize that this type of colorful concentration practice is not unique. Esoteric school practitioners always think they are engaged in practices higher than those found in other spiritual schools and religions. However, even the school of orthodox Buddhism, which most esoteric practitioners feel they are above, has various concentration practices quite similar to deity yoga visualizations. The basic technique is all about concentration in order to develop a stable mind. In order to concentrate you must banish wandering thoughts, and if you reach a state of concentration it means your mind has become relatively stable. From that stable basis it is possible to relax, introspect, and then realize emptiness - the empty basis of the mind. That is the basic technique. Once you understand it, you can realize there is nothing mysterious about it.

The most common mental concentration or visualization practices are the *kasina* meditations, and the white skeleton (body impurity) visualization that I have been emphasizing actually belongs to this category of techniques as well. In the *kasina* meditations (found in the *Path of Purification*, or *Visuddhimagga*) you practice concentrating on the colors white, red, yellow/gold, blue/green, light and so forth, and there is also a visualization practice for the fire, water, earth, wind and space elements, too.[126]

Related and yet entirely different from the colorful *kasina* visualization practices, there is also a special type of practice in Taoism where people try to absorb the chi or light essences of the sun or moon in order to transform their chi, which is yet another cultivation practice used at the early stages of the path. Practitioners in some schools visualize the lights of these celestial bodies, and in other schools they actually try to absorb their essences. In these absorption practices, mentioned in the book *Can Tong Chi* by Wei Bo Yang, it is related that you should only try to absorb the yin light of the moon around the fourteenth to sixteenth day of the lunar calendar when the moon is full, for at other times the practice is virtually worthless. Practitioners try to absorb the yang light energies of the sun only from the first to third days of the lunar month, too, so if there is a cloudy day or rainy weather during these periods then you are out of luck. You don't have many chances during the year to practice this sort of technique.

What you really need to do to correctly practice absorbing the essence of light is to simply imagine the light of the sun or moon in your body. This is a method much used in hatha yoga, and anyone can do this. If you're weak you try to imagine the light of the sun inside you, and if you have too much energy, you "cool off" by imagining moonlight within. You just imagine the light of the sun or moon wherever you need it in your body, and then you need not try to absorb any chi essences from outside. This is a visualization practice, too, that can be used as a method of cultivation.

You don't need to go and physically see the sun or moon to "absorb their essences" because you are always absorbing their energies anyway.

---

[126] People don't ordinarily realize that the first, second, third, and fourth dhyanas as well as the formless absorptions and white skeleton meditation are all considered *kasina* meditations. *Kasina* concentrations help you purify your chi and open your chi channels because of the attendant state of stable mind you try to cultivate, and this is another reason why people should practice the impure body white skeleton visualization method taught by Shakyamuni. Not only does mental stability transform your chi channels up and down the full length of your body, but it also prepares you for the higher stages of the path - namely samadhi where you forget the body entirely because the channels have been transformed. It is said that super-powers are often achieved because of the practice of these visualization techniques.

We are always absorbing the light of the sun, moon, stars and planets. Our physical bodies, with chi channels and chakras inside, are like molecules that absorb the light energies of the universe. Externally, one frequency of light causes our physical body to make vitamin D while another causes it to tan. Inside of us, who knows what those then invisible energies are responsible for doing?

The sun's energies are always passing through you, even if you are inside a house, but practitioners didn't understand this when reading the early Taoist books that mentioned these techniques. You can always connect with those energies through the mind. In visualization practice you try to reach a stable state of consciousness by concentrating on an image, and then let go, and that resultant state of emptiness leads to transformations in your chi and channels. This is what we are ultimately after.

In Shakyamuni's day, every monk was told to imagine that their mind and body became only sunshine as they were falling asleep, which is also an excellent related cultivation technique. This sort of practice is once again different from but related to the idea of visualizing colors in either *kasina* meditations, deity yoga, tantras and other visualization practices. Whereas the practice of visualizing rainbows can also be used in concentration practice, which helps open up the chakras and chi channels if a stable mind is attained, the idea behind visualizing the light of the sun and moon is to help transform the body's chi and consciousness as well. It is hard to visualize endless boundless light, and the only way you can approximate anything like that is by reaching a state of infinite emptiness.

In the white skeleton visualization you practice seeing the human body becoming only a bright white skeleton after all the flesh is stripped off and happily offered away. If you achieve one-pointed stable concentration on the final skeleton visualization, it will help to open all the chi and channels throughout the entire length and breadth of the body because your skeleton stretches everywhere.

Other practices have you imagine that your body transforms into the body of a beautiful deity. Yet other cultivation schools have you visualize all the chi channels and chakras within your body in multi-color form to accomplish the very same end. Some schools want you to visualize geometric shapes, such as mandalas, and others suggest complicated pictures such as the City of God or Jesus dying on the cross,[127] both being

---

[127] Some people who practice this incorrectly can develop stigmata in a subsequent life because they concentrated on that aspect of their visualized image, and did not learn to let go.

visualizations recommended by the Jesuits. If any of these visualized images become stabilized, that calm mental state, which is not empty but similar to emptiness in that wandering thoughts have died down, will assist in transforming all the chi throughout the entirety of the body.

While different, these practice techniques are similar. Many methods can be built on the same principles. If you can visualize a chakra or set of chakras with stability, as done in kundalini yoga visualizations, you are accomplishing the same ends. Furthermore, you are affecting the chi in those sections of the body because wherever the mind goes, chi will follow. With the skeleton and deity visualization techniques you are helping to transform your body's full set of chi channels, rather than just those in one particular area, because you are not focused on a small region. To properly practice, as soon as you "see" that you become a skeleton or deity you are practicing correctly. You don't have to hold on to the image with tremendous force so that strain shows on your face. You just visualize the image, you know the image, you hold it, and then release it to develop emptiness. As with anapana practice where you watch the breath, you repeat the process as necessary.

If you understand the principles of practice, you can create all sorts of visualization exercises, and perhaps someone will create more effective means in the future than what has already been transmitted in famous tantric texts. To start with, however, it is just common sense that one should always use what has worked in the past for countless people within a tradition. Nevertheless, with our modern understanding that all the chakras are linked together by channels, like atoms linked by chemical bonds within a molecule, you can use understandings like this as the basis for new one-pointed visualization practices to help transform your chi and channels. Many tantric visualizations are based on such principles. If you know the principles, you can practice with almost anything and as the results of visualization practice for the great scientists and inventors illustrate, the results can be outstanding. It is unfortunate that those individuals did not turn their efforts toward spiritual cultivation; as the case of Viktor Schauberger illustrates, one can be a scientist and spiritual cultivator as well.

Do not think that one tantric visualization is more powerful than another. It all depends on the individual and their karmic propensities. It is simply a function of science that chi transformations come about when you achieve a stable mind due to visualization practice. This happens regardless of the image you use to achieve stable concentration, though some visualizations are indeed easier than others to master and some have deeper meanings from the field of spiritual cultivation. Remember that the tantric transmissions offer proven patterns for visualization practice that have helped many people achieve mental stability and spiritual progress. One of the wisest things to do is just use the proven tantric visualizations that have successfully worked for countless people in the past and been blessed by enlightened masters and their lineages through transmission.

As with the white skeleton visualization practice, deity yoga visualization, or tantric concentrations, once a stable image is achieved you always release it and then mentally rest in emptiness. Visualization images employ color, as with mandala visualizations, because for many people this is a more effective way to engender a concentration state that leads to the samadhi of a stable mind. And once again the principles of cessation and witnessing apply always apply to this practice technique. You concentrate on visualizing something in order to attain cessation, which is the disappearance of the wandering thoughts of the monkey mind, and then relax the mind while maintaining awareness to practice witnessing.

It is said that if you succeed in the *kasina* visualizations on colors and the five elements, etc. you will often develop miraculous superpowers. This is because you can use any method of concentration as an entryway into developing the stable samadhi of the first dhyana rather than the mundane samadhi of just a quiet, empty mind. From samadhi, superpowers can arise and India has plenty of ancient yoga texts on these capabilities. By practicing these concentrations, after a long time you will end up transforming the chi and channels of your body, namely the body's five elements, just as Hercules does in the Twelve Labors through the simple cultivation of empty mind. That is the starting point and it proceeds onwards from there.

If you practice visualizing complicated mandalas of many colors, and then offering them away as done in Vajrayana, this is a similar concentration technique with the additional fact that you let go or offer away the imagination at the end of practice, as is done with the white skeleton visualization technique. Mandalas typically represent the functions of various chakras in one image just as the skeleton visualization represents all the chi channels of the body. If you see eight Buddhas or eight petals around a central mandala figure, that mandala usually represents the heart chakra and the *sushumna* channel running through its center. Twelve petals or deities surrounding a mandala's circular shape often represents the throat chakra, four deities around a central Buddha usually represents the root chakra, and so on. In complicated mandalas you will often see representations of multiple chakras stacked upon one another. If you mix mandala practice with mantra recitation on chakra points, and with breathing practices, you can transform your body quite quickly.

These are not secrets, but just cultivation methods not understood by the public because they have never been instructed in these matters. Success in being able to visualize colorful pictures with a stable mind requires concentration, namely the ability to develop a stable mind that can hold on to a vivid image without fluctuation. That's called "one-pointed concentration." The mind stays on a point without wavering. Concentration practice means to reach a state absent of mental wandering.[128] Guess what? Simply by watching your mind's contents, your mind will become quiet or absent of wandering thoughts, so that's another cultivation method, too. All these different methods are designed to lead you to the same state of an empty mind though they use different approaches to do so.

It's hard to master *kasina*, mandala, tantra and deity yoga visualizations because we are not used to developing mental stability. Human beings have problems concentrating for any length of time on anything, yet this is one of the proven roads for attaining samadhi or stable mind. However, once your channels start opening and your mind becomes emptier it's easier to develop an open mind and practice visualizations. This is a good skill to master. Gaining proficiency in cultivating traditional visualizations is no different than Nikola Tesla learning how to visualize the moving parts of his inventions.

Every mental problem, guilt, or suffering you have represents a knot, restriction or obstruction in your chi channels and chakras because of the connection between chi and consciousness. To have constant mental afflictions means that your consciousness, chi and channels have not yet transformed. Being able to readily mentally change shape, form, color and appearance as required in a visualization, or visualizations done in series, means you are cultivating a freedom of mind akin to emptiness

---

[128] A special point to note about the mandala and deity yoga visualization practices of Esoteric Buddhism is that the proper level of achievement, or target level of attainment, is the samadhi of infinite consciousness. However, most people who practice visualizations usually attain the samadhi of neither knowing nor not-knowing (the samadhi of neither thought nor no-thought).

that will enable you to let go of afflictions more easily. An empty mind leads to the transformation or purification of your chi, and meditation is the only real practice that deeply helps along these lines.

Pranayama practice, mantra recitation, the bhajan singing of bhakti yoga, and even karmamudra imaginings can generate some heat for the process of opening the channels but meditation is the foundational road you must practice in any path of spiritual cultivation. If you are virtuous and have the requisite merit and devoted practice, you can make extra fast progress in opening your channels if you receive the "blessings," "empowerments" or "abhisheka" from the Buddhas, Bodhisattvas, protector gods and heavenly beings (deities, devas, dakinis, angels, etc.). But this never happens unless you've performed lots of preliminary cultivation work, and have some inkling of the meaning of emptiness meditation. It is universal for practitioners to pray for this type of help in all religions, but only those who cultivate to a sufficient level can actually receive its full measure.

These empowerments from "on high" spoken of in religions are represented by the purifying waters of Kuan Yin's vase. In countless spiritual schools, an empowerment is represented by water that is poured out into your body to help purify and open up your body's channels, thus "washing" or "cleansing" it. These heavenly gifts of chi purification wash away impurities inside you that interfere with your cultivation progress and help to make your channels more open and flexible. This flexibility is the characteristic which Tibetan Buddhism calls "pliancy" or "physical suppleness"[129] that grows over time for all successful cultivators. Although the real empowerments seem like liquids poured into your physical body from above, unbeknownst to you, they are actually occurring within your own body. The multicolored medicine pills carried in a bowl by the Medicine Buddha Bhaisajya also symbolize this same type of assistance.

The event of deities pouring such chi substances into the bodies of practitioners is what is symbolized by the baptism in Christianity. This heavenly help is known as an "abhisheka" (sometimes abhishekam) and it is described in Vajrayana, Shingon (which calls it "pouring from the peak"), Hinduism, Jainism and Judaism as well. It is the "heavenly dan" which Chinese Taoist practitioners pray for, and it is only bestowed upon spiritual practitioners who have made sufficient cultivation progress, merit and vows. So Buddhas, Bodhisattvas and spiritual beings often

---

[129] Lao Tzu refers to pliancy when he notes that a baby's body is soft and gentle, and a man's body should become soft and flexible.

intervene to help practitioners open up their chi channels and fix their chi flows. This is what a Tibetan Vajrayana ceremonial empowerment is supposed to symbolize, but a genuine empowerment, or *abhisheka*, is the real thing.

Such blessings "from Heaven" seem like hot liquids[130] poured into your body from above, but despite the deceptive appearance so that individuals are less frightened, what you feel is happening within. As with people who pray for the spontaneous remission of a disease, such help is only possible when the individuals have the requisite fortune and merit, and are really working hard and who make great Bodhisattva vows to help all beings on the road of enlightenment. Countless cultivation schools describe the *abhisheka* empowerment because it is a non-denominational blessing bestowed upon cultivation practitioners who make it to the upper half of the Twelve Labors. We tend to prejudicially segment things in this world according to people's religion, but heaven is blind as to religion and helps anyone who makes sufficient cultivation efforts with virtuous objectives in mind.

It is said that the Great Lord Rama of Hinduism had to practice cultivation for fourteen years in the jungle before he attained such blessings, so this shows they are difficult to receive. The ceremonial *abhisheka* empowerments of religions only symbolize this event, but the real thing is achievable. While the *abhisheka* is what the baptismal ceremony within Christianity is *supposed* to represent, Christian religious functionaries have lost the knowledge of this meaning, as has happened in Judaism as well. If you cultivate sufficiently you might possibly receive this gift of grace. If you don't, then you will not. It's as simple as that. The *abhisheka* empowerment of heavenly help for transforming your chi and opening your chi channels is recognized in Hinduism, Jainism, Buddhism, Taoism and other religions because heavenly beings help without prejudice. It is only people who get stuck on the outer differences between religions and lose sight of their overall target.

Why is it found everywhere? Because people in all these schools cultivate spiritual practice in search of the same original nature, and spiritual help is something that is non-denominationally given. Bodhisattvas are not prejudiced like us but will help anyone who spiritually cultivates and wishes to attain the Tao. That is why so many people from so many

---

[130] The hot sensation is similar to the feeling of drinking liquor that seems to burn, but in this case the feeling is felt along a thin line that seems to be progressively cutting open the truck of the body from inside.

cultures and religions succeed in attaining enlightenment. Regardless as to what the major religions tell you, membership within a specific religious sect or group is not the important thing, and does not guarantee your salvation or a place in heaven. Personal cultivation practice is the important thing for a life not to be wasted. The religion you land in is a product of karma, just as are the genes that have produced your physical body that must be transformed on the path. Your religious affiliation is not the ultimate thing – personal spiritual practice is what is important. Spiritual practice is not about worship or following rules of discipline but about getting a direct experience of your true nature.

The *abhisheka* or empowerment given to human beings is symbolized in many cultures by libations of various healing substances (water, milk, honey, rose water, special oils, etc.) poured over statues such as the Shiva lingam in Hinduism. In Judaism it is indicated by the anointing of kings, prophets and the high Priests, pouring oil on the head. An actual *abhisheka*, however, is not like a forehead anointing or even the sprinkling of water on the head but like the pouring of a stream of hot water into the body's chest when you are on your back to help purify its chi and channels. It can feel like a liquid burning sensation as certain chi channel lines are opened in this way.

People sometimes experience a similar type of "baptism" as they sleep but rarely remember the process after waking up. It's often responsible for many "spontaneous" health cures as well, though you cannot count on receiving this help for a "spontaneous remission" if you lack the requisite merit. When it's your karma to suffer a particular disease because of past faults, there is sometimes very little that anyone can do unless you have cultivated hard and performed a lot of merit in this life. Karma that must be paid must be experienced, and even superpowers cannot avert it. However, the more charitable and meritorious deeds you have performed in the world, the more good you have done for others and the more people and other beings[131] you have helped in various ways, then the more the realm of consciousness can be stimulated and the more mundane strings that can be tugged to help you change a difficult karmic fortune. One should not expect miracles, however, because the mutual conditioning of cause and effect interacting from so many sources insures often makes difficult karma hard to alter for the better in a short period.

---

[131] The aggregate realm of consciousness, as one whole, does not just refer to human beings but *all* sentient beings.

If you receive an *abhisheka* empowerment, it does not mean that the path is easy from then on in. In fact, the heavenly beings overseeing and dispensing such assistance will test you, trick you and confuse you in countless ways to see what channels they must concentrate on helping to open. The transition phase of opening your channels this way can be emotionally and mentally difficult in the extreme, and the process lasts for a very long time. Having access to your memories, every good or bad deed you ever did will come up during the process, and you will be challenged on them. You will be temporarily exposed to all sorts of societal prohibitions you have fiercely adopted - such as not eating meat,[132] not drinking wine or refraining from sexual relations - to determine which channels you have forcibly shut close with hard rejection. A true master refrains from what is wrong naturally, without need of mental force or strain. This is why it is often said that samadhi is the highest form of discipline, and losing (falling out of) one's samadhi is the largest breech of discipline.

This explanation is the secret tie-in, by the way, to the meaning of "left hand" tantric paths which masters always warn that religious commoners simply cannot follow. Tantric sadhanas are not about breaking prohibitions, but about opening hard-to-open channels shunted off due

---

[132] Societies develop countless artificial prohibitions over time that we become afraid to break without realizing why the conventions were set up in the first place. For instance, many religious hygiene and dietary rules were built up over time because a master, or wise individual, realized that a rule would prevent many cases of illness and disease. The rules were invented by men, not by heaven. For instance, most people are right-handed and might not clean themselves sufficiently after defecating, so a "religious" rule might be made that one should always wipe themselves with their left hand. There is nothing wrong with eating fresh shellfish, but because seafood spoils easily and people were often getting sick from food poisoning, someone made eating shellfish a prohibition that later generations turned into an unbreakable religious rule. People strictly ruled by religious injunctions rather than wisdom and scientific, logical thinking lack even the basic wisdom required for the path and are not qualified to be spiritual leaders. We can even say they are at a *negative level* of spiritual understanding and attainment when they take rules as the spiritual path in itself or as inflexible injunctions from a higher power. It is by this overemphasis that individuals exhibit their lack of qualifications for spiritual leadership roles. They do not recognize that *true virtue is supple in regards to circumstances.* Such individuals cannot lead you to the Tao. You should always act with wisdom, virtue and compassion in all circumstances, and know that what those entail may violate the traditional rules of society in special circumstances, and yet violate them you must when the situation calls for it. No excuses need be made. There is nothing wrong with religion, but with the lack of human wisdom in doing what needs to be done in certain situations. As to the definite need and usefulness of religion itself for society, aside from its ability to lead one to liberation you must also remember the words of Benjamin Franklin who once wrote, "Think how great a proportion of mankind consists of weak and ignorant men and women, and of inexperienced and inconsiderate youth of both sexes, who have need of the motives of religion to restrain them from vice, to support their virtue, and retain them in the practice of it till it becomes *habitual.*"

to normal occlusions as well as any strong prohibitions you have forcibly adopted. Naturally you should always act with virtue and wisdom in all life situations, so this sort of tantra does not necessarily mean you indulge in prohibitions. Nevertheless, it is about opening difficult-to-open channels in a way not one in a hundred million could understand. Thus this type of path is never taught publicly and is only guided by enlightened beings, Buddhas and Bodhisattvas, who have vowed to help practitioners and protect the path and dharma of enlightenment. Sexual relations can be used in these routes to help transform the body's channels quickly. However, as the examples of the Sixth Dalai Lama and Adi Shankara (whose consciousness entered the dead body of a king to learn the "art of love" from his harem) indicate, only a spiritual practitioner of the right status can abandon prohibitions and engage in those techniques. Karmic consequences must always be paid; you can never escape karma. Lust or promiscuity are never any sanctioned path and so we must not take sex as the spiritual path because it absolutely, positively is not. You cannot even say it is part of the spiritual path. Movements of the lower torso do not lead to samadhi or enlightenment. The path has nothing to do with sex because celibacy is usually necessary for success, and there should be no disharmony or disorder in a body of monks and nuns because of sexual relations, which tend to break an order's discipline.

Shakyamuni Buddha and Tsong Khapa therefore wisely prohibited sexual activities for the body of monks and nuns, and the celibate life has become the standard rule for countless traditions because it is the wisest one and best one for achieving success in spiritual cultivation. Even for society, a lack of ethical codes or principles of conduct covering sexual relations, dietary matters, drinking, drugs, propriety and etiquette, and so on is extremely bad, certainly disorderly at best, and typically harmful to the good health and peaceful functioning of society. As an example, it is often said that teenagers are all hormones, so think what would happen if there were no adults or rules to guide their behavior? There are always negative consequences of various dimensions to unwise behavior, such as certain types of permissiveness that can hurt both oneself and others. One should therefore be careful never to promote a pathway that is ultimately destructive to society. A path that emphasizes the free indulgence of bodily matters without balance, even among willing participants, is certainly not the spiritual path nor necessarily conducive to health and harmony. What willing partners do is naturally a matter between themselves, but since cause and effect rules consequences such matters are always best guided through wisdom. In the realm of sensation, human beings always tend to go to harmful extremes.

To help open the channel pathways other beings must first see the lay of the land, and thus you will be thrust into all sorts of extreme situations where you are forced to go through enormous emotional situations or make incredibly large emotional decisions. While the enormity of the situations eventually dies down over time as more refined levels of channel structures are reached, I don't even want to go into the various initial extreme situations I was put through and what I almost lost during the process. The story of Naropa's twelve hardships comes to mind, and Father Abraham's dilemma falls into this pattern, too. The type of tension-release situations you will be subjected to all depends upon your mental traits, attachments and afflictions. For those who have gone through the process, it is easy to recognize this type of intervention in the story where Abraham was told to offer up his son. The original nature does not talk since it is not a person or being, so of course this was due to the intervention of heavenly beings. Abraham doubtless went through many other testing situations as well, similar in nature to what I have recounted, that were not even mentioned in the Bible.

If I really were to go into all the various types of emotional ups and downs, afflictions, pain and suffering you will go through from the genuine, rather than the ceremonial *abhisheka* empowerment, you might wonder why this transformative assistance is called a "blessing." Nevertheless, it is the most supreme of blessings in the world to receive this help in opening your channels, and it gets much easier to bear the process over time. Even with all the explanations that I am providing, you will never be able to figure out what the Bodhisattvas are doing with your chi and channels and why you are mentally being tested in all sorts of ways. They will test you, this way and that, so that they may determine what needs to be done, but you will never be able to determine the methodology. But with these words you will be able to keep your balance and sanity through the process when you are unfortunate not to be near your master.

My hope is that the true cultivation trail does not pass away from this world and that it takes hold in the West. However, the chances are that practitioners will not have the teachings or an enlightened master available to help them. Therefore, I am pulling back the curtains and providing as many explanations as possible for solo practitioners who get this far, knowing that without these explanations you would suffer greatly maintaining your balance through the process of body transformation. This is why the process is normally completed within a sealed retreat under the watchful eyes of a master who is present.

From his description of hearing a chorus of inner daemons and the fact that he became enlightened, we can surmise that Socrates must have gone through this type of experience because this is one of the typical accompaniments of the process. Abraham of the Old Testament, who heard voices telling him to give up his son as a type of spiritual test, definitely went through this same process which people mistakenly take as words from God the ultimate. He is certain to have gone through other testings as well which the Bible did not recount, otherwise it makes no sense that an intelligent man would follow voices he hears in his head. The Second Chinese Patriarch of Zen, Hui Ko, who heard a voice telling him it would not last long as he endured the pain of the chi penetrating through his skull bones, also went through this process as his chi channels were opened.

The famous twelve major hardships of the famous Tibetan cultivator Naropa, overseen by Tilopa his enlightened master,[133] exemplify some of the difficult experiences you might mentally be put through during this process. The single event reported from Abraham's life is just a subset of the overall process represented by Naropa's example, whose own commitment to attaining the Tao reveals why he reached such a high stage of attainment, as did Milarepa in his lineage. In receiving heavenly help in transforming the physical body along with its chi and channels, such as is asked for in countless traditions, you will really be put through the physical, emotional and mental ringers. You will see all sorts of things such as attacks by demons, visits by other beings, trips to heaven and hell, that are all fictitious visions. You should never believe anything you hear via "heavenly voices" during these experiences either, but every time you go through some difficulty due to these interventions yet more channel blockages will disappear and your chi and channels will further transform. Without this help – called heavenly *dan* in Taoism - it is very difficult to transform the body, and these explanations reveal some of the secrets behind true tantra.

The twelve hardships of Naropa, the empowerments of Yeshe Tsogyel, the testing of Abraham in offering his son, the Second Zen Patriarch Hui

---

[133] You can also read the story of Tilopa and his encounter with the Queen of the Dakinis and her retinue of thousands, which is similar to the tale of Krishna and the Yellow Emperor we have previously discussed. These stories all refer to the physical transformations of the body for individuals seeking the sambhogakaya attainment.

Ko who heard a voice during the painful time when his head channels were being transformed, and Socrates' chorus of inner daemons are all linked to chi and channel purification in conjunction with "heavenly" (Bodhisattva) assistance. These stories are all related to the accounts in the Buddhist scriptures of the pores of Bodhisattvas being the homes of countless other Bodhisattvas, but non-initiates cannot fathom the connection. Such assistance is not easy to obtain, it is never understood when received, and rarely discussed in full measure because common people would fear it and not believe it either. It takes a rare individual to reach these stages, and fewer still understand what is occurring as they happen.

Our fundamental nature doesn't "test" people because it is not a god, deity or personal entity. It is only sentient beings with higher attainments who can choose to help us. In other words, "God" does not test people, karma only happens. To say that the original self nature is testing you is just nonsense. Only a being, such as a Buddha, Bodhisattva, heavenly deity dharma protector (what you would normally call an angel, deva or dakini and daki), or human would interact with virtuous spiritual practitioners in regards to the Tao. They already know ahead of time who's qualified for assistance but must still put practitioners through difficult experiences, such as Abraham's or Naropa's, to see which sets of channels should be opened first. This type of assistance, and thus the difficult testings that will occur, can last a long time because the process of purification lasts a very long time. Most practitioners only report one or two of the most memorable experiences, and many don't even know that they are going through this transition with "Heaven's help."

Aside from the prerequisites of practicing virtuous ways, desiring spiritual progress and practicing spiritual cultivation to a sufficient degree, you really need the "right view" if you want to succeed in great awakening. It is safe to really throw yourself into cultivating the body only *after* attaining the right view of realizing that your true mind is ultimately empty, that you are not the physical body, and there is no such thing as an inherently existing person.

Your natural mind is empty and yet things appear in it. Despite these appearances, the fundamental, absolute, foundational essence of this ordinary mind is empty or pure in a way that transcends just an ordinary absence of thought. Our true self or the fundamental nature of what we are is self-illuminated, so from this natural empty awareness consciousness can arise. When consciousness is empty because thoughts die down, the mind merely is, the world does not manifest because there are no thoughts registering perception, but our absolute presence still exists. We say that the essence of consciousness can in some way become empty, but that emptiness isn't the same as the emptiness of space which has limits or borders. One can say that it is like a non-existence of ordinary phenomena, but can we call it a non-existence when the next moment that emptiness somehow gives birth to appearances? Appearances arise within it but it abides empty. We say it's empty, but it's not inert or dead because it gives birth to existence. Because it is luminous it is not mere inert emptiness. On the other hand, we cannot say it is alive because it does not fundamentally change, and hence it transcends the transient realm of birth and death that is consciousness.

The fact that something seems to arise (within the mind) and be there is what we call existence. On one hand you have this emptiness (non-existence), and on the other hand you have appearance (or existence). You also have the logical fact that what appears in the mind must be of the same nature as the mind. When you have no thoughts there is nothing to perceive, and so there is only awareness or consciousness (depending upon your terminology) without subject or object. In a state of pure consciousness without thoughts, nothing is perceived. When you perceive phenomena these are simply modifications of consciousness, and therefore identical with it. They are of the same nature as the mind because they are the mind. There is no inside or outside to it; you are always just experiencing mind.

As to the awareness or knowing that arises from the mind, this must be the function of the mind's underlying essence, whatever that essence is. If you think about it, what appears in the mind (thoughts, sensations, images, etc.) must also be one with its nature or essence. The manifestations of the mind are part of the mind, so they cannot be anything other than one with its nature. So the appearances of interdependent origination in the mind's empty true nature must be a unity. There must be an interdependence of inherent emptiness and dependent origination. The contents of the mind *must* be of the same nature as the underlying essence of the mind, and so both must be empty. This is why we say that emptiness and interdependent origination (all of existence, which is what we call "appearance," the universe, manifestation, "mind and matter," Thusness or the realm of cause and effect) must therefore be the same.

Unfortunately, you have to cultivate, cultivate, cultivate to get to the absolute base of the mind and verify this for yourself with direct experiential insight. It is not something you make up, not some dogma you adopt because of the creed of religion or teachings from various sages, but Truth you must awaken to through direct realization. You actually find the substrate of your True Self that is the essence of all mind and matter, all sentient beings and the universe.

Through spiritual cultivation you can discover that mind is ultimately experienced as a great original wakefulness without borders, without center, timeless and spaceless, that is intrinsically pure ... like a mass of pure awareness that is free of names and forms and free of liking or disliking. It is primordially empty and free, self-existing and complete in itself, and has always been present within yourself from the beginning. This is the basis of your mind and the five senses. It is self-luminous unbroken awareness that transcends the phenomena of birth and death that appear within it. It is an entirely one and unbroken state that encompasses all consciousness.

What supports it is the Supreme state of silence, stillness and purity, or True Self, that is unreachable by mind. It is not perceptible because it makes perception possible. Mind is one of its functions. What you are is beyond the mind and its contents, beyond being and non-being.

You are always that pure, eternal, equanimous, non-dual empty universal awareness (in terms of functioning) experiencing various transforming appearances, but you have to finally attain one of the degrees of self-realization, or *bhumis,* to realize this and the Source of the mind. To do so you must transcend the knot between the pure consciousness of undifferentiated being and the physical body, which is the ego or "I-thought,"[134] by diving into the source from whence the I-thought arises to find the True Self. For complete enlightenment, that realization must be perfect and complete without stain.

Shakyamuni Buddha explained that ignorance stands in the way of this realization – we are ignorantly clinging to the contents of the mind, to consciousness, and hence cannot readily realize its origins. Because of incorrect, deep seated habits developed over infinite past lives, which is why you are on this Earth rather than in a higher realm, you're clinging to the body and mind all the time. If you cultivate, you can start to achieve an independence of mental functioning which does not attach to the body because that attachment is just a habit. The body is eventually seen

---

[134] This is called the "seventh consciousness" in Buddhism, or "afflicted mind" because the belief in an inherently existing ego or self is an affliction or stain on the true Self original nature.

as just an experience of consciousness. Eventually you can detach from consciousness itself to recognize its ultimate source.[135]

Through proper meditation practice you will eventually achieve a degree of mental clarity and purity that enables this because your chi and consciousness will become pure, and you will reach a degree of mental stability because your channels clear and the chi flow through them becomes smooth. With this as a foundational basis, you might finally be able to "see the Tao" and understand the dharma like finally being able to see to the bottom of a lake because the ripples on its surface have all calmed. Or, you might cultivate peaceful samadhi states instead (that are manifestations of the mind) and still miss realizing the Tao, which means discovering its source. To see the Tao and realize these things is called prajna wisdom.

So even without any dharma teachings whatsoever, if your mind becomes clear, pure and calm you might see the Tao and self-awaken. This has happened to countless self-enlightened ones in the past, which is why great spiritual teachers have arisen from time to time and founded new traditions for people to help them attain the path. Self-realization is possible because the Tao is always there and salvation, or liberation, does not come from a creed or dogma. It comes from discovering your True Self, what you really, foundationally are. It is not an artificial dogma or man-made creation you adopt because of belief but your absolute nature you can realize through direct experience. The Tao is not a creation, dogma, religious invention or artificial teaching. It is not something made up. It is the underlying absolute nature, your True Self. This is what you awaken to because this is what you are, this is your true nature or fundamental face.

Many people have independently awakened throughout history, although the Stage of Study and Virtue Accumulation certainly helps people awaken who desire to cultivate, and having a teacher who knows

---

[135] In the *Surangama Sutra*, Shakyamuni Buddha explained what it is like to finally detach from the skandha of consciousness. He said one enters a state where absolutely nothing stains consciousness. One detaches from the fabric of *samsara* and the karma of transmigration. One can therefore contemplate any contents of consciousness without any attachment whatsoever, and free of consciousness all things are revealed. Having attained an identity with all things in the universe, including all beings, one can understand the source of all defilements and will find it to be thoughts. Shakyamuni said that the sense consciousnesses are all empty and no longer gallop about; because of their empty purity they are now interchangeable. Within and without there is perfect clarity, and body and mind are both clear like transparent glass. In the *Surangama Sutra* he also talked of ten great possible errors you might make when trying to detach from the skandha of consciousness, and ten errors of practice or interpretation when trying to pass through the other four skandhas as well.

the path is extremely helpful. But such men and women who have awakened are exceedingly rare. Remember, awakening is a self-realization as to what you ultimately are, what is truly your Real Self or original nature. Religion is not necessary for this awakening, although religion is supposed to preserve and disseminate the methods for people to cultivate and awaken to their True Self, or "God," and to help them along this road. Is your religion doing this for you?

After you awaken all sorts of miraculous abilities can arise because you have realized the source of all existence and are one with the base of all minds, all existence, all matter, all functioning. Sages assure us that you free yourself from pain and suffering, and all sorts of troubles come to rest because the true nature of the Self is peace. Buddhism speaks of this in detail though countless other sages from other religions mention this as well. They just substitute the word "God" or "Brahman" or "Allah" etc. for dharmakaya, Buddha-nature, dharmadhatu, absolute nature, fundamental nature, True Self, Reality and so on. As to how the body came about and how ignorance first arose in this endless universe, or as to information on all sorts of miraculous abilities of the body and mind, you'll have to go to the advanced Buddhist sutra sources for those discussions.

If you don't first "see the Tao" so that you can understand these matters and what the spiritual path is all about, you will almost always go astray in the form schools of Vajrayana, Taoism, tantric yoga, western alchemy, paganism, science and so forth, as they stress the physical body in cultivation. You'll continue to take the body as something real. Even to say you are "bodyless mind"[136] is partially incorrect because in using the term "mind" this refers to function rather than substance or essence. Awareness, or witnessing, is just a function of what is fundamentally real, of what you fundamentally are. The witness is not an experience by itself but merely registers the presence or absence of experience. It becomes an experience when the thought "I am the witness" arises.

We say we have a mind because we have awareness of consciousness, which are both functions of the original nature. Without this witnessing

[136] This is a good meditation practice in itself, to just take yourself not as the body or appearances within consciousness but as witness only – a dimensionless, timeless, centerless witnessing function. If you so detach from mental consciousness, the phenomena of the mind, to practice this, in time you can eventually realize the immense, pure, changeless ocean of pure awareness that is both mind and matter and yet beyond them. Through detachment your mind will purify and chi will change, just as in the Twelve Labors of Hercules, and you go through all sorts of gong-fu and eventually reach a stage of realization. This is true cultivation and true spiritual practice. The true road of religion should be teaching people how to do this.

of consciousness there would just be inert matter or emptiness. Yet there *is* witnessing, which we call awareness, and there is the miraculous existence of phenomena within consciousness, so one must come to understand the base of the functioning of witnessing by tracing it back to discover its Source. You cannot perceive that ultimate base because it is what makes perception possible. It cannot be reached by mind. It is beyond consciousness and therefore in consciousness you cannot say what it is. It is beyond conventional existence and the absence of existence, and hence free of birth and death or the rising and departure of thoughts. You can only be It, the Real Self, the underlying true nature. You are always It, the original nature which appears at a given point of space and time as the witness,[137] or "I am," which is a bridge between the pure awareness of the Self and the consciousness of the person. At the level of the absolute original nature there are no persons, entities or beings. They simply do not exist in reality. Furthermore, its ocean of pure awareness is not only undifferentiated but attributeless – neither virtuous or non-virtuous, neither pleasurable or painful and that is bliss. Neither good nor bad it is simply a functioning. It's what's operating, it's the true immortal body of what you are yet of course it is not a body in the conventional sense. This underlying pristine wisdom is self-aware, yet without ego, capable of inhabiting ("working," "appropriating," or "shining through") a body and consciousness yet not attached to it. As Zen master Lin-chi said, "One pure illumination functions as six interacting aspects (the five sense consciousnesses and discrimination)."

In relation to consciousness you can therefore say we are simply functioning awareness, but in relation to the universe you can say we are pure being, the Real Self or absolute original nature that has given rise to everything. Consciousness is a function or operational characteristic of our True Self, and arises as one single body. Within consciousness false thoughts sprout up that create the illusion of differentiation within that one body of impersonal consciousness. Due to more false thoughts

---

[137] The witness is like pure awareness that knows itself to be as nothing. This is why all enlightened beings awaken to the truth of no self, selflessness, or no ego which they call "emptiness." Emptiness means to be as nothing because that point of awareness lacks any substantial substance or essence and is empty of content, hence its stainless unchanging purity lacks any characteristics or attributes. We say that you are the witness or observer, but even that you are ultimately not, for you are actually the true underlying reality that has awareness (witnessing) as one of its functions, and That One is the ultimate potentiality of everything that has been and can be and yet is independent and free of all it gives rise to. You are Host, not guest, and yet the essence of guest is the Host. You can never know what It is, so the only way of knowing Host is to be It, which is what you already are, but shedding the false identification with a small self and actually realizing Host is what we call realization or awakening.

and attachments that pile upon one another over beginningless time, the illusion of an independent ego or small self is created which must be traced back to its source for there to be spiritual liberation.

In any case, consciousness is transient and ever moving, so is not real, and through insight consciousness can trace itself back to its roots of pure being, which can be known by a direct experience that lacks ignorance and illusions. That's why this is not just theory or surmise, for sages prove this over and over again throughout the countless cultures and religions, in this world and that world and in countless realms wherever there is sentience. They teach it but people don't understand, and out of compassion the awakened constantly intervene again and again to point the true way of spiritual practice and ways to awaken.

That real "pure being" is beyond ordinary existence and non-existence, and awareness is its nature. Experience is a state of mind while *being* is not a state of mind. Being, or beingness, is true existence, the True Self. It is what you are, experiencing the world through a small clouded filter until you awaken. There is no self other than this True Self. That true nature pervades all states but is not a state because it is independent and beyond space and time, matter, life and consciousness. It is not this or that. The true nature, Source or True Self is self-so, self-existent, self-manifest without a creator. It is complete and whole. It transcends everything and does not fall into either subjectivity or objectivity, birth or death, coming or going. It is the unborn potential of everything, the inexhaustible possibility for manifestation. Hence the original nature is called the Unmanifest or Unborn as well as the Unseen or Unknown (since gnosis of the essence is utterly impossible), and also the spontaneous, natural state. It is the natural state that is eternally self-existent, the underlying nature. It enjoys permanency whereas the manifest state is always marked by disequilibrium. The process of yoga, meditation, religious practice or spiritual cultivation – however you wish to word it – is to take you back to the underlying Source.

My words here are only to help get you started in the right direction. People don't make progress in cultivation because they never attain the right view, and are always holding on to other notions that actually inhibit their cultivation progress. They pursue superpowers and all sorts of other things other than to look for the base, the absolute nature, the foundational state, the Truth, the Self, the Buddha-nature from which we have mind, consciousness and awareness. How to find it? The practice words for the path are, "Let go, let go" while continuing to let consciousness shine without restriction. You are always experiencing It.

To attain perfect enlightenment you must achieve three things: complete realization of the dharmakaya, sambhogakaya and nirmanakaya, rather than just the dharmakaya alone. This trio corresponds to the mind, body and behavior. The nirmanakaya, for instance, entails the ability to skillfully project images or thoughts to any realm of consciousness, meaning even to what we call individual consciousnesses because they are all part of the one body of consciousness. It is proper to start cultivating the other two "bodies" of the sambhogakaya and nirmanakaya after you realize what the Tao is by mentally experiencing the truth of emptiness for yourself via a direct experience. That's the approach of Zen which stresses that you must work hard and first see the Tao. Then you can cultivate realization and start carrying out vows to better the universe and the state of sentient beings.

As Buddha said, you must verify and authenticate the Tao through personal experience. Don't just accept spiritual teachings out of devotion, but out of your own experimentation. Do not just swallow things on faith as the good sheep in the orthodox religions are ordered to do. You must be a lion, rather than a sheep, on the road of spiritual cultivation to find your true self. Because people "want to be good" by following some set of rules and regulations handed to them, they become "sheeple" who allow so much nonsense to continue to survive and propagate in the world. People just accept anything that somehow gets inculcated in a tradition and continue to stick to it, rather than use logic to reason things out and abandon what is false or simply replace what should be replaced. You must become your own lamp, and your own refuge, by letting truth be your light.

The only "belief" factor you should hold to within spiritual cultivation is called "clear belief." This belief arises within your own self naturally because of the self-verification of your own discoveries. It comes from the proving of the dharma through personal experience rather than from blindly accepting some dogma that one unquestioningly gets accustomed to from youth.

In short, you really need to be virtuous and be worthy to deserve *abhisheka* help for transforming the chakras and channels of your body, but this is not the highest form of spiritual blessing because enlightenment, or realizing the dharmakaya, is the supreme accomplishment and merit in the universe. Spiritual practice all starts with the right view from seeing the Tao and understanding the inherent emptiness of the mind, and from there, the body transformations all start coming about. People study the dharma to help learn how and why they should let go of thoughts, and after they learn detachment, they can start experiencing physical-spiritual gong-fu such as within the Twelve Labors.

People who work assiduously in Taoism, yoga, Tibetan Buddhism, alchemy and other spiritual schools typically get nowhere because they concentrate too much on purifying a physical body when it is not the true self. They are actually overly clinging to the body. Not realizing this, they do not see the Tao to be able to truly understand emptiness, which happens when your chi and mind become pure. Not understanding this, and not able to let go of the thoughts which screen the clear substrate of the mind, they never achieve the bodily transformations that they hope to attain.

All these experiences are just things that happen after you see the Tao and continue cultivating. You should pursue the route of purposefully cultivating the body to transform it only *after* you are able to experientially realize the Tao and the truth of non-ego, no body, and emptiness. That's why the high tantric teachings in Tibet, and the materials you are presently reading, are only given to people after twenty to thirty years of dharma study and preliminary practice because people typically need a large degree of study in order to understand things correctly. Yes, only after twenty years or more do they hear similar lessons. Actually, much of what you are learning in this tiny little book goes far beyond what is introduced to such practitioners.

It's enough to know when an *abhisheka* empowerment, baptism or blessing (known as a "*guan-ding*" in Chinese) occurs, it is to help you purify your body, so that you can free yourself of further physical obstructions in the chi channels. It helps purify your chi, channels and chakras and in Tibetan parlance, helps to make your body warm, soft and "pliant." True Vajrayana practitioners are always praying to the enlightened Buddhas for assistance on attaining several spiritual objectives, and these are the objectives you should seek, too.

First, they pray that their bodies become as soft and as healthy as a baby's body, so that the body poses no obstacles to spiritual practice. Lao Tzu has correctly noted that a young baby's body is the perfect example of the naturally pure, healthy yang chi we should aspire to attain through the road of spiritual cultivation.

Second, they pray for assistance that their chi channels all open and their bodies become flexible and warm. Once again, this happens to spiritual practitioners in all spiritual schools as a result of practice, but Vajrayana practitioners know the target from the start, and so like Taoists, they work hard at their practice and specifically pray for this to happen. Anything you can do in terms of stretching exercise, yoga, martial arts, bodywork and so on will help in this direction.

Third, they pray that their chi begins to circulate smoothly in their channels and meridians so that they can attain higher spiritual states and abandon errant personal behaviors. When your chi flows smoothly in your body, then your personality will soften and bad behaviors will tend to decrease. Emotional states are connected to the health of the body and your chi flow. Naturally, you cannot achieve a smooth circulation of chi flow with your spiritual cultivation unless your channels open, and that's what is happening in these Twelve Labors.

And fourth, they pray that they can cultivate the tummo fire, or yang chi kundalini arising, so that they can initiate this whole process and eventually reach the samadhi states of calmness and bliss. It first arises as the Nemean lion in the First Labor of Hercules when the root chakra becomes a bit unplugged, but we can see through the Twelve Labors that there are many stages to kundalini arousal, and yet most people don't realize this. This is actually the first book in existence that takes you through various cultivation methods and all the stages of the kundalini arousal from its initial arising on through to the opening of the channels, in the expected sequential order, and which links all the various dharma schools and their explanations not just through to the dharmakaya realization, but the cultivation of the sambhogakaya and nirmanakaya as well.

The Twelve Labors of Hercules, because they touch upon so many details, can be called the greatest explanatory book on all the sequential stages of kundalini arousal and chi and channel transformation in existence. You can find transformational teachings in ancient Vedic and Chinese texts but they are usually difficult to decipher. In short, you will not find its equivalent in the schools of Chinese Taoism, Indian tantric yoga, Judaism, Tibetan Buddhism or in any other spiritual school.

The physical "*guan-dings*" or *abhisheka*s that help you along these lines are hard to obtain, but even harder are the wisdom "*guan-dings*" of the Buddhas which are the highest to be sought after. As my teacher once related to me, the only real *abhisheka, guan-ding* or empowerment, is the last one given by all the Buddhas to someone about to achieve perfect and complete enlightenment at the very last stage of the path before Buddhahood. That's the one that everyone should vow to achieve.

Shakyamuni Buddha, in order not to promote attachment to the body or the view that physical purification is the road to the Tao, simply called all the transformations that occur along the path, including those arising from *abhisheka* help, "the purification of the five elements of the physical nature." When a vibration occurs in the body due to cultivation, some schools would say it is because of the chi (kundalini) or channels or *gunas,* but he would simply say it was the product of the five elements. He stressed that practitioners should cultivate by just letting things arise while you cultivate prajna wisdom. As you cultivate you should always be watching your mind (thoughts) to learn how to let go of consciousness and could adopt this practice of mindfulness to specific exercises such as watching your breath (anapana) or observing your physical body sensations. He taught direct realization into the mind's true nature, but also taught the cultivation of samadhi-dhyana[138] as an intermediate step to help transform the body and purify the mind, a tried and true route that has produced countless successes over the centuries.

The Buddhist cultivation path is extremely profound because it contains magnificent details and instructions largely absent in most traditions. Shakyamuni Buddha never said that you did not need to cultivate personal practice because you could rely on anyone else to enlighten you Buddha cannot do it, Jesus cannot do it, Krishna cannot do it, ... you have to awaken yourself through your own spiritual practice efforts. If you want to know what to expect as you cultivate, where the information is presented in an instructional form rather than in a narrative story form, there is no better book out there than *Tao and Longevity* by Nan Huai-chin and his English translator Wen Kuan Chu.

My personal fear is that the motivation of "worldly suffering" will not effectively inspire spiritual practice as it once did in days of old because there is now increasing worldwide affluence and prosperity. Our minds are ever more distracted or captured by modern technology such as video games, the internet, and all sorts of gadget wonders. Our bodies are becoming less fit as well - polluted by chemicals previously unknown to man, the nutritional content of our food is becoming weaker, we are being bombarded by excessive amounts of radio waves jostling our cells, and stress levels in society are increasing as is the pace of life. There are

---

[138] Every religion contains cultivation methods for producing a peaceful mind, which eastern schools call "abiding," "samadhi" or "dhyana."

countless other reasons that the road of spiritual cultivation may pass away. Unless the reality or existence of spiritual gong-fu is openly revealed to society, for demonstrations are a form of proof, and unless the road of spiritual practice is once again emphasized from a different angle, I fear it may pass away.

Today people live lives of wealth, health and abundance far beyond the norm of the last two thousand years, and so there is less motivation to cultivate because suffering has declined. People everywhere are becoming fascinated with technology and losing themselves in scientific marvels that are pulling them further away from peaceful lives, rich human relationships, healthy balanced living and spiritual progress. In addition to the destruction caused by modernization, three major spiritual schools have already been destroyed in China because of Communism, and modernization within India is sure to hurt the major Indian roads of cultivation practice, too. These are the traditional homes of the spiritual road, and so the foundations of cultivation are truly in jeopardy.

Despite all our advances, people are actually quite spiritually lost in the world. They don't know any of the non-denominational teachings and principles I have been talking about. They don't even know what the Tao is or what spiritual practice truly entails. Rather, they take orthodox worship and religious ceremonies and purity rules as their guides to attainment. You don't actually have to engage in worship of anything like this because you are already *That One*. People continually cheat themselves in all sorts of areas so they can excuse their errant behaviors, sleep soundly at night and not have to think badly of their behavior and the responsibilities they are shirking. People are lost and the world declines, but this is human being karma.

Today, people live lives of heightened anxiety and stress that lack any means for cultivating mental peace, and busy themselves with trivial things and false paths in lieu of higher concerns. They are not cultivating correct practice at all in nearly every religious tradition. The cultivation road will positively crumble during this century if a new way is not used to capture people's attention and direct it to personal cultivation practice. A new way is needed to harness people's spiritual aspirations with proof rather than unproved dogmas and superstition. And so the details behind the Twelve Labors are being revealed to you so that you can understand some of the verifiable physical transformations you will go through as you tread the correct spiritual trail (which you are supposed to be practicing in your religion). This is revealed along with all sorts of non-denominational details in hopes this non-sectarian universality prompts you to pause, rethink, and then wake up to acknowledge that there is something definite, non-nebulous and universal called the "spiritual path" which, though buried underneath orthodox religions, should be something you can definitely cultivate. It should be this way. It has to be this way. There should be something non-sectarian which is the crux of all genuine religions, and your own spiritual practice should be focused on this striving.

The many prior individuals who spiritually succeeded in the past became known as saints and sages, Mahasiddhas, Taoist Immortals, Arhats, Nath gurus, Bodhisattvas, avatars, prophets, holy men, and so forth. Most genuine spiritual schools have individuals in their lineage who achieved high levels of spiritual cultivation, and their teachings have certainly been left to us but people rarely read them. At the levels of enlightenment, those teachings are pretty much the same. At the level of dogma - developed by academics, intellectuals and pundits - we have a different story entirely where falsity has come in and religions have striven to differentiate themselves from one another. Unfortunately, it is the teachings of the enlightened ones which are most often ignored in favor of orthodox dogma that leads no one anywhere. If you are not familiar with the basic principles of the spiritual path and spiritual practice for enlightenment, frankly you better worry about the path you are presently following.

When someone attains the Tao and succeeds in transforming their physical body to a high degree, the common vernacular is to say they become "ascended masters" like the Yellow Emperor of China. In Taoism, the achievement of transforming the body is called "rising to heaven in broad daylight," something hinted at in the Bible for one or two individuals, but people don't know the actual meaning behind such words. The physical transformations experienced by Abraham, Hui Ko, Tilopa, Naropa and others all proceed in this direction, but there are many different stages of physical attainment possible on the road to the sambhogakaya.

The many female deities previously mentioned (Isis, Vajrayogini, Tara, Lakshmi, Anahita, etc.) are perfect examples of women who achieved these stages, just like men such as Krishna, Nagarjuna, Tsong Khapa, Tilopa, and so on. Melchizedek and Enoch are two examples from the Old Testament whose spiritual practice also enabled them to achieve some degree of success so that they could be "taken by Heaven." They weren't any holier or more special than anyone else who attained these achievements. They simply cultivated an empty mind to realize the Tao and achieved it, but were within a tradition which does not understand these things, and so the accomplishments were described in a mystical way that present practitioners still do not understand.

Whether we're talking about an Old Testament prophet, Taoist Immortal, Buddhist Arhat, Hindu Avatar, Confucian sage, Christian saint and so forth, any differences among the successes are due to the depth of their realization of the Tao, *for there are indeed different levels of self-realization.* Elijah in the Bible, for instance, had a higher degree of cultivation achievement in some dimensions than many other Biblical prophets, but that doesn't mean his actions, teachings or methods were the best or highest. And how did he stack up against a Tsong Khapa, Shankara, or Nagarjuna? The teachings these great ones have left us not only varies due to their degree of enlightenment, but because there are differences in what they could transmit to their audiences. This is another reason why I always encourage people to support sages and their missions, so they can do more, but ordinary people lack wisdom and usually support orthodox religious institutions rather than the enlightened.

Someone like Shakyamuni Buddha, who had hundreds of students with advanced samadhi attainments, could deliver much higher teachings than someone like Jesus or Moses, who both had uneducated audiences entirely lacking in any cultivation training or attainments. Therefore, just as you cannot teach kindergarteners the lessons fit for university students, if you want the highest teachings you must turn to the East and find teachers who had a large number of very high stage students, and an environment that could accept such teachings.

The actual truth of the Tao is singular, but the proficiency of teachers in terms of their teachings and degree of realization varies. Don't kid yourself saying that the past saints and sages are all the same, or alternatively say they are all different, or that they all reached the same degree of realization. There are indeed different levels of realization of one's self-nature, called the Bodhisattva *bhumis*, and just because a holy man is in *your* tradition does not mean his realization and teachings are the highest, or even complete. This is certainly a prejudicial view, and not the result of wisdom.

In the past, a "saint" was the typical name given to someone with samadhi attainments, whereas a "sage" was the term given to those who had some realization of the Tao. If you cultivate you, too, can achieve some proficiency in the Tao along these lines, and if you don't cultivate you certainly won't achieve anything except lay the foundation for yet another life, perhaps better or perhaps worse than this one. And that life will lead to another, and then another, and another, until at some point you finally decide to jump out of the net by cultivating, after which if you achieve self-realization you'll be able to come and go to do what you want as you please. But will you have the teachings available then, or just have another life of suffering in store? And what about the next life, which is right around the corner? You must start cultivating now before it's too late.

Anyone and everyone can achieve the Tao regardless of their religion. You just need to cultivate in the right way. Unfortunately, Orthodox Judaism, Christianity, and Islam have lost practically all knowledge of these stages of spiritual attainment and how to achieve them. Only the remnants of these teachings remain within their traditions. And whereas the path of attainment is often taught by the Sufis, Hasidics and Christians mystics, these are the very ones that the orthodoxy brushes aside and ignores, punishes, or persecutes. The individuals or sects within these three religions that actually teach cultivation are the ones which are brushed aside. Buddha said that human beings were topsy-turvy, and he was right. We persecute, or even kill, the ones who can most help us.

Spiritual progress all starts with a closing of the eyes and resolve to learn how to meditate by letting go of thoughts. There is only one road of cultivation, and it is not blanking the mind but learning how to let go of consciousness while maintaining awareness so that the mind naturally purifies. You can, through detachment, arrive at realizing its ultimate substrate. That substrate is the substrate of all minds, all beings, all existence. That is God, the original nature, your True Self, home. Prove it for yourself!

You always find the *same* stages of spiritual attainment, regardless of tradition, for people who truly tread the spiritual path. This information makes zealots uncomfortable because it calls into question their own supremacy claims and needs for ultra-orthodoxy. Cultivation is all done inside yourself and does not occur because of an outer religion or due to rules of purity and discipline. It requires personal wisdom and personal spiritual practice.

Naturally, some adepts in a tradition will attain a higher stage of attainment than others, but they always have to adapt what they can teach to make the lessons acceptable to their traditions. Sometimes they will simplify matters greatly, dumbing things down to allegorical basics, such as in Genesis, because the audience they are trying to teach simply does not possess enough gong-fu or wisdom.

The good thing is that *you* now know some of the non-denominational techniques for attaining spiritual progress, as well as some of the principles of the path and spiritual gong-fu you will attain along the way, so you are unlikely to be cheated anymore or mislead by all sorts of competing teachers and religions. Just follow Shakyamuni's principle of personal study and then verification by yourself, and you will surely understand what is true, or not true, in the end.

The adherents of most spiritual traditions typically claim their religion has something unique, different and supreme in terms of a spiritual salvation. However, the same stages of cultivation are being rehashed over and over again with other information thrown in to differentiate one school from another and match with social longings, human political aspirations and the environmental realities of the time. Underneath all the misconceptions and misinformation out there, the true spiritual way is scientific, non-denominational and non-sectarian. For it to be able to lead anyone to reality it *has to be* that way. It has to be natural, non-sectarian, non-artificial, and achievable without dogma. Hence, relax your mind, let go of the mind, watch your mind.

Just think about that, as well as all the ways that academics and religious functionaries without cultivation knowledge and attainments have messed up cultivation teachings again and again throughout history. Think of all the bloodshed and persecutions that have occurred, especially in the western religions. This is just another reason why people tend to turn away from the orthodox religions. People want a path they can practice, but the actions of human beings go against that very path.

If you say you must be vegetarian, recite so many prayers, participate in a particular ceremony, visit the holy land, or do this or that, these things will not lead you to the ultimate. They will gain you merit, but they do not lead you to the Tao. I'm not saying religions are bad or not helpful because society and the world certainly needs them, but I am simply asking you to ponder what your current practices are ultimately helping you to achieve. Furthermore, many ancient practices passed down in religion were customs developed for a different era, and one should use wisdom to abandon the false, the harmful, or the unfair and adapt to the times.

Put the words of the religious functionaries aside for a moment and start thinking for yourself about this matter, because it's your own life and future fortune you must consider. There are countless other spiritual paths with viewpoints quite different from your own, and the individuals within these religions are just as intelligent or virtuous as you are, or even more so, and just as vehement in maintaining the validity of their beliefs. Can all these conflicting dogmas be right, or is there something underneath the surface that isn't being recognized?

Nearly everyone gets attached to their religion and thinks its practices are supreme. Of course people think their country supreme, and attach superiority notions to their race and culture as well (not recognizing that with their next incarnation it all changes once again). The practitioners of body cultivation also think their method is the right way, but the big mistake comes in when they cling to their practices and try to bring consciousness into the body. For instance, one problem with form school yoga practitioners is that they usually get attached to these methods and think they actually have a really existent bodily form when it is all an empty appearance. Rather than help break the perception of the body, their practices often amplify the perception of being the body and create a habit where there wasn't one previously.

In spiritual cultivation you must become liberated from the perception of being a physical body to realize that mind is everywhere and that all that you experience is mind, and let go of the concept of a being, personality, life and existence. If you keep dwelling in form you will not succeed in any spiritual practice or spiritual tradition. Your true mind is everywhere, so it is not confined to a body. The problem with many of the spiritual schools which cultivate form is that people develop the tendency of bringing consciousness into the body when consciousness is actually everywhere, and the purpose of cultivation is to realize this fact by breaking the mistaken identification with the body and body consciousness. Then you can finally attain the Tao.

The ultimate purpose of cultivation is to reach the foundational source of life and consciousness and discover the true Self (or True Self) rather than to cultivate the body. By practicing to bring consciousness into a body you often create a habit of believing that the body is real. You create a strong, sticky habit of attachment and clinging that you'll follow life after life. That's why the esoteric schools point out the importance of finally realizing nirvana where emptiness and clarity are one. It's the dharmakaya realization that's important. There are ways to specifically cultivate particular body attainments, but these roads are only safe for those with the right view.

You can break the habit of attaching to a bodily form if you are wise and practice the mental detachment of not dwelling, and if you work hard enough you will realize that you are not the physical body, not any type of body or form, and should not attach to a body or any form including those of purified chi or light that arise out of cultivation. You want to be cultivating the Tao which is empty of all characteristics, attributes, marks, signs, or phenomenon. That means it is absent of a body.

The orthodox school of Buddhism avoids an entire host of problems connected with body cultivation by having you practice mental dhyana meditation as a road to attainment. With success, you end up cultivating the purity of the mind and let the body do its thing and transform on its own. It's just like striking a match to light a fuse. Once you get the fuse lit, you give it no more thought but let it burn on its own. So, once the River chariot rotation and other chi circulations in the body start going because of your "letting go" practice, you simply practice emptiness meditation and let the body undergo whatever transformations naturally happen.

Once you can get those rotations going, which is the important thing, you can forget about tantric body cultivation techniques and simply continue to cultivate empty mind. If things bog down, you can often speed up the process, or get it started again, through a variety of tantric techniques used just in a pinch. That's why masters in the esoteric schools sometimes use sexual cultivation, although the monk's, hermit's or sadhu's path of asceticism use different means. It's like stoking a fire to get it to flare up, and after that happens you don't need to stoke it anymore. If you mantra and pray for help, of course the Buddhas and Bodhisattvas will help those who wish to cultivate to achieve self-realization, but they can only help to the degree that you practice. The monk's life is easiest for cultivation, and so many take on the robes so they can cultivate to attainment without any other worldly concerns to distract their time and attention.

This discussion of *abhisheka* empowerments, deity yoga and tantra concerns topics beyond Hercules' accomplishments in the Twelve Labors. Through such means, you can quickly open the tiniest of your chi channels and chakras – a stage after Hercules' final attainments - and fully transform the earth, fire, water, wind and space element chi of the body. Those saints who display incorruptible bodies after their death have achieved a measure of success in this direction. However, if you keep clinging to the body and think it's real or continue to believe that you are the body or possess a body, you are spiritually lost.

Nevertheless, this vehicle of ours, the physical body, must transform on the path of spiritual cultivation, and what is happening in this Eleventh Labor is the purification of the crown chakra and chi channels in the head. Hercules has been seeking the garden of the Hesperides, and after learning its location he sets off to find it. Naturally, he experiences various adventures along the way.

One of the more famous adventures is that Hercules meets Antaeus, son of Poseidon, and is forced to wrestle with this foe. This wrestling is exactly the task of unwinding the channels and chakras we have been describing over and over again. It's like pulling plastic saran wrap off some tightly wrapped item. Each time you unbind the channels, the old wrapping of viscous chi around the channels seems to be pulled away and discarded and in a little while an empty chi body seems to rise into the sky and float away in imaginary vision, a process partially described in the *Song of Solomon*. After a long time of this "purification of the five elements," the chakras and channels are freed of obstructions to the chi flow circulations and you fell the newly opened circulations every time they occur.

With this knowledge, you can now understand that paying for and attending books, tapes and courses on "how to open the chakras" are ludicrous. You must simply cultivate the pure state of mind we call internal peace or emptiness (since wandering thoughts are relatively absent), which causes your yang chi to arise and open all the chi meridians naturally, and then you must cultivate yet further so that you do not hold on and permit the yang chi to freely run through all the channels and drives out the impurities. No medicine, music or what not can accomplish this other than emptiness meditation, pure and simple. But you are so used to holding on to consciousness that you do not even know what it means to "let go," and hence cannot experience an empty state where you "see the Tao." That's the problem.

Some schools teach mantra practice, or prayer, to quiet the mind so that the yang chi can arise and "light the fuse." Some schools teach vipassana meditation so that wandering thoughts die down and the yang chi arises. Some schools, such as in the kundalini yoga traditions, teach one-pointed visualizations and pranayama methods to stir the yang chi into forcibly arising. Some "left hand" schools teach non-ejaculatory sexual yoga to help raise one's yang chi so the chi channels can be flooded to help open and harmonize complete circulations, or karmamudra visualizations when a partner is not available, but this is only done in special circumstances within the tantric schools of cultivation. Obviously, many schools and methods abound, and Buddha summarized them into ten great paths.

In Hercules' story, the stages of unwinding the channel restrictions (what Tibetan Buddhism calls the "untying of knots") are called "wrestling," and so we have the story of his wrestling with Antaeus. In wrestling you are pulling and pushing your opponent, and that act of tugging is what you often seem to be doing with the chi wrapped around your channels at this stage. After each unwinding of the channels and chakras, the old layer of chi is discarded and the shape of the whole inner complex seems to rise and float away – which is the meaning of Hercules having to lift Antaeus from the ground in order to beat him at wrestling. After a set of channels and chakras become unwound, the strong pumping of the root chakra from underneath seems to push out the entire imaginary chi body that's been released, and it slowly rises out of the body and disappears.

The very first time this entire structure is discarded - and I mean very first time – your entire inner chi body will seem stuck in the buttocks and shoulders. If you have ever seen a turtle walking as if it's straining to come out of its shell, that's the effort you must remember the first time you reach this stage of ejection. As the discarded chi body rises into the air you will be able to see the two large channels which branch off into the legs, and this is why I always recommend you cultivate the entire body (including the feet) using some full body visualization technique like the white skeleton visualization or a Vajrayana tantra of a Buddha. You might also practice anapana and Taoist inner viewing as well with a greater or lesser degree of success. Otherwise, it is hard to loosen the lower trunk channels, and there may be some initial difficulties in getting through this stage.

To help prepare you for all these things and help you make spiritual progress quicker than is typical, I always tell people interested in spiritual cultivation to engage in several simultaneous cultivation practices that don't take a lot of time but cover all the bases: mantra, anapana and pranayama, the white skeleton visualization, and pure vipassana meditation practice. Since you can mantra silently throughout the day, this takes no time at all. Pranayama practice can be performed in a few minutes on a daily basis, like the brushing of your teeth, so that it seems to take no time at all. The only time that needs to then be scheduled is for the skeleton visualization and anapana or mental vipassana, and yet these can be unobtrusively done whenever you have a few minutes free, even while at work since no one will know what you are doing.

Along with merit making and watching your behavior as a form of mindfulness practice, the combination of these different meditation practices will help you reach higher spiritual stages rather easily. In particular, make sure you concentrate on the feet, hands, buttocks, ribs and shoulders in the skeleton visualization, pranayama and anapana or body observation practices. These are all areas people tend to neglect, and your attention to these areas helps to open up the channels in these regions. Remember that where the mind goes the chi goes, so any progress achieved through these methods is self-explanatory.

All of these cultivation techniques are non-denominational if you're still stuck on, "It's not in my religion." These practices are human being science, not religion. Remember that ultimate success in spiritual practice depends upon realizing the meaning of "letting go" and "empty mind," so anything along these routes is a proper meditation vehicle as long as you understand the principles and do not cling. How can resting the mind, letting go, or being natural be wrong ... or even denominational? As to visualizing the body, there is nothing wrong with that.

The mental result you achieve through these practices, called "emptiness," "peace" or "tranquility," does not mean nothingness, annihilation or extinction. It simply means thoughts have died down, and there is now a bit of freedom from mental attachments. Along with this new freedom and degree of open mind the level of noisy mental background chatter and negative self-talk will decline as a result of your channels opening and your chi becoming purified.

If your chi purifies, then consciousness will purify, and if your consciousness purifies (becomes empty), then your chi will in turn purify. The connection is that simple, which is why both routes of cultivating either your chi or your consciousness are used throughout the world's spiritual schools. Because your breathing (respiration) affects your thoughts and chi, this route is common within religions. In all cases of mental calming, thoughts will always still arise as you need them and they should, for you should never suppress thoughts to try and achieve an empty mind. You should never try to suppress emotions but can cry and enjoy whatever situations arise because those reactions are part of the field of manifestation of reality. You simply won't be stuck on thoughts and emotions. If you cultivate correctly, you will gradually attain the peacefulness, clarity, and effectiveness of a Zen master. Thoughts arise, you act, they depart. There is no sticking to them, so we say you become natural, effortless and spontaneous.

Eventually, with time, you will pass through various stages of these channel purifications because of your practice. Initially the inner body of channels that is discarded from the body looks like a bent hockey stick because of the inwards bending of the *du-mai* spinal channel with the sacrum. In consecutive stages this bending eventually straightens out as the chi channels underneath become unfurled. The shape of the entire configuration of channels and chakras improves with each unwinding of the inner chi body that is discarded and ejected. In progressive fashion the discarded structure might remind you of the shape of a scorpion or lobster (because of an initially undifferentiated blob of hand chi), salamander,[139] vajra and then crystal chandelier. The world's cultures have represented the shape at various ejection stages with their own culturally pertinent symbols.

The root chakra and sacral chakra start pulsing at critical stages of this initial process of purifying the channels and produces what is called "Zen sickness." When Zen sickness arises you cannot sleep[140] because the root chakra is unplugged and sacral chakra is pumping your chi which is moving furiously throughout your body. You are absolutely flooded with vitality in every cell of your body – absolutely everywhere. You seem temporarily filled with boundless energy and "inspiration" – a fact

[139] See Emblem XXIX of the *Atalanta Fugiens*.
[140] My teacher told me that some cultivators drink wine when this happens so that they can become tipsy and fall asleep when they feel the need for sleep is overwhelming. However, he just stayed awake through the process until after a few days the energy died down and he could fall asleep once again. Following his example, I chose his route as well and after about three or four days the ability to fully sleep returned; short naps did occur during this period but it seemed like there was no sleep at all, and it was easy to lose track of time during this stage. Either route is fine, but you must be forewarned that there are countless stages past this one where you cannot seem to sleep for days because of all the chi and *shen* transformations occurring within the body, and you may long for sleep. You are never hurt because of an unfulfilled longing for sleep, but you quickly learn that sleep is simply a habit. You will sometimes suddenly and unexpectedly nap for a few minutes or so during these stages, and will always fall asleep when necessary for the amount of time required by the body (so you are never hurt and have no need to worry), but it will often feel as if no time passed and you did not sleep at all. As the example of the Second Zen Patriarch Hui Ko showed, lacking a master you might even hear voices telling you what to do during these stages so that you do not worry about the physical chi and channel transformations.

noted in countless spiritual schools, especially the Celtic tradition. You have thousands of things to say and anything you say, think or write may tend to come out in verse. I once thought that the rhythm of the verses might be related to the rhythmic pulsation of the chi, but am not sure. The tendency to talk, write or sing in rhythm at this stage eventually dies down in several days time as the channels become freed of their obstructions. One will pass through one large, and possibly several smaller occasions of this phenomenon when going through these stages, but they happen in close proximity to one another and after it disappears it never returns.

This event, from the opening of the root chakra at a certain level, is repeated several times during these purification cycles and might possibly be the origin behind Celtic legends of bubbling brooks that provide inspiration, but we cannot know for sure. Remember that all spiritual school adherents experience the exact same states of gong-fu but they simply describe them differently to match the local cultures and traditions.

Sometimes when the chi layers are released around a chakra you will see a shining blue orb like a tiny marble or smaller. The tiny orb looks like a bright blue pearl with a shining halo, and seems to float off from chakras that have just been uncovered. Sometimes a string of these blue pearls, connected with what seems to be a thin thread, come off together as the old channel coverings are split open across an area that had several chakras in series. One should offer these to Buddhas (enlightened teachers) when this happens, just as the dragon king's daughter offered her pearl to the Buddha in the *Lotus Sutra*.

There are many phenomena that appear during the process of purifying the inner chi body or *kosha* layers, and these are just a few. The Buddhist sutras have descriptions scattered throughout many texts, Taoism has descriptions, Hinduism has some descriptions, tantric yoga texts have some descriptions, and even the Bible records some stages of the process. It's only after you reach these stages with your own gong-fu progress that you can correctly identify those descriptions and understand the genuine meaning of these texts.

If you work hard, you can finish the process of initially opening the heart chakra, "seeing the Tao," experiencing Maitreya's "Big Knife wind" and purifying many of your channels of obstructions in just a little over a month's time once your chi starts significantly coursing through the central channel. From the Fifth Labor to the Twelfth Labor of Hercules actually only takes some four to five weeks of round-the-clock cultivation effort after the process commences. This is best passed through while you are in retreat and divorced from daily worldly concerns.

This is truly when you should take off work for awhile and just meditate in retreat to complete the process. If you refuse to go into retreat at this and other crucial times, you will probably end up prolonging the process by many years. You should "strike while the fire is hot" and complete most of these transformation when they are occurring one after the other. For those who aren't monks or nuns, this takes a certain discipline to leave the world aside for this short period of time, but when will you get the chance again? Never.

After the majority of Hercules' labors are finished, it does not mean that your cultivation is done or that success in attaining enlightenment is assured. Neither does it mean that you will attain steady samadhi either, although you will briefly experience a small taste of many samadhi-like states during this process and will start to understand the meaning of many cultivation texts from your experiences. Going through all these labors simply means that you've laid a good physical foundation for possible success in samadhi attainments and attaining enlightenment, or self-realization. You still have much more cultivation work to do.

Thus in this Eleventh Labor, the description of wrestling, as mentioned, refers to unwinding the layers of chi wrapped around the channels. When Hercules wrestled with Antaeus, son of the earth goddess Gaia, and beat him by lifting him aloft from the ground, the contest was said to be one of Hercules' most difficult. That's because when Antaeus touched the earth he would wax stronger. Only when lifted aloft did Antaeus become weaker, finally giving Hercules his chance to crush him. This detail symbolizes the fact that it seems as if you must struggle a bit to pull off the chi from around the channels at this stage or they will spring back because of stickiness. That springing back is Antaeus' ability to renew himself each time he touches the earth. This meaning may seem farfetched to the uninitiated, but becomes perfectly clear once you start experiencing the unwinding of the channels yourself, as does the meaning of other Herculean labors. Every time Hercules wrestles with someone in the Labors it means that chi obstructions are being pushed or pulled away from the channels.

After this is all done you will have a better physical foundation for spiritual cultivation attainments. However, once again you must remember that this still isn't the Tao or samadhi even though you will in all likelihood have bumped into semblance samadhi states when going through this entire process. There's more cultivation work to be done for that attainment – lots more – but now much higher spiritual stages are within reach. You've experienced many of the tantric, Vajrayana and Taoist stages of transformation, but the fruit of the Tao is still out of reach.

These higher accomplishments are the deep emptiness-wisdom attainments rather than the purification of the body, chi, channels and chakras, but purifying the inner subtle body helps you attain them. If your chi is not pure, then consciousness is hard to purify, and hence the physical path that proceeds involves the purification of the chi and channels. If you could just detach from the body altogether, you would get the Tao instantly, but most people cannot, so they have to go through preliminary work before that attainment.

The physical body will also continue to transform for many years after these Twelve Labors, but the process at those stages is much more refined than the events Hercules is currently experiencing. The chi continues to rotate through all the channels until the circulation becomes so smooth that it seems to subside or disappear, and then at a certain point of progress a new cycle of opening at a deeper level will suddenly occur. When that new cycle commences you will often feel the River Chariot rotation flaring up again, the circulations in the arms and upper torso will be felt, and then the channels in the legs at this more advanced level will finally seem to recommence their circulations after the upper *ouroboros* circulations are felt. The full rotation of chi circulating in all the body's channels will then be felt, and in time this will all seem to quietly disappear once again after it smoothens and seems to diminish. This process is repeated over and over again over the years, and can sometimes even be stoked into action through skillful activities of which emptiness cultivation is paramount.

Once again, the highest attainments in cultivation are not physical gong-fu attainments like this but prajna wisdom attainments that enable you to realize the Tao - the original fundamental nature of everything - through investigating consciousness with insight and then realizing the empty nature of the mind. If you cultivate prajna wisdom by studying the dharma, you can attain all these stages of physical gong-fu far easier by applying wisdom rather than using strength, as Hercules had to do, because you'll understand that all you need to do is let go. The highest stage individuals can easily detach from their body and consciousness to realize the Tao, because their wisdom is so high, and then they work on cultivating the body rather than visa versa.

Great Zen masters succeed because they study the dharma assiduously. Next, they work extremely hard to abandon the habit of clinging to thoughts by learning how to let go while letting their awareness shine. That's meditation practice, mindfulness practice, introspection, witnessing, vipassana, whatever you want to call it. Because they ignore everything except their pursuit of the Tao – dropping mind, body and sensations - they realize enlightenment quickly and then allow their bodies to transform naturally so that they attain the sambhogakaya. It is because of cultivating wisdom and applying it, such as someone who studies Vedanta or Consciousness-Only would do, that they can succeed where so many others fail.

Through dharma study they cultivate prajna wisdom or insight. With those lessons or instructions behind them, they can analyze their mental experience, realize its falsity and then let go of it to reach the underlying state of ultimate non-production, or non-arising, that ultimately gives birth to consciousness. That's what we call returning to the Source, "becoming one with God," and what Christians call "theosis," "divinization" or "deification." The cultivation path and its culmination in enlightenment is actually the purpose of Christianity, although most Christians remain entirely ignorant of this process and its potential. Nonetheless *this*, rather than worship, is the purpose of Christianity despite followers kept in ignorance, and when you read the biographies and autobiographies of Christian saints you will find that they also want people to attain this same state of unity or realization. You will also find that they passed through similar stages of gong-fu.

Everything you see, touch, think and experience in any way whatsoever is just your mind. You are not seeing the room around you with its objects but rather, you are experiencing your own consciousness. You are just seeing your mind. Consciousness is always self-consciousness so "in being conscious" you are essentially conscious of yourself. This is all you, your mind. How so? Your senses turn everything into mental images of consciousness, so you only ever are experiencing your own consciousness or mind. You only ever experience your own mind and never anything else. It is not the world but your own consciousness that you are presently experiencing. Everything you see ... it's all just you.

Here is what you eventually realize through cultivation after your chi and channels all purify and transform to their healthiest state, as they should, when you properly practice meditation. In the whole universe, you are always experiencing just ephemeral scenery flowing across a stationary base of clear, pure, pristine, empty awareness which is called the "clear light" in Tibetan Buddhism. That base is always there and never moves. It is free from all content, and so is sometimes called no-mind and sometimes mind since it knows consciousness. In its stainless purity is no sentience and no mistakes of ignorance; it is not the entity of anything. Even the idea of me and otherness are absent in that pure, pristine, ever functioning empty awareness. It doesn't arise from the mind but is the mode of subsistence of the mind. It is primordially self-so, unmade, unborn, unfabricated, unpolluted, stainless, pure, immutable, empty and yet a great unhindered vividness that is self-luminous or illuminated so that we can call it pristine wisdom or the mind of enlightenment. *That is what is always there* and the distinctions made by religious theories and dogmas are all falsities simply meant to lead you to a realization of that one true mind.

To go beyond this unpolluted awareness is the Supreme or absolute nature, which is its essence – one with it. If you detach from that moving scenery you can eventually experience that clear base of awareness that is always you, always there. Going beyond, you can find that this awareness in turn has its root in the original nature because witnessing is just another one of the endless functions of the original nature. The road to this realization starts with witnessing. Furthermore, you will find that the ephemeral scenery you experience is just an ungraspable Indra's net of infinite cause and effect[141] that never rests where everything participates in the existence of everything else and the substance of everything is

---

[141] Everything is the way it is because the entire universe is the way it is, participating in all its details of existence; the entire universe is therefore reflected in every event through infinite cause and effect interdependence. You can also say "in every event the universe is reflected because the universe is as it is," and so the ultimate cause of anything is untraceable or unknowable. Here is no particular cause of anything because the All participates in manifesting everything; one single body arises because of the mutual conditioning that performs al the "parts." When you don't know something it is called ignorance, so we can say that the source origin of the universe is ignorance, unknowable. To trace the fundamental cause is impossible, and we cannot talk about a real cause of something unreal. This apparent universe is one single body wherein the entire universe infinitely contributes to every event within it, no matter how minor. It is one connected dream wholeness. While many religions say this world is unreal, including Christianity and Hinduism, you might in particular want to study the *Flower Ornament Sutra* (*Avatamsaka Sutra*) or Buddhist *Hua Yen* school to understand this connectedness in detail and the lack of any part having an existence on its own.

empty. The plot of the scenery story is always correct, because of the interlinkage of cause and effect, but the story is a fiction. As you witness it you can realize it is like a dream and the true you is beyond it. It is an interdependent existence that is in no way ultimately different than emptiness. The true reality is that no thing has any being on its own. Rather, all existence is rooted in being.

Where does mind come from and what is its ultimate substrate that is always there? In other words, where does consciousness ultimately come from, and how do you jump out of this realm of dualities to find its source?

If you can find that Source, you can become free of pain and suffering because it is only through consciousness that we experience pain and suffering. The Source is formless, free of suffering and at peace.[142] Even the "ego" or "I-thought" is just consciousness, so it will always experience suffering and affliction. It's just a bunch of thoughts we hold onto, a mode of consciousness rather than anything solid or real, which is why you cannot ultimately find the ego when you look for it. Upon enlightenment the identification of the "I-thought" with the underlying pure witness snaps, and the personality and "I-thoughts" only continue as part of the objective world. What you think of as your person is just a reflection in the mind of the witness, which is itself just a mode of being. This is why

---

[142] That body of awareness is free of pain and suffering, and unaffected by like or dislike or any other emotions or thoughts that appear within consciousness. It totally accepts the present moment. It is like space, unaffected by what appears within it, and therefore not affected by appearances. Therefore it is often compared to a mirror that simply reflects images but is unaffected by them. It is beyond the mind and its various states and conditions. It can use memories but memories or phenomena cannot use or affect it, or bias it in any way. It is therefore undistracted by the assumed separations and distinctions that constitute a person. It can view all consciousness with the equipoise of perfect detachment. It can observe the sources of attachment and desire without feeling any attraction itself. Mental troubles therefore do not reach it, afflictions and suffering are absent within it. The pain and suffering of life therefore disappear through the road of spiritual cultivation to reach this true one. They are "out there" while the witness is always "here," unaffected, permanent, solid, real. Thus the trio of *sat-chit-ananda*, or being-consciousness-bliss of Hinduism, is somewhat explained. The *chit* is this universal stainless, non-moving, empty awareness that gives rise to consciousness, knows consciousness and is one with consciousness without being affected by consciousness. The *ananda* or bliss is the absence of suffering within this true nature, meaning peace. Bliss is something always there and not something which comes and goes. You are always bliss but never blissful as a characteristic or attribute. The *sat* or being or Truth or existence is the Self, which is what this is. Or, we can call this the function of the true self depending upon our level of explanation. The original nature is the True Self, purity, permanence and bliss of Buddhism mentioned in the *Nirvana Sutra*. The wrong tendency we have been following for innumerable lives has been to attach to the I-thought that arises because of conditions, and that wrong identity has caused untold pain, suffering and misery. Spiritual cultivation is a way to break that road of misery and regain realization of our true self which is absolute and ever present in all experiences.

the practice of witnessing meditation, or cessation-witnessing, is essential for spiritual practice as it enables there to be an eventual separation of the Self from ignorance. But where does the I-thought of ignorance first come from and why?

You can only find the answers to these questions through the practice of meditation which causes thoughts to eventually die down because you watch consciousness without impelling thoughts forward. You just observe what happens in the mind, and in time the extraneous mental chatter will die down from non-interference. As your mind purifies because the internal dialogue passes away, your chi will purify and as your chi becomes purified your mind will become purified. As mind becomes pure, empty or still, from that stillness, or yin state, yang will be born and so your kundalini will arise. Why? Because chi and consciousness are linked, because yang gives birth to yin and yin gives birth to yang and you are still within the realm of these dualities. Then all these transformations will come about due to cause and effect. It all starts by witnessing the contents of consciousness, and then the purification proceeds naturally.

If you abandon a firm hold on the idea of being a witness or self, you can finally attain union with the original Self of everything. That is what you are because you are not an ego. That eventual realization of the fundamental nature, or "union with God," or "finding your fundamental face" is the ultimate purpose of spiritual practice, but how will that ever happen through the attendance of worship, through "faith" or by virtue of membership in a group that thinks of itself as "select" due to some covenant? It won't. The saints of every tradition tell you to seek direct union with the original nature through spiritual practice, but the religious professionals today seem to bar the way by promoting mistaken notions and practices instead. The situation in the field of religion is entirely topsy-turvy, just as Buddha warned.

When wandering consciousness quiets down there will be silence in your mental space, but the stillness or peace you will experience will still be just another experience of the mental continuum. That silence is still a mental construction, image, mark or sign and not your original nature. It is the flip side of busyness in the mental continuum, and still belongs to the realm of duality. Mental silence or peace may seem empty of thought but this emptiness is not yet true emptiness. It is just a mental phenomenon of quiet that is contrary to mental business. How do you find where it ultimately comes from?

All you can ever experience in life is just your consciousness until you penetrate via investigation to find its source. You never directly experience the world but just a conscious image of the world ... your own consciousness, your own mind. Since this is one hundred percent true if you think about it, what about the ultimate substrate of consciousness? Where is it? What is it? Is it universal? Can its existence explain matter, which Einstein's work shows is really just condensed energy?[143]

That ultimate substrate is something everyone shares because consciousness originates from the same source. If all the different schools and religions talk about one original nature then it must be the same one original nature, the One-Without-A-Second. That's what you must come to realize on the road of spiritual cultivation. That is the goal of all spiritual practice and religious activities. Call it God, the original nature, Allah, the primal source, the fundamental state, dharmakaya or any other synonym you like. The one original nature or True Self is the same thing across religions even though they have tried to radically differentiate themselves from one another.

All consciousness comes from That One as just another of its infinite functions. It is ungraspable and cannot remain stationary. The functions and appearances or aspects of conventional reality also seem real but they too are ungraspable for you cannot freeze anything into a stationary state that stays. They have no fixed, stable, unmoving true reality, hence they are "empty" of true existence. Whether or not Hercules got to this realization is unknown because his story only talks about the physical

---

[143] Taoism and Hinduism assert that everything in the universe is energy, or chi, which agrees with modern physics. Or we can say physics agrees with the higher cultivation teachings because physics simply derived the authenticating math to the prior teachings. In spiritual cultivation you must actually experience a principle to prove or authenticate it whereas science likes measurements. The world is not "real" as an assemblage of matter and energy but is an effervescent appearance, empty of true substance, that is inseparably one with consciousness and the original nature. Furthermore, the various cultivation schools also assert that all chi is accompanied by light, though not necessary a physical light, so you can talk about either chi or light and be speaking about the same thing. The typical mention of light is not about photons, but about the self-illumination of the original nature, its capacity for clear awareness. This pristine awareness is like light in that light is itself invisible and colorless in a room, yet illuminates everything. You never see the underlying awareness either which makes consciousness possible, from which manifestation becomes possible (since it is only known if consciousness is present), and yet it too is always there unnoticed. Hence in Christianity, *John* 1:5 was able to say "God is light" because John reached that stage of realizing the pristine awareness from his own work at spiritual cultivation. The Koran contains very similar words. By putting your mind in tune with God, you can actually end up transforming the physical body to that same stage of realization, too, which is what cultivating the sambhogakaya is all about at the higher stages of attainment. Of course to get that far your physical body has to go through many stages of purification.

gong-fu accompanying the earliest physical transformation stages of the path. Nevertheless, to transcend the phenomenal world of transient relativities is the ultimate target.

In this labor, Hercules also eventually arrives at the place where Zeus had chained Prometheus on a rock as a punishment for stealing the "secret of fire" from the gods. The secret of fire which Prometheus gave mankind is a symbolic way of referring to kundalini cultivation within the Intensified Practices stage of the cultivation path. Prometheus, like Hercules, is considered a great cultural hero because he brought these gifts to humanity, so you can see once again that the people who succeed at cultivation and make the knowledge available to the public are really the great heroes of mankind.

Zeus (who also stands for yang chi) had bound poor Prometheus to a mountain and every day an eagle would come to tear open his flesh and eat his liver.[144] After this gnawing the eagle would fly away, Prometheus would grow back his liver and skin, and the next day he would endure this torture all over again. Perhaps by this story the Greeks knew, as the Chinese and Indians do, that the liver regenerates itself. Perhaps they knew that angry thoughts are connected to the liver or that liver energies usually represent impure yang chi, something we previously encountered. In any case, the most appropriate meaning of this story concerns a phenomenon of cultivation that you will experience over and over until your yang chi is finally purified.

Prometheus' suffering on the rock is due to the release of yin chi from the body that is locked within the joints and channels. Until you transform your body enough, yin chi is always locked within all the channels, bones, joints, and interstitial spaces of even the warmest and healthiest human body. It can finally be released or transformed only after your yang chi (kundalini) makes its way to these places. When that happens in a substantial fashion, there is a particular phenomenon you may experience again and again at the earliest stages of the path that is similar to the chills and shivering of a serious flu or even malaria. It's like a "detoxification reaction" but it happens because yin chi is suddenly released from the body in voluminous amounts.

If you cultivate meditation by sitting in a cross-legged lotus posture, which is always recommended, there may arise various instances where

---

[144] Many schools use the liver to represent the body's unpurified yang chi since the liver involves the chi flows dealing with anger and aggression.

a tremendous cold seems to be released from your body, usually starting from the legs, that causes tremendous shivers and shaking. Those feelings of cold, which last just a few minutes, might even be severe enough to cause a chattering of the teeth. The only remedy to this sudden giant release of cold yin chi from the body,[145] without any recourse to herbal medicines that might immediately help open the body pathways, is to lie in bed for a short time as the chi leaves the body. You can lie on your back (as Prometheus did) or on your side, but in either case you'll be shaking furiously and shivering for a few minutes as the cold yin chi departs. This, too, is part of the necessary sequence of body transformations. It represents a violent departure of the yin chi all at once.

Prometheus, the teacher of kundalini cultivation, suffers this fate because every now and then when the yang chi reaches a new set of obstructed channels in his body he must go through this shaking discomfort as the area opens and the impure chi escapes. The situation *is* definitely comparable to being chained on your back while an eagle eats your liver in that there's no way to avoid the event and you just have to let go and bear it. Again and again it will happen through the course of your cultivation until you are finally free of all the yin energies to the deepest levels of chi purification. It's nothing painful, but indeed an occasional nuisance for a few minutes of teeth chattering and violent body shaking, and in this story it's represented by the daily scourge of Prometheus having his liver gnawed until yang chi Hercules comes at this stage of cultivation and finally frees him of the vestiges of yin.

In gratitude for freeing him from this affliction, Prometheus tells Hercules the secret to being able to get the apples of the Hesperides. That secret is to send the giant Atlas into the garden after them instead of going himself. If any mortal steps into the garden, Prometheus warns that he would die instantly. Prometheus relates that Atlas hates holding up the sky so much that he would readily agree to fetch the apples in order to pass this burden over to Hercules. Hence, before we go further, we need to know who this Atlas character is in order to understand this part of the story.

Atlas was the son of Aether, one of the primordial elemental gods. Aether was the god of space, heaven or the sky which to us should mean

---

[145] This is another type of yin chi that causes sickness in the body, such as cancer, when it is not transformed or expelled through the practice of meditation. *Kumbhaka* pranayama together with meditation practice are two of the best ways to rid your body of hidden illness that eventually become chronic disease, but science and the public do not yet recognize this fact.

emptiness or empty mind. Atlas' mother was Gaia, goddess of the earth, which means that Atlas was the son of both heaven and earth just as we encountered in the very beginning of our story. He represents us because he is standing between Heaven and Earth, a concept well familiar to those conversant with many ancient philosophies. Mankind is born of the earth element, and yet with cultivation he can rise to the heavens and become a heavenly being because that, too, is part of his nature and potential. We saw that with Typhon, who represented untransformed man, but now we are presented with Atlas who represents a higher level of cultivation even though the method he uses, we will find, is incorrect.

Atlas holds up the heavens, but the proper method for spiritual practice is to cultivate an empty mind where thoughts calm down naturally rather than to hold on to an image of emptiness, as symbolized by Atlas. When you mentally let go and let awareness shine without impediment, as is proper, thoughts die down just as they should and your consciousness and body both transform. The habit energy of mentally clinging interferes with the body's natural chi flows, so it obstructs and inhibits those flows from assuming their correct circulations. The habit of identifying with a particular physical shape as the self also holds the body back from reaching an optimal state of perfection. When you stop interfering with the natural chi flow in your body by detaching from consciousness to realize empty mind, which means letting go of even images of emptiness, it will eventually attain a natural state of peaceful and harmonious perfection.

Following Prometheus' advice, Hercules arrives at the place where Atlas is holding up the heavens. Just as Prometheus had predicted, Atlas readily agrees to get the apples for Hercules if Hercules in turn assumes his place, with the weight of the world literally on his shoulders. What this all means is that only by cultivating emptiness – by "holding up the sky" – can someone enter the garden of the Hesperides. An ordinary mortal cannot get the apples but only a cultivation practitioner – Atlas who is cultivating emptiness - and so the many petals (apples, or peaches in other cultivation schools) of the crown chakra in the head cannot open unless you practice meditation.

Atlas has to get the apples for Hercules because Atlas is always cultivating emptiness – he holds up the sky or empty space. But there's a point about this most people miss: Atlas can only get the apples when he cultivates true emptiness rather than false emptiness. When he holds up the sky he is clinging to an image of emptiness in his mind, but when he gives up that practice of holding on to emptiness he can finally get the apples because he's finally experiencing true emptiness. Just let it go, stop holding on to emptiness and you can experience the true emptiness of the mind and its fruits.

Atlas retrieves the apples from the garden and then tells Hercules he'll take them back to Eurystheus himself. Now our hero Hercules is in a quandary, for who knows what Atlas will do after delivering the apples.

The Greeks in their cultural stories loved men who could outwit their opponents rather than just defeat them with brute strength, such as in the story of Odysseus and the Trojan horse or Odysseus and the Cyclops, so it's not surprising that a bit of cleverness is worked into the story here. In the Arabian story of Aladdin, who tricks the giant genie back into the bottle, we find this same admiration of quick thinking as well. In the story of the Twelve Labors, Hercules reveals his wit by agreeing to the proposal, but asks Atlas to hold up the sky temporarily so that he can arrange his cloak as a pad to make it more comfortable. Atlas unthinkingly puts the apples down on the ground and takes the sky back from Hercules again, after which Hercules simply picks up the apples and departs.

This story reveals a very important lesson about the right type of cultivation which I have been emphasizing because people make this mistake all the time. "Emptiness cultivation" does not mean that you should suppress thoughts or not use thoughts and become dull or dim-witted like Atlas. If you refuse to use your mind you will become as easy to trick as Atlas was. Unfortunately, most people who try to cultivate emptiness try to suppress thoughts and become a little dull headed, so they make this mistake. The condition for enlightenment is the natural total absence of thoughts, not their repression. If you try to suppress thoughts in cultivation, in the subsequent life you will tend to be a little bit slow or dim witted because of this mistake.

Spiritual master after spiritual master tell you not to suppress thoughts to reach "no-thought" on the spiritual trail because this is not the correct meaning of emptiness. It means not dwelling in thought, but letting thoughts arise according to situations and circumstances, and acting on them naturally. If you do not cling to thoughts the mind will empty out, and you will experience silence to the degree of your detachment, along with your chi and channel purification. Thoughts will still arise, but they will arise from a background of a very quiet mental state that is colloquially called "no thought" or emptiness.

As you reach higher stages of spiritual training from simply letting go, then because of your chi and channel purification this experience of emptiness will become even more profound. The mind becomes bright, clear, alert and pristine and also what we would describe as open, spotless and free. At the level of an Arhat, thoughts seem almost non-existent, and so body and mind seem to pass away, but they do indeed still arise. Obviously the chi flow through the channels must be extremely smooth to get to this level, which represents a remarkable degree of cultivation work.

You should therefore never try to cultivate a state of stale emptiness or solid blankness as the path of spiritual cultivation, but must always let thoughts freely be born. Wisdom, or understanding, must always be freely born and allowed to function because you are not a dumb animal who just follows their instincts. You can cultivate and attain realization precisely because you can have wisdom, insight or understanding (all synonyms) into the nature of the mind, and can detach from thoughts to realize their ultimate source.

The mind is ungraspable so you should never try to turn it into blankness or stupor. The mind with its memories is there, so you do not try to get rid of it but just act wisely. It is simply that sages have discovered that the proper use of the mind means that you do not try to dwell in any mental state or phenomena but just let thoughts arise and function, and so keep doing that. We say "no thought" and "empty mind" as just colloquial expressions to help you let go and understand the way to spiritually practice.

In short, the mind does indeed quiet down during the process of correct spiritual practice, but you don't attain this quiet through thought suppression. Thoughts will always arise, should arise and must arise. Consciousness is thoughts. A Buddha simply knows all the thoughts that arise in his or her mind quite clearly. In fact, it is said that a Buddha, being entirely out of consciousness or "transcending consciousness," can know the minds of all sentient beings and now you can understand why. Buddhas get to the stage where they transcend consciousness so they can know all consciousness.

As the great Zen master Lin Chi said before passing away, "The continuous flow of thoughts in the mind does not stop, so what can you do about it? True boundless awareness can be said to resemble the original nature. Because it is beyond name and form (consciousness), people cannot realize It. After splitting a hair with a sword, hone the sword at once (after the mind gives birth to thoughts according to need, let them go and the mind will return to become empty once again)." The state of emptiness when thoughts depart is perfect peace and bliss. You are always that, which you must come to recognize, but you should not identify with that through clinging. This is what is naturally always there. It comes from the true you which transcends even the realization of that empty pristine awareness.

As the Sixth Patriarch of Zen exclaimed upon his enlightenment, you just let the mind be born while not clinging, not dwelling. Atlas, on the other hand, was clinging to empty space, a type of thought suppression, so in not thinking at all he easily got tricked. His mistake warns us not to suppress thoughts to arrive at an artificial emptiness, and so there he is stuck holding up the sky. There he is trying to cultivate emptiness, but is he really?

You don't have to hold up the sky because the sky is already empty – there's nothing to hold on to. He's just incorrectly holding on to empty space. If you think you must cling to emptiness to cultivate emptiness, you're making a big mistake. You cultivate by not abiding, which means you simply let go. You abide by not abiding.

As a Buddhist story explains, there was one particular Bodhisattva who sat for ten full eons cultivating no-thought but who never got the Tao (achieved enlightenment, self-realization) from his long effort because that isn't the proper way to practice. You can arrest the movement of thoughts but as soon as the concentration ceases your thoughts will rise once again. You have to ask yourself who or what is having this experience, and search for the source rather than cultivate the samadhi of no-thought. Whenever you reach a state of silence, peace, quiet, emptiness or stillness from your meditation practice, you have to inquire who is experiencing this emptiness.

Those who suppress the mind by clinging to a state of no thoughts, rather than abide in the naturally empty state of the mind without clinging to thoughts while letting them arise, make this mistake. They mistakenly believe that the cultivation path is all about suppressing thoughts or becoming muddle headed to experience emptiness. Tsong Khapa warned that if you suppress thoughts as a cultivation habit you can end up becoming reborn as an animal because their consciousness is similarly dull.

One of the cardinal principles of science, or cultivation, is the fact that everything is always changing and ungraspable, like a dream or illusion, so just let it go. Act as appropriate, but let the mind transform because none of its states can stay. This is what human beings do wrong – they cling. When it's time to be sad then be sad and when it's time to be happy then be happy, but don't cling to any such mental states. The mind is free not because it is empty, but because it does not cling.

Once you realize this deeply, you can just let everything be born while you mentally abide nowhere, as is truly natural. Everything you are experiencing right now is your mind anyway, so there is no center. Just let go and then you will be free and natural. No one is binding you except yourself. Look for an ego and you cannot find it. In that realization of its non-existence you are discovered to be free.

What we typically do with our minds is to follow the stream of thoughts down all sorts of alleys and think that's natural, but when you don't cling everything still functions, nothing is lost, and you can find peace in the midst of worry, affliction and still accomplish everything and more. Shakyamuni Buddha said we are topsy-turvy in that we mistake our thoughts as something real rather than taking the empty nature of the mind that is always there as what's real. That empty nature always stays, so that is what is real rather than the ephemeral picture show of thought images that we cannot even remember from last week. When we say empty nature we are not talking of stillness, for that stillness is still a duality opposed to the birth or existence of a thought. Empty means empty of all phenomena, even images of emptiness or space. It is something you can only realize through cultivation practice for to stop at stillness is the mistake of Atlas.

Thoughts are like birds that fly across the sky. Birds leave no traces of their flight in the sky, and yet when we cling to thoughts we are essentially trying to create traces in the sky that cannot fundamentally exist. You can try to make the image of a whirling fire brand into something real and solid, but you can never succeed at it despite all the machinations you ever perform.

People hear this but only realize the meaning of the words when they actually cultivate spiritual practice enough to experience it for themselves. Your chi channels have to open and your chi flow has to become smooth enough, and your chi pure or clear enough, to start bumping into states like this. Only then can you realize what is really going on beneath a human being's normally busy mind, for due to ignorance humans cannot recognize any of this but must be taught this through the dharma, and then cultivate to prove it. This is just a scientific result, which is why the true spiritual path is non-denominational. Everyone experiences this and recognizes the truth of the path I have been describing when they cultivate far enough and high enough. Search and you will find that the past masters of countless traditions have said this as well. It is a universal realization because it is true.

Some cultivators, when they reach a stage where they experience the extinction of thoughts, become Arhats who want to cling to the quiet side of the Tao forever, calling the whole world that arises in the mind an illusion. Thus they try to silence their mind stream so that they will never be reborn here, instead of letting the mind of awareness naturally flow and function. They desire just the unmoving, peaceful, stillness side of the Tao we call "emptiness" and have disdain for the moving side called "existence."

However, emptiness itself becomes an illusion when you cling to it, as Atlas' story illustrates. Mentally identifying with something as the supreme reality only fabricates an image, and leads not to the attainment of the supreme reality you seek. Furthermore, after your karma of experiencing that created image of peace is used up, out you will come again from enjoying that particular samadhi.

The highest Tao is simply to let go and function without clinging whereupon you will attain unqualified formlessness and be free within all realms. The highest Tao is an empty mind of detachment that still gives birth to wisdom and understanding but never engages in clinging to the thoughts that are experienced. You don't cling to emptiness, and you don't cling to whatever arises in the mind; rather, you simply function with ease. Neither the one-sidedness of Shiva or Shakti is correct, neither existence nor non-existence is correct, neither yin or yang is correct, neither the real or unreal is correct, neither emptiness or existence is correct. The ego is replaced by wisdom on this road, meaning that insight or understanding still arises and always will. There is always still functioning.

Non-clinging is the real Tao. As Lao Tzu said, the Tao that can be named is not the real Tao because the real true nature is beyond consciousness and cannot be described. There is actually no person clinging, no process of clinging, and no object to be clung to, so you practice letting go to eventually reach the point where you abandon everything and abide in the natural state that transcends consciousness and is pristine, pure, unfathomable, eternal and yet the appearance display of reality still arises. That appearance is inherently one with the emptiness. It's hard to reach this understanding unless you learn how to let go and not mentally dwell. Reaching this realization, one becomes the equivalent of a sage, an enlightened being, a Buddha.

As expected, our hero Hercules outwits Atlas, who had cultivated a false emptiness by suppressing his thoughts (that's why he's holding up the heavens on his shoulders), or we can alternatively say he's made emptiness into an image like space and incorrectly holds to it. When Hercules carries the apples back to Eurystheus, the court finds that no ordinary human beings can keep these fruits, because they represent attainments from cultivation, and so they are then returned to the gods.

In summary, for this Eleventh Labor Hercules must obtain the golden apples of the Hesperides nymphs protected by Ladon, a dragon with a hundred heads. This means he must open up the crown chakra in the head including all its countless chi channel branches, which is extremely hard to do. That will help silence thoughts even further. Although pranayama practice can help at this juncture, only someone who truly cultivates emptiness can achieve this.

After the impurities around the crown chakra soften and are discarded, all the tiny channels and chakras in the head can start to open but only if you practice correctly and reach some stage of emptiness, meaning selflessness. Hercules gets Atlas, who is holding up the heavens of space, to retrieve the apples for him, meaning the task is achieved through some degree of empty mind cultivation. With the fruit of his labors attained, Hercules then returns triumphantly to King Eurystheus.

THE TWELFTH LABOR: CAPTURE CERBERUS THE HOUND OF HADES

[2.5.12] A twelfth labor imposed on Hercules was to bring the watch dog Cerberus back from Hades. Cerberus had three heads of dogs, the tail of a dragon, and on his back the heads of all sorts of snakes. When Hercules was about to depart to fetch him, he went to Eumolpus at Eleusis, wishing to be initiated into the mysteries. Hercules was not permitted to see the mysteries because he had not been cleansed of the slaughter of the centaurs, so he was cleansed by Eumolpus and then initiated. Then he set off to Taenarum in Laconia, where is the mouth of the descent to Hades, and he descended through it. When the souls in Hades saw him they fled, save Meleager and the Gorgon Medusa. Hercules drew his sword against the Gorgon, as if she were alive, but he learned from Hermes that she was an empty phantom. And being come near to the gates of Hades he found Theseus and Pirithous, him who wooed Persephone in wedlock and was therefore bound fast. When the two beheld Hercules, they stretched out their hands as if they should be raised from the dead by his might. And Theseus, indeed, he took by the hand and raised up, but when he would have brought up Pirithous, the earth quaked and he let go. Hercules also rolled away the stone of Ascalaphus which had been pinning down the gardener. Wishing to provide the souls with blood, he slaughtered one of the kine of Hades. But Menoetes, son of Ceuthonymus, who tended the kine, challenged Hercules to wrestle, and being seized round the middle, had his ribs broken; howbeit, he was let off at the request of Persephone. When Hercules asked Pluto for Cerberus, Pluto ordered him to take the animal provided Hercules mastered him without the use of the weapons which he carried. Hercules found him at the gates of Acheron, and cased in his cuirass and covered by the lion's skin, he flung his arms round the head of the brute, and though the dragon in its tail bit him, he never relaxed his grip and pressure till it yielded. Thus Hercules carried it off and ascended through Troezen. But Demeter turned Ascalaphus into a short-eared owl, and Hercules, after showing Cerberus to Eurystheus, carried him back to Hades.

The twelfth and final labor of our hero Hercules was to capture Cerberus, the fierce three-headed Hell Hound, and bring him back from Hades alive. The ancient Greeks believed that when a man died his soul went to the underworld, the kingdom of Hades, and dwelt there for all eternity. Cerberus guarded Hades, so just the thought of Cerberus would frighten ordinary men.

It is said that Cerberus possessed the tail of a dragon, which once again is a reference to a chakra. On his back were the heads of all sorts of snakes, which you can now easily surmise symbolized various chi channels. Since Cerberus had three heads we also know that he in some way stands for the juncture of three chi channels because guard dogs always represent the entranceway into, or juncture of chi channels in the Twelve Labors. They guard a division of a channel into multiple sections. However, because Cerberus has this tail and chakras he definitely represents something more than just this.

Cerberus was born to the fire-breathing giant Typhon and the half-woman half-serpent Echidna. Cerberus guarded the gates to the underworld, which means the gate between life and death. The gate to life or death in the body is the root chakra because it is the source of ascending chi life force. When that source dries up, a person dies.

You can unplug the root chakra to various degrees when you start purifying your channels but it's only when you start working through the deeper levels that you can uncap the root chakra and get to see the chi source of life wavering over the chakra's mouth. Shakyamuni Buddha mentions that any person who reaches this point in spiritual cultivation will now have the opportunity to gain control over where they will be reborn in their next life, but of course the true mastery over this issue, and its relationship to the volition skandha, does not happen at this preliminary level of purification.

In the story of the Twelve Labors, we first started with the monstrous body of Typhon, who represents our own unpurified physical nature. To this point we have opened countless channels, cleared them of obstructions and purified the chi to help transform this initially impure physical nature. Now we have reached the point where we come to the source of life force chi within the body, and thus the topic of life and death arises, which also has a relationship with the volition skandha. Cerberus, who guards the underworld, represents something connected with this stage of attainment.

Because this is the last labor, it makes perfect sense that Cerberus would be connected with some final stage of attainment that the Greek public could understand, rather than really high cultivation phenomena, and thus we have this topic of life and death in the Twelfth Labor. Few spiritual schools are conversant in the topics of the four dhyana or the sambhogakaya, or even enlightenment, so this is the highest topic a Greek audience could handle. With this understanding as our background, now we can truly decipher the meaning of Cerberus.

Cerberus is a scary creature, and the key to his decipherment is his three heads. The rest of his body, including a tail with snakes on it, of course represents chi channels because of the many branches, but which main energy channel? Several areas of the body might fit this description, but one fits best.

Just as Geryon's two-headed dog Orthus represented the conjunction of two chi channels, Cerberus represents the conjunction of three chi channels near the perineum or root chakra. This is where we find the source of life in the body, which takes us all the way back to Hercules' First Labor wherein the Nemean lion represented the yang chi of the body, and the bottom of the ocean where the Monkey King Sun Wu Kong first found his magic staff. This magic staff had the ability to control the ebb and flow of the ocean's tides, and like the story of the Nemean lion its attainment represented the unplugging of the root chakra.

Now the Chinese Taoists commonly use the symbol of a three-legged toad in many cultivation teachings. They say that the three-legged toad represents the accumulation and transformation of the three essences *jing*, chi and *shen* that everyone experiences on the cultivation path. In most of these representations the toad holds a round coin in its mouth that is connected to a fishing line that stretches upwards. That thin string or fishing line represents the *sushumna* central channel.[146] The Chinese coin in the toad's mouth, which has an empty square cut out of its center, represents the root chakra. The four sides of its inner square represent the chakra's four petals just as the four sides of a Tibetan mandala represent these four petals as well. This is where the *du-mai*, *jen-mai*, left and right channels all interconnect. Because the root chakra gives rise to kundalini, it is often represented by the color red, a red triangle (symbolizing fire), or a four sided pyramid which captures its four channels on the base.

The three-legged toad, which some equate with a man's scrotum because of its shape and natural references to sexual energy, connects with the *jen-mai* heading down the front of the body, also known as the channel of descent. Since the *jen-mai* front channel is also connected with the third eye and brow chakra near the top of the head, this is one possible explanation for Cerberus who has a dragon head on his tail.[147] We might also note that the *sushumna* branches off from the root chakra into two sections that proceed down the legs to the feet, and in many cultivation traditions, the feet are associated with the underworld.

All of the symbolism now perfectly fits to identify Cerberus as follows:

- The generative organs themselves, located near the root chakra and symbolizing the topic of life and death, are often represented as a triplex structure
- The *sushumna* runs upwards to the crown chakra (which was the dragon of Ladon)
- The *jen-mai* runs upwards into the brow chakra (which could also be a dragon)

---

[146] Some cultures use the symbol of a bucket and well to represent the *sushumna central* channel and root chakra above the perineum. The well rope, or *sushumna* channel, hangs down and reaches the water below (the root chakra), and that water (chi) can be pulled up through the bucket. The Chinese *I-Ching*, for instance, uses this symbolism.

[147] Pictures of Lao Tzu and the Long Life Taoist Immortal often show them holding a wooden staff capped with a dragon head. This represents the fact that kundalini rises in the body to the head.

- All of the above are involved with the root chakra - the gate of life and death
- The *sushumna* itself breaks into two parts that run into the feet, which are often used to symbolized the underworld in various traditions, and so we have three channel branches to match the three heads of Cerberus

At this stage of cultivation it is still hard to open up the chi flow into the leg channels fully. Opening the leg channels is akin to transforming one's death karma and hell karma according to many cultivation traditions, so there are many good points for choosing this interpretation. In short, Cerberus the three-headed watch-dog of Hades represents the protrusion of the root chakra channel with its inverted Y-shape division into two channels proceeding downwards into the feet.

It is particularly difficult to open up all the chi channels in the legs, including the knee joints,[148] ankles, and the soles of the feet, which eventually happens only after years of cultivation practice beyond this stage of attainment. In any case, this interpretation of Cerberus' identity fits all the facts and makes the most sense, but rather than insist on one interpretation or another, for this last labor I'm going to deviate from the normal pattern and leave it to you to decide when you reach this stage yourself.

In this Twelfth Labor Hercules has to descend into the netherworld, the realm of death. This is a place where Hercules reasons that his great strength might not help him because Hades means life is over. If he enters

---

[148] This is yet another reason why meditators are encouraged to sit in a full lotus posture, which helps to progressively soften and open up the knee joints. The difficulties involved with opening the knee joints are also why Tibetan Vajrayana practitioners often make 100,000 prostrations to help soften the knees. The story of Yeshe Tsogyel offering away her knee caps illustrates the difficulties with opening the knee area as well, which only fully occurs past the stage of Hercules' Twelve Labors. Some devout Buddhists make walking pilgrimages to holy sites, making full kneeling prostrations every few feet of the way, which also helps to transform the knees, too. Martial artists who practice the horse stance posture get help towards this end from their training as well, which also helps open up the inner leg channels. Basically, it is very difficult to open up the chi channels in the knees. Even my teacher, who was a martial arts champion, often told me how difficult it was to truly open up his leg channels completely and the extent to which he practiced. One day after many years of effort, he decided he was finally going to tame his legs and open them fully so he sat cross-legged in a bell tower without moving until the channels suddenly opened all the way through, after which he said his legs were blissful and he felt as if he was walking on air. Naturally this is something you should not do because without many years of prior training and practice you might hurt yourself from the strain of sitting cross legged for many hours. As the case examples of Milarepa and Shakyamuni showed, during cultivation you should never subject your body to extremes or you will hurt it.

Hades, our hero realizes he might not be able to return to the land of the living. He, therefore, decides to protect himself by being initiated into the Eleusinian Mysteries – the spiritual cultivation school of the time that taught people about immortality - so that he can learn how to enter and then exit the underworld alive. The actual experiential meaning of the mysteries becomes more clear from the achievements of this labor. It involves how to escape the clutches of death by passing this stage of cultivation.

Hercules, therefore, traveled to Eleusis to be initiated in the mysteries, which required that he first be cleansed of his previous crime of killing the centaurs. This purification meant that his previously impure chi and channels were now sufficiently purified and that he had overcome most of his animal passions and lower nature symbolized by the centaurs, who were half-man and half-animal. His initiation into the mysteries now, after all this time, therefore marked a definite stage of purification or completion in the progress of his body cultivation. So at this time, he is finally introduced to the mysteries because he has accomplished all the necessary stages of preliminary purification gong-fu.

In other words, after all these previous spiritual gong-fu attainments, Hercules is finally ready to understand the real meaning of the mysteries because he has attained the preparatory purification. He is ready to experience, master or attain what they teach. As far as the Greeks were able to communicate about the foundations of the spiritual path, Hercules' journey was nearing completion for the laying of this foundation.

What is the spiritual path all about? It is about more than the Greeks could possibly represent in this story, for the Twelve Labors of Hercules only describe the stages of chi, channel and chakra purification prior to samadhi and yet higher spiritual attainments. Those higher attainments are not described at all, just a hint at heavenly immortality. But long life or immortality is not the spiritual path. The spiritual path is actually about penetrating through the fog of the false I-thought and finding the essence of where the concept of "I-ness" or beingness ultimately originates from. If you trace the I-concept back to its source, you are on the road of true spiritual practice.

The notions of being real separate beings, personalities, egos, selves etc. are all false, incorrect thoughts because they entail the concept of separateness or independence. We might feel that all the individual minds that we experience each have a separate consciousness but they are really just part of one whole body of consciousness and the underlying clear awareness that can know consciousness is still not the original nature or ultimate foundational original essence. Our fundamental essence even transcends consciousness, which is why Buddha says he knows the minds of all sentient beings, but you must travel the road of tracing consciousness back to its ultimate source to find that fundamental essence. That is why the spiritual journey entails cultivating mental purity.

The path is not about suppressing thoughts to create mental dullness or an image of emptiness in consciousness, but of letting go of thoughts as they arise so that consciousness clarifies and the underlying pristine awareness that knows consciousness can eventually be recognized. When one realizes the base of awareness, cultivation becomes effortless until one becomes a fully enlightened Buddha. That is the route. So no one attains the ultimate end of recognizing God or the Source without cultivating a pure mind,[149] and you can only reach that through the practice of meditation and virtue. You might recite prayers or engage in other religious exercises, but the spiritual activities that produce results are the ones that follow the *cessation-witnessing* principles of meditation.

The thought of being a life, ego or "I" is a big barrier in spiritual cultivation, just as is the idea of taking the human body as your real self or identity. Many cultivation schools, such as Vedanta, Zen and Buddhism, tell practitioners that to realize enlightenment and experience the True Self, their real self which is the original nature or fundamental essence, practitioners must transcend the false ego or I-thought to find its source. You give up holding on to the false ego, or small self and only then can you realize the True Self. Only then can you win self-realization and spiritual liberation.

You must give up the small false self to find the True Self, dharmakaya, Womb Matrix, God, Brahman, Ein Sof, original nature, Source - call it our "fundamental essence" or "original nature" or whatever you will. On that journey it is easy to get lost in the gong-fu experiences or superpowers and mentally go astray, especially at this stage of the journey where Hercules will encounter the source of life and death in the human body. That is why Hercules must take some special precautions here. This stage of cultivation has linkages to the volition skandha of Buddhism, and it is easy to get confused when progressing through this stage of attainment.

Whatever you believe is the cause of birth and death in the universe is something you might encounter in visions at this stage of cultivation.

---

[149] You can always experience visions and various purified states of mind on the cultivation trail, but that is not true attainment. Spiritual practice is cultivating to realize or penetrate through to the ultimate absolute source behind all consciousness.

While it is seemingly simple to pass through many other visionary experiences prior to this one, your mind may see all sorts of confusing imaginings concerning the source of life on earth or in the cosmos, a topic which is connected with the phenomenology of this labor. In particular, you might see the physical source of human life in the body at this level of cultivation, but not the ultimate source. We are still just talking about chi rather than the original nature, which is not a phenomenon that can be "seen." Nonetheless, entering Hades and coming out again is akin to reaching the physical source of birth and death for the body, so this labor marks a milestone in cultivating towards the Tao.

After learning the mysteries from Eumolpus, Hercules then comes to the entrance of the underworld at Tanaerum in Laconia and starts his descent into the nether regions. Laconia is probably a reference to the location of the perineum (and root chakra) because you can see on a map that Laconia is located at the bottom of the major Greek land mass, and the perineum is located at the bottom of the body's upper trunk. Many of the places mentioned in the Twelve Labors are references to our body in some form or another and in this case the reference is to our root chakra, the source of life or death in the body.

On the way into the deep cave, Hercules comes to a bench where Theseus and Pirithous are sitting. Historically, the strangers Theseus and Pirithous became such great friends that they felt like brothers. When younger, they both wanted wives and foolishly pledged to carry off the daughters of Zeus. Whether or not this action was truly the product of courageous daring, or simply youthful folly inspired by sexual desire, either way, such details definitely have connotations of the root chakra. Seeking wives, Theseus decided to steal Helen of Sparta, and Pirithous wanted to steal Persephone, the wife of Hades. One wanted an earthly beauty and the other the wife of a god.

Hades, through his magic, captured both these men and caused it so that they had to sit on a bench next to each other forever. The two friends were still sitting there as Hercules came along, and they lifted up their arms as he passed, asking for his help in pulling them free. Hercules lifted up Theseus to free him but he could not move Pirithous, and so Pirithous had to remain in the underworld.

This part of the story is very easy to understand when you go through this stage of attainment, and is even mentioned in the *Surangama Sutra*. It signifies that Hercules reaches a purification of the root chakra chi at a deeper level than in previous cycles, and completely frees it from some final layers of obstructions. At this level of channel purification, you might be able to see a cap on top of the root chakra which looks like a crystal dome formed of solidified *jing*-chi. After that cap lifts off, underneath the wiggling "chi of life" or "life force chi" can be seen. The cap that rests on top of the chakra is not a perfect half sphere but is a bit bumpy and irregular in shape, but a semi-translucent cap nonetheless.

In some Chinese schools, the vital chi seen at the root chakra after the cap is removed is described as a "galloping horse" or "wandering heat haze." It is something that just wobbles there when the cap is removed, and is unpredictable in its jiggling movements. When you observe this chi after its irregularly formed clearish domed cap comes off, you will see that it stays somewhat centered on the hole of the root chakra. It will softly shimmer while randomly wiggling forwards and backwards, left and right with its own unpredictable Brownian motion. It is not like a burning jet flame of gas that stays perfectly centered over its source, but more like a soft haze in a blobular, half-spherish sort of shape that shakes and wobbles wandering this way and that.

Shakyamuni Buddha simply said you will eventually find the source of life when you reach the point where you are purifying or breaking through the volition skandha. Although it is not definite that you are breaking free of the volition skandha at this time, Shakyamuni's words on this feat are an excellent lesson rarely encountered or heard, and so I will relate just a few of his words to you because you can find the rest in the *Surangama Sutra*. Its teachings on the skandhas can help you pass through many of these labors.

People tend to experience thoughts about creation and destruction, or birth and death, when passing through this stage because the chi energies are involved with the source of life and death in the body. Since your chi (life force) remains in your body until you die, Pirithous, who sought an immortal wife, represents that yang chi just wiggling there over the root chakra, and so he cannot be pulled from the bench. He must remain there. As for his close friend Theseus, he represents the cap or plug of solidified *jing*-chi that is pulled off, and so he is able to be taken away.

One more thing about Pirithous, the one who could not be removed and who got in this situation in the first place because of his sexual desires. When you reach this stage of cultivation, your body is hot everywhere and the sexual desire is extreme. The rising yang chi, if you mentally connect it with your imagination, can lead to a torment of sexual desire.

The only way to pass through the pull of sexual desires is through the willpower to refrain from physical indulgences at this stage. Just let it go.

Three things might help you in this situation. First, you can imagine that you are a golden Buddha like Amitofo or Ksitigarbha.[150] Through your visualization, which also entails trying to match their boundless mind of compassion, or simply offering your problems over to them and letting go, you might then be able to maintain discipline while imaginary sexual involvements arise. The yang chi involved with sexual imagination at this stage may help open up the channels, as Vajrayana maintains, so there is nothing wrong with their arising. That is natural. However, the breach of discipline in losing one's semen at this point will not help your cultivation but impede it.

The second way to deal with sexual desire during cultivation in general is to imagine stripping off everything that surrounds your white bones[151] and offer it away. Then you will be left with just a set of bones in your imagination, which you can imagine become dust, and then empty space as you take the visualization further. If you imagine you are just a set of bones and nothing else, sexual desire cannot grab you or harm you or provoke you to do anything because bare bones cannot engage in sexual relations. Lacking flesh and organs, you will have no sexual equipment with which to fulfill sexual desires! The same goes for empty space. Perhaps the highest method for dealing with sexual desire is to finally experientially realize that you are not the body and have no body because you are just bodyless awareness, and then sexual desire is something you can witness, detach from, and it will pass you by. However, it is hard to practice this great method unless you have constantly been practicing emptiness attainments and your channels have already opened to some degree.

Always remember to end any visualization technique with an empty mind – there's no body, no space, no mind anymore but just awareness – and then you can succeed in spiritual cultivation. The cultivation path

[150] Ksitigarbha is also known as Dizang in Chinese, meaning the Earth Store Buddha. He is also known as the Hell Buddha. He appears in the form of a monk because he compassionately ministers to those in the hells while not having hell karma himself. Although he ministers in the hells, the sutras state that he remains active in countless worlds across the universe by emanating billions of nirmanakaya to help sentient beings change their errant ways and achieve enlightenment.

[151] As is taught in Shakyamuni Buddha's white skeleton visualization technique, which is traditionally called body impurity contemplation. In some versions of this technique you can imagine that your bones burn with fire, and then turn to ashes which are blown away. First you form a stable visualization that encompasses the entire body, and next you release it so that the mind becomes empty, which is letting go.

is always about letting go and not dwelling in any mental scenarios or states of consciousness that arise. The trick is to use these methods to get started with your cultivation and after your channels open sufficiently, in time your mind will become free and quiet naturally. All the methods of visualization used in spiritual practices are designed to help you attain mental stability, or one-mindedness, and then that quiet calm state is released (no longer held on to) so that you become mentally free, open and silent. The channels open in the process and from that opening you can attain higher empty states of mental purity.

The third method for dealing with sexual desire is to simply cultivate emptiness by letting go. If you can manage to remain empty and do not cling, those energies will work to open your chi channels dramatically, which is one of the basic principles of sexual cultivation. This is the easiest method of the three, but also might be the hardest of the three alternatives when sexual desire grabs you. That is why Shakyamuni Buddha often approved of his students practicing meditation in charnel grounds where they would see dead bodies decomposing everywhere. Seeing these repugnant scenes all around, they could handle the sexual desires that arose due to their ascending yang chi because, seeing dead bodies in states of decay, they were able to cultivate a state of detachment.

If you don't triumph over sexual desire you will always remain in a hell of torment, sometimes of your own making. Just consider how Pirithous and Theseus were willing to risk the consequences of traveling to Hades because of lust. Because the root chakra represents sexual urges and the life force, and sex is the source of life in a physical sense, we are dealing with the very foundation of life in this difficult labor. Of all the labors of Hercules, this Twelfth Labor is probably the greatest one to accomplish because overcoming the pull of sexual desire, especially the flow of yang chi from the root chakra, is one of the biggest obstacles in cultivation. If you can let go, that chi can be utilized to open up your channels. If you succumb to the loss of your *jing* or elixir, you will have to wait until sufficient force once again builds up.

There is also an earthquake in the story when Hercules frees Theseus from the bench, and this is something you may actually experience if you get this far in your cultivation. The *Surangama Sutra* of Buddhism, which is the Orthodox Buddhist school's equivalent to the esoteric texts within Vajrayana, states that when you are freeing yourself from the five skandhas there comes a time during these purifications where it feels like an earthquake occurs. That often happens right around this stage of attainment.

The earthquake-like shaking does occur in your body, and you will indeed feel it, but it is not something that happens in the physical world. People read the Buddhist sutras which state that earthquakes would occur at certain instances when the Buddha taught, and they think this is all nonsense. However, when you experience this particular phenomenon, it will indeed feel like your entire body AND the whole building and your surrounding area start to shake for a few moments, but it will only be happening within you. During Buddha's time there were some actual earthquakes attributed to his teaching, as well as at Jesus' death, but in this case Hercules is referring to an earthquake of chi that you feel internally that might even cause you to fall down. When it happens you'll swear it was an earthquake but it was just an internal chi and mind phenomenon.

Buddha says the earthquake will cause the palaces of ghosts and demons to tremble and topple down, but practitioners don't realize that this refers to the yin chi structures within their own body that are finally being purified. Your own body is like an entire world but people do not realize it. Others will not feel this chi earthquake, only you and other beings made of chi, but the event is so strong that you might have to grab the sides of the building you are in to prevent yourself from falling.

There is also a minor story in this Twelfth Labor about the gardener Ascalaphus who is freed by Hercules and then turned into an owl. This short story is there for a reason, but the meaning is not easy to decipher. Some may say it represents an astral body attainment[152] that can travel almost anywhere like a bird, something also often incorrectly taken by many schools to be the final fruit of spiritual cultivation. It might also represent the enlivening of another type of chi flow as well, and this is probably the case because it fits all the relevant characteristics of one particular phenomenon.

---

[152] In Chinese Taoism, this is known as a "*yin-shen*" attainment, an invisible and intangible chi body that can travel the universe. After three years of cultivation, it can manifest in a material form others can see and touch, whereupon it becomes a "*yang-shen*." The *yang-shen* body double phenomenon is documented in countless spiritual schools, especially the yoga schools of India (and even various Christian monks), but we cannot go into the details of this attainment. However, it is a fact that many practitioners, especially in the western schools, mistakenly assume that this body is the ultimate spiritual attainment because they are ignorant of higher samadhi attainments and supreme enlightenment, which seems to be the case in Hercules Labors. See Emblems VII, XXIII, XXXVIII of the *Atalanta Fugiens* which contain related teachings.

The opening of the third eye, which has two side wings (like an owl) and is usually represented by lunar yin phenomena (when owls are active) in cultivation schools, is probably represented in this part of the Twelfth Labor. The third eye, or Ajna chakra, sits in front of the "garden" of our story, which is the Garden of the Hesperides representing the many chi channels in our head. The brow chakra sits above it, often symbolized in Indian culture by a very giant circular piece of gold jewelry worn by women on their forehead. You can see such jewelry worn by beautiful women in Indian movies. This brow chakra could actually be our stone under which Ascalaphus is imprisoned.

We say that the third eye is sealed shut before it is opened, and this is similar in meaning to a rock imprisoning a gardener beneath it. Once the rock is rolled away by Hercules, however, the gardener is freed and turned into a winged owl. Since the "owl" encapsulates the yin nature of this channel, as well as the chakra's two side wings, this part of the story can indeed represent the opening of the brow chakra and then the Ajna chakra below it. The brow chakra is represented by the boulder since the brow chakra is larger and more circular in shape.

In Taoism the opening of this region is often represented by the opening of a cave or cavern. This is because it actually feels like there is an indentation in the forehead at this region when the relevant channels are opening, and you will actually feel this "cavern" from time to time during the earlier cultivation stages. However, the Indian schools don't like this representation of a hollow space, even though that's what it temporarily feels like. They just refer to the Ajna chakra as a circular moon or chakra having two wings. In the west this chakra is said to be connected with our pineal gland, which has lunar connotations again, and so all the representations are apt regardless of which tradition we turn to.

After dealing with Theseus and Pirithous and rolling away the rock pinning down Ascalaphus, Hercules finally meets Pluto (Hades) in the underworld and asks permission to bring Cerberus back to the surface. Pluto agrees under the condition that Hercules overpowers the beast without using any weapons except his own strength. This is because there is absolutely no way you can force these two leg channels to open. You can only keep cultivating emptiness to let go, and then these channels will finally open. You are the one who has to do it because no one can do it for you.

Just as Hercules wrestled with Menoetes upon entering Hades (which means he pulled off the chi surrounding some channels just as he did previously when he wrestled with others), Hercules wrestles with and then overpowers Cerberus. Flush with success, he carries Cerberus out of Hades through a cavern entrance in the Peloponnese, and eventually brings him back to Eurystheus.

Essentially, Hercules opens up a fuller degree of the *jen-mai* channel circulation down the front of his body (through the brow and Ajna chakras), clears open the gate to the source of life and death to see the life force chi wobbling there, opens the channels downwards into his two legs, and then leaves Hades with new life. Taoism directly says that a cultivation practitioner will extend their life and can become an Immortal only when they fully open the channels into the feet at this level, and Hercules finally achieves this. This is essentially the story of the Twelfth Labor.

King Eurystheus was incredibly frightened at seeing Cerberus and amazed that Hercules could even complete this underworld labor. He was so frightened that he finally ceased giving our hero troubles and released Hercules from any more tasks. Our tale of spiritual gong-fu, culminating in a triumphant discovery of the source of the life force within the body and its circulation even into the feet, is now complete. As always there are greater degrees of this opening that occur over many years of further cultivation going into the future, but this is where the Greeks ended the story.

Although the legend of the Twelve Labors doesn't explain what happens when you proceed yet further in opening the chi channels, to proceed this far is considered quite a cultivation achievement in preparing one for the Tao. Unfortunately, we cannot say this is the Tao or that you really have broken through and perfectly purified any of the skandhas or *koshas*. That would be a mistake. You have only made a dent in this direction and laid a good foundation because there is much work left to do, and there are many years of cultivation work lying ahead.

Hercules still has not yet achieved samadhi and certainly not enlightenment or self-realization. It would be nice to say so and make these claims, but to be accurate he has not really completed the stages necessary to fully transform the physical body. There is still much work to be done, but Hercules has passed a major milestone in this direction. We can say that Hercules has definitely cultivated the initial physical foundation for stable samadhi achievements, but still has many years of work ahead. Actually, in the Greek myths it is only after many more years that Hercules is finally made immortal, too.

Many people think they are enlightened if they reach this far, but this is still just a partial achievement. The great Chinese neo-Confucian Wang Yangming comes to mind at this part of the story because he was another great cultural hero who made the mistake of assuming he attained the Tao. Although one of China's four great Confucian masters,[153] he did attain some degree of the Tao but not ultimately self-realization. Nevertheless, his teachings effected a tremendous impact on the culture of countless Asian countries. If you reach this far, you are not yet able but can become a person who can impact culture to a great positive degree, and even a Bodhisattva protector if you continue cultivating and so choose. It all depends on your efforts, compassion, wisdom and commitment. In having shown you many others who have previously succeeded in countless cultures and who had chosen to become cultural saviors and protectors, I personally hope the Bodhisattva way is what you choose.

As a caution, another great Confucian scholar that people often think reached some stage of the Tao – Zhu Xi – didn't get anywhere near this ultimate target at all. He, too, greatly affected Chinese culture but in a negative way. Like Aristotle, Zhu Xi was extremely intelligent but totally removed from any spiritual cultivation attainments. Zhu Xi should be considered simply an intellectual rather than a sage or cultivation adept. His intellectual explanations of Confucius' teachings totally destroyed their cultivation content, and he made terrible interpretative mistakes that crippled the Confucian path of enlightened spiritual cultivation, causing its decline, because he lacked any sort of actual spiritual attainments himself. As an intellectual, however, his writings became the official guide to Confucius just as the academic writings of Thomas Aquinas (another religious great of profound intellectual capacity but without any spiritual gong-fu or attainment) became a guide for Christianity. Many Jewish and Islamic scholars have similarly shaped their faiths without any genuine spiritual understanding or spiritual attainments at all, also harming their cultivation traditions in the process. The same pattern of a twisted loss has followed Christianity practically since its inception.

This same event of the true dharma becoming buried - as a result of the contributions of so many "learned men" inventing dogmas and writing interpretations devoid of cultivation knowledge and attainments - has plagued Judaism, Islam and Christianity practically since their inception. The eastern religions have experienced this too, but Bodhisattva masters can easily, independently arise within these traditions, since they don't

---

[153] The other three include Confucius, Mencius, and Zhu Xi.

have to fight a power structure and its propaganda machine, and correct matters from time to time. It reminds me of the situation today where we have all these people lecturing on spirituality from the pulpit and none have even the slightest cultivation attainments to know what they are talking about. These are the people we take as our teachers in Judaism, Islam and Christianity, but they are leading everyone astray.

Lacking anything even remotely near any of these true spiritual attainments, everyone charismatically bandies about his or her intellectual interpretation of the Old Testament, New Testament or Koran. Christianity has so many sub-sects because of this that they can hardly be counted. However, no one offers any insight into the real spiritual cultivation lessons within these holy books or the cultivation path you must follow for genuine spiritual attainments. Unfortunately, this is to be expected and is a sign of the poor karma of people born into these traditions, which historically appear to have been constantly at war with one another.

You need a lot of merit just to come in contact with true cultivation teachings and great wisdom to recognize their correctness. As the accomplished masters of countless spiritual streams have consistently stated, it is *very hard, in fact extremely difficult* to come into contact with true cultivation teachings, or even the information within this small book. Why you even have the merit to encounter this material, in the face of the billions who will never hear of it, I do not know. You need great merit to encounter the high dharma teachings and real wisdom to accept them, study them and put them into practice. As my teacher says, it is easy to develop the merit for becoming super rich or very famous if you really want that, but very difficult to develop spiritual merit for enlightenment unless you really cultivate and study and support the true dharma.

That is our path that lies ahead – continued study of cultivation materials, such as the Buddhist sutras, along with intensified meditation efforts according to the proper principles of cultivation practice. As to Hercules, we must salute and applaud him for his spiritual progress in the Twelve Labors and for the cultural contribution and example he subsequently provided for western civilization. That contribution is really the important thing because using your strengths and abilities to help others, including your cultivation accomplishments, is the ultimate achievement in spiritual cultivation and purpose of the spiritual path. They are all you, so why should you not devote your efforts to helping all other sentient beings?

Everyone knows the names of Socrates, Confucius, Lao Tzu, Buddha, Jesus, and Krishna not just because they succeeded in their spiritual cultivation, but because they greatly contributed to human culture as a result. That is the sign of a true Bodhisattva hero who does great things for humanity. Just by living they made a great contribution to humanity because they attained the Tao.

You can become like this yourself if you succeed in your own cultivation and so choose. In the Buddhist scriptures you can read the history of so many Buddhas and Bodhisattvas who have succeeded at enlightenment and subsequently devoted themselves to accomplishing great things for humanity and in countless other worlds. Arhats do not choose to do this because they want to cling to the peaceful clear side of *nirvana*, failing to recognize that there is no difference between the emptiness of the original nature and its functioning appearances. The path of the Bodhisattva hero is clearly taught in Buddhism whereas Vedanta just states the target, Taoism describes living naturally according to the way, and Confucianism describes how you can cultivate in every day daily life and make a contribution to humanity as well. The universe lasts forever and you are bobbing up and down without purpose, typically engaged in meaningless activity, until you choose the path to become enlightened and then work for others, who are really just you. It is time to start on this quest.

Many great enlightened ones have left us their mantras which act as a sort of password that cuts through the body of consciousness to connect with them so that we may receive their enlightening help. They cannot enlighten us, since we cling to ignorance, but only help us in our own efforts at self-realization. Our mind is the confused one, so we have to purify it ourselves. If the Buddhas and Bodhisattvas had the power to enlighten us they would have done so already, but people have to make the efforts to save themselves by awakening. Nevertheless, of the many deities and protectors we have already mentioned and described, many have chosen the Bodhisattva path to help those who spiritually cultivate. We may call some of these great ones "pagan" because they came from traditions different from our own, but the enlightenment way actually has no religion attached to it. The question to ponder deeply is whether your current religion and spiritual practice is a pathway helping you attain self-realization at all.

Hercules' example inspires people and is just one of the many types of contributions that spiritual cultivators can achieve for mankind. The fact that he eventually became fully divine suggests that he completed a fuller course of spiritual cultivation than recounted in the Twelve Labors, but we will have to look at the subsequent details of those journeys, and what they would entail, at another time.

If we want to understand how to proceed further ourselves or want more details of the process Hercules went through in this last labor, we can certainly turn to other information sources to flesh out the rest of the story. As mentioned, one such source is the *Surangama Sutra* where Shakyamuni Buddha explains what transpires as you break through the skandhas. He also warns practitioners of the many by-roads of error through which they can go astray in spiritual practice. I cannot recommend this source enough along with *Tao and Longevity*, which explains many of the physical changes according to Taoism. While Vajrayana texts take one to the opening of the central channel, there is not much material in print taking one far past that accomplishment, but many of those materials are within Taoism. Yet for the very highest stages, we once again must turn to Mahayana Buddhism and the sutras which explain the beautified bodies and Buddha lands of many great Bodhisattvas and Buddhas.

The school of Vajrayana, tantric yoga and Taoism all contain teachings on the body's physical transformations as you cultivate toward self-realization, and explain how to perfect the sambhogakaya reward body. You will not find this guidance in the western religions, and yet all these same transformations will occur to those practitioners, too. The knowledge we have gone over is all part of the non-denominational science of human beings and their potential. The eastern schools just cited commonly talk of body cultivation and physical transformations on the path, but if you want to know cultivation basics and the proper type of mental practice you are best advised to turn to the writings of Vedanta, Zen and Mahayana Buddhism.

It is not that Zen, Mahayana Buddhism and Vedanta are greater or better than western schools or even the other eastern schools, but if we are benchmarking for the best explanations then in my opinion these schools reveal the enlightenment pathway most clearly. They reveal so many aspects that we did not even discuss in this book. If you follow their guidance, you will avoid the danger of divergent religious roads leading you astray.

As Shakyamuni Buddha said in the *Lotus Sutra*, "All the Buddhas want to enable sentient beings to open up their enlightened perception and make it pure and clear, and so they appear in the world. They want to show sentient beings the perception of the Buddhas, and so they appear in the world. They want sentient beings to awaken to the perception of the Buddhas, and so they appear in the world. They want to enable sentient beings to enter into enlightened perception, and so they appear in the world."[154] Buddhas can do anything they choose in the universe, but with all the choices available this is what they choose. I hope this observation makes you think deeply.

One always hopes that their life has some meaning in the end, but countless sages have said that your purpose should be to achieve self-realization rather than to become famous, rich, powerful or accomplish great deeds. They have said that our life should be centered on this task of self-realization - attaining spiritual enlightenment - and that a blessed life is one where an individual spends time on this pursuit.

Confucius called this the task of the "great learning" that we should always be pursuing in life, and said it is the central pivot around which all human life should revolve. I hope that the examples from Hercules' labors have given you faith in the universality of this path, that you realize it is the true crux of what religion is supposed to be about, that all genuine spiritual schools talk about it, and that cultivating is the hero's way.

---

[154] *Working Toward Enlightenment*, Nan Huai-Chin, (Samuel Weiser, York Beach: Maine, 1993), p. 78.

CONCLUSION

While it might seem to be a let down to hear that by his last labor Hercules still did not achieve enlightenment or self-realization, there is no problem with this at all. Who said we had to have a complete description of the physical gong-fu that appears on the way to self-realization, or that he actually had to attain enlightenment in just these Twelve Labors? Our set of twelve lessons are perfect for revealing what they do cover, which is a certain set of preliminary stages of the path dealing with chi and channel transformations, and we should be extremely thankful to even have the teachings they contain.

Hercules went through many gong-fu stages and experienced many spiritual phenomena that various cultivation schools all commonly describe, such as the well-known "kundalini awakening," so the story of his labors offers us many instructional lessons. In fact, after studying countless cultivation traditions we can honestly say you would be hard pressed to find a clearer sequential description of the standard gong-fu you can expect on the spiritual path in any other spiritual school or tradition.

One thing missing from the Twelve Labors, however, was teachings on meditation and the four dhyana that are usually achieved well past these stages of mental and physical purification. These samadhi states are something Hercules would get a slight inkling of during the Twelve Labors, but they are not something he could cultivate with stability until he passed through all these labors and then proceeded further with his cultivation efforts. In the Twelve Labors he lays a foundation for attaining the Tao, but he does not yet attain it.

To spiritually cultivate, the first step is to arouse the life force of the body by cultivating a quiet mind. Because of a quiet or empty mind the life force then subsequently arises without any forceful effort required on your part. This is what we call a kundalini awakening, or more properly, we say that your yang chi arises. From that initial start, both your mental consciousness and physical body will then begin to go through many stages of purification before you can achieve the four dhyana and spiritual enlightenment.

The four dhyana of spiritual cultivation, which many saints experience, are as follows:

- In the first dhyana your coarse thoughts settle down and you start to experience profound mental quiet along with mental joy and physical bliss, the bliss being possible because your chi and channels have all opened and transformed to some degree, and because you can now let go of the body.
- In the second dhyana your chi comes to a rest and you experience more refined states of joy and physical bliss than in the first dhyana due to a higher stage of mental and physical purification.
- In the third dhyana even your pulse will come to a rest, with your heart beat slowing to just a few beats per minute, and the physical bliss is even more refined than anything experienced previously because you can almost forget the body entirely.
- In the fourth dhyana your mind will become so calm and tranquil that there is no feeling of mind or body anymore. Mind and body both drop away.

Hercules was laying the foundation for these spiritual attainments in the Twelve Labors, but did not yet reach this far as the samadhi-dhyana attainments. If you want to learn more, Buddhism provides explicit details of the many steps to these attainments, though of course the four dhyana are also found in Taoism, Hinduism, Christianity, Vajrayana, Judaism, Islam, Jainism, Confucianism and many other spiritual traditions as well. The spiritual states of samadhi and dhyana are the common gong-fu of the spiritual path, but not yet the Tao.

Hercules did not achieve the four dhyana in his Twelve Labors, and he did not achieve enlightenment either to become ultimately free of the realm of birth and death. He passed through many spiritual stages of preliminary chi purification, but he only laid a good foundation for attaining the Tao of self-realization, which is something few achieve. Many spiritual practitioners and religious greats in history only achieved one or more of the four dhyana, and very few achieved the highest stages of true enlightenment. The Twelve Labors are an easy task when compared to this most difficult of pursuits.[155]

Nevertheless, the story does recount many types of the sequential stages of gong-fu you will encounter along the spiritual path, and these experiences are not religion dependent. If you cultivate sufficiently you can experience them, and if you do not cultivate you cannot experience them. That is the real meaning of "grace." Grace means heavenly assistance for spiritual attainments that comes because of hard work and diligent effort on your part. The best chance for receiving such grace is if you set for yourself a devoted meditation schedule.

The experience or attainment of spiritual gong-fu is as simple as that; effort is required rather than study, belief, membership in a group or natural "holiness." In short, you must cultivate meditation. It is not that spiritual gong-fu does not exist because you have not experienced it. Search the stories of countless spiritual greats from countless traditions and you will find that they describe the same stages of attainment, which attests to the non-sectarian existence of spiritual gong-fu and the fact that there is a science behind its manifestation or achievement. You simply do not experience these stages yourself because you have not cultivated hard enough, long enough or high enough yet.

While the gong-fu experiences of the spiritual path are common or shared phenomena, you should not be wed to any of the specific interpretations I have provided for the Twelve Labors. Who was Hippolyte or Cerberus really? What did Molorchus, Pholus, Eurytion, Theseus, Pirithous, or Ascalaphus really represent? Who really knows? Although the sequential correspondences to stages of cultivation are exact, only the author of the Labors - and there are various versions to the stories – knows what he really intended.

Frankly, any of my interpretations can change because every now and then I come upon some new fact about this or that Greek character which was not available to me previously. Those facts might add details that would cause one to switch an interpretation from one spiritual phenomenon to another. In life I have made numerous interpretative mistakes in my own cultivation so I don't consider these interpretations

---

[155] Most people fail at attaining enlightenment because they still cling to consciousness on the spiritual path despite attaining dhyana. This is why you most often hear instructions such as let go, be natural, no effort, stop clinging, or do nothing at all. If you dwell in any type of form, such as taking the body to be your self or taking samadhi as enlightenment, you will not ultimately succeed.

definitive and perhaps one day a realized master will correct them or add additional helpful comments.

In the meantime, one thing is for sure. I can assure you without any doubt that Hercules' Twelve Labors do indeed describe the sequential spiritual gong-fu that you will experience on the cultivation road. The general sequence of gong-fu events is correct and the major details of the path are exactly as described. Cultivation gong-fu varies somewhat according to the individual, but there is a commonality to the stages that comes shining through the Twelve Labors. Once you go through these stages you will immediately recognize their descriptions yourself, and so meditation is the spiritual practice I encourage you to engage in.

The important lesson from the Twelve Labors is for you to spiritually cultivate yourself, achieve some of these progressive stages, and make the identifications for yourself *because you experienced them*. As my teacher always says, you must *prove* spiritual teachings for yourself. You must *verify* them through your own personal experience. You must *authenticate* all the teachings of spirituality through practice and then attainment. Don't just read about them because faith isn't enough, belief isn't enough, and study isn't enough.

Most people never prove anything when it comes to the path of spirituality but simply remain lost in a soup of religious beliefs that we have been born into and become accustomed to so that they take them as what's real. In addition, the religious road of worship is certainly inadequate for helping you attain real spiritual progress. Even if you totally accept cultivation teachings upon reading them, that belief is worthless to you without the commitment to practice and the progress from practice. Even when true spiritual cultivation information comes your way, without meditation practice another life of opportunity is again wasted.

As a final tribute to Hercules, let us try to review his story and summarize some of the major events on the spiritual trail that you can expect when you first start to cultivate, and let us try to throw in some helpful hints that may assist you in your own cultivation efforts, for that's what it is all about.

In the First Labor, Hercules awakened the yang chi of his body at the root chakra. When that happens, this chi travels up the *du-mai* to the head, and then comes down from there coating the outermost layers of your body so that you feel like you are being sealed in. This actually happens just as described. The experience will help you understand a later stage where you feel like your body is an empty sack without any bones or innards, a stage of achievement which many masters tell you to try to cultivate. The great master Tsong Khapa often spoke of this practice, as does Taoism, and I have experienced it many times myself.

Next, Hercules starts emptying the chi channels of their dirty, impure yin chi innards or obstructions. The clearing out of the channels is symbolized by the Lernean hydra growing new heads one after the other. This emptying of the channels can happen to a greater or lesser extent depending on the depth of your cultivation work. For instance, many people at this stage will actually see the dirty chi squeezing out from the tip of their toes in the feet, or fingers, something mentioned in Tibetan Buddhism because it particularly focuses on the purification practices of the path. Hercules also starts feeling the pumping of the heel chakra in the Second Labor. This can happen at this time but is usually felt in strength a little later.

All these events so far are commonly described in various cultivation schools. The most important thing to know is that the white skeleton visualization practice is a preliminary preparation that will help you more readily reach these stages. Anapana practice will help, too, and of course you must practice witnessing meditation. In terms of a complete set of cultivation practices to help you achieve great progress, I always recommend that people practice the white skeleton visualization technique along with mantra, vipassana, pranayama, sexual discipline, behavioral correction and charitable offering if they really want to succeed on the spiritual path.

If you have the right practices and make the right effort with the right heart, you can succeed in record time. You just need to keep to a schedule and do a few things really well. I do not want anyone to waste as much time as I did when younger because I had an insufficient practice schedule and non-existent understanding of the path. All the different schools and techniques confused me as well until I found a great teacher. This book is my chance to transmit some of what I now understand to you.

By the time of the Third Labor, with his chi channels somewhat emptied and opened (it's just considered a superficial degree of opening at this stage), Hercules starts making more significant inroads into transforming his yin chi and the chi channels of his body, represented by the Cerynian deer that had golden horns and hooves of bronze. The feet are very hard to open on the spiritual trail, and thus the deer had hooves of bronze in this labor. The golden crown chakra or many channels in the head, represented by the antlers, are also difficult to open but that happens at a later stage of the story. For now you just begin to recognize that they are there.

After the chi channels are somewhat opened and the chi somewhat transformed at this stage, which does indeed take quite a bit of meditation work, a new stage of Hercules' raw, unpurified yang chi starts to come up. Thus we then have the fierce Erymanthian boar that had to be conquered in the Fourth Labor. When the raw yang chi first starts coming up, it is certainly not purified, so the experience can be emotionally irritating as the channels clear. People initially experience headaches or emotional outbursts when first learning how to handle this sort of energy. The yang chi is coarse or raw, and unpurified yang chi that arises is not necessarily the smoothest thing to deal with. At every stage of the path a new level of refined yang chi will arise, and this is the first degree of any marked significance.

At this stage herbal medicines might help you open up your liver and reduce angry outbursts or feelings of irritation due to errant liver chi flows. Detoxification regimes, in general, can help your body and should be used. Remember that physical detoxification efforts, especially in today's "age of pollution," are something wise to do even if you are not a spiritual practitioner. Typically you do not spend much time working at herbally detoxifying the physical body at the higher stages of the spiritual path because you don't want to lose energy at that point. Everything is done via chi. Of course you will take medicine when you get sick, but when it comes to body purification at the upper stages of the path you usually just let the chi do the cleaning for you unless you have a superior knowledge of herbal medicine that helps. However, anything you can do at these lower stages to clean and detoxify your body – whether the liver, colon, skin or other body organs - will help your appearance, health, longevity *and* spiritual progress.[156]

---

[156] It is quite pitiful to see the incredible paths people will pursue in order to maintain a youthful appearance. Our bodies become like cesspools as they age (the ancients called them stinking bags of filth) because they accumulate all sorts of physical and chi toxins. Meditation will unclog the chi channels, and together with herbal detoxification and pranayama, these are the only things that can really improve the health and appearance of the body and restore youthful vitality at a deep level. Silicon implants and plastic surgery, botox, cosmetics, hormones and all sorts of other methods may artificially stave off the outward appearance of aging, but these interventions result in a plasticized, "dirty looking" countenance. Everyone can spot the artificial interventions. For ordinary people not pursuing the Tao such interventions are the way of the world, but for those who want to reach the level of a master they must never implant foreign materials in their body (steel pins, silicon implants, etc.) because

The task of detoxification is one of the major lessons I have added for the Fourth Labor because it should be something you are doing in life anyway due to all the chemicals we are ingesting today. With yearly detoxification efforts, any nation would see fewer cases of illness and chronic disease, but people always act on these matters when it is too late. Detoxification should become a regular yearly part of human culture, like celebrating a birthday, Thanksgiving or Christmas once per year. In the earliest stages of the spiritual path, almost all your energies go into transforming your physical body so whatever you can do to help in cleansing matters will be a blessing to your regular health and spiritual practice, too.

The cultivation changes of the Fourth Labor mean that you have been doing your spiritual practice religiously – mantra, meditation, anapana, pranayama, and the white skeleton visualization – and you cleaned out some of your channels and your yang chi (kundalini) is now arising. Now you must divert the rising yang chi into the central channel. When that happens ... Bingo! The central channel can finally open.

The Augean stables in the Fifth Labor are therefore cleaned in a single day because when the chi enters the bottom of the *sushumna* it will push out the obstructions within it so that the *sushumna* empties in a short while. In real life you will feel the pumping of impure chi gunk from out many of the channels (or may see it in a visionary process) for several days when you reach this stage, and afterwards the purification of all the related channel orbits will finally be within reach due to that crucial cleansing. The preliminary stage of coarse *sushumna* cleansing, when it first opens, takes a few days of continuous meditation to complete. You will feel and see all sorts of chi extrusions from the channels and chakras during and after this event. Of course the complete set of subsequent transformations after the opening of the *sushumna* take years to work through because it requires a long time to totally transform all the chi, chakras and channels of the body and purify its five elements.

---

foreign objects are too difficult to transform. In short, if you want to look younger and feel better at the same time, take detoxification herbs and start practicing pranayama and meditation for as little as 30-40 minutes a day. Meditation leads to better health and longevity rather than a sickness prone life marked by pain and debility that is typical of the current medical approaches to life extension. As you get older the impure chi obstructions in your channels harden and affect your appearance, as well as mentality. When it finally clears out – which only meditation can do – the body becomes more flexible and its light can appear once again. Your appearance and personality will both change for the better. But if you don't clear out the chi channels then your body will continue to age by collecting dirty, poisonous channel obstructions and blockages and you will suffer the normal aging consequences of debilitation.

There are countless Hindu yoga and Buddhist Vajrayana teachings on how to initially open the central channel, but if you don't engage in the proper preparatory intensified cultivation work prior to this stage then it just is not going to happen. This is true regardless of your tradition. In other words, you do not have to follow the traditional Vajrayana methods to open the central channel, but if you don't do sufficient preparatory work involving specific cultivation exercises, then it really is not going to open. When it does open you will experience many visionary phenomena, and the event is so momentous that the local Protector Gods in the area might rejoice by producing various atmospheric phenomena. It might rain or snow and various dragons, and dakinis and devas in the sky might be seen flying around celebrating and carrying banners.

People typically practice emptiness meditation along with mantra recitation and *kumbhaka* pranayama for years to reach this stage. They practice the nine-bottled wind practice, vase breathing, vajra breathing and so on.[157] They constantly recite *proven* mantras that have helped countless others to succeed. All your prior practice efforts finally bear fruit with this event. However, you must maintain a steady commitment to meditation practice to get this far even though it may seem like nothing is being accomplished along the way and you feel your effort is insufficient. All of a sudden your cumulative cultivation work will catch up with you and then you will achieve a tremendous breakthrough like this even though you may have felt like you were not making any progress at all.

My personal advice is to always chant the Zhunti mantra to help purify your channels and open the heart chakra, and practice the white skeleton visualization technique. I also encourage you to read the Buddhist sutras and biographies of Vedanta saints to increase your wisdom and knowledge of the path; practice the relevant sections within the *Six Yogas of Naropa* on opening the central channel; practice vipassana mindfulness meditation;[158] and keep cultivating even if it all seems hopeless. I never knew what I was doing when I was younger but I had faith and persevered because my teacher said it was important, so

---

[157] It is my hope that the field of freediving, where people learn to hold their breath for extreme lengths of time under water, and the invention of glossopharyngeal insufflation (lung packing) for this sport, might after some experimentation help produce entirely new pranayama techniques that can be used in the preparatory stage of intensified meditation practices for spiritual cultivation.

[158] You might try a different emptiness meditation practice each week from among the 112 methods described within the *Vijnanabhairava Tantra* of Kashmir Shaivism, also known as the *Vijnana Bhairava*.

I'm passing this advice on to you as well. If you simultaneously practice a number of different cultivation techniques according to a schedule, wherein those techniques aim at providing an experience of cessation-witnessing from different principles (mantra quiets the mind, vipassana mindfulness results in a natural subtraction type of mental quieting, visualization ties up consciousness to produce quiescence, pranayama works on physical channel openings, the meditation practices within the *Vijnanabhairava* aim at a direct experience of emptiness, etc.), you will make ultra quick spiritual cultivation progress.

With your *sushumna* central channel now somewhat opened, thoughts will start to quiet down because chi will start to flow through it into the brain. That silence or emptiness is the meaning of chasing away the toxic Stymphalian birds, which is the essence of the Sixth Labor. We colloquially call this type of mental quiet that you experience "samadhi" but it's not the real samadhi of the four dhyana yet. It is just the mundane samadhi of reduced mental chatter and quieter mental state that some schools call peace, tranquility, silence and so on. This is the sort of quiet you can attain from religious practice, though of course at a much deeper (quieter) level.

You still need a lot more meditation practice to attain the real samadhi states of spiritual training called the four dhyana, and that is when all sorts of spiritual powers will come out. The attainment of such powers is far past the events recounted within Twelve Labors, but you will bump into many "semblance" samadhi states while going through the Twelve Labors. The Sixth Labor represents a stage where you can finally achieve and maintain some of this mundane mental peace and quiet with some stability. Your mind will have reached a degree of emptiness or quiet that is easy to naturally maintain.

By the end of the Sixth Labor you will have opened up the central channel along with the *du-mai* and *jen-mai*, so a new stage of yang chi can be experienced. Also, after you have opened up the central channel you can somewhat open the heart chakra and other chakras upon its length along with their attendant chi channel circulations that hitherto have been unreachable. Previously there was no way for the chi to fully enter into these channel networks, but now access is available to you for cleansing.

Your spiritual gong-fu attainments are proceeding exactly according to schedule and following the typical, standard sequence experienced by most practitioners. By the Seventh Labor, the yang chi has spread itself into a fuller circulation of the channel orbits, and all is proceeding nicely. All the yang chi is arising in your body, and this is the bull that comes out of the sea. You don't need to know how to do anything at this stage other than to keep meditating. Just keep practicing to let go and more and more channels will open. Essentially, in the Seventh Labor, you are told not to cling to any stage of attainment or any phenomenon that arises, and you will continue to make progress in the purification of your chi and channels.

"Let go" means not dwelling in any mental states that arise because dwelling impedes the transformations of chi and inhibits your spiritual progress. Clinging means you effectively cling to chi and channels and hamper the flow of your chi through its cleansing orbits. So you don't need to know any teachings about chakras, chi, the skandhas, illusory bodies or so on. Forget that stuff and just cultivate meditative emptiness all the way – letting go of each and every stage, phenomena or experience of spiritual attainment that arises. What could be simpler? Nevertheless, you are now deeply smack in the middle of opening the chakras and channels, purifying the body's five elements, or harmonizing the physical nature.

One of the phenomena that occurs during this process is Maitreya's Big Knife Wind, which is the Eighth Labor, known as the traditional kundalini awakening. This is a stage when ascending chi cuts open all the tiny chi channels in the flesh. When this happens you feel like you are being ripped into pieces. We are not talking about opening the big channels like the *du-mai* and *jen-mai* but all sorts of tiny channels that cross the body everywhere like a net. The man-eating mares of Diomedes in the Eighth Labor are nothing else other than this uncomfortable stage of purification. The phenomenon is unmistakable when you go through it. Although uncomfortable, it is nothing you cannot handle and subsides after three or four days of heat and soreness.

The major chi channels of your body are now opened, and countless tiny minor channels are also somewhat opened after the experience of the Big Knife Wind, which is what people typically think is the traditional kundalini awakening. It is time to reach yet another stage of transforming yin chi to yang chi, and open the other major auxiliary channels in the body. Hercules therefore obtains the belt of the Amazon Queen Hippolyte in the Ninth Labor, which she wore across her chest, and then he's on his way to the Tenth Labor.

Don't think that "opening a chi channel" here means completely opening a subtle energy channel. All the way to the final achievement of the sambhogakaya there is cycle after cycle of chi purification and the opening of more and more and tinier and tinier channels at more and more subtle levels of chi. It takes years to open up all the channels corresponding to the most advanced stages of spiritual practice. We are only discussing the initial kick starting of the process in the Twelve Labors.

Along the way, the transformations of chi purification that occur can produce all sorts of phenomena, and Hercules is only describing the beginning stages of this whole process. At the upper end of the process we have all sorts of achievements such as rainbow bodies, *yang-shen* attainments, bodies that can disperse into chi to reassemble elsewhere at will, and even more. The Twelve Labors just introduce you to the introductory phenomena of the physical purification aspect of the path. Naturally the mental aspect is more important, but we are describing the physical gong-fu in Hercules' labors.

At this point past the Ninth Labor, you have gotten the scaffolding of the chi channel structure of the body somewhat opened and cleared of obstructions. You've opened the left and right channels and can now differentiate your yin chi from yang chi. You have initiated the River Chariot rotation and can actually feel the microcosmic circulation in the body. Now it is time for shooting the big guns – to get the kundalini to course through the *sushumna* and activate the major chakras along this route heading into the brain.

That's the story of claiming Geryon's cattle in the Tenth Labor. The yang chi arises, heads up the *sushumna*, through the chakra orbits, and on into the brain. Once this main channel opens, other channels can now open more completely and the chi can flow throughout the body to find a new equilibrium of flow. The key is unplugging the *sushumna* circulations first.

When the yang chi reaches the head in the Eleventh Labor, you are finally in the garden of the Hesperides where there is the golden crown chakra with all its petals as well as the forehead brow chakra and Ajna third eye chakra. There are other chakras that need opening as well such as the brahma-randhra chakra and Buddha-randhra used by Bodhisattvas in the back of the head. There is a flower bud at the top of *sushumna* which opens, and this is also where the *jen-mai* starts turning down through the nose and heads towards the lower regions of the body.

Reaching this far means you have attained some of the physical fruit of the Tao. Congratulations, because it's hard to get this far, but remember it still is not the Tao.

As far as the Greeks are concerned, to this stage Hercules has done the preliminary coarse dredging work of opening up most of the chi channels you need to open to lay a good foundation for the spiritual path, which ultimately deals with life and death. This is coarse work, though, and not refined because it takes years of continual channel opening and chi purification for the really high stages of the path. However, this is laying down the initial physical foundation for actually cultivating the sambhogakaya reward body of purified chi. Hercules succeeds in opening up the rest of the *jen-mai* and the chi paths to his feet in the Twelfth Labor, along with a further clearing or "unplugging" of the root chakra, so his preliminary spiritual foundation is laid for the attainment of the four dhyana and ultimately the Tao.

Hercules has laid a good foundation for attaining the Tao by opening up his chakras and channels, but he hasn't achieved it yet. Through this path, rather than through the path of prajna wisdom that investigates consciousness to find the ultimate substrate of the mind, he has to continue cultivating. He must wait through many years while feeling the chi revolve through the orbits of his channels as it opens new regions and transforms into a higher stage of excellence that matches with the most purified state of pristine consciousness. Every time he reaches a new degree of letting go of consciousness (which includes body sensations), a new set of hitherto blocked chi channels can now open. As the chi suffuses throughout all the channels during this period he will begin to feel physical bliss in every cell, and he must learn how to let go of thoughts, the body and ego to attain the first dhyana.

If he continues cultivating and the body sufficiently transforms from the chi rotating and continually opening up channels at deeper levels, it can reach a state of purity or incorruptibility so that it does not decay upon death. Some adepts reach a physical stage where they can transform the body into light upon their deaths, shrinking it over a matter of days and leaving behind only a few remnants of hair or fingernails. Some adepts, at a sufficient stage of attainment, rise into the sky and demonstrate the eighteen transformations of an Arhat before they pass away, proving their mastery over the five elements of the body. Then they most often let the fire element burn their bodies and reduce them into ashes. Some seem to have their bodies dissolve into space. A Zen master might simply say he is leaving and then die right then and there on the spot – an extremely high stage as well which most people do not fathom.

There are many possible demonstrations of one's mastery over the five elements of the body after one reaches certain levels of samadhi attainment. It all starts right here with the "kundalini awakening," Taoist transformations, or completion stage yogas mentioned in these Twelve Labors. The Tao school, Indian yoga schools, Vajrayana Buddhism, Shintoism, Hinduism, Egyptian mystery schools, western alchemy, Jewish mystical stages of attainment, Christian saintly stages, Sufi stages of attainment, Confucianism, and so forth are all within these Twelve Labors because the gong-fu of the spiritual path is one hundred percent non-denominational. The practitioners of all these schools would benefit greatly from studying these materials, and then realizing that the relevant teachings are everywhere.

Cultivating is all about the process of breaking the habit of mentally clinging to thoughts, attaching to the sensations of the body, and holding on to consciousness itself. You always get results on the spiritual path but if you get wrapped up in them like a cocoon then you get nowhere. Just mentally let go of whatever happens. After everything settles and clears due to the process of letting go, what is ultimately revealed at the base of it all is something permanent and real that never moves. But until your mind is clear, until your consciousness is purified, you cannot realize this.

If you practice letting go long enough, then eventually you will experience some stage of emptiness and your kundalini will spontaneously arise in your body. Rising kundalini, or yang chi, will open up your channels and chakras and you will start to experience sensations in the body and this road of gong-fu if you work hard enough. Of course you must persistently cultivate an empty mind that does not cling in order for the process to deepen and continue. From that better unobstructed chi circulation, the mind can in turn become more stable and pure so that you can attain the dhyana. Ultimately, as consciousness purifies and your awareness remains bright, with wisdom one can detach from the mind and body altogether to attain self-realization.

By the end of the Twelfth Labor Hercules has cleared his major channels of obstructions and initiated the free rotation of his chi through all these orbits, but he cannot stop cultivating if he truly wishes to succeed in spiritual realization. He must continue to practice meditation and letting go while searching for the ultimate source of consciousness.

At his stage of attainment, Taoism describes the physical aspects of cultivation as a transformation of chi and *shen* into emptiness as his mind and body both transform to their natural states of purity and he starts to experience the pristine awareness of the mind. Buddhism always calls the physical transformations during cultivation the purification of the five elements of the body since there are five types of chi that transform, but the key to success in this process is to continue cultivating a mind that does not cling. The body is not you, but just a receptacle used by consciousness that transforms to purity and bliss after you start to cultivate.

If we were to summarize the spiritual cultivation path we would have to say something like the following: it is all a path of mentally not clinging to consciousness and searching for its source while letting consciousness function without impeding it. Of course, people don't know how to let go or even how to become still to mindfully witness or watch their mind. That is the problem in the first place for all spiritual practice, and that's why you are taught to meditate or perform other spiritual exercises.

People do not even recognize that they are holding on to consciousness to begin with, which is why the practice of meditation is so important as a spiritual training vehicle. If you learn to let go, your yang chi will eventually arise naturally and start transforming the five elements of your physical nature, i.e. your chi, channels, chakras and consciousness which entail various layers, sheaths or refinements called *koshas*. Every school describes these things differently but they all refer to the very same process since it's non-denominational. In this book we have used terminology from Hinduism, Taoism, Buddhism, and other schools to reflect this universal nature.

It is simply a basic fact that your chi and consciousness are linked, and it is because you are subtly holding on to consciousness that your yang chi is inhibited from arising and circulating as it should. When you let go of that clinging, the natural circulation of your chi that should exist will resume and reassert itself, clearing obstructions away in the process. This is what opens up your channels.

After the chi components of your subtle body are purified from this process and the chi channels are all cleared, your unobstructed chi will automatically start rotating through the macrocosmic and microcosmic circulations in the body of its own force, and you need not perform any special cultivation techniques other than continuing to meditate and let go. Your personality will transform as bad thoughts and bad habits drop away, and you will be within reach of cultivating higher states of human perfection.

You will continue to experience the rotation of the chi in the channels for many years as it continues to transform the body to greater degrees of purity. It's very hard to get to the stage where you do not feel the pulsation inside the head channels anymore, which some schools call "brain breathing," so that you can totally forget yourself and attain the highest spiritual stages. However, it is only a matter of time, and continued cultivation, until all chi channels open and their chi flow becomes smooth and harmonious. As this happens you must always detach from, rather than block, the physical sensations that occur on the path, but of course some are harder to let go of than others. The fact that we are always feeling sensations of the body, and thereby identify these constant feelings as part of our self rather than recognizing they just represent a body that is appearing within consciousness, is what makes cultivation difficult.

The physical body is not you because consciousness is actually everywhere, but like a shadow the body comes along on the path. Without a physical form, consciousness cannot manifest to know the world, and so the Unmanifest needs the Manifest to know itself. As you start to mentally cultivate, the five elements of the body will transform, and the body itself can be cultivated so that its constitutional elements return to their purest ultimate form. We say they return to the Source because the real sambhogakaya is where there is no body at all. All sorts of sensations, memories, emotions and mental garbage will come up as the chi channel pathways in the organs and viscera open, and you must continue to let go of these consciousness arisings because they are not the real you and do not ultimately mean anything either. Most spiritual practitioners have no idea what the Tao is, and thus they get caught up in body sensations as they cultivate and thus always remain lost within the sensation skandha.

After you get the whole process of chi circulation initially kick started, you do not need to engage in any special cultivation technique other than the continued meditation practice of letting go and then investigating consciousness. In time, with proficiency at detached mindful vipassana practice in watching the contents of the mind as they arise and depart, you will break through consciousness to reach a stage of non-ego.

Although the whole process of spiritual cultivation is really "emptiness cultivation" at each and every step of the way, Buddhism (including the Zen school) teaches that anapana is the topmost technique for quickest progress at attaining dhyana for even the highest stages of the path. This is the technique that Shakyamuni Buddha cultivated during his retreats. Anapana is also the technique which he taught to his son, his best student Mahakasyapa, and to his closest attendant Ananda. This is an instruction that my teacher gave to me because he said he wanted me to know the top method of the Zen school, which someone might not point out to me, and so I also want to pass this information on to you.

In time, the entire coarse physical body of an expert cultivator can eventually be transformed into chi, or energy. This is what it essentially is, just as Einstein's equations tell us. Of course this was true before Einstein deciphered this principle and encapsulated it in mathematical equations, but for some reason people only seem to accept explanations if we associate them with mathematics and science, which is why I have bothered to go over these physical transformations with such detail. Remember that I am only going over the lower physical gong-fu stages of the path, and not the transformations of consciousness along the way to self-realization. These are the more important thing because that's the whole point of the process. We are only describing the Yogacara half of the Yogacara-Madhyamika full explanation of existence and emptiness, and we only seem to be over-emphasizing these physical events because that is what this story is about. May you not take the emphasis in the wrong way.

Our flesh is just condensed chi, so naturally the coarse flesh of a practitioner can be transformed if you cultivate many years in the right way. Miraculous changes can come about, and superpowers as well, but they all follow principles of science. Many masters, however, do not choose to cultivate the purified sambhogakaya and so do not achieve complete enlightenment. Essentially, when you open up the chi channels and re-enable the natural rotation of your chi, your body can start to transform to match its highest state of natural perfection. But if you refuse to continue practicing letting go, you will impede these transformations.

You can call "letting go" by the term "spiritual cultivation," but then again it is just being natural, so there is nothing artificial about this practice and really no effort involved. It is perfectly logical as well because just as air cannot be grasped, consciousness cannot be grasped. "No effort," which occurs when you break the almost invisible habit of clinging, is the meaning of being natural. Therefore the "methodology" we have discussed, if we choose to call it a method or methodology, is ontologically significant because it is one hundred percent non-created, non-invented, non-artificial. You do not have to be taught it because it is just there, always available. It is not created like a scripture or dogma, and this is why people can awaken to realize the Tao.

You don't have to learn anything particular on the spiritual road except how to remain natural, and then you can awaken. And because chi and consciousness are linked, a human body going through this process of detachment and the subsequent attendant purifications can demonstrate all sorts of miraculous transformations. Depending upon how well you cultivate, you can eventually reach greater and greater states of samadhi and superpowers involving chi and consciousness.

Taoism states that the process of your chi transforming into spirit (*shen*) after the opening of the chi channels takes about nine months, and fully transforming *shen* (spirit or awareness) to emptiness takes approximately three years of further cultivation refinement. In those three years you can develop the ability to generate a *yang shen* emanation body, which is the ability to project a physical body double that can appear in other locations at will. This is unlike an invisible astral body because other people can actually see and touch it.

The *yang shen* achievement explains the stories from many spiritual traditions, including from the western orthodox religions, of masters who could physically appear to their students in faraway locations and then instantly disappear. These stories all represent this same cultivation achievement because the *yang shen*, once again, is a non-denominational attainment. Remember, none of this stuff is sectarian because *this is the cultivation path inherent to human beings*. Religion is supposed to lead you to enlightenment, and through all these various stages of gong-fu accomplishment. If your religion does not do so, you are not being well served.

The *yang shen* is just another natural human phenomenon or capability found within the scope of the science of human beings, but its attainment is only within the reach of those who spiritually cultivate to a sufficient level. Just as some people can win an Olympic medal because they practice a sport to a state of excellence, only those who spiritually practice to a state of mental purity and transform their bodies can attain these special abilities. These individuals are not freaks of nature but perfected human beings, so rare they are. Naturally, such individuals are not going to discuss these accomplishments with you or demonstrate them openly and get into all sorts of trouble. And once again, these abilities are not the path either but simply possible achievements within the path for those who choose to cultivate them.

The process of "returning emptiness to the Tao" or "breaking through emptiness to return to the Tao" takes a further nine years of spiritual cultivation effort, and many saints in various traditions have achieved this, too. But in terms of achieving complete and perfect enlightenment, which entails the attainment of all three Buddha bodies completely, my teacher has stated many times that over the last two thousand five hundred years only five or six individuals have attained it.[159] It is very difficult to become a fully and completely enlightened Buddha. Moses, Jesus, Mohammed, Confucius, Lao Tzu, Socrates and many other greats definitely achieved a degree of the Tao, but it is difficult to achieve the complete and perfect enlightenment of full Buddhahood.

Treading the spiritual path entails *the mental practice of learning how to let go through meditation, the resultant purification of your body and consciousness, the correction and ennoblement of your behavior, and then compassionately working for others - this is the spiritual path!* There is nothing in this description about attending the church, synagogue, mosque or temple for worship, ceremonies, rituals and services, and yet they can be an integral part of the process if you need them or desire them. Since you now know the proper principles, you can turn that attendance time into real spiritual practice.

As to the fact that your body transforms because of spiritual practice, this is something you should not concentrate on or worry about because it just happens along the way. The transformations, so to speak, just

---

[159] This does not mean that fully enlightened Buddhas, other than Shakyamuni, have not also come to teach in the various traditions of the world over time. The Sixth Patriarch of Zen, for instance, reached full Buddhahood (enlightenment) in eons past. Buddhas do not just appear in the streams of Buddhism, Vedanta, Sufism, etc. Enlightened Bodhisattvas and Buddhas arrive all the time in this world, constantly taking rebirth in religions where and when it's possible to uplift their dharmas and help the people awaken. However, like us they are limited by the karmic circumstances of the "outside paths" which do not stress the quest for enlightenment, and therefore can only conventionally teach in limited ways while performing their invisible enlightening activities. When Shakyamuni talks of the next Buddha Maitreya in the sutras, unlike other religions that expect a world savior to arrive, he is not just announcing the arrival of another teaching Buddha. He is announcing a situation where the karmic timing allows the simultaneous rebirth of all sorts of Bodhisattvas, Arhats and samadhi attainees at the same time who wish to arrive for teachings so that they make further progress in their spiritual practice. Such circumstances where so many advanced practitioners can assemble at the same time, and when the complete dharma can be openly taught without corruption or restraint, are rare indeed. This is how the coming of the Buddha Maitreya differs from other religious greats expected to come – whether those expectations are truth or not. It means the full dharma can be taught once again because there will be a karmic situation pregnant with the opportunity and which also allows the assemblage of countless enlightened adepts coming together. As explained, it is hard to produce such great auspicious circumstances where the good karma of so many beings is aligned.

come along for the ride. Physical transformations are not the cultivation path itself but just something that occur along the way. They are like a shadow that comes along as consciousness becomes purified, and not the cause of purified consciousness although of course there is a connection between purified chi and purified states of mind. There is nothing you need to know or do to "cause" gong-fu to occur, and you do not need to guide these transformations in any manner (although there can be little tricks now and then for breaking a plateau where the going seems slow or a bit stuck). Simply cultivate in the right way and they will occur quite naturally.

During the true process of spiritual practice, all sorts of physical transformations will naturally occur to your chi and channels, and you will achieve all sorts of spiritual gong-fu. For example, Jesus performed all sorts of miracles that were also seen in many other traditions because they are common gong-fu capabilities for certain stages. If you cultivate to the same stage of attainment then you can perform them, too. It is not that they were possible because Jesus was uniquely special, for then we would have to deny any accounts of such things from countless other traditions. You cannot just say that superpowers occurred or "miracles" happened for practitioners of one religious tradition but not for others. There are stories of such phenomena occurring in countless traditions pre-dating Jesus, and various cultivation texts go into the details behind the attainments.

When Jesus was pierced in his side while on the cross, it is said there was an outflow of blood separate from water which indicates a particular stage of physical transformation. When the Twenty-fourth Indian Zen Patriarch Aryasimha was beheaded, out flowed a white milky substance[160] which indicated yet another stage of physical transformation due to many years of cultivation effort. Even higher, after many years of physical transformation from cultivating emptiness (after the channels clear and the full microcosmic and macrocosmic circulations commence), a person's physical body can transform entirely into chi, or energy. Many supernormal powers become possible along the way.

This is an accomplishment of advanced Buddhist Arhats, Hindu Mahasiddhas, Taoist Immortals, and saints from other traditions. Typically, we call all these individuals "Arhats." When they stick around

---

[160] This phenomenon corresponds to a transformation stage of the bone marrow. If the body is cut at this time, a white liquid will flow out. This stage has been reported of many masters, especially in the schools of Taoism, Indian yoga, Zen and Tibetan Vajrayana, and is sometimes seen represented in Chinese martial arts movies.

to assist in humanity's welfare, returning in incarnation after incarnation out of a desire to help the world and human beings in attaining enlightenment, we call them "Bodhisattvas." When they cultivate high enough, these individuals can actually achieve the stage where their own physical body can disperse into energy and instantly appear elsewhere at will, which is different than a "*yang shen*" body double. This is possible because everything in the universe is ultimately consciousness and chi (energy), so no distance barrier is involved. Thought is the same thing as an instantaneous transmission.

The universe arises in the mind and is essentially consciousness. Matter and mind have the same ultimate source which the process of spiritual cultivation allows you to ultimately discover. However, consciousness has a flip side component of chi, or energy, that can be of a highly subtle, purified and ultra refined nature. If you cultivate consciousness you end up cultivating the chi, or energy of the body, because of this connection, and this is what accounts for all these transformations.

Everything is really consciousness, or energy, and for humans we have to think of the body as chi energy that has become physical flesh. The bodies of heavenly beings are also made of chi, which is why people cannot see them, and the higher the heaven the higher the degree of purity or refinement to that chi. On the spiritual road the flesh can become consciousness or energy once again due to the cultivation of mentally letting go, and that's the result of high spiritual practice aimed at returning to the Source.

Everything is "God-stuff" so nothing in the universe is more God-stuff than anything else or less God-stuff than anything else. Everything is ultimately the original nature which is the underlying essence or substance of reality. Recognizing the original nature through the route of cultivating meditation, which lets consciousness function as it should, one can eventually "realize the source without stain." We then say that "one returns to the Source," which of course are just nonsense words since the Source is that which one always is, hence there is no returning or actual attainment of anything. There is no individual attaining anything, no process of attainment, and no attainment. There is no one desiring enlightenment nor anyone liberated. It is all just the original nature; you are always the Self so you can never be ignorant of the Self, hence any striving to find the Self is just imaginary ignorance.

Conventionally, however, there is an unenlightened individual reading this book right now, and there is a spiritual path. There is awakening or self-realization. Realization can be cultivated and achieved. On this spiritual path there is no such thing as annihilation except for the extinction of ignorance. Awareness is a function of the original nature and cannot be obliterated. You can only block or suppress knowing, which is incorrect.

Pristine clear awareness is a natural function of the original nature. The base of existence is naturally aware. You are that pristine awareness, or we can more correctly say you are the original nature, the ultimate potentiality of which consciousness is just one of its functions or expression. It is the potentiality of everything because it is beyond consciousness, and hence is the unmanifested while consciousness is the manifested. When we say "empty mind" or "emptiness," it only means you reach a point where consciousness seems empty because you reach that base state of awareness, and that emptiness, which is like a nothingness since there is no underlying substance or energy matrix involved, can still miraculously give birth to thoughts when necessary. You are It, the original nature beyond all attributes. You are pure being upon which consciousness rises like a wave on an expanse of water, and through that consciousness the world appears. Thoughts appear and disappear in your light, but you transcend them, and they cannot describe the real you. Whatever is seen in consciousness is only a play on the screen of the mind, and you are essentially neither male nor female but that light of awareness.

Thoughts provide a world, and so we say It gives rise to "miraculous existence" because without this pristine base awareness there would not be anything we call life or existence. Miraculous existence is the manifestation and expression of the underlying fundamental Source and its nature of self-illumination, which gives rise to consciousness. However, you must never attach to the thoughts of consciousness because that constitutes a drop into ignorance or *maya* that obscures presence.[161] The universe is all names and forms, thoughts or consciousness, whereas the

[161] Witnessing or presence is always in the *here*, always in the *now* but you obscure this living vividness by mental attachments. While witnessing experiences consciousness, you are not the *skandha* of consciousness or its contents. Consciousness, as a single body or wholeness, is just a dream-like experience and not your true self or true nature. Your true self has non-moving stainless awareness that knows consciousness. Consciousness, however, is a falsity like a dream you cannot grasp and which passes by since it lacks the never changing stability of the true nature. You are actually the light within which it appears, and that light is the functioning essence of reality, a bodyless pristine awareness. The "I am" is actually It announcing its existence through the apparent existence of what seems an individual self; all beings, in saying "I am," are actually referring to the very same source without realizing it. Consciousness is a falsity that simply appears as the man infestation of the One Source. The awareness is its functioning while the underlying nature or essence is empty, formless, unknowable.

true you transcends them. Cultivators who make progress realize, "the world is there because I am," meaning they recognize that the I-sense is the first thing to arise within consciousness, and then all else arises. The fundamental nature, the fundamental unity or unicity gets separated into the duality of subject and object with the arising of the "I am." From that duality of subject and object, all else is born. Hence, you are what is prior to consciousness, which is pure awareness, the self-illumination of pure being. Since the functioning of consciousness naturally arises, we should not try to destroy or obliterate consciousness to find the thought-free Source. Just learn how to let thoughts function without clinging to them and then the I-sense will dissolve and you will be liberated and free.

You must not try to suppress thoughts on the spiritual trail to reach a state of no-thought that matches the empty nature of pristine awareness. You must always act according to the exigencies of the moment in perfect freedom without any attachment. And by the way, if that means breaking the normal orthodox behaviors of society (such as Talmudic or Sharia disciplinary rules or religious injunctions) because your actions are necessary or just the right thing to do, such as pulling a mule out of a ditch on the Sabbath, then you just break those artificial rules. None of these things are universal rules. They don't exist in ultimate reality. They are just exigencies and conventions which were invented by man according to time and place, and should change with time and place. They are not the Tao, not the road to the Tao or the practice of the Tao. You must learn to become free of such notions and just do what is proper to do at the moment it needs to be done. This is the highest true spiritual practice, but unfortunately much of humanity is locked in inferior religious notions.

As to the contents of knowing, the contents of consciousness are always being transformed which is why they are not the true reality. Truth or reality never changes but is constant, whereas consciousness always changes. Consciousness is always transforming and therefore neither consciousness nor its contents (objects) are the immovable, pure, stainless, eternal underlying source essence that does not fall into either existence or non-existence. Awareness is not the original nature either, but just one of its functions.

The original nature has the self-luminous function of awareness, and by investigating and understanding consciousness we can guide ourselves to find our underlying True Self. While you can surely cultivate different states of consciousness, your pristine awareness that always underlies consciousness - which is an innate functioning of the original nature - cannot be annihilated or obliterated. Awareness always exists whether or not consciousness exists, and it is by this natural illumination that you know the transformations of consciousness, which are like movie images that flash across a screen, the screen being mind's empty true nature. When we go to outdoor movies we can see pictures flashing across the screen, but nothing is real except the screen. The screen is empty and clear, pictures pass over it, and then it's as clear and empty as it was before. The pictures aren't affected by the screen nor the screen by the pictures.

If you so cultivate so as to finally trace consciousness (or pictures) back to its ultimate source (the screen), you will eventually find perfect union with the original source nature (God, the Father, Allah, Brahman, True Self, Source, Ein Sof, dharmakaya, etc.) where there is no small self or knowledge of a small self. There is no sense of being a separate person. By abiding in that realization through non-abiding you will detach from pain, suffering, misery and every affliction that is not YOU but just a fleeting moment of conscious thought. What we ultimately are - unicity-absolute-subjectivity that has the nature of awareness – cannot suffer because there is no objectivity in it, and only objects can suffer or have an experience. That is what we are; no entity is involved in what we are!

What is happening on the screen of consciousness-awareness are just pictures that are not the real you, nor actually really happening to the real you. They are passing illusions there to be witnessed. Free of attachments to "I-knowing," the underlying true you is pure, eternal, blissful and universal True Self. It was there before the Big Bang, is there now, and will always be there. That wholeness cannot know itself and is unaware of itself because there is no independent subject and object in its unicity, which are necessary for there to be knowing, so is not aware of its existence unless consciousness arises. Consciousness simply arose, as a wave does on a body of water that's always present, and through consciousness the ultimate "I" witnesses manifestation. All of consciousness or manifestation is It. That consciousness is the highest God that an individual can *conceive*, but consciousness is actually a function of the original nature rather than its true essence.

When Jesus said, "The Father and I are One," it is because he reached this attainment of the Tao. That is why he could say, "I am the way, and the truth and the life. No one cometh to the Father but by me." "Before Abraham was I Am" also refers to the underlying original nature and its manifestation of beingess or awareness-consciousness. Of course ordinary people do not understand the meaning of these phrases, but he simply spoke of the same realization as the enlightened Zen masters or Vedanta sages of East, which is why westerners should study the eastern religions. He reached a stage of self-realization so he could say this.

Jnaneshvara explained of his enlightenment, "As I approached God, my intellect stood motionless and as I saw Him I became Himself."

When the Muslim al-Hallaj said, "I am the eternal Truth," it is because he also reached a degree of this attainment. When you achieve enlightenment then you are the Source and recognize what It is, which is you. You recognize that you are the ground source, or fundamental essence and so you can say these things. The first words Shakyamuni Buddha spoke after birth, showing a stage of realization prior to his incarnation, was "Above and below, I am the only honored one." He is the only honored one because he is the original nature; consciousness is not destroyed but functions with complete purity upon perfect enlightenment, and thus he is the only honored one.

When Krishna said "Even those devotees who, endowed with faith, worship other gods, worship me alone," it is because he attained enlightenment to the Source, or real Self, as well. This is your True Identity. When Krishna says "All are my expressions" it is because he has attained realization of his actual identity as the original nature, and every being is that same original nature. The knowledge "I am" in every sentient being, arising from the original nature, is also your self. So you and I can also say what Krishna said upon self-realization, for at that time we can experientially realize that the Self of all beings is what we truly are and there are no independent small selves in actuality. The life that flows through all beings is you. You can say, "no I is separate from me" because upon self-realization there is no sense of being a separate person anymore. There is no sense of being a separate entity, being, person or life. The entire universe is yours.

Krishna, in speaking this way, is simply speaking from the standpoint that he is the source of all manifestation, which is the identity of the original nature. From this standpoint you are the unmanifest foundation of all manifestation, the functioning of all manifestation, the manifestation and the perceiving of the manifestation. You are the absolute essence, its functioning and appearance. However, you cannot just read these words but must discover this for yourself with a true, direct, experiential realization. That is called realizing your True Self, or self-realization.

The fundamental nature, which is not an entity or thing, assumes the roles of all sentient beings and matter in manifestation. In enlightenment we come to recognize that fundamental source of what we ultimately are, which is peaceful, pure, blissful and free. Fundamentally we are the beingness of every sentient being in the cosmos; we are the entire expression - and also what is unexpressed. Realization is like a mountain of gold; you realize that you are that mountain of gold, and so every particle of gold is yourself. Thus you can say "every being is part of myself."

When Mohammed talked of submission to Allah — the absolute, eternal ground of being prior to all existence — he was also speaking of the original nature because he reached a stage of attainment. All beings who awaken have the same message to tell.

When the Bodhisattva Samantabhadra said, "the root of all things is nothing else but one Self ... I am the place in which all existing things abide" and "everything is Me, the All-Creating Sovereign, mind of perfect purity ... I am the cause of all things. I am the stem of all things. I am the ground of all things. I am the root of all things," it is because he, too, realized this attainment. As the source of universal awareness, all consciousness is you, all events are yours, all bodies are yours.

All these individuals mentioned reached some stage of enlightenment, some degree of self-realization, some stage of the Tao. However, you must be careful if you assume that they all achieved the same level of realization. As Buddhism clearly points out, there are ten different levels of self-realization possible to a *jnani*, called the ten Bodhisattva *bhumis*, before the nirvana of perfect and complete enlightenment.

If we talk about the finer details, sometimes these ten stages are broken into thirteen levels of realization. For instance, Jesus and Mohammed were just around the first *bhumi* at the time of their teaching. With Moses it is possible that he achieved enlightenment but a multitude of factors, including criticisms of him within the Bible itself (which might also be explained away by a people who didn't want to accept his highest message), raise the question whether he achieved anything more than a dhyana attainment. Lao Tzu reached a much higher stage of self-realization than Confucius in terms of the *bhumis*, but the merit from Confucius' teachings far outranks any of Lao Tzu's contributions because of their impact on society. Adi Shankara, Nagarjuna and Tsong Khapa are examples of individuals who reached extremely high stages of self-realization. People always think the founders of genuine spiritual traditions are those with the highest attainments in those traditions, but that is not so. Who said it had to be that way? They were simply individuals with spiritual attainments *and* the requisite karma which allowed deep spiritual teachings for a people to take hold.

Krishna, Samantabhadra, Jesus, al-Hallaj, Bodhidharma, ... as a personality, none of these individuals is God. However, there is no difference between God and these individuals for the same reason there is no difference between God and you - because you are God only. God is you, the subject, and these individuals have realized that non-difference.[162] You are everybody and every thing. Through the spiritual practice of looking for their True Self, the sense of "I am" for these individuals dissolved into the sense of being a witness only, which then dissolved into the realization "I am all," which eventually became the One. As the saying in Islam runs, "Whoever knows himself, he knows his Lord." Hence upon enlightenment we say they shared the same "fundamental face." There is no separation between them and any other being. There is no separate "I" and no "other." One realizes the Source, True Self or fundamental substrate which is not a person or being or entity, and speaks directly as if identified as the True Self. This is a sage,

---

[162] There is an original state before the "I-amness" came. The beingness of the "I am" depends on something, which is the absolute nature itself. The Absolute "I" or true beingness nature becomes the manifested "I" of consciousness, but the only thing functioning is consciousness – there is no entity involved. You are part of the function of the total manifestation, and its entirety defines your personality as in an infinite Indra's net of interdependence. Since everything participates in defining you, you have no nature of your own. Even your personal responsibilities are the duties of the All. There is nothing independent or separate about you or your awareness. There is only one single, homogenous, undifferentiated underlying awareness that "shines through the vehicle of people." Because of that pristine awareness we can say there is consciousness and therefore existence, or being or "I-amness." Without consciousness in the universe we would have inert existence, or nothing at all. Its essence would just be whatever it is without any knowing. Through false thoughts and wrong thinking in that consciousness which arises, imaginations develop that postulate out separate sentient beings and we attach to these false notions. Individuality is just something that has been imagined whereas the underlying substrate is pure and clean, empty of substance, unmoving, stainless, universal and free. Consciousness over endless time becomes confused, tied up in knots, and the road of spiritual practice becomes that of tracing your individual consciousness back to its substrate source, for that is what you are. This is when we say you become enlightened by directly experiencing the true reality of what It is without the obscuration of individuality. The problem is that the "I am" (seventh consciousness) within you hangs on to the body and mind as its identity, and this affliction of clinging screens the true self-nature. You therefore must free yourself of these attachments on the spiritual practice road of letting go, dropping everything, being effortless and being natural. You are that original state before the "I-amness" came. The manifest comes out of the Unmanifest, and you are therefore that Unmanifest nature. That which is there prior to the appearance of this body and consciousness is your true identity, correct? That is your True Self, fundamental nature or fundamental face.

an enlightened being who has reached self-realization. For all intents and purposes they are now the operating, functional Self in the guise of a human being because the separation of false individuality is now gone and the Real can reassert itself fully, without the contamination of ignorance.

With these individuals – and for anyone who achieves enlightenment – we can say they are not even a being anymore but the beingness of all beings, the ground from which all grows or arises, and so they can talk in the way they have spoken. This is why your spiritual study should once again be non-denominational.[163] The expression through the body is, of course, individualistic and that is where your problem of understanding and interpretation lies. Because of the existence of the absolute nature countless incarnations have come and gone but the Absolute has remained untainted by the movement of all these incarnations. It is not bothered because it only has one state.

A sage once explained this, whose words will help make this clear. When there is awareness with an object, we call it "witnessing." Witnessing, or observation, starts the cultivation path and is awareness of an object. When there is also self-identification with the object, such a state is called a "person." This is why you do not attain self-realization, because you attach to thoughts, sensations, the body and so forth and identify them as a self. In reality there is only one state - one single undifferentiated state. When distorted ("afflicted") by self-identification it is called a person. When colored with the sense of beingness, it is the witness. When colorless and limitless, it is called the Supreme or Self or fundamental nature. That is what you truly are, and it is ignorance to consider oneself as a self; we only talk of the "self" or "ego" in a colloquial sense in order that the communication and transmission of the dharma becomes possible.

---

[163] For instance my own teacher is called a "Zen master" but never considers himself a Buddhist, which is my path as well. However we both extensively rely on Buddhism to explain countless spiritual matters because it is extremely thorough and scientific in laying out the aspects of the spiritual path. If you want to discuss body matters in detail, however, you can turn to Taoism, yoga, Vajrayana and science. If you want to discuss proper behavior you can turn to Confucianism, Christianity and the Bodhisattva ideal. If you want a very direct and clear explanation of enlightenment you can also turn to Vedanta. For meditation practices you can turn to countless traditions for as Kuan Yin's many arms illustrate, the number of methods is virtually limitless. Look at this book – it is a Greek source discussing the stages of the path. It is a perfect example of why you can and should pull from the clearest and best for your purposes, which calls for a non-sectarian study and practice of the spiritual road. As long as a method is virtuous and hurts no one, use what works best!

In the Absolute there is no individuality. Yet you are the absolute nature, you are God, and to abide in the Self is godly. From the absolute standpoint there is no other existence other than the impersonal Self, the absolute nature, the Absolute. Individuality is an illusion and when that illusion disappears, what remains is God, the Absolute. These individuals have reached the egoless, impersonal Absolute absent of the "I am" and the speaking emerges out of a seamless realization of this True Self, emanating out of a state where there are no words. The witnessing directly knows its true nature and from prajna wisdom, or "insight," the fact "I am." You recognize that you are the ultimate observer by direct insight, not by thoughts. The "I" is not an individual.

If we wanted to make definitions we could say that the real formless consciousness alone is God, the sole being-reality-existence, and this formless consciousness or pure consciousness is "awareness." We can also say that God identifies himself through the "I am," since crudely put that is the recognition or announcement of this awareness through the filter of the false self. The "I am" is actually the contaminated underlying witness, and we say "contaminated" or "afflicted" because without contamination there is no thought of "I am." We are in the Absolute is timeless, spaceless, unconditioned, without attributes, but *That* cannot know itself because it has nothing objective about it. The universe arises because the self-so illumination of this absolute nature, this natural awareness, is there and gives rise to the consciousness "I am," which is the "I am that I Am" mentioned in the Bible. This indicates the underlying truth of the "I am." What-I-am is not aware of its existence until the "I am" arrives, and so what you are conventionally is "that I am," which is in turn the primordial beingness that lacks any notions of existence or non-existence, self or other. Such notions only arise because of consciousness.

We can say that the awareness by which you perceive the world - that "I" or identity or little "I am" - is God to match the terms people normally use (since this is what gives rise to manifestation), but it isn't truly a being, self, entity or anything like that. All things define everything else s it can have no nature of its own. It is just a finger pointing to the true Reality, and is just a functioning of the underlying beingness or primordial essence. Your underlying awareness that sprouts "I am" is also that original, basic existence for it has the capacity of awareness or illumination. The Absolute "I" or True Self becomes manifested in form, and that I-consciousness can awaken to realize its nature through the road of mental investigation we call spiritual practice.[164] It is because these individuals cultivated and realized the original nature, which is just yours and my True Self (because we are all *That One*), that they became godly and upon stabilizing that realization they could say these things. Every sentient being can awaken to say that "all manifestation is my expression" (meaning the expression of the original nature with which they finally identify) from recognition-realization of the Source; Everything Here Now (True Thusness) is no different from the unicity of the Source. To discover the Self and abide in the Self is thus the purpose of spiritual practice.

It is so rare to encounter an enlightened individual such as these few examples that you might go for millions of lives and never meet one or hear the dharma. The only thing you might have is the road of religion to help you, and which of those roads has any of this information or is guiding people along these lines? The most important thing is to have an enlightened master to be able to help you see your own mind and recognize your true nature. Usually people pay their utmost respect to singers, actors, athletes, the mega-rich or even heads of state, yet these people cannot save you in any way. In spite of their excellence they cannot find peace themselves, and cannot point to that which is your true nature. They have no merit at all when compared to a sage. The Chinese and Indian cultures understand this, but not the western world.

In the *Sutra of 42 Sections* Shakyamuni Buddha once revealed a ranking scheme we should take to mind when dealing with sages: "It is better to feed one virtuous man than to feed one hundred bad men. It is better to feed one who cultivates the spiritual road than to feed one thousand

[164] The "I am" is real, whereas consciousness is not. The "I am" is a way of announcing pure underlying Being that has the function of awareness, or awareness that is the nature of pure being (is the essence of pure being). The "I" or identity with this pristine, self-so body of awareness-essence is there even without the "am," so it is there whether or not there is consciousness or not, whether you say "I" or not. That "True I" is beingness. It's the only thing Real. It is formless, empty, stainless, self-so and illuminated so it can experience a universe of consciousness. That awareness is sometimes called "clear light" or spiritual light in various traditions, and while you first identify this light on the road of cultivation, the highest realization also considers it a guest rather than the ultimate Host, a functioning you should not identify with or cling to. Hence the highest cultivation path is effortless or natural, letting consciousness function without attachment and not identifying or attaching to awareness either as this, that or something else. There is nothing to hold onto, nothing real within consciousness and the Source needs no clinging since it is self-so. In the purest awareness all identities and characteristics are lost. There is just effortless functioning where there are no longer *bhumis* or grades of realization.

virtuous men. It is better to feed one stream-enterer or Srotapanna[165] than to feed ten thousands of those who observe the precepts of good conduct. It is better to feed one Sakradagamin, or 'once returner,' than to feed one million Srotapannas. It is better to feed one Anagamins, or 'non-returners,' than to feed ten million Sakradagamins. It is better to feed one Arhat than to feed one hundred million Anagamins. It is better to feed one Pratyekabuddha (self-enlightened man) than to feed one billion Arhats. It is better to feed one of the Buddhas, either of the present, or of the past, or of the future, than to feed ten billion Pratyekabuddhas."

There is a similar scheme warning about the bad karma earned for physically harming a sage. In terms of hurting an individual, one should also remember that hurting someone's reputation or disturbing them by giving them troubles also earn bad karma. A sage who decides to stay and help mankind has only that one goal, and one should ask how to assist and support and free them for that work rather than hinder them or criticize them. Clear the way for them and then not only you but the world can receive dharma teachings. The respect we should show to a sage, who can help us out of the false realm of reality, far exceeds what we normally show to the rich, powerful, athletic and entertaining who are at the bottom of this pyramid of rankings.

Many people think they are extremely smart or clever, but we are nothing compared to a sage who has transcended the limits of the mind. The wisdom of a sage is so vast, their strategies so powerful and advice so effective that the emperors of old would beg the enlightened to serve in their courts. They would even travel on foot to seek out their advice, and properly humble themselves in their presence because these masters had overcome the world. Without going into countless case examples, which we can readily pull from the Indian and Chinese cultures, we will simply summarize matters saying that many of the greatest kings of the past succeeded only because they heeded the advice of a sage, and openly admitted it. It is not just kings who need sufficient merit to have a sage available for consultation, but nations

---

[165] The four stages of spiritual attainment are called the Srotapanna, Sakradagamin, Anagamin and Arhat. The Srotapanna, or stream-enterer, reaches enlightenment within seven rebirths due to their stage of cultivation attainments in realizing that there is no such thing as a self. The Sakradagamin, or "once more to come," will at most return to the human world one more time. The non-returner, or Anagamin, having overcome sensuality, does not return to human or any unfortunate world lower world after death. Then there is an Arhat, who achieves a degree of nirvana or enlightenment. We call this self-realization because they realize their True Self, or dharmakaya, also called the absolute nature, God, and so on. These stages are mentioned in the *Diamond Sutra* and various other sutras.

need sufficient merit as well. When a nation, religion, or culture is to fail, it will get the leaders who would ignore the advice of sages even if it were available. The only ones who could turn around matters are the ones ignored or refused.

Sages are selfless and do not seek anything for themselves; they transcend consciousness, so that they are able to see the whole of karma including the outcome of any policies and plans. This is why they always know the right policies that will bring unity, peace, and prosperity to any country, business, family or group. Having detached from fleeting consciousness to find his never changing real Self, a sage has become all. He has abandoned delusions and falsities so won't be bothered by them in his activities, and therefore his actions become virtuous. Losing the small ego, the sage is fair, unbiased and unselfish. Sages are probably the only people in the world really qualified to be kings or prime ministers because of their wisdom and the fact they are truly devoted to helping the people, but because of good or bad karma a country gets the leader it deserves.

Most people who think they are qualified for social, economic, political and strategic planning roles – sometimes simply because they are already in such positions, or just want to be - are usually far from qualified. Thinking they are qualified and lacking humility, such people usually ignore the views of the most qualified. The highly qualified usually have exceedingly humble positions far removed from the citadels of power, and advocate far reaching wise policies which work by cause and effect principles that the straight-line orthodoxy usually cannot comprehend. The policies that will most often preserve, protect and prosper nations are not usually advocated by the moneyed or self-interested because they usually just want more for themselves. Thus are the twists and turns of karma.

Many rulers of the past have readily credited their success to a sage; sages should always be consulted if great deeds are wished to be done or great choices are to be made. In any case, putting these issues aside the same principle arises that if you really want to be able to truly help the people of the world you must vow to become enlightened and work towards self-realization. Only the enlightened have the liberating power necessary to solve the world's ills because they are out of it. Alternatively, if you just want to truly end personal suffering and help yourself, you must also work to become an enlightened being, a sage, a Buddha, a self-realized one. Whether it is for the self or for others the target must be the same. The only one who can save others is the one who has saved himself or herself.

The mood of a nation and even the weather can change because of the presence of a sage, but people don't believe these words because they simply don't understand the levels of cultivation achieved. On just a local level, their bodies have transformed to such a degree that they can give off chi and light that will help calm you and open your own channels in their presence, and thus people often feel peaceful just sitting near them. If you want to transform a situation into something better, such as change the fortune of a person or nation, seek the advice of a sage. The advice of a true sage, who knows what karma can be changed and to what degree and by what methods, is worth more than the wise advice of thousands of intelligent advisors. However, it seems that only Easterners tend to know this.

Sages themselves tell us that we must strive to realize the underlying egoless reality of our true Self, because that is what we truly are. This will truly bring us peace and bliss. This achievement is the actual purpose of all religions and spiritual strivings. We must also salute those sages who have already attained this goal, regardless of their religion, because it is our own self-nature they have realized. Being free of birth and death and the realm of consciousness, they are the only ones who can help us escape the endless pain and suffering of the cosmos. In terms of the conventional reality of the cosmos, these are the highest beings. They are far greater than rich men, powerful conquerors or kings and deserve your utmost of respect.

Then again, you must understand that everyone is fundamentally enlightened and so no one is to be belittled. A butcher, prostitute, jailer, soldier ... anyone can become awakened and choose the path of the Bodhisattva who returns to work for humanity even though they have achieved stages past that of the non-returnee. As personalities they will exhibit noble behavior, but the enlightened are not perfect Greek statues devoid of human blemishes and imperfections. Because of the necessary inheritance of the physical body with its genes, and because of growing up in a particular culture with its own influences, they will have unique personalities, customs, habit energies and quirks just like you or I.

A sage might even do things you disapprove of or make mistakes, which we might call faults or errors, just like everyone else. No one said an enlightened sage must know the answer to all questions either or that their solutions are perfect, for there is no such thing as perfect yin or yang. However, by switching their attention they can know the contents of consciousness of any being, and thereby help solve your problems. They are enlightened and can help you achieve the Tao, and you are focusing on the superficial if you emphasize such things. Unfortunately, most people develop strange idealized notions of sages and lacking any true wisdom, do not understand this.

The purpose of yoga is actually to take the practitioner back to realize their fundamental Source, their fundamental self-nature, their real Self, what they truly are. The purpose of religion is to take adherents back to their Source so that they can know their True Self. The purpose is to help people become able to recognize their fundamental substrate so they experientially know what they truly are. Just to say "You are God" is not enough because the words are meaningless without a direct realization of this fact and an understanding of what this means. The purpose of spiritual cultivation is to take practitioners back to this one Source of mind and matter, of all sentient beings and consciousness. Its whole purpose is to help you discover your ultimate original essence, what you really ultimately are underneath everything.

That fundamental substrate is your original nature or real Self or true identity, and realizing your original nature or true Self is called spiritual enlightenment or SELF-realization. It is self-illuminated which is why there is awareness, and it is omniscient. All matter and consciousness comes from It. In spiritual practice you search for your self by trying to penetrate through to the root of consciousness, so the route involves being conscious and tracing consciousness and awareness back to their primal source as far as it goes. One travels the path of discovering the witness, next the pristine awareness, and then the pure being or fundamental essence. The path is all about this, and this is the road I hope you choose to tread. In Hercules' Twelve Labors, we have simply discussed some of the preliminary yoga and sequential stages of chi and channel transformations that occur along this royal road. Please do not get lost and forget the main objective.

The ultimate basis of reality can indeed be realized. It transcends thinking and consciousness although it is often called "Mind" because it is empty of everything and awareness is one of its functions. It is through the avenue of investigating consciousness with wisdom and tracing it back to its source that you can realize this ultimate fundamental source of existence, or True Self, the absolute nature. It is experienced as a pristine, all-pervasive, all-encompassing unmoving, stable, imperceptible because formless, timeless, pure wakeful awareness. Beyond that, no one can actually describe It or say what It is.

In cultivating the Tao you are not cultivating a phenomenon, object or state such as gong-fu but an underlying freedom of natural awareness that is primordially empty and free, intrinsic and self-existing without any stains. You can compare it to a single changeless mass of pure awareness, free from all the mental patterns of name and form. It is entirely one indivisible whole, and the only way of knowing it is to *be* it. Thoughts or consciousness or the ordinary mind of mentation cannot reach it. It is the true unshakeable, immoveable, permanent pure reality. It is not perceptible because it is the very thing that makes perception possible. It is not a thing, and does not fall into either being or non-being, existence or non-existence. On the road of spiritual practice one finds the underlying empty true awareness, and with further progress awareness dissolves into pure being which is beyond existence and non-existence.

Our underlying true nature, or pure being, does not abide in any state, so you can only arrive at the realization of *true reality* if you practice not clinging when knowing arises and just let awareness function.[166] On this road consciousness will purify, just as your chi will purify, and you will be able to attain self-realization. The ultimate universal bliss is the underlying original nature, source of awareness and free of misery, pain and suffering – all names and forms. Witnessing still exists upon self-realization, functioning still exists but the limitations of identity broaden to become that Real Self. This is what people are actually seeking to discover throughout life, and yet they do everything else except cultivate to attain this because of so many reasons, including the fact that it is so very difficult to encounter direct teachings on this true spiritual path.

---

[166] Conventionally we are speaking of a "you" here – a being, personality, ego or life – but in terms of the original nature, absolute or true reality, there is no such thing. To say there is an individual person, ego or entity is just a way of talking to help you gain comprehension. In terms of the original nature, these are just false divisions of consciousness because the true consciousness is just one body of consciousness without divisions. You can reach knowledge of that one undifferentiated body of consciousness as you pass through the ranks of cultivation. The root source of that body of consciousness is itself empty of all phenomena. It is not conscious but gives rise to consciousness. It is contentless, empty, effortless, spontaneous, beyond birth and death or beyond our beingness and non-beingness, existence and non-existence, consciousness and unconsciousness. We say It is unknowable, indescribable, imperceptible or incomprehensible because It is unreachable by thoughts or mind. You cannot perceive It because it is what makes perception possible; it is what stands behind perception. The mind therefore cannot reach It. It is what it is – the True Self, timeless reality, original nature, fundamental essence.

Self-realization is not an invention or artificial dogma or creation but a discovery, from letting go, of what you truly are. People fall into so many false roads created by ordinary men of religion rather than the paths of liberation taught by enlightened sages.

The fundamental self essence, True Self, true existence, true purity, true bliss, and true permanence does not fall into either existence or non-existence, emptiness or form. Hence, cultivating Shakyamuni's Tao is the solution to ultimately ending pain and suffering – a fact confirmed by the statements of hundreds of saints from countless traditions who have also finally attained enlightenment.

In the meantime, for those who do not achieve the Tao or even cultivate the spiritual path, your life should still entail the same activities. You should still be working unselfishly to improve the state of the world and lives of others so that everyone encounters richer states of peace and happiness and leaves behind states of suffering. If you cultivate just to attain the Tao for yourself we say you have the mind of an Arhat. If you cultivate to attain the Tao but also work to help others attain it and improve their lives, we say you have the mind of a Bodhisattva. Those who succeed in their cultivation and who stick around, coming again and again to help us as teachers of religion and culture, are the Buddhas and Bodhisattvas.

There are many levels to the spiritual attainments of Arhats since becoming an Arhat involves mastering the first, second, third or even fourth dhyana and also realizing some degree of the Tao. All these levels can involve *siddhis* or superpowers if the Arhat chooses to cultivate them, whereas many Arhats do not specifically set out to do so (ex. Confucius, Socrates, Nisargadatta, etc.). Buddhas and Bodhisattvas all have the Arhat attainments, but are called Buddhas and Bodhisattvas because they completely shed the concept of the ego and have compassionately chosen to keep being reborn in the world to help sentient beings awaken.

Because Arhats in their cultivation often purify the chi of their body and penetrate through to the source of the five elements, many learn to gain control of the five elements. Before their death they often rise into the air and exhibit the ability to transform their body into water or fire,[167] two famous examples being Buddha's student Ananda as well as Elijah of the Bible whose departure was symbolically described as a chariot of

---

[167] Traditionally there are "eighteen transformations" that they can typically demonstrate upon their death. They usually do not demonstrate these accomplishments earlier so as not to mislead individuals into thinking that gong-fu abilities are the Tao, the purpose of the Tao, or road to the Tao.

fire. Enlightened Zen masters, on the other hand, usually demonstrate that they are in control of death by dying at a time and place of their choosing in a dignified but unusual way. When we look at the great enlightened Sufi saints from Islam, such as Adbdul-Qadir Gilani who definitely attained the Tao and transformed his body, they often chose this method as well.

If someone becomes a master and transforms their body sufficiently through spiritual cultivation through the routes mentioned, then upon death their physical body also will not decay like a regular human body. Rather, their dead body can exhibit the common spiritual phenomenon of incorruptibility, as was seen in the cases of the Christian monk St. Francis of Assisi, the Hindu master Paramahansa Yogananda, the Buddhist Zen master Hui-neng and the Tibetan sage Tsong Khapa. Countless examples of incorruptibility can be offered, but until now no one ever explained why this non-denominationally occurs to the bodies of saints and sages.

This non-denominational phenomenon has been seen in almost every religion. It is simply due to the fact that the chi channels have become thoroughly purified from the transformations we have discussed. Some masters also cultivate their energy and bodies in such a way that they can attain superpowers, such as the ability to fly, which was the case of the Christian monk Padre Pio, the Chinese Taoist Lu Chun-yang and the Tibetan sage Milarepa.

All sorts of things are possible if you cultivate the body's energies, but cultivating the body is not the way to the Tao. Once again, it is something one should concentrate on cultivating *after* they see the Tao. Otherwise, people who take physical cultivation as the spiritual path or run after superpowers always get absolutely nowhere. The most that can happen is that they become a bit healthier or better athlete, but that's about all. The physical gong-fu aspects of spiritual cultivation are things which happen naturally as you cultivate and which just naturally fall out of the path. That is how you should view them.

As you can readily surmise by now, the stages of the spiritual path are non-denominational, as is their attainment, and there are all sorts of levels to these attainments, too. To attain or not attain a true stage of spiritual progress like this is all a matter of someone's wisdom and cultivation efforts. How far you proceed is also a matter of your commitment, so the decision is all up to you. For instance, some Arhats cultivate superpowers and others do not. Some cultivate the body with special techniques in the sense of using fertilizer to help a tree grow faster, and others do not but simply let it transform in a slower but natural fashion because all they care about is union with the original nature; they have no worries about the time constraints of their age and feel no urgency to complete all the Buddha bodies. However, for the complete Tao you must cultivate realization (dharmakaya), transform the body (sambhogakaya), and activate compassionate behavior (nirmanakaya) for all beings because they are all the same base. They are all you.

Many spiritual schools don't describe the Arhat attainment level, and two major reasons pop out as to why. First, quite a few schools do not have adepts in their lineage that reached this far. Buddhahood, or perfect and complete enlightenment, is even harder to attain and so even less frequently described. You will not even find it in Islam, Judaism or Christianity. As my teacher often told me, since Shakyamuni's day only a few individuals have attained all three enlightenment bodies – the dharmakaya realization, sambhogakaya and nirmanakaya – for complete, perfect enlightenment. When you have all three Buddha bodies, the six spiritual powers, the four wisdoms of the Buddhas from the transformations of consciousness, the physical attainment marks of a Buddha and all eighty Buddha virtuous qualities, this is the completion of the sambhogakaya. When your cultivation reaches a stage where you are able to generate hundreds of millions of transformation bodies, this is the nirmanakaya accomplishment.

The second reason the Arhat attainment is missing in most religions is that they do not have clear teachings to help you attain any stage of dhyana or non-ego, or even specify these as target objectives. So even if someone reached this far in a tradition, if they did not leave teachings behind then no one has a path to follow.

Most of the western schools, for various reasons we won't go into, have even shed themselves of the very teachings that would help someone attain the highest spiritual stages of attainment. How unfortunate this is, but this is the karma of the western spiritual streams. If you want enlightenment teachings to be available in the future, it is totally up to you to do something about this. Why does everyone think the responsibility rests on someone else? Why do people believe that without making the efforts themselves that they will have the merit for the fruit? It is impossible to come upon true dharma teachings if you do not support them and protect them when you find them and their teachers. All that seems to be protected today are grand religious institutions and activities for social welfare.

An individual who succeeds on the spiritual path does not actually belong to any specific tradition but to *all traditions* because they achieve union with the original nature, and yet people do not even support such teachers within their own traditions, let alone others, but just contribute to religious buildings, organizations and causes that do not point to the ultimate or lead people to the ultimate. They complain about the organized religions and yet do nothing to educate the people.

Should you ever encounter a sage, then it is your own duty to support and protect them and their teachings. Sages *are* the original nature, so they do not belong to a religion. A religion is just an outer garb for the day, like the clothing you wear for the weather. Come a new life and it's a new country, race and religion you'll enjoy again - it's as simple as that.

Whether Jewish, Christian, Muslim, Buddhist, Taoist, Hindu or whatever, the enlightened only wish to help humanity and lead people to the Tao, which is what religions maintain they are after. The knowledge of cultivation dies because ordinary people do not protect it or promote it. Socrates was killed, Jesus was killed, al-Hallaj was killed, Milarepa was killed, … humans have a propensity to kill the enlightened rather than protect the dharma.

Many spiritual traditions also do not emphasize the Arhat's supernormal abilities either, because they correctly focus on the mental, consciousness aspects of the spiritual path. This is the route by which you make spiritual progress, for everything comes down to consciousness and behavior in the end. If you focus on the physical, material aspects of the path, hardly anyone ever attains the first steps of true spiritual progress that Hercules achieved. As Confucius pointed out, cultivation starts with watching the mind and correcting one's behavior. From witnessing one's mind you can reach a state of cessation, or mental calming, and from that state you can achieve samadhi and wisdom. All of the gong-fu stages experienced by Hercules will also occur, but the spiritual path is transmitted as that of watching one's mind and behavior. How could the path be more humanistic?

The path is not about the body, superpowers or the like but about realizing the source essence of your mind and body, and then functioning with compassionate selfless behavior in the world along with teaching this path to others. Why not support *that* for a change and the individuals and institutions actually doing that?

People talk about the unity of religions and the intersection between them is in the common stages and practices of the path, and yet this is precisely the information which no one supports, propagates and protects. People want to accumulate the merit for success on the path but they never use their minds - which they readily apply to chasing money or sex or power or fame - to figure out how to support the true enlightenment pathway. And yet they always expect to encounter the dharma in the future. Frankly, their thinking escapes me.

During the entire process of advanced spiritual development, which goes far beyond the content of the Twelve Labors, a cultivation practitioner who works hard enough can finally recognize the underlying, always present basis of their own mind. All the phenomena you see, feel, smell, taste or hear are just consciousness and not the original essence. Without the mind you cannot know any of these things, so all phenomena arise because of the mind. You must trace the mind back to its source. You must first find the witness and then go beyond the witness. As the Delphi Oracle says, *gnothis seauton*, "know thyself," which not only commands us to practice the simple meditation technique of observing our minds (witnessing) to police our thoughts and behavior, but indicates final objective our finding our true nature. This attainment is called by many schools "true knowledge."

Awareness or witnessing allows you to start to experience the consciousness of all your thoughts with a presence you previously lacked. The underlying knower of the mind is just a witness which does not interfere in anything, and transient things pass by. This realization usually accompanies a more advanced stage of chi channel transformations, although people can sometimes achieve it when they deeply study just the teachings on enlightenment by themselves.

With time, eventually Hercules would be able to let go of any attachments to the feelings of his body, which Buddhism calls the body-consciousness, and drop the view of being a body to realize that the true "he" was actually mind only. Mind has no shape, no form, no location, no attributes. What appears in the mind appears because of circumstances, and all of reality participates in those circumstances; every thing that arises does so because it is arising together with every thing else through infinite interdependence, with every thing participating in the existence of everything else. The original nature has the function of consciousness, and human beings mistakenly take that function as their small false self rather than finding the real True Self that they are – God, original nature, Supreme Self, Allah, Buddha-nature, Parabrahman, Universal Mind, Absolute Reality, Absolute Truth, Tathagatagarbha, dharmadhatu,

Source, Ein Sof, Self of Thusness, dharmakaya, nirvana essence, however you wish to word it – that transcends consciousness.

Through spiritual cultivation you can regain that unity without the obstruction or pollution of ignorance, and thus mental afflictions will melt away as you practice meditation. The final realization is that of purity, bliss, permanence and True Self. The methods for attaining that realization, and the various stages of the path, are not really factors of religion or belief but phenomena that belong to the larger "science of human beings" and its methods of moral, spiritual and humanistic cultivation. To create peace, harmony and prosperity in the world, this is what you must support.

Perhaps Hercules attains the Tao later in life (becomes enlightened) because Greek legends say he is eventually made immortal.[168] In any case, the set of transformations we have already covered in the Twelve Labors must suffice for now. In fact, the Twelve Labors of Hercules are the clearest and most complete description of the initial physical gong-fu stages of the path that can be found among the world's spiritual traditions, and it is surprising that this fuller story came from the Greeks rather than the Eastern spiritual traditions.

Perhaps this is due to the predominantly material emphasis of the labors, which is something I must warn against time and again because a majority of people will definitely take this material the wrong way. Usually we just get bits and pieces of the spiritual gong-fu transformations described in other traditions, such as from autobiographies, but the Greeks have welded it all together in one fine story. It is a great story from which you can teach many aspects of spiritual cultivation.

Unfortunately, the stories within the labors did not go into much detail on the methods Hercules actually used in his cultivation, which are perhaps the most important details for us to learn. Yet perhaps this is best, for meditation practices might have been of little interest to Greek audiences, and the story might not then have survived. The story of an incredibly strong fighting hero who conquers all sorts of monsters and challenges is a much more fascinating tale, is it not? It was crafted in a wonderful way that has kept the transmission of spiritual information alive, and so it succeeds.

---

[168] Reaching a state of seemingly physical immortality due to body transformations, while possible, is not the Tao. However, immortality in the sense of becoming a heavenly being was a way of indicating the highest spiritual achievement possible that the Greek public could envision.

On the other hand, where can we find those consciousness teachings? If you turn to the Eastern spiritual schools you will readily find the relevant complementary consciousness teachings for the spiritual path rather than the physical aspects we have just covered.

That, in essence, is a short synopsis of Hercules' Twelve Labors. I have tried to go over these stages of gong-fu in a manner that makes them clear for you, and which will help you with your own cultivation. You will go through these stages if you cultivate correctly with commitment as they do occur after the right amount of proper practice. The truth behind the labors is that these stages of gong-fu happen quite quickly after one another because they are connected in a stream of chi and channel transformations that get kick started after you open the *sushumna*.

From the time of opening up the central channel on through Maitreya's Big Knife Wind, the opening of the auxiliary channels and on through the Twelfth Labor, we are actually only talking about a sequence of thirty to forty days typically experienced during seclusion or retreat. If we expand the time period to include certain other related phenomena not mentioned but still felt strongly, in total we are talking less than three months, or one hundred days, while you strongly feel the channels opening and the *jing* initially transforming into chi. Naturally the process of transformation continues for many years after this initial period.

You should try to remain celibate through this process despite the extreme sexual desire that will arise due to the yang chi kundalini. And remember that to open up all the channels and chakras to a greater degree after this initiatory period still takes years of meditation practice cultivating emptiness. The chi will continue to revolve through the channels and the higher your stage of emptiness, the more channels will open and the more refined your chi will become. It all starts with the labors which are experiences that can be concluded within about a month's time.

If you really want more information on the mental and physical transformations of the path, I suggest you read *Tao and Longevity* by Nan Huai-chin and Wen Kuan Chu, and *How to Measure and Deepen Your Spiritual Realization*[169] by Nan Huai-chin and William Bodri. *Twenty Five Doors to Meditation*, by William Bodri and Lee Shu-mei, gives explanations of over two dozen meditation methods you can use to get started on the path. I also recommend the *Vijnanabhairava Tantra*, from

---

[169] An alternative is to read both *Working Toward Enlightenment* and *To Realize Enlightenment* by Nan Huai-chin. Many other helpful texts can be found at MeditationExpert.com.

Kashmir Shaivism, which offers over one hundred different ways to try to cultivate emptiness. If you sincerely try a different method each week, the newness of each technique, in attempting to teach you how to let go via a different angle, will do just as much as Abhidharma analysis to help you stay out of the rut of mentally clinging during meditation practice.

The *Surangama Sutra* spoken by Shakyamuni Buddha would also be most helpful because it contains more information on many of these sequences of transformation, particularly the information on what happens as you break through the five *skandhas*. Some of the stages experienced by Hercules are also mentioned in the *Lotus Sutra* and *Surangama Sutra*, but even ardent Buddhists do not know it. The *Diamond Sutra* and *Vimalakirti Sutra* would also be of much benefit to study to help you understand the mental aspects of the path.

The Six Yogas of Naropa by Glenn Mullin is a valuable book that can help you gain an understanding of basic tantric yoga practice for spiritual cultivation. This book contains a commentary by the great enlightened master Lama Tsong Khapa on how to open the central channel, which is the basis of most tantric yoga practices. This is what you really need to know if you want to understand early Indian and Tibetan traditions.

If you want to cultivate the royal spiritual road, I recommend that you create a simple every day schedule of mantra practice, the skeleton visualization, vipassana, pranayama and merit making. Those practices alone, at just an hour a day, will put you far ahead of all other spiritual practitioners in existence, including ardent religious attendees. As you gain proficiency in understanding the empty nature of the mind because your chi channels open, you can practice more tantric style visualization techniques like those mentioned by Lama Tsong Khapa. However, you must understand that complicated Vajrayana visualization practices such as the Chakrasamvara, Guhyasamaja, Vajrabhairava, Vajrayogini, Yamantaka, Heruka, or Kalachakra tantras are in many ways similar to practicing the very simple and basic white skeleton visualization technique, which together with the information in this book, may be far more helpful to most people. You do not need to engage in complicated tantric techniques, although they may appeal to some people, and should not think they embody mysteries or principles absent in other schools and traditions. If you understand the basic principles of spiritual practice, the simplest road followed with intent is often best because on complicated roads people usually get lost.

How much you can achieve with such practices is all a function of your wisdom, merits and practice efforts. What helps is having not a good teacher, but an enlightened teacher. The Vajrayana practices of Tibetan Buddhism offer many meditation practices for helping people cultivate the spiritual path. However, you must understand that, as a practical matter, most practitioners who become immersed in Tibetan Buddhism lose their way and begin to think that cultivation practice is mysterious and involves complicated exercises. Nothing could be further from the truth. This is why I emphasize a return to science and a concentration on the basics when it comes to all matters of spiritual cultivation. This keeps the path clean and pure and free of superstition. This is the direct road to progress, and it is unfortunate it is not championed by the western religions. The curtain has been lifted; all these phenomena are now the province of science. You now have the linkage between the stages of Taoism, tantric yoga, Vajrayana, western alchemy and Judeo-Christian cultivation, as well as the methods to attain these stages and the ultimate purpose of path as well.

In terms of understanding the one common target of spiritual enlightenment held by all true religions, there are two books from the school of Vedanta that I also encourage you to read so that you comprehend the ultimate spiritual objective. The first is *Be As You Are: The Teachings of Sri Ramana Maharshi* by David Godman, which is excellent.

All the books by the Indian sage Sri Nisargadatta Maharaj are also excellent without exception, but perhaps his most popular book is *I Am That: Talks With Sri Nisargadatta Maharaj*, which is another title I highly recommend. After you read these truly non-denominational books, you will understand what enlightenment is and what the spiritual path is all about. The Zen school has this very same emphasis, but most people who study Zen miss the target because they don't truly understand the old translations of various Zen dialogues and their Chinese or Japanese cultural references. Practitioners of Zen today should first study Mahayana Buddhism and I highly recommend the Consciousness-Only school teachings as well. For this no book is better than *Three Texts on Consciousness-Only*, published by the Numata Center.

For those inclined to study more about the original nature and the aspect of manifestation we call consciousness and matter, or ignorance and *maya* (*samsara*), three books come to mind that are highly relevant. Today's university "philosophy majors" don't know any of the materials within these texts even though the ancient pursuit of philosophy was actually the road of cultivation to discover the Source through direct realization. The three books that would be helpful are therefore *Traditional Theory of Evolution and Its Application in Yoga*, by Manmath Gharote, Parimal Devnath and Vijay Kant Jha, *The Awakening of Faith* (*Attributed to Asvaghosha*) translated by Yoshita Hakeda, and *Fundamental Mind*, by Mi-pam-gya-tso. I also recommend *Vasistha's Yoga* by Swami Venkatesananda.

If one were to search for similar discussions in Judaism, Christianity and Islam, you would have to mostly turn to realized Kabbalah authors, Sufi sages, and the writings of Plotinus or Pseudo-Dionysius the Areopagite. The little one might find from orthodox sources would have usually been penned by scholars, rather than by realized sages. These writers had to toe the party line by keeping explanations strictly in line with their holy texts and accepted dogmas, regardless as to whether they were somehow deficient or mistaken. Most western religions have been greatly crippled by such dogmatic restrictions. Even the "revolutions" we have sees in the western traditions were typically reinterpretations by theologians and religious thinkers without any stage of Tao attainments at all, and so they still didn't point to the Source, teach how to cultivate attainment, or go into any of the stages and challenges of the path. The typical situation is still that of the blind leading the blind.

If you do not know the target of spiritual practice, then it is hard to get your bearings, know how you should be practicing, and know where to place special efforts. Sri Nisargadatta Maharaj, without any regards to sectarian religion, speaks words that clearly reveal what enlightenment, or self-realization, is all about. Because he attained the Tao and his contemporary teachings had little need for extensive translation efforts, they readily describe the final objective of spiritual practice in a way that hits home for English speaking audiences, and which you might miss if you were to study translations of ancient writings from Buddhism or Zen, which I also highly recommend. The translations of Lu Kuan Yu are excellent in this regard.

Basically, it all comes down to the following: The spiritual path is about the one cosmic objective of self-realization, or enlightenment. All beings are seeking this one great objective. They are all trying to become Buddhas, even though they may not know it. The universe is moving in such a way that all beings eventually attain enlightenment.

To achieve the Tao you must cultivate meditation. You must cultivate an empty mind that does not cling - that is still alive, awake, aware, open and unsuppressed - by which you can eventually realize the source of consciousness that transcends ordinary mentation. If you trace consciousness and then awareness back to their source, you can attain the Tao. That ultimate source is what you are. It only seems you are a separate individual or life because that underlying one awareness peeks through the vehicle of the body, and you screen its pristine nature because of false clinging so that you lose recognition of what you truly are. You are the presence of clear awareness that is constantly at the base of everything that you experience, and through the road of spiritual cultivation you will find that this underlying awareness is the same one, homogenous whole for what we call "all individuals." "All individuals" is not really a truth in fact, but just a way of speaking since individuals do not truly exist – it is only this underlying pristine illumination that is real and never changing. There is no one seeking enlightenment and no one attaining it, and from the absolute standpoint there is no awareness, consciousness or matter either. Everything is *you*, so there is no reason to be selfish and greedy about your life. To end the pain and suffering, you simply have to discover your pure true nature that is absent of the pain and suffering. Awareness, of course, will still function as it should. In the underyling Oneness we call pure being, consciousness arose, and in consciousness the world appeared. The appearances of consciousness are subjective to an apparent individual who lives in their own small world of consciousness because they have contaminated the pristine awareness with false clinging and attachment, and screened the source. One has to discover through cultivation the substratum of all experience, and abide in the state prior to the arising of consciousness that is always ever present there. You are that pure being, the Source, with no need to rely on anything.

As you properly cultivate spiritual practice to uncover your true nature, your chi will transform and your body will go through all sorts of purification stages that make it easier for you to realize your original nature, your True Self. You will feel these transitions quite clearly. The Twelve Labors of Hercules primarily describe these stages of gong-fu, or stages of physical and inner subtle body purification, rather than the practices Hercules used or transformations of consciousness he experienced. They describe what happened to his chi, chakras and channels as the five elements of his physical nature became purified and harmonized. You will go through similar experiences if you, too, cultivate the path sufficiently. It only takes time and practice. It has nothing to do with your religion or membership in any group or sect, or any beliefs you hold. If you just become natural and effortless, by letting go of internal attachments to consciousness, this will all happen to you.

It is as simple as that. It is as hard as that.

My hopes are that you choose to cultivate with wisdom and without prejudice, and ultimately succeed at some stage of spiritual attainment. As I mentioned previously, it is said that several hundred Arhats who succeeded in enlightenment once walked out of one of Shakyamuni Buddha's lessons when he said there was a higher stage of attainment than what they had already reached. He was speaking of the vows to become a Bodhisattva and endlessly, tirelessly, compassionately work for sentient beings in all ways to relieve them of their sufferings and help bring them to the fruition of enlightenment. Even his number one student, Mahakasyapa, was initially taken aback when he heard the vast responsibilities that the Bodhisattva path entailed in terms of service and commitment.

Nevertheless, some people who succeed in cultivation take this route. I have pointed out many instances of the great protectors of countries and religions, who like Hercules, became cultural heroes because they succeeded in their cultivation and decided to take upon themselves this mantle of responsibility. Many have become dharma protectors because life is all about this one task of awakening, and making it better for all beings while helping them to eventually awaken. You can also read of the many past vows of various enlightened Buddhas and Bodhisattvas which include the many ways in which they helpfully intervene in the affairs of human beings and other sentient beings in the universe over the endless eons to come. To reach this stage you have to cultivate all three Buddha bodies of dharmakaya, sambhogakaya and nirmanakaya, and in this book I have introduced a little of the path to these attainments.

My sincere hope is that you choose this Bodhisattva path of cultivation and service as your own inspiration in life until you attain the perfect and complete enlightenment of Buddhahood, something only five or six have been able to do since Shakyamuni's time. It all starts with simple meditation practice.